Mapping Precariousness, .
Insecurity and Uncertain]

The condition of precariousness not only provides insights into a segment of the world of work or of a particular subject group, but is also a standpoint for an overview of the condition of the social on a global scale. Because precariousness is multidimensional and polysemantic, it traverses contemporary society and multiple contexts, from industrial to class, gender, family relations as well as political participation, citizenship and migration.

This book maps the differences and similarities in the ways precariousness and insecurity in employment and beyond unfold and are subjectively experienced in regions and sectors that are confronted with different labour histories, legislations and economic priorities. Establishing a constructive dialogue amongst different global regions and across disciplines, the chapters explore the shift from precariousness to precariat and collective subjects as it is being articulated in the current global crisis. This edited collection aims to continue a process of mapping experiences by means of ethnographies, fieldwork, interviews, content analysis, where the precarious define their condition and explain how they try to withdraw from, cope with or embrace it.

This is valuable reading for students and academics interested in geography, sociology, economics and labour studies.

Emiliana Armano has a PhD in Labour Studies at the Department of Social and Political Sciences in the State University of Milan, Italy.

Arianna Bove is a Lecturer in Politics and Ethics at the School of Business and Management, Queen Mary, University of London, UK.

Annalisa Murgia is Associate Professor in Human Resources Management, Leeds University Business School, UK.

Mapping Precariousness, Labour Insecurity and Uncertain Livelihoods

Subjectivities and Resistance

Edited by
Emiliana Armano, Arianna Bove and Annalisa Murgia

LONDON AND NEW YORK

First published 2017 by Routledge

2 Park Square, Milton Park, Abingdon, Oxfordshire OX14 4RN
52 Vanderbilt Avenue, New York, NY 10017

Routledge is an imprint of the Taylor & Francis Group, an informa business

First issued in paperback 2018

British Library Cataloguing-in-Publication Data
A catalogue record for this book is available from the British Library

Library of Congress Cataloging in Publication Data
A catalog record for this book has been requested

ISBN: 978-1-4724-7156-7 (hbk)
ISBN: 978-0-367-21874-4 (pbk)

Typeset in Times New Roman
by Saxon Graphics Ltd, Derby

Contents

List of contributors vii

Mapping precariousness: subjectivities and resistance. An introduction 1
ARIANNA BOVE, ANNALISA MURGIA AND EMILIANA ARMANO

PART I
Subjectivities: a cartography of experiences **13**

1 **The precariousness of work in postcolonial Africa** 15
FRANCO BARCHIESI

2 **The Chinese Dream and the precarity plateau: why industrial workers are looking to entrepreneurship** 31
BRANDON SOMMER

3 **Hybrid areas of work in Italy: hypotheses to interpret the transformations of precariousness and subjectivity** 47
EMILIANA ARMANO AND ANNALISA MURGIA

4 **The French Business and Employment Cooperative: an autonomy factory?** 60
MARIE-CHRISTINE BUREAU AND ANTONELLA CORSANI

5 **Against precarity, against employability** 70
IVOR SOUTHWOOD

6 **The 'academic career' in the era of flexploitation** 82
GEORGE MORGAN AND JULIAN WOOD

7 **Coping with uncertainty: precarious workers of the Greek media sector** 98
MANOS SPYRIDAKIS

8 **Stories of precarious lives** 110
JOANNE RICHARDSON

9 **Precarious Japan** 122
STEFFI RICHTER

PART II
Resistance: social movements against precariousness **135**

10 **The two endings of the precarious movement** 137
DIMITRIS PAPADOPOULOS

11 **The precariat for itself: Euro May Day and precarious workers' movements** 149
ALEX FOTI

12 **Fake it until you make it: prefigurative practices and the extrospection of precarity** 157
VALERIA GRAZIANO

13 **'Precariedad everywhere?!' Rethinking precarity and emigration in Spain** 170
MARIBEL CASAS-CORTÉS AND SEBASTIAN COBARRUBIAS

PART III
Conceptual outlooks **187**

14 **Working for nothing: the latest high-growth sector?** 189
ANDREW ROSS

15 **Labour, (in-)dependence, care: conceptualizing the precarious** 199
ISABELL LOREY

16 **Encoding the law of the household and the standardisation of uncertainty** 210
ANGELA MITROPOULOS

Index 227

Contributors

Emiliana Armano has a PhD in Labour Studies at the Department of Social and Political Sciences, State University of Milan. Her research focuses on the intertwining of work processes and production of subjectivity in the context of informational capitalism with a social enquiry and co-research methodological approach. She has published several essays, recently (with Annalisa Murgia) *Le reti del lavoro gratuito. Spazi urbani e nuove soggettività* (2016) and (with Federico Chicchi, Eran Fisher, Elisabetta Risi) *Boundaries and Measurements of Emerging Work. Gratuity, Precariousness and Processes of Subjectivity in the Age of Digital Production* (2014).

Franco Barchiesi is an Associate Professor in the Department of African American and African Studies at the Ohio State University, a non-resident Fellow at the Hutchins Center for African & African American Research, Harvard University, and an International Visiting Research Associate at the University of the Witwatersrand, Johannesburg. His latest book, *Precarious Liberation: Workers, the State, and Contested Social Citizenship in Postapartheid South Africa*, is the recipient of the 2012 C.L.R. James Prize from the Working Class Studies Association. He is also a senior editor of *International Labor and Working Class History* and a co-editor of *Rethinking the Labor Movement in the 'New South Africa'* (2003). Barchiesi's current research is focused on how liberal ideas, processes of state formation, and labour regimes shaped the racialization of the Atlantic world in the late nineteenth and early twentieth century.

Arianna Bove is a Lecturer in Politics and Ethics at Queen Mary, University of London.

Marie-Christine Bureau is a sociologist at the Lise-UMR 3320 CNRS-CNAM. She works on the local implementation of public policies, but also on work changes and new forms of autonomous work. Recent publications include: *Un salariat au delà du salariat?* [Labour institutions beyond salaried employment?] (in collaboration with Antonella Corsani, PUN, 2012) and *Reconfigurations de l'État social en pratique* [Reconfigurations of the Welfare state in practice] (in collaboration with Ivan Sainsaulieu, Presses Universitaires Septentrion, 2011).

Maribel Casas-Cortés, PhD in Cultural Anthropology at the University of North Carolina at Chapel Hill, is writing a monograph on social movements in Europe dealing with precarity. She has been actively participating in and reflecting upon precarity struggles in the contexts of the university, early public education, migration and emigration. Previous writing on precarity movements include: 'A genealogy of precarity: A toolbox for re-articulating fragmented social realities in and out of the workplace', in *Rethinking Marxism* (2014).

Sebastian Cobarrubias is Assistant Professor at the Department of Global, International and Area Studies at the University of North Carolina in Charlotte. Based on his activist participation in the *Counter Cartographies Collective (3Cs)*, he has contributed with writings such as 'Drifting through the knowledge machine', in Stevphen Shukaitis *et al.* (eds), *Constituent Imagination: Militant Investigations and Collective Theorization* (AK Press, 2007). Together with companion and co-author Maribel Casas-Cortes, he is currently working on processes of borders outsourcing and precarity.

Antonella Corsani is Associate Professor at the University Paris 1 Panthéon-Sorbonne, and a member of IDHES UMR 8533. She works on neoliberalism, work changes and transformations of the wage relation. Recent publications include: *Un salariat au delà du salariat?* [Labour institutions beyond salaried employment?] (in collaboration with Marie-Christine Bureau, PUN, 2012).

Alex Foti created the Milano May Day Parade centred around young precarious workers and contributed to spread the EuroMayDay Network in 2001–2010, which put precarity and precarious labour on the political map. He co-wrote *ChainWorkers* (2001) and authored *Anarchy in the EU* (2009). He writes frequently on social movements and European politics after the Great Recession on Nettime. His current affiliation is with the Liège-based collective Precarious United.

Valeria Graziano is a cultural theorist, practitioner and educator whose research is mainly concerned with inventing post-work alternatives. She is currently a Postdoctoral Research Fellow at Middlesex University. Her background is in visual culture and critical organization studies. Her PhD (Queen Mary, 2015) looked at different notions used to conceptualize the pleasure of being in common, such as sociability and conviviality. Her postdoctoral research project considers the role of prefigurative practices and of imaginal procedures within the organizational lives of collectives. Valeria has been active within a number of militant research initiatives, including the Micropolitics Research Group and the Carrot Workers Collective.

Isabell Lorey, political theorist at the European Institute for Progressive Cultural Policies (eipcp), and editor of *transversal texts*. She is Professor for Gender Politics at the Institute for Political Science of the University of Kassel. She taught social and cultural sciences, feminist and postcolonial theory at the

Humboldt-University in Berlin and the Universities of Vienna and Basel. Her research interests focus on the precarization of labour and life in neoliberalism, social movements, critical theory of democracy and representation, and political immunization. Her recent books include: *Figuren des Immunen* (2011), *Regierung der Prekären* (2012), *Kognitiver Kapitalismus* (2012), *State of Insecurity. Government of the Precarious* (2015).

Angela Mitropoulos works at the University of Western Sydney. She is a queer Marxist philosopher and she has written on precarious work for some time, including in *Precari-Us?* (2005) and more recently in *Contract and Contagion: From Biopolitics to Oikonomia* (London: Autonomedia/Minor Compositions, 2012). Her current book project is titled 'Infrastructures of Uncommon Forms'. She was a founding member of Left Alliance, xborder and has been involved in a variety of campaigns including noborder camps and antifa.

George Morgan works in the School of Humanities and Communication Arts at Western Sydney University. His research interests range from urban studies to Aboriginality and post-colonialism, to precarious labour, especially in the creative and knowledge sectors, to the politics of moral panics. His books include (as sole author) *Unsettled Places: Aboriginal People and Urbanisation in New South Wales* (Wakefield Press, 2006); and as editor (both with Scott Poynting), *Outrageous: Moral Panics in Australia* (ACYS Press, 2007) and *Global Islamophobia* (Ashgate). His book, *The Creativity Hoax*, co-authored with Pariece Nelligan, will be published by Anthem Press in 2017.

Annalisa Murgia has been the Scientific Coordinator of the EU-FP7 project GARCIA: *Gendering the Academy and Research: Combating career Instability and Asymmetries* at the Department of Sociology and Social Research of the University of Trento. She currently works at the Leeds University Business School and she is the Principal Investigator of the ERC Starting Grant Project SHARE – *Seizing the Hybrid Areas of work by Re-presenting self-Employment.* Her research interests include work trajectories and fragmented careers, with a focus on knowledge workers, precariousness and the social construction of gender in organisations.

Dimitris Papadopoulos is a Reader in Sociology and Organisation in the School of Management, University of Leicester. His work in science and technology studies, social theory and sociology of social change has been published in numerous journals and in several monographs, including *Experimental Politics. Technoscience and More Than Social Movements* (Duke University Press, 2017), *Escape Routes. Control and Subversion in the 21st Century* (Pluto Press, 2008), *Analysing Everyday Experience: Social Research and Political Change* (Palgrave, 2006) and *Lev Vygotsky: Work and Reception* (Campus, 1999/Lehmanns, 2010). He is currently working on Chemical Futures, a study of the becoming-ecological of chemical practice.

Joanne Richardson is a theorist and video artist currently living in Berlin. She has written essays on experimental film and video, net.art, tactical media, free software, intellectual property, and the radical left, and has edited two books on digital culture. From 2002 to 2009 she was the director of D Media (www.dmedia.ro), an artist-run organization in Cluj, Romania, that has produced numerous events and more than 10 experimental documentaries. Her videos reflect an ongoing interest in globalization, nationalism and post-communism, and manifest a critical perspective toward the status of documents, history, and memory.

Steffi Richter studied Philosophy at the Lomonossov University of Moscow; she holds a PhD in Japanese Philosophy at the Humboldt University Berlin, a habilitation at the Ludwig Maximilian University Munich, and an Associate Professorship at the State University of Tokyo. Since 1996 she has been a professor for Japanese Studies at the University of Leipzig. Her research focuses on consumer culture and modern identities, 'Cool Japan', historical revisionism in East Asia and Japanese intellectual history. Since spring 2011 she has been co-organising a website providing translations of Japanese texts related to the 3/11 triple disaster in Fukushima, and researching precarity in postmodern societies.

Andrew Ross is a social activist and Professor of Social and Cultural Analysis at NYU. A contributor to the *Guardian*, the *New York Times*, the *Nation*, and *Al Jazeera*, he is the author of many books, including *Creditocracy and the Case for Debt Refusal*; *Bird On Fire: Lessons from the World's Least Sustainable City*; *Nice Work if You Can Get It: Life and Labor in Precarious Times*; *Fast Boat to China-Lessons from Shanghai*; *No-Collar: The Humane Workplace and its Hidden Costs*; and *The Celebration Chronicles: Life, Liberty and the Pursuit of Property Value in Disney s New Town*. He is also the editor of *The Gulf: High Culture/Hard Labor* (available from OR Books).

Brandon Sommer is a PhD candidate at the International Institute of Social Studies in The Hague. His research interests lie in the areas of industrial and labour transformation in newly industrialized zones as well as precarious work, especially in China.

Ivor Southwood is a loading bay operative and writer living in the UK. He is the author of the book *Non-Stop Inertia* (Zero Books, 2011) and the blog Screened Out (http://screened-out.blogspot.co.uk).

Manos Spyridakis is Associate Professor of Social Anthropology. He teaches Anthropology of Work and Economic Anthropology in the Department of Social and Educational Policy at the University of the Peloponnese. He is the author of the monograph *The Liminal Worker. An Ethnography of Work, Unemployment and Precariousness in Contemporary Greece* (Ashgate, 2013).

Julian Wood was born in London and educated at Exeter University and the University of London. He emigrated to Australia in 1992 and now lives in

Sydney. He is currently teaching and researching sociology at the University of Sydney. Julian has researched and published in a number of areas including; gender, masculinity studies, the sociology of knowledge and the sociology of the media. His current research interests include the changing world of work and the conditions of academic precarity.

Mapping precariousness: Subjectivities and resistance

An introduction

Arianna Bove, Annalisa Murgia and Emiliana Armano

Mapping Precariousness is an investigation of the experience of precariousness and the forms of subjectivation and counter-subjectivation it gives rise to.

In the past decade, interpretations and approaches to the question of precariousness have proliferated amongst scholars of different disciplines as well as social movements across the globe. With an international scope and a focus on subjectivity, the present book aims to offer different perspectives on the phenomenon as it gives rise to a variety of responses and interpretations that are shaped by the historical trajectories and geographical locations of the subjects affected by it (Lee and Kofman 2012; Breman and van der Linden 2014; Atzeni and Ness 2016).

Reconstructing the fragmented history of the concept of precariousness is not a straightforward task. In a way, the term has been in use since the beginning of critical political economy. Traces of it can be found in the works of Karl Marx, especially *Capital*.[1] Max Weber also made use of the term in *Science as Vocation*, to describe the new condition of researchers resulting from the alignment of the German academic system with the American model.[2] From the early 1960s, precariousness became the object of conversations in social movements and academia. The women's movement of Bologna, Italy, adopted the term in the context of demands for better working conditions (Betti 2013).[3] In the same decade, the *International Labour Review* published an article by Paolo Sylos Labini entitled 'Precarious Employment in Sicily', which presented a category of poorly paid and irregularly employed workers connected to but also wider and more heterogeneous than that of *lumpenproletariat* (Sylos Labini 1964). Then the debate on precariousness disappeared from academic discourse for nearly three decades[4] and in the 1990s researchers based mainly in France and Italy began to use the term again.[5] In the meantime, precariousness became a key word for social movements, especially the Italian movement of 1977, where students and protesters called themselves 'precarious' to mark their distance from parties concerned exclusively with protecting the salaried industrial working class (Lerner *et al.* 1978; Berardi 2009; Fumagalli 2011; Shukaitis 2013).

It was not until the end of the 1990s that a proliferation of theoretical developments of the notion of precariousness and of social enquiries and auto-ethnographies of the condition began to be documented in the Italian militant research journal *I Quaderni di San Precario*, giving expression to struggles against precariousness. At that point, the academic debate lagged well behind social movements, as it was largely concerned with retracing the paradigm of flexibility and labelling as 'ideological' those standpoints that had assumed precariousness not only as their research object, but also as the interpretive framework of their analysis of the changes that labour market transformation effected on the production of new collective subjects. Therefore, the idea of investigating precariousness arose from social struggles (Neilson and Rossiter 2008; Betti 2014; Murgia 2014) that can be located within the political tradition of the global justice movement. Amongst social movement actors, there was a high level of awareness that various forms of precariousness were proliferating and of the need to fight against them with new political tools, as well as a strong desire to produce better analyses of the subjectivities involved. This is the political background we recognise our work as being part of and situated in.

Now the debate on precariousness has also entered the academic arena (Barbier 2005; Fudge and Owens 2006; Kalleberg 2009; Lee and Kofman 2012), where it has taken on a transnational dimension partly thanks to research sponsored by international institutions such as the International Labour Organisation (ILO), the European Foundation for the Improvement of Living and Working Conditions (Eurofound) and other research initiatives supported by the European Union.

This 'institutional' strand of research conceptualises precariousness as a condition that is at the antipode of what has been known as the 'standard employment relation' (SER). SER was a normative standard for countries following the models of Keynesianism and Fordism in the post-war era, largely motivated by the objective of ensuring that as many people as possible had access to consumer goods and were granted a minimal purchasing power, ensured by a degree of certainty of continuing employment, job security and work regulation, and some control over labour conditions, intensity, and remuneration by means of representation on platforms of negotiation with employers (Vosko 2010). The standard employment relation was the way in which the 'Labour Question', a cause of great concern for political leaders and industrialists, was to some extent temporarily resolved during the post-war period; to some extent because falling outside of this standard were swathes of informal labour markets populated primarily by women and migrants. However, this was only a temporary solution or compromise. From the 1960s and 1970s, the standard employment relation came under attack in the name of greater flexibility.

Advocates of greater flexibility in employment relations have been informed by two sets of ideas. The first, the neoliberal agenda, has been discussed at length (Dockès 2006; Molé 2012; Standing 2011; Perlin 2011). The neoliberal model understands working class organisation as an impediment to progress, and the SER a temporary concession to the demands of workers, a burden that needs lifting for the sake of economic growth. This notion of progress tends to see the SER as a stepping stone to a new stage of deregulation and flexibility in labour relations, and the condition of precariousness experienced by growing numbers of people as the flipside of flexibility and a necessary evil. This narrative also accuses critics of such condition of backwardness and nostalgia (Strangleman 2007).

Under a mantel of calls to entrepreneurship – a celebration of a culture of 'danger' and risk-taking – the neoliberal critique took the form of a veritable assault on the wage form itself; working should not de facto entail getting paid. Rather, out of necessity work must be reinstated as something that workers should feel grateful to be in receipt of (Perlin 2011; Southwood 2011). Neoliberalism thus, in its partial critique of the state, tried to alleviate the burden of social responsibility from business and clear the way for all kinds of new work arrangements aimed to free employers from the duty to give cause for hiring and firing and in many cases even paying wages.

Although this set of ideas has become dominant in the academic debate, where a critique of precariousness is formulated as a critique of neoliberalism, a very different set of ideas has informed arguments demanding flexibility. It is possible to discern in the literature a rich and populous strand of thought that acknowledges the struggles of the late twentieth century that refused work and the identity made between work and life (Bologna and Fumagalli 1997; Fleming 2014; Lazzarato 2016). These comprised political and cultural critiques of the permanent contract as a life-long commitment to one type of work, or one industrial sector, and much more. It meant women refusing being reduced to their reproductive abilities. It called for flexible hours, work from home, part-time arrangements, where severing the connection between work and life was a demand for freedom from standardised work time (clocking in and out) and place (office, factory). It also comprised challenging the idea of wealth, forcing us to consider the whole of society as making a contribution to the economic success of a nation. The linking of work with citizenship, civic duty, was questioned by a generation that saw work as a mode of discipline and repression (Ackroyd and Thompson 1999; Barchiesi 2011; Berardi 2009; Weeks 2011).

But of these two sets of ideas, the dominant one is the former, that severing the wage from work has in fact sanctioned the identity of work and life (and worklessness and death). In the neoliberal agenda, work is not a means of securing economic subsistence, and a generation of workers is at work for nothing but the development of their human capital. Whilst employers enjoy flexibility, employees experience precariousness, etymologically a condition of being in receipt of some favour (work). Compliance is thus ensured.

This divides commentators into at one end those who regard the SER as a point of reference and a 'solution' to precariousness, and at the other those who systematically question the organisation of work and life built on the premises of Keynsianism and Fordism, and then many stances in between. For this reason, there exists a wide variety of definitions of the concept of precariousness, some of which are conflicting (Neilson and Rossiter 2005; Gill and Pratt 2008; Puar 2012; Armano and Murgia 2013; Cingolani 2014; Lorey 2015). With no pretence at exhaustiveness or systematisation, we here wish to outline the main phenomena that this condition is said to designate, to explain the remit of our project in this book.

In the current debate, precariousness is theorised in one or more of the following ways:

- An ontological and existential problem, informed by the assumption that we are all contingent beings and in life there are no guarantees (Puar 2012). Here precariousness describes the fragility of human corporeal existence, well thematised in the work of Judith Butler (2004) on the aftermath of 9/11 in the United States. In these terms, recognising precariousness entails an ethical encounter, an understanding of 'the precariousness of the Other' essential to the constitution of vulnerability and interdependence as prerequisites of being human.
- A watchword used for decrying worsening labour contract conditions, the demise of trade unions' influence over labour reforms, or the growing endorsement by successive governments of all dispositions and past legacies, whether social democratic or liberal in orientation, of an aggressive and unforgiving neoliberal agenda. In this understanding, the term is elected to provide a voice and visibility to the effects of what to some appears to be a silent takeover of industrial relations by employers at the expense of employees (Fudge and Owens 2006; Kalleberg 2009). Here precariousness is an umbrella term that describes different work situations, from self-employment to part-time, temporary employment, internship and zero-hour contract work; designating a condition that is atypical and contingent, characterised by uncertainty, unpredictability of income streams, insecurity, vulnerability, lack of protection and regulation (Crompton *et al.* 2002; Blossfeld *et al.* 2005).
- A condition inherent to contemporary global capitalism that allows for the production and reproduction of capital as a whole. In this perspective, insecurity, informality and precariousness represent a dominant mode of governance (Mitropoulos 2004; Neilson and Rossiter 2008; Breman and van der Linden 2014) implemented by different means. For instance, an increasing number of people find employment outside of conventional work arrangements, in global cities or as crowd workers in the digital economy, arrangements that are made invisible by the global dynamics of contemporary capitalism (Atzeni and Ness 2016).
- An experiential condition investing a person's life as a quality inherent to that person and his/her specific position. The new spirit of capitalism is based on the self-identification of workers with the products of their labour (Boltanski and Chiappello 1999) and the putting to work and valorisation of emotional and relational skills (Morini 2010). In this framework, the analytical focus is on the process whereby individuals are required to be masters of their own destiny and entrepreneurs of their selves and lives (Ross 2009; Dardot and Laval 2009; Armano and Murgia 2013), a process that aims to turn citizens into entrepreneurs of their own human capital, and thus gives rise to forms of subjectivation and construction of the self that rely on fragmentation, individuation, and the logic of the enterprise. Following a rhetoric of

self-realisation, the system of discipline and obedience typical of Fordism is here overturned thanks to the interiorisation of the principles of merit and the 'praising of skills' (Lazzarato 2012).

- A way of recognising and organising a collective actor and new forms of political struggle and solidarity that reach beyond the traditional organisational models of political parties or trade unions (VV.AA. 2004; Tarì and Vanni 2005). In this sense, precariousness can be seen as 'not only oppressive, but also as offering the potential for new subjectivities, new socialities and new kinds of politics' (Gill and Pratt 2008: 3). This is the *class in-the-making* that Guy Standing, popularising a term already widely in use amongst social movements, calls 'the Precariat' (2011). In this sense, the growth of the precariat is not merely a result of changes in the labour market and an increase in temporary contracts; it is also driven by the transformation of production processes, the rights connected with them and, above all, the deliberate governance strategies of capitalism. Therefore, this term is not meant to identify a distinctive socioeconomic group, but to point to the potential to construct an identity and an imagery for the collective experience of precarious subjectivities.

This brief survey gives us a glimpse of the multidimensional and poly-semantic nature of the concept of precariousness, of the ways it traverses contemporary societies in multiple contexts, from industrial to class, gender, family relations as well as political participation and citizenship.

Mapping Precariousness aims to present an inquiry into the phenomenon in three main parts. Part I – *Subjectivities: a cartography of experiences* – investigates precariousness as a driver of the process whereby risk is damped onto individuals in multiple ways: financial, social, existential. Part II – *Resistance: social movements against precariousness* – follows the narrative of how the 'Precariat' has come to develop a variety of forms of political actions and expressions of collective subjectivity. Part III – *Conceptual outlooks* – presents a series of proposals to reconsider the way we understand precariousness from a theoretical, epistemological and political point of view.

A pilot project of *Mapping Precariousness* was developed in 2010 and published in two volumes (Armano and Murgia 2012). This focused on collective responses to precariousness in Italy and Europe and aimed to build a network of agents within and outside the academia who interpreted precariousness in terms of subjectivity and biographical and experiential narratives. The present volume aims to cast the net wider and expand this network of mappers.

The thread uniting all chapters is an accent on subjectivity and how it intersects the ongoing transformation in the experiences and representations of those affected by precariousness. These are hard to discern through the statistical measures of sociological findings on labour market trends. Far from providing a comprehensive map and an exhaustive definition, we aim to continue a process of mapping experiences by means of ethnographies, fieldwork, interviews, content analysis, where the precarious define their condition and explain how they try to withdraw from, survive within or embrace it. What follows is a brief overview of the contents of the chapters.

Subjectivities: a cartography of experiences

Part I surveys international standpoints and a heterogeneous set of industries, economic sectors, political experiences, and regions characterised by different histories of labour relations, legislations and welfare provisions, that are also currently confronted with different economic pressures. These are investigated with the aim to begin to help dissect points of commonality and difference between regions and sectors. What emerges from China, Romania, Japan, Africa, the United Kingdom, Australia, Greece, Italy, France, the United States, Spain, and sectors ranging from factory work, to IT, education, journalism, care, unemployment and prison, is a moving picture, not a snapshot, but stories of an ongoing process that is transforming society and our relation with work and life in significant ways.

Part I opens with a displacement of the discourse on precariousness: away from Eurocentric accounts of development progressing from the social democratic aspirations of the SER to the precarious work relations of neoliberal policies, in 'The precariousness of work in postcolonial Africa', Franco Barchiesi charts the trajectory of the imposition of waged work in Africa and the experience of those who resist full proletarianisation as a form of colonial rule, to highlight that 'capitalist command is constitutively precarious'.

In 'The Chinese Dream and the precarity plateau: why industrial workers are looking to entrepreneurship', Brandon Sommer then transports us to China, the region of Guangdong, and shares his findings from fieldwork and interviews, seeking an explanation for the rise of entrepreneurialism that he tentatively ascribes to the institutional instability, poor prospects for retirement, and ineffective market mechanisms conjuring up to push industrial workers into self-employment and small business ventures, from one form of precariousness to another. The ambivalence here is this threshold between the possibility of experiencing an autonomous self-organisation and the subsumption of one's subjectivity as it gets put to work. Emiliana Armano and Annalisa Murgia further explore this ambivalence of the experience of precariousness of self-employed workers and freelancers in 'Hybrid areas of work in Italy: hypotheses to interpret the transformations of precariousness and subjectivity'. Reporting on their interviews, they investigate the way precariousness makes inequalities more entrenched and significantly changes the subjectivities involved by demanding an entrepreneurial internalisation of the logic of command.

Marie-Christine Bureau and Antonella Corsani are also concerned with the rise of self-employment but, writing from France, in 'The French Business and Employment Co-operative: an autonomy factory?' they give us a snapshot of the possibilities of moving beyond the identification of self-employment with precariousness and individualisation and present us with the experience where self-employed workers share their risks in return for some protections.

In 'Against precarity, against employability', Ivor Southwood examines the relationship between precariousness and the recent discourse of employability within the remit of social policies implemented in Britain, where it functions, particularly through the provision of welfare and education services, as a mode of governance and legitimation of precariousness and accustoms young people to accept social and economic inequality and conform to the increasing demands of the labour market.

In 'The 'academic career' in the era of flexploitation', George Morgan and Julian Wood examine the condition of precariousness in academia with an ethnography and case studies of the higher education sector in Australia, to investigate the effects of the rise of managerialism and precariousness on new entrants into the profession.

Manos Spyridakis's 'Coping with uncertainty: precarious workers of the Greek media sector' reports on a prime example of the sort of experimentation that the experience of the struggle against precariousness can give rise to, discussing his interviews with the workers of a major TV channel in Greece during the crisis.

In 'Stories of precarious lives', Joanne Richardson offers us the transcripts of a documentary assembling ten portraits of Romanian women working in different countries, questioning the dominant discourse on precariousness and its disregard of the gender and economic inequalities that separate the first and third worlds of Europe.

Steffi Richter closes this cartography with 'Precarious Japan', an outlook on a new 'lost generation' and the ways it makes sense of its conditions of economic and social uncertainty, with a focus on how they voice their plight in publications and through forms of self-organisation.

Resistance: social movements against precariousness

As we have mentioned, as a watchword the concept of precariousness has emerged from and was developed in the context of European social movements, their theory and activism. Because of this, Part II includes analyses of their politics and practices of self-organisation. The term 'precariat' was first evocatively adopted in 2000 by various sections of the Italian social movement (Frassanito-Network 2005; Mattoni 2015) to designate a new fragmented subject and both give it a voice and harness its potential to act politically. From 2000 onwards, a series of activists' interventions gave rise to the singular and lively experience of Euro May Day, a Europe-wide coalition. These movements believed that those excluded from income and rights could unite and represent themselves with no recourse to traditional forms of representation. Thus, initially, 'precariat' was not an analytical category and precariousness described a subjective condition: the existential condition and experience of shared meanings of a whole generation, rather than a particular group identifiable by a particular social or employment status. Part II charts the genealogy of the resistance to precariousness in social movements from Euro May Day to the present. Their political agenda is plural and includes making precariousness visible to policy makers and public opinion, creating spaces and services that assist those affected by it, and organising collective struggles against it.

Part II opens with Dimitris Papadopoulos's 'The two endings of the precarious movement', where we are presented with two interpretations of the forms of struggle against precariousness in social movements from Euro May Day to the present. Following an initial phase of struggle against worsening contractual and working arrangements, in 2008 Papadopoulos sees the beginning of a new phase of struggles where precariousness is associated with the financialisation of life and its bio-economic subsumption under systems of rating and evaluation. Rather than the impasse diagnosed in the following chapters, Papadopoulos here sees a leap in the movement against precariousness that with the crisis broadens the scope of its demands, yet still struggles to find a voice.

In 'The precariat for itself: Euro May Day and precarious workers' movements', Alex Foti offers a reflection on the 'precariat' as a political subject. Whilst Guy Standing defines the precariat as the sum of all those at risk of job insecurity, and Andrew Ross as the sum of service labour in the North and informal labour in the South, Foti's definition of the precariat is 'the sum of people working precarious jobs in dependent and formally independent employment, as well as those experiencing unemployment'. Tracing the trajectory of the Euro May Day movement against precariousness and its legacy, Foti insists on the need for this category to overcome 'leftist mythologies of the industrial working class'.

In 'Fake it until you make it: prefigurative practices and the extrospection of precarity', Valeria Graziano investigates the apparent stalling in the processes of composition of a political subject that recognises itself as precarious, and ascribes it to an underestimation of the micropolitical dynamics of the struggle in past movements, to put forward a new strategy of recomposition that relies on a micropolitics of solidarity and sociability.

In 'Precariedad everywhere?!' Rethinking precarity and emigration in Spain', María Isabel Casas-Cortés and Sebastian Cobarrubias reflect on the experience of recent social movements in Spain, and report on the dialogue between struggles against precariousness and migrants' struggles. Exploring the staggering rise of emigration from Spain that followed the global crisis, they show how precariousness can be identified not only as the cause of emigration, but also as the condition of all migrants in destination countries, thus furnishing important points of commonality between emigrants and immigrants in Spain and beyond, whilst questioning the identification of work with citizenship and rights.

Conceptual outlooks

Part III, far from attempting to provide a theoretical systematisation of what emerges from the cartography of experiences and the narratives of social movement actors, instead hopes to solicit new research trajectories and the use of innovative theoretical tools to make sense of precariousness, with a heuristic and explorative agenda.

In 'Working for nothing: the latest high-growth sector?' Andrew Ross discusses the way in which precariousness has spread to affect a whole generation and such a growing number of workers that it would no longer seem appropriate to see it as an 'atypical' condition. If anything, Ross contends that it signals a strong trend in labour relations towards the large scale de-regulation of the labour market and progressive financialisation of the economy. In this context, Ross discusses the trend towards the increasing exploitation of 'free labour'.

In 'Labour, (in-)dependence, care: conceptualizing the precarious', Isabell Lorey introduces three analytical categories: precariousness, precarity, and governmental precarisation, and focuses on the ways these help distinguish between the socio-ontological and legal-economic realms from those where the ambivalences of freedom and subjection intersect.

The volume concludes with Angela Mitropoulos's 'Encoding the law of the household and the standardisation of uncertainty', a theoretical discussion of precariousness as a mode of governance. A unique angle on the political epistemology of precariousness, the closing chapter charts a genealogy of the category in discourses on statistical measures and spontaneous order.

The present book hopes to furnish new tools, empirical and theoretical, to understand the condition of precariousness as it unfolds across borders, and we would like to thank all contributors, including all the participants in their inquiries, for joining this project and continuing the work of mapping new subjectivities and resistances.

Notes

1 In Chapter 25 of Book I of *Capital*, Marx writes: 'The higher the productivity of labour, the greater is the pressure of the workers on the means of employment, the more precarious therefore becomes the condition for their existence' (Marx 1990: 798). For more on Marx's theory of working-class precariousness, see Jonna and Foster (2015).

2 'Thus the assistant's position is often as precarious as is that of any "quasi-proletarian" existence and just as precarious as the position of the assistant in the American university' (Weber 1946: 131).

3 In 1963, an intervention entitled '*Graduale superamento delle forme di occupazione precaria e delle attività meno produttive*' [Gradual overcoming of forms of precarious employment and less productive activities] (Betti 2013).

4 An exception is the 1989 publication of Rodgers and Rodgers (eds) *Precarious Jobs in Labour Market Regulations.*

5 See Robert Castel (1995), Alain Supiot (1999), Sergio Bologna and Andrea Fumagalli (1997), Luciano Gallino (1998), Pierre Bourdieu (1998), Luc Boltanski and Eve Chiapello (1999). A contribution to the debate also came from Richard Sennett (1998), Ulrich Beck (1999) and Zygmunt Bauman (2000).

References

Ackroyd, S. and Thompson, P. (1999) *Organisational Misbehaviour*. London: Sage.

Armano, E. and Murgia, A. (eds) (2012) *Mappe della precarietà*, vols 1 and 2. Bologna: Odoya.

Armano, E. and Murgia, A. (2013) The precariousnesses of young knowledge workers. A subject oriented approach. *Global Discourse* 3(3–4): 486–501.

Atzeni, M. and Ness, I. (2016) Precarious work and workers resistance: Reframing labor for the 21st century. *Working USA* 19(1): 5–7.

Barbier J.C. (2005) La précarité, une catégorie française à l'épreuve de la comparaison internationale. *Revue française de sociologie* 46(3): 351–71.

Barchiesi, F. (2011) *Precarious Liberation. Workers, the State, and Contested Social Citizenship in Postapartheid South Africa*. New York: SUNY Press.

Bauman, Z. (2000) *Liquid modernity*. Cambridge: Polity Press.

Beck, U. (1999) *Schöne neue Arbeitswelt. Vision: Weltbürgergesellschaft*. Frankfurt: Campus.

Berardi, F. (2009) *Precarious Rhapsody. Semiocapitalism and the Pathologies of the Post-Alpha Generation*. Edited by E. Empson and S. Shukaitis. Translation by A. Bove, E. Empson, M. Goddard, G. Mecchia, A. Schintu and S. Wright. London: Minor Compositions.

Betti, E. (2013) Precarieta e fordismo. Le lavoratrici dell'industria bolognese tra anni Cinquanta e Sessanta. *Culture del lavoro 1*: 17–45.

Betti, E. (2014) La precarietà del lavoro come fenomeno storico: un approccio di genere. Prime riflessioni metodologico-storiografiche. *Memoria e Ricerca*. maggio-agosto: pp. 51–71.

Blossfeld, H.P., Klijzing, E., Mills, M. and Kurz, K. (eds) (2005) *Globalization, Uncertainty and Youth in Society: The Losers in a Globalizing World*. London: Routledge.

Bologna, S. and Fumagalli, A. (eds) (1997) *Il lavoro autonomo di seconda generazione. Scenari del postfordismo in Italia*. Milan: Feltrinelli.

Boltanski, L. and Chiappello, E. (1999) *Le nouvel esprit du capitalisme*. Paris: Gallimard.

Bourdieu, P. (1998) La précarité est aujourd'hui partout. In P. Bourdieu, *Contre-feux*. Paris: Liber Raison d'agir, pp. 95–101.

Breman, J. and van der Linden, M. (2014) Informalizing the economy: The return of the social question at a global level. *Development and Change* 45(5): 920–40.

Butler, J. (2004) *Precarious Life: The Powers of Mourning and Violence*. London and New York: Verso.

Castel, R. (1995) *Les Métamorphoses de la question sociale. Une chronique du salariat*. Paris: Fayard.

Cingolani, P. (2014) *Révolutions précaires*. Paris: La Découverte.

Crompton, R., Gallie, D. and Purcell, K. (eds) (2002) *Changing Forms of Employment: Organizations, skills and gender*. London: Routledge.

Dardot, P. and Laval, C. (2009) *La Nouvelle Raison du monde. Essai sur la société néolibérale*. Paris: La Découverte.

Dockès, P. (2006) Metacapitalismo e trasformazioni dell'ordine produttivo. In Vercellone, C. (ed.) *Capitalismo Cognitivo. Conoscenza e Finanza nell'Epoca Postfordista*. Roma: Manifestolibri.

Fleming, P. (2014) *Resisting Work. The Corporatization of Life and its Discontents*. Philadelphia: Temple University Press.

Frassanito-Network (2005) *Precarious, Precarization, Precariat? Impacts, traps and challenges of a complex term and its relationship to migration*. Available from: http://05.diskursfestival.de/pdf/symposium_4.en.pdf [Accessed: 15 August 2016].

Fraune, D. (2015) *The Refusal of Work. The Theory and Practice of Resistance to Work*. London: Zed Books.

Fudge, J. and Owens, R.J. (eds) (2006) *Precarious Work, Women, and the New Economy*. Oxford and Portland Oregon: Hart Publishing.

Fumagalli, A. (2011) La condizione precariat come paradigm biopolitico. In Chicchi, F. and Leonardi, E. (ed.). *Lavoro in frantumi. Condizione precariat, nuovi conflitti e regime neoliberista*. Verona: Ombre corte, pp. 63–78.

Gallino, L. (1998) *Se tre milioni vi sembran pochi. Sui modi per combattere la disoccupazione*. Torino, Einaudi.

Gill, R. and Pratt, A. (2008) In the social factory? Immaterial labour, precariousness and cultural work. *Theory, Culture & Society* 25(7–8): 1–30.

Jonna, R. J. and Foster, R. B. (2015) Marx's theory of working-class precariousness – and its relevance today. In C. Fanelli and J. Shields (eds) *Precarious Work and the Struggle for Living Wages*. Special issue of *Alternate Routes: A Journal of Critical Social Research*. 27: 21–45.

Kalleberg, A.L. (2009) Precarious work, insecure workers: Employment relations in transition. *American Sociological Review* 74(1): 1–22.

Lazzarato, M. (2012) L'uomo indebitato. Roma: Derive Approdi.

Lazzarato, M. (2016) *Experimental Politics. Work, Welfare, and Creativity in the Neoliberal Age*. Edited by J. Gilbert. Translation by A. Bove, J. Gilbert, A. Goffey, M. Hayward, J. Read and A. Toscano. Cambridge, MA: MIT Press.

Lee, C. and Kofman, Y. (2012) The politics of precarity: views beyond the United States. *Work and Occupations* 39(4): 388–408.

Lerner, G., Manconi, L. and Sinibaldi, M. (1978) *Uno strano movimento di strani studenti. Composizione, politica e cultura dei non garantiti*. Milano: Feltrinelli.

Lorey, I. (2015) *State of Insecurity: Government of the Precarious*. London: Verso.

Marx, K. (1990 [1867]) *Capital: A Critique of Political Economy*. Translation by B. Fowkes. London: Penguin Classics.

Mattoni, A. (2015) The many frames of the precarious condition. Some insights from Italian mobilizations against precarity. In D. della Porta, T. Silvasti, S. Hänninen, M. Siisiäinen (eds). *The New Social Division. Making and Unmaking Precariousness*. Basingstoke: Palgrave MacMillan, pp. 233–48.

Mitropoulos, A. (2004) Precari-Us?. *Mute. Culture and Politics after the Net* 29: 88–96.

Molé, N. J. (2012) *Labor Disorders in Neoliberal Italy. Mobbing, Well-Being, and the Workplace*. Bloomington: Indiana University Press.

Morini, C. (2010) *Per amore o per forza: femminilizzazione del lavoro e biopolitiche del corpo*. Verona: Ombre corte.

Murgia, A. (2014) Representations of precarity in Italy. Collective and individual stories, social imaginaries and subjectivities. *Journal of Cultural Economy* 7(1): 48–63.

Neilson, B. and Rossiter, N. (2005) From precarity to precariousness and back again: labour, life and unstable networks. *Fibreculture* 5. Available from: http://five.fibreculturejournal.org/fcj-022-from-precarity-to-precariousness-and-back-again-labour-life-and-unstable-networks/ [Accessed: 15 August 2016].

Neilson, B. and Rossiter, N. (2008) Precarity as a political concept, or, Fordism as exception. *Theory, Culture & Society* 25(7–8): 51–72.

Perlin, R. (2011) *Intern Nation. How to Earn Nothing and Learn Little in the Brave New Economy*. London: Verso.

Puar, J. (2012) Precarity talk: A virtual roundtable with Lauren Berlant, Judith Butler, Bojana Cvejić, Isabell Lorey, Jasbir Puar, and Ana Vujanović. *TDR/The Drama Review* 56(4): 163–77.

Rodgers, G. and Rodgers, J. (eds) (1989) *Precarious Jobs in Labour Market Regulation: The Growth of Atypical Employment in Western Europe*. Belgium: International Institute for Labour Studies.

Ross, A. (2009) *Nice Work if You Can Get It: Life and Labor in Precarious Times*. New York: NY University Press.

Sennett, R. (1998*) The Corrosion of Character. The Personal Consequences of Work in the New Capitalism*. London: W.W. Norton & Company.

Shukaitis, S. (2013) Recomposing precarity: Notes on the laboured politics of class composition. *Ephemera* 13(3): 641–58.

Southwood, I. (2011) *Non-Stop Inertia*. Winchester: Zero Books.

Standing, G. (2011) *The Precariat. The New and Dangerous Class*. London: Bloomsbury Academic.

Strangleman, T. (2007) The nostalgia for permanence at work? The end of work and its commentators. *Sociological Review*. 55(1): 81–103.

Supiot, A. (1999) *Au-delà de l'emploi*. Paris: Flammarion.

Sylos Labini, P. (1964) Precarious employment in Sicily. *International Labour Review*. 89(3): 268–85.

Tarì, M. and Vanni, I. (2005) On the life and deeds of San Precario, Patron Saint of precarious workers and lives. *Fibreculture Journal* 5.

Vosko, L. F. (2010) *Managing at the Margins. Gender, Citizenship, and the International Regulation of Precarious Employment*. Oxford: Oxford University Press.

VV.AA. (2004) Middlesex Decalration of Europe's Precariat, Available from: http://five.fibreculturejournal.org/fcj-022-from-precarity-to-precariousness-and-back-againlabour-life-and-unstable-networks/ [Accessed: 17 January 2017].

Weber, M. (1946 [1922]) Science as a vocation. In Gerth, H.H. and Wright Mills, C. (eds) *From Max Weber: Essays in Sociology*. New York: Oxford University Press, pp. 129–56.

Weeks, K. (2011) *The Problem with Work. Feminism, Marxism, Antiwork Politics, and Postwork Imaginaries*. Durham: Duke University Press.

Part I

Subjectivities

A cartography of experiences

1 The precariousness of work in postcolonial Africa

Franco Barchiesi

Whose precariousness? Wage labour, racial governance, and African refusal of work

In mainstream sociological analyses of the transformations of work, 'precariousness' has emerged as a distinct pathology, which has not only degraded, on the wake of the global neoliberal onslaught of the late twentieth century, employment conditions and benefits, but also determined harmful consequences for social compacts supposedly premised, at least in older industrial countries, on fair rewards and security for labour. Yet a look at the history of work in colonial and postcolonial Africa offers a substantially different picture, one in which progressive social compacts have never counterbalanced, for the majority of the continent's proletariats, capitalist exploitation, and work has rather been experienced in peculiarly despotic forms. From Africa's history, precariousness comes therefore into sharp relief as persistently and paradigmatically constituting labour and its experiences as such. The ordinary precariousness of wage labour was defined and strengthened not only by economic forces such as the continent's continuous dependence on international markets for mineral and agricultural raw materials, which stifled the emergence of domestic accumulation and the expansion of wage labour; powerful extra-economic factors were also at work, namely colonial modalities of racialized subjugation with which, even when exploited as workers, the domination of Africans and their positioning as hyper-exploitable labour forces were primarily justified on account of their blackness. In the postcolonial reality, the dehumanization of African producers has found a parallel in the way in which vast numbers seeking avenues for survival in the circuits of self-employment and the 'informal' economy have remained the target of state predation and repression.

Despite the limited benefits that specific groups of African workers could contingently claim in various times and locales, an African working class was never conceptualized, from a governmental standpoint, as an autonomous counterpart in negotiated productivity and redistributive deals. Although of colonial origins, such modalities of domination were confirmed by postcolonial rulers, which, despite enforcing a formally deracialized equal citizenship, largely embraced the labour regimes and forms of state discipline of their colonial predecessors. Yet, this chapter also argues, the typicality of precariousness in colonial and postcolonial Africa was not confined to labour exploitation and control, but also characterized African workers' responses to waged employment. Far from relating to precariousness as a condition of powerlessness and subordination, African commodity producers have historically opted for contingent and casual labour relations or self-employment as ways to subvert capitalist work routines and thus implicitly criticize wage labour, which has consequently been heavily questioned as a pathway and signifier of human fulfilment and social inclusion. The precariousness of work in Africa thus undermines working for wages as a putatively progressive norm as well as a social condition through which capital reproduces itself.

During the past decade the concept of 'precarity' has gained prominence, not only in labour studies but also within broader theoretical efforts at understanding the changing place of work in political and social orders writ large. Debates on precarity have in fact foregrounded the predicament of insecure, unprotected, poorly remunerated, and highly exploited jobs as a key dimension of collective existential conditions in dire times of global austerity and persistent capitalist crisis. Thus Guy Standing (2011) invokes 'the precariat' as the possible harbinger of new social compacts, requiring a departure from the obsessive productivism underlying older generations' experiments with full-employment welfarism. Without such a shift, he warns, precarious and restless youth would remain a 'dangerous class', fodder for all sorts of right-wing political adventures. Others are more optimistic as to the political possibilities of precarity *sans* official institutionalization through the state's discourse of social rights and deals. Neilson and Rossiter (2008) regard precarity as a concept that defines the politicization, most evident in southern European social movements during the 2000s and now resurfacing in anti-austerity mobilizations, of precarious employment. The condition of precariousness thus transcends the realms of sociology of work and industrial relations, embracing an entire existential reality, requiring new political concepts. For Neilson and Rossiter, precarity as a political concept indicates that Fordist and Keynesian experiments were temporary and now bygone exceptions, products of a political imagination, including ideas of work-based social inclusion and organized labour itself, anchored to the past. Judith Butler (2004) identifies in vulnerability, rather than stability, the promise of a new and critical political community resting on a collective opening up, which she terms 'ecstatic', to each other's precariousness, rather than on the ultimately illusory quest for individual integrity and security, to which, I would add, employment has provided a crucial vehicle throughout the twentieth century.

Precarity is juxtaposed, across these debates, to a past, or at least an 'elsewhere' – be it understood as a temporary historical episode, a progressive yet defunct phase, or a nostalgically evoked but now superseded 'normal' some still deem worth fighting for – in which commodity-producing work supposedly provided rights, community cohesion, subjective selfhood, and social integration. Even scholars of Africa, as a continent that hardly witnessed the type of full-employment social-democratic strategies of older industrialized capitalism, have recursively commented on the devastation wrought by forty years of structural adjustment programmes and neoliberal policymaking by focusing on their making the world of work more precarious, thus invalidating earlier developmentalist dreams of job creation and the 'postcolonial social contract' (Carmody 2002: 53). Loyalty to the ethics of waged work and an employment-centred representation of the social order are what, on the other hand, motivate the intervention in the postcolonial space of international bodies, especially the 'decent work' agenda of the International Labour Organization, and the plethora of non-governmental organizations intent on 'formalizing' informal economies. As a critical counterpoint, Ronnie Munck (2013) invokes a 'view from the South' on precarious labour, which would require a departure from Eurocentric understandings of 'regular' waged work as a social norm and notions of the precariat, *à la* Standing, as a potentially dangerous class, an image that would pathologize precarious workers, thereby blocking their political possibilities.

Among such possibilities, I contend in this chapter, is the radical critique of wage labour allowed by a focus on precarious work throughout Africa's history of insertion in global capitalism, colonial white rule, and postcolonial turn to neoliberalism. Wage labour as such appears across the continent during the twentieth and early twenty-first century as a reality constitutively characterized by instability, violence, and suffering while remaining, at the same time, hollow, fragile, and uniquely contested. Experiences of working for wages also problematize the continental predicament of blackness and how, during the almost two centuries that follow transatlantic emancipation, black bodies have continued to be put to work through coercive modalities that belie their juridically 'free' status, hence exploitable by capital, in the wake of the abolition of slavery and colonial conquest. Emancipation and colonialism were closely inter-related, as European powers drew from abolition ethical justifications for the subjugation of Africa (Hall 2002; Blackburn 2011). Such ideological modalities have, on the other hand, continued to operate in the ways in which international financial institutions subjected the continent to the violence of structural adjustment under pretences of fostering the productive virtues and budgetary discipline of its inhabitants, assumed to be in need of perpetual external guidance. The representation of African labour as an indistinct black aggregate also underpins, in most dramatic forms, the socioeconomic violence through which the lives of countless migrants are made utterly disposable as they face the lethality of aiming for the southern borders of the European Union (Saucier and Woods 2014). Anti-blackness has crucially determined the precariousness of wage labour in Africa, yet it remains a largely neglected aspect in need of deep investigation (Barchiesi 2015). A look at precariousness as persistently and essentially constitutive of wage labour in Africa outlines, nonetheless, the continent in the specific terms of a space where precarious employment is not merely occasioned by the productive functions it historically performs, being rather indexical of racialized modalities of rule fortified by a global and paradigmatic dehumanization of blackness.

The unique tangle of racialized subjugation and economic exploitation African workers confront means that the analysis of labour relations has to take place, in this case, without the comfort of comparison with pasts in which work has originated anything but existential precariousness. Even at times, such as the post-war welfarist parenthesis, when employment seemed to deliver to Western proletariats opportunities of social mobility and recognition, in Africa waged employment has been unavailable as a building block of possible social compacts. Working for wages itself, with the limited stability it occasionally allowed, has been mostly limited to urban areas, transportation nodes, government employment, portions of commercial agriculture, specific plantation-type economies – especially in 'settler' colonies – mining areas, and scattered industrial pockets, notably at the continent's northern and southern edges (Freund 1988; Ferguson 1999; Austin 2005). Following decolonization, the political elites of newly independent nation states committed themselves to projects of socioeconomic development, which remained nonetheless predicated upon the supply of primary commodities to world markets. African rural producers could mostly satisfy such requirements through complex articulations of commodified and non-capitalist production relations, especially centred in local lineages and communities, which, under the authority of elders and notables, retained nominal control of the land (Berry 1993; Bernstein 2010).

Large numbers of those who were unable or unwilling to eke out their subsistence in rural economies subject to the volatility of international markets, coercive surplus extraction by the state, and the patriarchal rule of professedly 'traditional' local African authorities moved to the urban areas where, faced with a general context of stifled industrialization and lack of economic diversification, wage labour remained volatile and uneven. As a result, many found avenues for survival in self-employment, casual jobs, and in what by the early 1970s came to be represented as the 'informal economy' (Hart 1973; Agier *et al.* 1987; Meagher 1995). The phase of structural adjustment programmes, inaugurated by the World Bank and the International Monetary Fund in the late 1970s, exacerbated such trends while international financial institutions fostered policies of economic liberalization geared at reinforcing Africa's position as a supplier of primary exports. Already limited contingents of workers for wages, primarily in government jobs and limited service or manufacturing sectors, were dealt heavy blows by public spending cutbacks, the erosion of public safety nets, and the opening of markets to foreign competition. Off-the-books and 'informal' economies, often emerging through the decentralization and outsourcing of productions on a local as well as global scale, partially counterbalanced the shrinking wage-earning populations, while leaving many in a state of persistent joblessness and generally forcing the participation of women and often children in widely unregulated and usually exploitative urban economies (De Miras 1987; Lourenço-Lindell 2010).

The trajectory of wage labour in Africa invites us to an analysis focused on historical continuities, which greatly complicates the meaning of 'post' colonialism. The precariousness of African work is 'post' colonial to the extent that it has challenged imaginaries of rule – emerged in the colonial context and transmitted to independent nation states – geared at positing wage labour as a condition to make Africans governable and productive. To challenge that paradigm of governance was not only the limited penetration of waged work itself. More importantly, as they were enforced among non-white populations in oppressive and unrewarding forms, wage labour and capitalist work ethics were resisted by Africans in ways that turned precariousness from a condition of vulnerability into a weapon against capitalist discipline. African workers' use of contingent, casual, and intermittent jobs as modes of refusal of work and resistance to full proletarianization also questioned anti-colonial imagination in places where wage labour was most deeply entrenched. Thus in South Africa, for example, the development of African nationalist, socialist, or trade unionist opposition to racial segregation was predicated upon grounding social transformation agendas onto the putatively modern subjectivities, self-consciousness, and respectability generated by commodity production for the market (Barchiesi 2012.) Black escape from or avoidance of full-time waged employment was therefore simultaneously perceived as a threat by the colonial state and by African elites striving to mould the 'native' into a political actor worthy of popular sovereignty.

Left historians of African labour have been traditionally concerned, in their analyses of the limitations of the wage relation, with the unevenness and limitations of capitalist employment, which they regarded as a necessary guarantor of proper forms of class struggle, from trade unions to working-class parties (Sandbrook and Cohen 1975; Gutkind *et al.* 1978). It was then easy to cast, within such normative frameworks, African refusal of wage labour as a premodern and atavistic phenomenon, a 'resistance to proletarianization' operating as a fetter on the full deployment of socioeconomic antagonisms. As a result, the representation of African precarious work as a pathology was reinforced, thwarting attempts at understanding precariousness as potentially subversive of the wage economy across the colonial and postcolonial condition. Placing precariousness at the core of the history of commodity-producing work in Africa would allow, instead, to reveal how capitalist command itself, and not only workers' lives, is constitutively precarious. At stake is then the potential of African labour history to destabilize and 'provincialize' (Chakrabarty 2000) the centrality of work and 'job creation' in capitalist modernity writ large.

Casual work and the destabilization of colonial capitalism

Contrary to the precepts of liberal political economy and the moralistic celebration of the 'dignity' of work in the discourse of European colonialism, Africans entered wage labour as the outcome of neither self-evident economic rationality nor a logical movement, dictated by income and productivity differentials, from pre-capitalist to capitalist production. Working for wages was the historical product of economic coercion, land expropriation, and colonially enforced taxation and unequal access to capital and infrastructures. Wage earning has also been largely experienced by local populations as intermittent and interspersed with multiple income-generating strategies, including informal trades and small-scale cultivations. Across diverse production contexts, ranging from formally independent commercial agriculture in West Africa to highly capitalized European-controlled mining in the central and southern regions of the continent, it was indeed 'casual' rather than 'permanent' workers who pioneered the introduction of the wage relation. Where European rule legally abolished slavery, as in polities along the Gulf of Guinea, reluctance by the freed slaves to work for wages turned casual jobs into the only viable labour market (Austin 2009). Similar conditions prevailed in the initial development of copper mining in Katanga (Higginson 1989), where refusal to work in often deadly conditions turned labour recruitment into an almost insurmountable challenge for European companies. Casual work, or systems like the employment of migrant workers on labour contracts, to be annually renewed, for a specific number of months, as in the South African mines, gave capital key advantages in exploiting a labour force whose costs of reproduction could be shifted onto pre-capitalist household and community networks, but also required some loss of control over the production process. As Luise White (1997: 437) commented, 'casual labour – the work men could do a few days a week or a month to eke out a living – might have been exploited, but it was beyond employers' control'. Early colonialism thus foregrounds a theme that would then shape subsequent African labour history: to confront capital and the state African workers did not necessarily have to become a full-time 'working class' (Cooper 1981). Indeed, collective reluctance to becoming a working class sustained identities, strategies, and demands that eschewed stable occupations or workplace-based organizations. The predictable operations of a capitalist labour market, and the turning of the casualness of the wage relations into a deepening existential precariousness for workers, were in the end the gradual products of a forceful erosion of independent peasant production, which exacerbated the vulnerability and lack of alternative for African wage seekers.

It is worth emphasizing that the penetration of the wage form cannot be grasped in terms of a linear and inexorable advance of 'proletarianization', but was rather uneven and contested, remaining largely incomplete to this day. In the final decades of colonialism and in the process of decolonization, urban areas became battlegrounds for competing agendas or labour control. Until the 1930s, the main colonial powers, Britain and France, had generally preferred African casual employment in the cities as an alternative to resident and potentially organized working classes. The structure of urban colonial economies, which revolved around unskilled black labour in sectors such as waste collection, domestic services, or the docks, with highly variable workforce requirements, seemed to corroborate such recruitment strategies (Waterman 1982; Willis 1995). Yet the movement to the cities of large numbers of migrants, for which casual and precarious jobs were often preferable to oppressive conditions in rural areas where forced labour was still widely practised, presented for colonial authorities an urgent problem of governance. Many newly urbanized Africans escaped the rigid categories informing the colonial gaze. They were neither 'urban' nor 'rural', rather continuously moving across social networks spanning both contexts (Ferguson 1999). Since even casual employment in the 'formal' economy could not satisfy the growing demand for jobs, arrivals in the city increasingly took on self-employment, in either unregistered 'informal' activities – hawkers selling fish, vegetables, milk, and charcoal by the roadside, or carpenters, water carriers, and rickshaw operators – or practices – such as sex work and liquor brewing – in the uncertain crevices between legality and criminality. Casual, precarious, and unregistered jobs came then to be regarded by European rulers as pathways to a dangerous 'underclass' of youths who had lost most linkages with rural tribal authorities and lived in mushrooming shack settlements evading the monitoring enabled by the official urban grid (Burton 2005).

Compounding the social fears generated by rapid urban change, new formations of uncontrollable precarious workers avoided wage labour, rather seeking in casual and self-employed occupations, now abundant in cities that constituted key linkages between the continent and the world economy, opportunities to evade capitalist work rhythms. By World War II, colonial discourse had decisively turned to regarding African casual work as a problem rather than an asset. White-ruled states thus placed greater emphasis on regular waged employment as a purportedly ethically superior condition, conducive to thrift, personal responsibility, and modern consumption and family patterns. Despite their apparent epistemic solidity, such ideological shifts revealed the difficulties European administrators faced in dealing with African refusal of work and the nagging realization that 'capital and the state had not created a reserve army of the unemployed, but a guerrilla army of the underemployed' (Cooper 1981: 41). Fred Cooper's (1987) classical study of African dockworkers in Mombasa documented the role casual jobs played in African life-strategies throughout the transition from the consolidation of the colonial state to policies that opened the door to decolonization in the second post-war years. As local officials tried to enforce registration and regularization for the port's labour force, African migrants evaded the scheme and preferred, often aided by African team leaders, undocumented day labour, even in periods of shrinking opportunities and growing hardships, such as during the Great Depression. A strategic use of precarious employment, which allowed access to multiple sources of income, provided in that case a better weapon against capitalist discipline than prospects of bargaining within a full-time waged job.

Late colonialism, after World War II, saw determined efforts by British and French administrators to come to terms with the urban 'labour question', as strike waves by organized African workers responded, for the first time, to worsening living and working conditions determined by intensifying exploitation in the interest of European reconstruction. A mix of repression and reforms – including social and housing policies and the extension to African workers of statutory minimum wages, working conditions, family allowances, and retirement pensions – was intended to meet the challenge. The reforms were, however, by and large aimed at formal, largely male, city workers. They did not cover agricultural labour, casual employees, and vast areas of off-the-books economic activity, where, as in the case of petty trade, women were preponderant.

Female dominance of 'informal' city commerce in basic necessities, such as food and clothing, is long-standing across the continent, where in many cases – of which Ghana is exemplary (Clark 1997) – it has enjoyed cultural and juridical recognition since precolonial times. In the context of colonial and postcolonial urbanization, 'market women' have, moreover, provided cheap goods and services that have proved vital to the everyday subsistence of casual and precarious workers (Robertson 1997). By excluding women in the informal sector, as well as workers deemed not permanently employed or urbanized, late colonial reforms imagined African working classes modelled after the European post-war experience. It was the hope of colonial officials that African trade union organizations would then orientate themselves toward apolitical demands for wages and working conditions predicated upon male breadwinning as sustaining broader household and consumption relations (Cooper 1996). A system of 'industrial relations' geared at hitching labour conflicts to the train of capitalist development was supposed to replace workers' opposition to European rule. By limiting themselves only to the small minority of workers in regular waged jobs, however, colonial reforms only deepened the precariousness of the majority, thus reinforcing the problem they presented to state and capitalist governance.

Postcolonial Africa, or the precarity of capital

Although decolonization was to a significant degree forced on European rulers by African workers and peasants whose demands could only have been satisfied, or repressed, at a prohibitive cost, African independences started, during the 1960s, as essentially negotiated processes without significant revolutionary ruptures. The African rulers of new nation states inherited the governance apparatus and social policy arsenal of former colonial powers, to which they continued to provide primary commodities and raw materials. Several independent states criminalized refusal of work and unregistered employment by keeping in their statutes legislation against 'vagrancy', evicting informal markets, and enforcing compulsory labour programmes for the youth (Keese 2014; Kinyanjui 2014: 23–26). The regime that remained quintessentially opposed to black rule and black workers' rights, apartheid South Africa after 1948, devised an 'urban labour preference' policy aimed at encouraging industrial employers to hire black urban township youths, instead of letting them opt for intermittent or illegal occupations. In the end, the 'urban labour preference' failed due to the refusal of its intended targets to take up factory jobs, which forced capital to increase its dependence on rural migrants (Posel 1991: 82–90, 158–64).

In the rest of the continent as well, despite the fact that more and more governments went to power representing black majorities desiring change, the official glorification of wage labour stood dramatically at odds with ordinary peoples' material practices and social experiences. In fact, despite few exceptions as in Nigeria during the 1970s' oil boom and copper mining in Zambia, the predicament of waged workers after independence was largely unfavourable across the board. Even before the neoliberal onslaught of the 1980s, urban wage levels from Accra to Kinshasa shrank, as trade unions were increasingly co-opted by new authoritarian regimes and the choice by regular workers and their families to moonlight in multiple self-employed jobs became necessary to mere survival (Sandbrook 1977). Late colonial social reforms and provisions such as medical care, food rations, and housing subsidies started to be rolled back as international prices for African raw materials declined at the onset of global recession in the 1970s.

The decline of African waged employment has been mirrored, over the past half century, by a growing scholarly and expert interest in the informal economy. The world of street vendors, small repair shops, or producers of shelter, food, and clothing outside the factory is unquestionably precarious to the extent that it is unregistered and unregulated, thus remaining the perennial potential target of police repression and state exactions of all kinds. To the rising neoliberal opinion, however, the informal economy also promised an untapped reservoir of entrepreneurial vitality and an anchor to social stability through the provision of jobs for unskilled and otherwise unemployable citizens. A range of undocumented economic activities that in the recent colonial past had been integral to the African subversion of wage labour became then the stake for capitalist strategies of governing the postcolonial present, which neoliberalism presaged as a 'post-wage' era of generalized, cut-throat individual competition.

In fact, already in the 1980s researchers found that informal or unregulated occupations were not merely synonymous with casual self-employment or petty commodity production, nor were they exclusively an outlet for social marginality (Roitman 1990). Instead, formal enterprises and multinational corporations took to outsourcing among unprotected workers, operating across increasingly uncertain boundaries between 'formal' and 'informal', key aspects of production and logistics. In a sense, reliance on local subcontractors and their vulnerable employees in the supply lines of textile companies, as well as the process of offshoring call centres and global tourist conglomerates, verged on a certain 'informalization' of formal enterprises operating on African soil (Hibou 2009).

The advent of structural adjustment programmes in the late 1970s and the adoption in virtually the entire continent of the neoliberal policies imposed by the World Bank, the International Monetary Fund, and Western donors, brought cuts to public spending, the downsizing of government employment, and market liberalization. As the ranks of wage labour were slashed, workers' living conditions worsened as a result of steep rises in the prices of basic necessities, currency devaluation, the termination of food and fuel subsidies, and the erosion of public social services. The need to diversify income-generating strategies to ensure the survival of families led many waged workers into multiple undocumented activities, while women and children also had to increase their economic participation in precarious occupations of all kinds, often to replace wages lost by male household members (Meagher 1995). International financial institutions propagandized the informal economy as a realm of entrepreneurial self-realization and accumulation liberated from the fetters of authoritarian and corrupt states. The neoliberal celebration of informality endorsed integration in global markets and was part of a broader rejection of earlier developmental hopes of breaking once and for all with the dependency inherited from colonialism.

Idealizations of African entrepreneurialism by American or European technocrats and Western-educated African policymakers resonated with erstwhile colonial images of economic and productive virtue, which external powers had once also spread as a means of salvation for black populations otherwise deemed incapable of self-determination. A remarkable shift was nonetheless now at work inasmuch as self-employment, rather than the wage relation, gained ground as a socioeconomic norm.

The economic necessity that forced workers into informal jobs revealed nonetheless a reality of pervasive poverty. Conditions in the few areas of manufacturing employment reflected what Andræ and Beckman (1991: 161–4) detected among textile factory workers in Kaduna and Kano (Northern Nigeria). In that case, self-employment opportunities in small-scale repairs or transportation, once provided by access to monetary wages allowing the purchase of materials and machinery, had shrunk under conditions of downsizing and austerity, fostered by foreign competition, which also made demands for higher remunerations more difficult. Far from sustaining postcolonial myths of self-empowerment and enrichment, movements between formal and informal jobs took place, with very few exceptions such as urban food agriculture for home consumption, under the sign of harsh self-exploitation through longer working hours and decreasing returns. Additional determinants of precariousness for informal activities were the uncertainty of their juridical status, which made them highly dependent on protections and patronage by state officials, and the social subjugation of the self-employed and their employees, who relied for their financial means on external actors, including household elders, artisanal 'guilds', or religious associations (Lourenço-Lindell 2010). Thus in Senegal, for example, the Islamic Sufi order of the Muridiyya, whose work ethic had configured the relationship between *marabout* (leader) and *talibé* (disciple) into one fusing the imperatives of piety and commodity production, legitimized the increasing use of young followers in a range of activities from begging to street trade (Marfaing and Sow 1999). Morice (1987) concluded that the multiple ways informal workers operated questioned and blurred established and neat juridical taxonomies, such as 'apprentices', 'own-account workers', or 'family helpers', adopted by the International Labour Organization and policy experts.

The caste-like organization of professions thus often gave the notion of 'apprentice' a remarkable elasticity, making it coincide with dependent young employees subject to authority derived from age hierarchies rather than labour contracts, regardless of actual access to training. Neoliberal postmodernity validated in the end the persistence of hierarchies premised on despotism, nepotism, and servitude, which ironically superseded the modern wage form and its institutionalization in colonial and post-independence states. Long-standing socioeconomic forms of exploitation, often packaged and legitimized as timeless precolonial 'traditions', could thus be flexibly resurrected and repurposed for the goals of local and global capital. Abstracted from their original social contexts, however, these modalities accentuated precariousness, reinforced by their high levels of numerical and functional flexibility as a counterbalance for the lack of capital and the volatility of markets, which make investment plans difficult. As suggested by the Senegalese examples cited above, as well as studies in the growing business of small-scale unlicensed urban transportation (Hugon 1982), new generations' access to capital to start their own businesses remained, furthermore, contingent upon their elders' benevolence, especially in cases where decisions to establish independent families as an alternative to being employed in the household rely on the approval and financial means made available by family authorities. The resilience of networks of accumulation centred on age hierarchies was nonetheless enabled, despite their fragility, as Julia Elyachar (2005) showed in the case of craft production in Cairo, by the fact that informal webs of social obligations steeped in long-standing artisanal identities could provide assets and connections allowing older craftsmen to survive the competition of entrepreneurs entering the sector mostly to escape neoliberal austerity.

In the early twenty-first century, the informal entrepreneurial paradigm glorified by international agencies and non-governmental organizations stands starkly at odds with what are often severely undercapitalized and unskilled businesses. They remain a frequent destination for populations undergoing a process of 'de-agrarianization' in which the conditions of migrants to the city are underpinned by the loss of agricultural self-sufficiency, the decay of rural–urban support networks, or the erosion of family resources necessary to look for better jobs (van Dijk 1997). Structural adjustment has been especially detrimental for market women, who suffered as a result of declining terms of trade for food staples, lower monetary incomes for poor and working-class customers, and the growing competition from men engaged in street-selling after being laid off from waged jobs (Clark 1997).

It is in the end a paradox of economic liberalization that accumulation strategies presented in official parlance as 'entrepreneurial' and predicated upon creativity, improvisation, and 'social capital' triumph precisely at a juncture in which neoliberal policies undermine the very social institutions – the family, education, employment, political patronage – that have for long facilitated economic initiative in Africa (Weiss 2004). The changing precarity of work thus becomes symptomatic of a more general precariousness of capitalism in the neoliberal age. James Ferguson (2006) hinted at that much in his critique of idealizing narratives that see Africa as 'converging' toward the fold of allegedly Western-driven globalization. To him neoliberal Africa reveals rather a jagged and uneven landscape in which capital, rather than uniformly 'flowing', 'hops', capturing raw materials and social cooperation networks in specific areas, leaving others in conditions of poverty and neglect, administered by a mix of hollowed out, austerity-abiding states, humanitarian agencies, and various militarized forces. The continent seems thus to announce powerful counter-trends liable to shape the uncertain future of capitalist globalization.

As neoliberal rationality has contradictorily and simultaneously promoted and disavowed entrepreneurial ethos in a world of fierce competition and evanescent success, other repertoires have legitimized precarious self-employment. Thus religious discourse in the booming Pentecostal churches has presented economic sacrifice and enterprise as sacred duties in a divinely ordained pursuit of earthly riches that foretell God's ultra-mundane favours (Hasu 2006). A peculiar form of what Weber termed 'mundane ascesis' thus gives new strength to neoliberalism in the form, somehow at odds with its claims to economic rationality, of a 'millennial capitalism' (Comaroff and Comaroff 2001) which, it is important to emphasize, is not necessarily congruent with the expanded reproduction of capital. Faced with the imponderables of the informal economy's business cycle, those, probably still a minority, who manage to eke a meaningful income out of it often prefer to use their earnings for purposes of consumption or strengthening social connections, rather than reinvestment (Rizzo 2011). Consumption drives are also often underwritten by specific informal activities occurring in the form of crime or illegal traffics; therefore, informal entrepreneurialism confronts neoliberal governance with new sets of problems, rather than just producing orderly capitalist conducts and subjects. No matter how beneficial the smuggling of mineral resources, drugs, or human beings can prove to global capital, they can well contribute to the already widespread fragility of the social, political, and psychic structures of local accumulation. The hyper-capitalism heralded by neoliberal informality could thus ironically show signs of its own self-dissolution.

The question remains open as to whether and to what extent such contradictions are inhabited by new collective subjectivities announcing some form of politicization of African precarity. Precarious workers and students, to whom structural adjustment denied income and prospects, have played prominent roles in repeated cycles of struggles since the 'IMF riots' of the 1980s. They have been, however, hardly capable of shaping the outcomes of such struggles beyond the reclamation of 'good governance', which, resulting in shallow liberal democracies during the 1990s, maintained an unyielding commitment to market liberalization and privatization. More recently, precarious workers and the unemployed have reclaimed a role in the Arab Spring, by infusing anti-authoritarian demands with a language of dignity and social rights. Yet, in a context of persistent state repression, armed conflict, and the rise of Islamist politics, social movements born out of precarity have found, even when defining themselves as such, only limited spaces for political initiative (Emperador-Badimon 2013). An instructive example is Morocco, where both retrenched mineworkers in the historic working-class stronghold of Kourigba and the movement of the *diplomés chômeurs*, educated youth for whom the lack of access to secure jobs represents a stark betrayal of all that postcolonial freedom promised, were in fact ultimately forced to perform a delicate balancing act. Their reasons for outspoken support for political change along the Arab Spring lines had there to be moderated by the need to maintain open channels for government assistance and employment, otherwise possibly endangered by an excess of activism (Bogaert 2015).

On the other hand, the indeterminate border between informality and illegality points to the persistent vitality of African self-employment. Despite the precariousness and hardship that continue to shape it, the informal sector has decisively energized key dynamics underscoring Africa's recent macroeconomic growth. The main beneficiaries are still countries dependent on the extraction of resources, oil and minerals, in high demand from emerging economies such as those of the BRICS countries (Brazil, Russia, India, China, and South Africa). Mining has witnessed – especially, but not only, in war zones where direct investment is risky for established transnational corporations – a resurgence of 'artisanal' operations, in which low-technology manual businesses, often unlicensed and uncertainly regulated, engage large numbers of youths working long hours in dangerous conditions while dreaming of rapid self-enrichment (Bryceson 2015). They generally do not see themselves as 'career' miners, but rather envisage the purchase of clothes, cars, or electronics in the city as the natural destination of their earnings. In the case of Katanga (Democratic Republic of the Congo), Timothy Makori (2013) found that the proclivities to conspicuous consumption by young artisanal miners were somehow underscored by a critique of their parents' work ethic and devotion to wage labour in a nationalized post-independence economy whose emancipatory promises were largely unfulfilled. Networks forged in the informal economy have also underwritten the strategies of those who tried to respond through transnational mobility and migration to the strictures of African accumulation. Thus relations between *marabout* and *talibé*, for example, have spanned globally as Senegalese migrants sell their wares on the streets or Paris and New York, where they acquire business linkages and know-how of technologies and products geared to African appropriation, often through smuggling and counterfeiting (MacGaffey and Bazenguissa-Ganga 2000).

In the end, however, attempts to define and conceptualize the informal economy in the neoliberal terms of an emerging African entrepreneurship are eluded not only by the precarious conditions in which informal employment takes place but also by the fact that its precarity does not stand as an alternative to the vulnerability of wage labour. Small informal entrepreneurs continue, in fact, to hire waged workers under highly exploitative conditions. At a deeper, ontological level, the precarious continuum between self- and waged employment is materially experienced in the hardships of families that have to rely on haphazard combinations of both in order to merely survive. Having a member in waged employment, as opposed to entirely relying on odd and contingent jobs, thus provides a household with scant protection against the ravages of economic liberalization. The precariousness of waged work was most painfully confirmed, in 2012, by the police massacre of striking mineworkers, once a vanguard of working-class organization and militancy, at the Lonmin Marikana platinum mine in South Africa, historically one of the continent's strongholds of capitalist accumulation. The strikers demanded work with dignity and decent wages, thus merely holding capital accountable for the promises with which it brought wage labour to Africa to begin with. The deadly ferocity meeting those demands reminded black workers, in its tragic recurrence, that their precariousness has much to do with how global capital retains the option of making them ultimately fungible and disposable.

References

Agier, M. Copans, J. and Morice A. (eds) (1987) *Classes ouvrières d'Afrique noire*. Paris: Karthala.

Andræ, G. and Beckman, B. (1991) Textile unions and industrial crisis in Nigeria: Labour structure, organization and strategies. In I. Brandell (ed.), *Workers in Third-World Industrialization*. Brandell, New York: St. Martin's Press, pp. 143–75.

Austin, G. (2005). *Labour, Land, and Capital in Ghana: From Slavery to Free Labour in Asante, 1807-1956*. Rochester, NY: University of Rochester Press.

Austin, G. (2009) Cash crops and freedom: Export agriculture and the decline of slavery in colonial West Africa. *International Review of Social History* 54(1): 1–37.

Barchiesi, F. (2012) Imagining the patriotic worker: The idea of 'decent work in the ANC's political discourse. In Badsha, O. Erlank, N. Lissoni, A. Nieftagodien, N. and Soske, J., *One Hundred Years of the ANC: Debating Liberation Histories Today*. Johannesburg: Witwatersrand University Press, pp. 111–35.

Barchiesi, F. (2015) Precarity as capture: A conceptual deconstruction of the worker-slave analogy. In Saucier K. and Woods, T., *On Marronage: Ethical Confrontations with Anti-Blackness: Africana Studies in the Twenty-First Century*. Trenton, NJ: Africa World Press, pp. 177–206.

Bernstein, H. (2010) *Class Dynamics of Agrarian Change: Agrarian Change and Peasant Studies*. Halifax: Fernwood Publishing.

Berry, S. (1993). *No Condition is Permanent: The Social Dynamics of Agrarian Change in Sub-Saharan Africa*. Madison: University of Wisconsin Press.

Blackburn, R. (2011) *The American Crucible: Slavery, Emancipation and Human Rights*. London: Verso.

Bogaert, K. (2015) The revolt of small towns: The meaning of Morocco's history and the geography of social protests, *Review of African Political Economy* 143: 124–40.

Bryceson, D. F. (2015) Youth in Tanzania's urbanizing mining settlements: Prospecting a mineralized future. In Resnick, D. and Thurlow J., *African Youth and the Persistence of Marginalization: Employment, Politics, and Prospects for Change*. London: Routledge, pp. 85–108.

Burton, A. (2005) *African Underclass: Urbanization, Crime and Colonial Order in Dar es Salaam, 1919–1961*. Athens, OH: Ohio University Press.

Butler, J. (2004) Beside oneself: On the limits of sexual autonomy. In Butler, J., *Undoing Gender*, New York, Abingdon: Routledge, pp. 17-39.

Carmody, P. (2002) The liberalization of underdevelopment or the criminalization of the state? Contrasting explanations of Africa's politico-economic crisis under globalization. In Logan, B. I., *Globalization, the Third World State and Poverty-Alleviation in the Twenty-First Century*. Aldershot: Ashgate, pp. 47–62.

Chakrabarty, D. (2000) *Provincializing Europe: Postcolonial Thought and Historical Difference*. Princeton: Princeton University Press.

Clark, G. (1997) *Onions Are My Husband: Survival and Accumulation by West African Market Women*. Chicago: University of Chicago Press.

Comaroff, J. and Comaroff, J L. (eds) (2001) *Millennial Capitalism and the Culture of Neoliberalism*. Durham, NC: Duke University Press.

Cooper, F. (1981) Africa and the World Economy. *African Studies Review* 24(2/3): 1–86.

Cooper, F. (1987) *On the African Waterfront: Urban Disorder and the Transformation of Work in Colonial Mombasa*. New Haven, CT: Yale University Press.

Cooper, F. (1996) *Decolonization and African Society: The Labour Question in French and British Africa*. Cambridge: Cambridge University Press.
De Miras, C. (1987) De l'accumulation de capital dans le secteur informel. *Cahiers des sciences humaines* 23(1): 49–74.
Elyachar, J. (2005) *Markets of Dispossession: NGOs, Economic Development, and the State in Cairo*. Durham, NC: Duke University Press.
Emperador-Badimon, M. (2013) Unemployed Moroccan university graduates and strategies for 'apolitical' mobilization. In Beinin, J., and Vairel, F., *Social Movements, Mobilization, and Contestation in the Middle East and North Africa*, second edition. Stanford, CA: Stanford University Press, pp. 129–48.
Ferguson, J. (1999) *Expectations of Modernity: Myths and Meanings of Urban Life on the Zambian Copperbelt*. Berkeley: University of California Press.
Ferguson, J. (2006) *Global Shadows: Africa in the Neoliberal World Order*. Durham, NC: Duke University Press.
Freund, B. (1988) *The African Worker*. Cambridge: Cambridge University Press.
Gutkind, P., Cohen, C. W. and Copans, J. (1978) *African Labour History*. Beverly Hills, CA: Sage.
Hall, C. (2002) *Civilising Subjects: Metropole and Colony in the English Imagination 1830-1867*. Chicago: University of Chicago Press.
Hart, K. (1973) Informal income opportunities and urban employment in Ghana. *Journal of Modern African Studies* 11(1): 61–89.
Hasu, P. (2006) World Bank & heavenly bank in poverty & prosperity: The case of Tanzanian faith gospel. *Review of African Political Economy* 110: 679–92.
Hibou, B. (2009) Work discipline, discipline in Tunisia: Complex and ambiguous relations. *African Identities* 7(3): 327–52.
Higginson, J. (1989) *A Working Class in the Making: Belgian Colonial Labor Policy, Private Enterprise, and the African Mineworker, 1907-1951*. Madison: University of Wisconsin Press.
Hugon, P. (1982) Le développement des petites activités à Antananarivo. L'exemple d'un processus involutif, *Revue canadienne des études africaines* 16(2): 293–312.
Keese, A. (2014) Slow abolition within the colonial mind: British and French debates about 'vagrancy', 'African laziness', and forced labour in West Central and South Central Africa, 1945–1965. *International Review of Social History* 59(3): 377–407.
Kinyanjui, M. N. (2014) *Women and the Informal Economy in Urban Africa: From the Margins to the Centre*. London: Zed Books.
Lourenço-Lindell, I. (2010) Introduction: The changing politics of informality, collective organizing, alliances and scales of engagement. In Lindell I. L., *Africa's Informal Workers: Collective Agency, Alliances and Transnational Organizing in Urban Africa*. London: Zed Books, pp. 1–30.
MacGaffey, J. and Bazenguissa-Ganga, R. (2000) *Congo-Paris: Transnational Traders on the Margins of the Law*. London: James Currey.
Makori, T. (2013) 'The Ethics of Excess: Consumption, destruction, and their limits in artisanal mines in Katanga Province, Democratic Republic of Congo.' Paper presented at the Annual Meeting of the African Studies Association, Baltimore, November 21–23.
Marfaing, L. and Sow, M. (1999) *Les opérateurs économiques au Senegal: entre le formel et l'informel 1930-1996*. Paris: Karthala.
Meagher, K. (1995) Crisis, informalization and the urban informal sector in sub-Saharan Africa. *Development and Change* 26(2): 259–84.

Meagher, K. (2010). *Identity Economics: Social Networks and the Informal Economy in Nigeria*. Woodbridge, Suffolk: James Currey.

Morice, A. (1987) Ceux qui travaillent gratuitement: un salaire confisqué. In Agier, M., Copans, J. and Morice, A., *Classes ouvrières d'Afrique noire*. Paris: Karthala, pp. 45–76.

Munck, R., (2013) The precariat: A view from the south. *Third World Quarterly* 34(5): 747–62.

Neilson, B. and Rossiter. N. (2008) Precarity as a political concept, or, Fordism as exception. *Theory, Culture & Society* 25(7/8): 51–72.

Posel, D. (1991) *The Making of Apartheid, 1948–1961: Conflict and Compromise*. Oxford: Clarendon Press.

Rizzo, M. (2011) 'Life is war': Informal transport workers and neoliberalism in Tanzania 1998–2009. *Development and Change* 42(5): 1179–206.

Robertson, C. C. (1997) *Trouble Showed the Way: Women, Men, and Trade in the Nairobi Area, 1890-1990*. Bloomington, IN: Indiana University Press.

Roitman, J. L. (1990) The politics of informal markets in sub-Saharan Africa. *Journal of Modern African Studies* 28(4): 671–96.

Sandbrook, R. (1977) The political potential of African urban workers. *Canadian Journal of African Studies* 11(3): 411–33.

Sandbrook, R. and Cohen, R. (eds) (1975) *The Development of an African Working Class: Studies in Class Formation and Action*. Toronto: University of Toronto Press.

Saucier, P. K. and Woods, T. P. (2014) Ex aqua: The Mediterranean basin, Africans on the move, and the politics of policing. *Theoria* 141: 55–75.

Standing, G. (2011) *The Precariat: The New Dangerous Class*. London: Bloomsbury.

Van Dijk Meine P. (1997) Economic activities of the poor in Accra. In Bryceson D. F. and Jamal, V., *Farewell to Farms: De-agrarianisation and Employment in Africa*. Aldershot: Ashgate, pp. 101–15.

Waterman, P. (1982) *Division and Unity among Nigerian Workers: Lagos Port Unionism, 1940s-1960s*. The Hague: Institute for Social Studies.

Weiss, B. (2004) Contentious futures: Past and present. In Weiss, B., *Producing African Futures: Ritual and Reproduction in a Neoliberal Age*. Leyden: Brill, pp. 1–20.

White, L. (1997). Cars out of place: Vampires, technology, and labour in East and Central Africa. In Cooper, F. and Stoler, A. L., *Tensions of Empire: Colonial Cultures in a Bourgeois World*. Berkeley: University of California Press, pp. 436–60.

Willis, J. (1995) 'Men on the spot', labour, and the colonial state in British East Africa: The Mombasa water supply, 1911–1917, *International Journal of African Historical Studies* 28(1): 25–48.

2 The Chinese Dream and the precarity plateau

Why industrial workers are looking to entrepreneurship

Brandon Sommer

This chapter will discuss an unlikely group of would-be entrepreneurs looking to take advantage of the Chinese Dream – industrial workers in Guangdong. Industrial workers in Guangdong are facing a precarity plateau; even though material hardships are minimized workers find it difficult to continue to reduce insecurity because they face limited social and economic mobility. The precarity plateau puts particular pressure on older workers to find alternatives to waged labour in spite of an adequate availability of employment.[1] The concept of the *precarity plateau* helps to contextualize the meanings of precariousness for industrial workers in Guangdong to explain the reasons for the arrival of entrepreneurship programmes as an alternative, albeit insecure, path for workers. I will interrogate the ways in which entrepreneurship is offering opportunities to reduce precarity for some, while for others, like industrial workers in Guangdong, it may be undermining their best interests. I will answer this question by explaining the late arrival of entrepreneurship to the Chinese economy and describing how it has surpassed waged work as a particularly desired type of work in China. Next, I will detail the methods used to collect data for the empirical portion of the work. Then, I will discuss what precariousness means for industrial workers in Guangdong and describe the context in which workers are turning to entrepreneurialism. Finally, I will discuss the type of entrepreneurship that is being created in Guangdong for factory workers and its implications for precarity.

Variegated tracks – the rise of the entrepreneur and the displacement of the worker

During Mao's time, industrial workers were considered socialist heroes; their labour was the harbinger of a modernized China. Social benefits were directly tied to State Owned Enterprises (SOEs) to reward workers for their help modernizing China (Gallagher 2005). Agricultural workers, it was assumed, would be able to fend for themselves; despite the fact that the communist revolution was won on the backs of agricultural workers, industrial workers were awarded a special place in the regime (Pun 2007; Blecher 2009). Today, this position has changed and entrepreneurs are the new socialist heroes (Guiheux 2007, 2013). Entrepreneurs are extremely important in the new economic system; their creativity and ingenuity is perceived to be driving China's steep climb up the path of modernizing the economy. Meanwhile industrial workers have been largely abandoned by the state with the dismantling of the Iron Rice Bowl.[2] However, differently from ignoring the plight of agricultural workers who could rely to a certain extent on subsistence farming, the ignoring of industrial workers who have nothing to fall back on is beginning to lead to social upheaval. In recent years China has seen growing labour protests, alerting the provincial and central governments to the necessity of addressing the root causes of precarity, as workers who supported the 'Chinese economic miracle' demand their fair share (Lee and Zhang 2013).

The Chinese Dream: context and content of a new discourse

One of the government's attempts to minimize this unrest is through the Chinese Dream project and the promotion of entrepreneurship. Invoked routinely by the current president of China, Xi Jinping, the Chinese Dream project perpetuates the belief that with hard work and an entrepreneurial spirit one can take advantage of China's rapid economic growth (*The Economist* 2013a, 2013b). Although vague in definition, the concept of the Chinese Dream has been regularly used by President Xi and by the Chinese public since November 2012. The term is an important indication that China is increasingly turning wealth creation into an individual responsibility by promoting entrepreneurship (*The Economist* 2013b).

Defining entrepreneurship along the norms of the Chinese Dream

Along with the Chinese Dream project come new concrete policies to support it, including the 'Start and Improve Your Own Business' (SIYB) programme (modelled after the ILO programme of the same name), which includes subsidies to start and run businesses (Xu 2014). Additionally, one of the newest policies, part of the 12th National People's Congress (2013–2018), is to allow private banks to facilitate lending to small and medium-sized clients. Further, in April 2015 the State Council issued a directive to improve entrepreneurship. One of the key objectives of this directive is to assist migrant workers to return home to become entrepreneurs (*Sina News* 2015). Both of these policies can be seen as ways for average Chinese people to play a part in the Chinese Dream and although start-up business success rates are not high (Sweeney 2015), the attractiveness of creating one's own Chinese Dream is an incentive for many.

In 2001 Jiang Zemin – the President and Chair of the Chinese Communist Party (CCP) –opened membership in the CCP to private entrepreneurs; this was seen as an important step in legitimizing and emphasizing the role of entrepreneurialism in Chinese society (So 2009). Guiheux explains that entrepreneurialism has transitioned from being prohibited in the Maoist era to representing more than 10 per cent of Chinese society and being a serious political and economic force among its highest levels (2013: 123). Entrepreneurs are celebrated by the state as heroes, such that with little risk to the state they generate jobs and reinforce the hope of the Chinese Dream even for those who are workers (Xu 2014). Many workers are responding by approaching entrepreneurship as an opportunity for increased social mobility at the expense of other strategies to reduce precariousness such as forming durable social movements to negotiate within their current workplaces.

Methods, data and discussion[3]

While investigating precarity among industrial workers in Guangdong in fieldwork conducted in the summer of 2014, I discovered that a surprising group of would-be entrepreneurs emerged: older factory workers. This was surprising not because factory workers should be any less captivated by the Chinese Dream project; rather, it was surprising that workers who were among the most precarious of all industrial workers and had experienced the greatest precarity throughout their work careers would chose a path seemingly fraught with insecurity and instability. For this project research was conducted in Guangdong province in southern China. The two main research sites are part of the Pearl River Delta region: Shunde in Foshan and Dongguan. Fieldwork took place from June to September 2014. Notably, research sites are at the centre of China's attempts to change the growth model through industrial upgrading whereby policymakers are trying to increase the amount of value-add that the region captures (Yang 2012). This is leading to conflicting policy decisions around precarity.

Interviews

Interviews with workers were structured as life histories that specifically focused on the transition through education and especially emphasized workers' lives once they began to work for a wage or once they were responsible for their own livelihoods through agriculture. The sample included 37 workers: 16 from Dongguan and 21 from Shunde. Of these, 23 were women and 14 were men, ages were divided between three main groups: 18–24, 25–34, 35+. In order to ensure the representativeness of the sample, workers were selected from a variety of industries from small, medium, and large enterprises. Industries included textiles, foodstuffs, electronics, home appliances, and machinery as well as some from the service sector.[4] The sample is purposely limited to low wage industrial workers to understand precarity among this subset of workers who are the backbone of economic growth in China. Interviews were also conducted with 13 factory owners from a variety of sectors, including textiles, foodstuffs, electronics and machinery. Sixteen additional interviews were conducted with other interested parties for the purpose of understanding the socio-political situation and in order to assist with contextualizing the workers' life histories.

Contextualizing the meaning of precarity in Guangdong Province

Precarity is often used in the Western context to describe the informalization, casualization and contractualization of the Standard Employment Relationship

(SER) (Vosko 2009; Arnold and Bongiovi 2013). In the Chinese context, the near destruction of the communist version of the SER came in the late 1980s and early 1990s.[5] The creation of precarious employment was itself an intrinsic part of the strategy of the Chinese developmental state, shifting workers from secure employment in SOEs through the Iron Rice Bowl, since the Deng Xiaopeng era, to highly flexible employment as part of the new regime to ensure economic growth (Lee and Kofman 2012). Informal work, brutal working conditions and low pay were all features of the Chinese developmental state and in many ways continue to be present in some form. Additionally, a two-tier migration system caused massive social dislocation as mass migration was, and continues to be, a key necessity of the developmental state to meet the needs for labour in the low wage manufacturing sector (Lee and Kofman 2012).

In response to the social dislocation and labour abuse, new laws and policies were introduced (see for example Friedman 2014). Although there is much debate on the effectiveness of the laws, precarity in China has begun to shift from being mostly about poverty to a precarity similar to Vosko's precarious work: 'uncertainty, instability, and insecurity of work in which employees bear the risks of work (as opposed to businesses or the government) and receive limited social benefits and statutory entitlements' (Vosko quoted in Kalleberg and Hewison 2013). In addition, China's labour issues are in some ways unique. Rather than seeing the evolution of the developmental state as a process of deconstruction of the welfare state, as is happening in the West, the Chinese example is a haphazard and, for all intents and purposes, instrumental creation of aspects of a welfare state to further the interests of the developmental state. Thus, the state is culpable for the creation and the management of this precarity as it simultaneously attempts to maintain internal stability through policy resulting in a particular form of precarity. The state manages this precarity by balancing the role of the developmental state and the quantitative generation of jobs against the need to maintain internal stability (Friedman 2014; Lee and Zhang 2013). Notably, precarity grows as workers get older which normally excludes them from the labour market, forcing them to rely on the incomplete formation of the welfare state. The absence of a fully formed welfare state is especially evident in the poor quality and inaccessibility of social services for migrant workers who make up most of the labourers in Guangdong. Yet, workers manage their precarity by leveraging a variety of networks and institutions to attempt to mitigate against current or future increases in precarity, albeit within existing constraints.

Defining precarity and the plateau

The analysis of Dörre (2014) and Castel (1996) explains the extent to which precarity can be controlled/resisted from the perspective of different actors. Dörre (2014) calls precarity a relational concept linked to one's position in relation to both cultural and social norms. Underscoring the relational aspect of precarity, Castel (2002) explains that mediating relationships are a way to understand the interrelated connections workers have with the economy, society and their culture.

A combination of mediating relationships forms the basis of the social contract that provides workers with some security, predictability and insurance that can cushion them from the unpredictability of the market (Castel 1996). However, social contracts presuppose a certain degree of citizenship. For industrial workers in Guangdong, citizenship is highly restricted in terms of access to and quality of benefits which limits both the quantity and quality of mediating relationships as a means to combat precarity (Yu and Hu 2013; Lee and Kofman 2012).

Mediating relationships in Guangdong face two important restrictions: a lack of industrial citizenship and the absence of legitimate union bargaining power (Chan and Siu 2012) which reduce the availability of mediating relationships for industrial workers in Guangdong, causing a plateau in precarity reduction as market mechanisms on their own fail to improve security for workers beyond a basic minimum. This leads to a specific definition of precarity for industrial workers in Guangdong as the following: access to minimal, uncertain and haphazard safety nets characterized by weak relationships between a worker, the employer, the State and social institutions. The absence of these mediating relationships means that workers are often subject to the arbitrary whims of the employer and local government officials among other things (Lee 2007). While precarity, especially for the newly proletarianized, continues to be reduced, new forms of precarity are produced as new subjectivities are created. The situation is causing workers to look for other means of precarity reduction and one of their strategies is entrepreneurship.

Pushed into entrepreneurship?

In what follows, I argue that workers are being *pushed* into entrepreneurship, a process that especially affects older workers, for two main reasons. There are also a host of valid reasons why workers of all ages are *pulled* into entrepreneurship including escaping the drudgery of highly controlled working environments (Chan 2012b; Boltanski and Chiapello 2006), and increasing control of one's future (Gibb and Li 2003) among other reasons. However, here I want to highlight the particularities of the push factors. I will argue that many workers are pulled into entrepreneurship in attempts to ease persistent precarity, the plateau, which workers may feel hopelessly unable to alleviate because market mechanisms are not doing enough. Thus, workers seek to change their current position within society, and the government highly encourages this transition through entrepreneurship.

The two reasons that workers are being pushed into entrepreneurship are *institutional instability*, which results in increased precariousness for workers in their old age and insecurity regarding retirement, and *ineffective market mechanisms*, minimizing social mobility and industrial citizenship.

Institutional instability: social insurance

In the Guangdong context older workers are those above 35 years of age. For this group stability is highly important as the economic and social demands of parenting increase. Also workers begin to think more seriously about retirement (legally 50 years of age for women and 60 for men),[6] thus workplace benefits become increasingly important. In an interview, a worker in the food industry describes the uncertainty of his retirement, due in one year's time: 'I want to go back home when I pay the social insurance for 15 years. I still have one year left. I am going to raise goats.' When asked about how much he would receive from social insurance per month, he responded, 'The new policy now says male worker can get the rewards at 60 years old. I'm not so sure how much. It may be about 2,000 rmb.'[7] And when pressed whether that would be enough, he responded, 'Of course not! That's why I am going to raise goats' (Int 42w[8]). Another example is Ms. Hu who works in a jeans factory and is 55 years old. She also expressed her fears for the future because of the limited time she has left to work and her limited earning capacity:

> Ms. Hu: I plan to work until the boss thinks I'm too old.
> B: How old do you think that would be?
> Ms. Hu: Sixty I think.
> B: Why are you going to continue to work that long? You are over fifty. You can retire already.
> Ms. Hu: Our family needs money, and the retirement money isn't enough.
> (Int 45w)

The relative position of older workers depends on their ability to negotiate internal structures with the businesses they work for, the choices they made previously and the skills they have accumulated, along with a good deal of luck. Their marketplace bargaining power (Schmalz and Weinmann 2014) is very low due to their relatively advanced age compared to the age desired by the labour market (18–25). As a generation, this group of workers is increasingly involved in labour disputes because when the stability of their workplace is compromised, they are often the most vulnerable with the most to lose. When asked if it is hard to find a job, this car parts factory worker explains: 'It's hard to find a job when you are old like me' (Int 50w). Having a stable job for at least the last 15 years of employment is extremely important under the current context as workers must contribute at least 15 years of social security to receive state benefits. Additionally, the one-child policy has caused workers to worry about their retirement as their adult children, who are in many cases themselves the only child in the family, find it difficult to handle the double burden of taking care of their parents and their own children. Thus, grandparents try and stay in the workforce for as long as possible. The jeans worker interviewed previously discusses her fears for the future: 'I'm afraid that my children would not take care of me. And I'm not so sure I can save enough money to take care of myself, but at least I have my retirement money' (Int 45w).

Insecurity regarding whether workers would actually receive their retirement money was central in one of the largest strikes in modern China: the case of Yue Yuen, where older workers became very involved in the strike. In 2014 more than

40,000 workers went on strike in Gabou, Dongguan at Yue Yuen, a Taiwanese company, the largest sport shoe manufacturer in the world (Merk 2008). One of the main reasons behind this strike was the embezzlement of social insurance payments by the local government and the company. This strike galvanized older workers who, up until that point, had not been important actors in strikes in Guangdong. Older workers gave their support because social insurance payments were compromised, raising important questions about whether their past contributions to pensions would be realized and whether they could survive on the monthly pension payment (Schmalz *et al.* 2017). The Yue Yuen strike underscores the increasing importance of social insurance as a means of security for older workers. When asked about whether she will benefit from social security, a worker at Yue Yuen explains, 'I'll have to wait and see. The government has made a commitment. I will only know if they will honour that commitment after my retirement' (Int 63w). A lack of confidence in the system is becoming more apparent and in some cases this is forcing workers to look outside the system to garner more security; this is one of the main drivers pushing workers towards entrepreneurship.

Workers are squeezed from multiple angles by their children, parents, and increasingly an understanding that their relevance and importance to the labour market is diminishing. They are also discouraged by the characteristics of the labour market because of the convergence of decreasing marketplace bargaining power, along with business and/or government undermining policies, such as social insurance and stable employment, intended to provide security to workers. This is particularly destabilizing because workers have oriented their lives and work careers to these characteristics as a necessary complement to their meagre salaries, yet in many cases those benefits simply do not come or come in a form that is not expected. This is clearly articulated in the way workers discuss their prospects for the future, which seems highly precarious. Thus, precarity is created for older workers through an unstable and haphazard implementation of social security along with weak marketplace bargaining power. This is why older workers are increasingly looking outside of wage labour for alternatives to provide security.

A failure of market mechanisms: the plateau

The second push factor is a failure of market mechanisms leading to a stagnation of social and economic mobility. In economic theory, as the supply of workers gets smaller or demand increases without a proportionate increase in supply, wages and working conditions should improve. For industrial workers in Guangdong, wages and working conditions have improved but now they appear to be plateauing despite a high demand for workers. Since 2004 there has been a labour shortage in Guangdong mostly caused by a lack of workers migrating from the countryside to feed the high demand for workers in urban areas. These shortages peaked especially around 2010 (Chan 2010). However, with a massive working-age population of 981 million (16–64) and at least 100 million workers surplus to agricultural needs, representing 44 per cent of the total agricultural labour force, there are serious questions about what is causing the labour shortage and how it impacts precariousness (Chan 2010; Yang *et al.* 2010; Zhan and Huang 2012). This is an excerpt from a factory owner in Dongguan explaining the evolution of the labour shortage.

> In the early years, employees received very little benefit compared to how hard they had to work, because at that time there were way more workers than factories needed. That was about 15 years ago. The working conditions were very bad. [...] Now, it is very hard to find workers. It sometimes takes me one or two months to find a good worker. [...] Back in the old times, if you put up a recruitment ad to find one worker, 200 people would wait in a line to apply. And the worker would probably have to have some connections to get into the factory.
>
> (Int 8o).

This excerpt underscores the marked contrast, in a short time span, of how the labour shortage is affecting factories in Guangdong.

Evidence of the improved wages and working conditions can be found in official data. Figure 2.1 shows the average wage of selected regions in Guangdong as reported by official statistical agencies of the national and Guangdong governments. It demonstrates that wages have more than doubled since 2005, which also lends support to the view of the factory owner quoted above. However, one must be somewhat suspicious of these numbers because they indicate that through the 2008 global financial crisis the growth of wages did not slow, yet there was significant evidence of mass unemployment during that period (Chan 2010; Kaiming 2013). More problematically and not shown in these figures is that wages are highly tied to incentives, composed of fixed and variable components that are significantly influenced by business performance. In interviews, I found

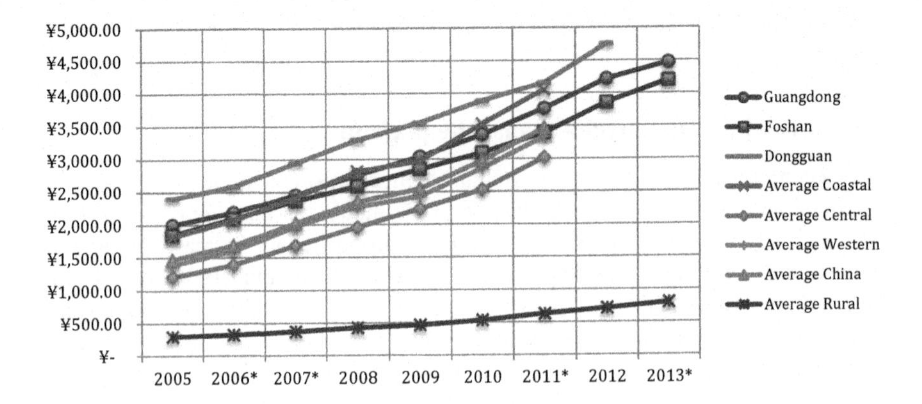

Figure 2.1 Average real wages selected regions in Guangdong (All China data, 2015)

* Guangdong Statistical Yearbook, various years.

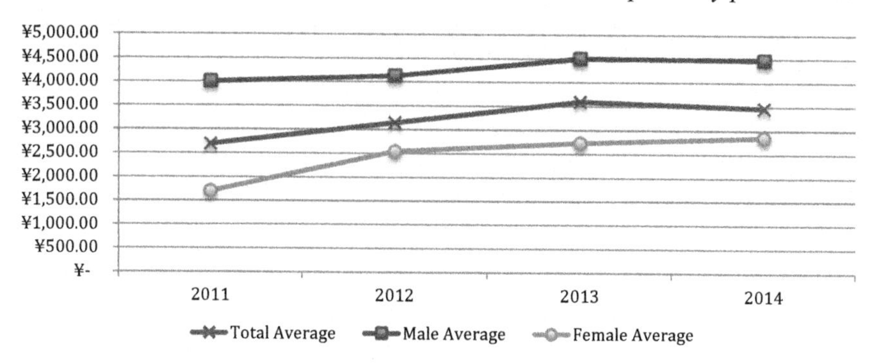

Figure 2.2 Average income interview respondents 2014 n=25, 2013 n=13, 2012 n=13, 2011 n=7

that on average 33 per cent of wages were made up of a variable component which fluctuates with enterprise output. Workers' salaries can be quite unstable, especially when external shocks impact business output.[9]

Figure 2.2 displays the average income as reported by respondents from the interviews: 25 respondents reported their incomes in 2014, 13 in 2013 and 2012, and 7 in 2011. Figure 2 shows a slightly different story to the one illustrated by Figure 2.1. Whereas Figure 2.1 shows a strong upward trend, Figure 2.2 represents a flatter profile and a lower average salary. Figure 2.2 is representative of the type of workers that were involved in this research project. The incomes reported by respondents in the sample are also supported by other recent studies in the region (see for example Butollo 2013). This suggests that even though aggregate incomes are rising due to the labour shortage, perhaps as economic upgrading creates new opportunities for the highly educated, industrial workers seem to be left out of this increase.[10] This is the other important factor pushing workers to entrepreneurialism.

Workers' strategies and the increasing importance of entrepreneurship

One important way that industrial workers have traditionally reduced precarity is through associational power. Associational power is the power of collective workers' organizations: trade unions, representations of workers on boards of directors, workers' councils and informal collective organizations (Wright 2000). In China this type of power is limited because there is only one union, the All China Federation of Trade Unions (ACFTU), which is institutionalized as an arm of the Communist Party. Other forms of organization are heavily restricted. The role of the Guangdong trade union is growing in importance as collective bargaining has been recently permitted, and the CCP is increasingly putting pressure on the union to quell workers' growing unrest (Int 58r).[11] However, a lack of proper representation leads to the continued problem that workers' demands rarely reach decision makers. Typically, much of the associational power in China is expressed through illegal wildcat strikes because of restrictions on the ability to organize and strike. However, the long-term effects of these strikes are limited by high turnover and relatively aggressive tactics by government and businesses to remove 'troublemakers' from factories, which continues to undermine industrial citizenship (Chan 2012a). Thus, the impact on precarity reduction is minimal in Guangdong except for in rare and spontaneous instances of wildcat strikes.

While associational bargaining power (Schmalz and Weinmann 2014) and unionism have not proven to be reliable mediating relationships, many workers believe entrepreneurship may be.[12] Entrepreneurship has grown dramatically as well, from being virtually non-existent in the 1980s and early 1990s to being a large part of the economy. Enterprises not controlled by a majority state ownership accounted for more than 70 per cent of GDP output in 2008 (Ahlstrom and Ding 2014). The pace of growth is often so rapid that from the inside timescales shrink; in most interviews a long period of time was around two years. If their lives are not improving or changing dramatically, it can be easily understood why workers are getting restless. When asked about her fears for the future this electronics worker explains, 'What I'm thinking is, the world is making progress every day and I can't be left behind' (Int 28w). As dramatic change continues to be a key feature of the Guangdong economy, little has changed in the remuneration for workers or their prospects because of a lack of the important mediating relationship of associational bargaining power. This situation leads workers to explore new opportunities.

Workers try entrepreneurship in a variety of different ways, either as small business ventures in Guangdong or opening businesses in their hometowns or other third-tier cities. The increased accessibility of starting up a business means that the benefits of working for a wage in private enterprises are negligible compared to the possibility of controlling one's own future through entrepreneurialism. Additionally, jumping between entrepreneurial and waged work is quite easy because of the labour shortage. Despite earning 2000rmb and having failed at an entrepreneurial venture two years earlier, Mrs Yang explains her continued desire for entrepreneurialism:

> B: Can you talk about your future plans?
> Mrs Yang: I want to work here for two more years and start my own business in my hometown.
> B: What kind of business?
> Mrs Yang: I would like to produce security bars or open a store to sell groceries.
>
> (Int 35w)

Mrs Yang typifies the administration's desire to create more entrepreneurship and her responses are typical of the majority of the respondents of her generation who are looking to entrepreneurialism as a form of stability in retirement (as opposed to relying on social benefits). Yet there remains a high degree of precariousness as her ability to earn wages, if the venture fails, will decrease, as the older she gets the more difficult it is to find a job. Mrs Yang is representative of many workers interviewed who were frustrated with the status quo and were looking for entrepreneurial opportunities to circumvent it (Int 21w, Int 35w, Int 36w, Int 39w, Int 49w, Int 53w, Int 73w). The revolving door between wage work and entrepreneurship created by the labour shortage provides workers with a small security blanket against poverty. However, surprisingly the labour shortage does not seem to be enabling social and economic mobility. Rather it seems to be creating conditions under which workers jump to a hopefully less precarious place through entrepreneurship.

Overcoming the plateau

In an attempt to overcome the precarity plateau, workers are choosing entrepreneurship. This specific form of entrepreneurship is a response to particularities of the Chinese context for workers. Baumol *et al.* articulate a category of entrepreneur called the replicative entrepreneur who 'produce[s] or sell[s] a good or service already available on the market [and …] represents a route out of poverty, a means by which people with little capital, education, or experience can earn a living' (Baumol *et al.* 2007: 3). Guiheux (2007) provides evidence of these replicative entrepreneurs in China by detailing an extensive list of categories of this type of entrepreneur who are forced into work after the companies they work for, mostly state-owned enterprises, are closed. And while these categories link with many of the attributes of the industrial worker-turned-entrepreneur in Guangdong discussed in this study, including selling existing products already on the market, little capital, education or experience, workers are not impoverished in the sense of the entrepreneur by reasons of survival (Berner *et al.* 2012). Therefore, other explanations are needed to understand the complexity of the Chinese construct of the worker-turned-entrepreneur and the reasons for the push to create more entrepreneurs in China.

Moore (1997) explains that in the transition from traditional to modern society the 'rationally self-interested, profit seeking, individualistic entrepreneur' is considered the ideal actor to break down traditional social barriers that impede modern commerce because of their eagerness to break from traditional social relations and seek greater profit. This definition on its own does not stand up in the case of workers in Guangdong because many small businesses rely heavily on family labour due to limited access to capital and other factors. Additionally, many worker/entrepreneurs in Guangdong occupy a complex social position being, on the one hand, fully proletarianized but, on the other hand, maintaining one foot in the countryside: they have a *dream* to go home one day or perhaps take a business idea and transplant it to their hometown (Lee and Kofman 2012; Chan 2010). Entrepreneurship also represents an escape route if things go really wrong.

However, Moore's (1997) definition certainly helps to link the entrepreneur to the concept of the Chinese Dream. Destruction of the traditional and its replacement by the modern and moderately prosperous future is at the core of the Chinese Dream. Thus, entrepreneurship is the path by which this dream can be realized. Furthermore, the ideal entrepreneur is not reliant on state transfers or social benefits. Therefore, by being self-sufficient, the entrepreneur is the ideal type of citizen for the modernization of China. Being self-sufficient highlights one of the paradoxes of entrepreneurship in China, as entrepreneurs are given virtually complete economic freedom yet their political freedom is strictly controlled. In fact, this type of entrepreneurship relieves pressure from the state by providing an outlet for aggrieved workers to have economic freedom through entrepreneurship (Chen 2002). Thus the category of self-reliant entrepreneur is unlikely to push for political change as their precarious position within wage labour and beyond forced them to turn their backs on collectivization in place of individual economic freedom.

Guiheux explains that, 'the transformation of workers into self-reliant and enterprising labourers is not indicative of the absence of power or governance, but is a technique of governing where the regulation and management of subjects happens through freedom' (2013: 124). In this way, Guiheux highlights the ironic win-win of entrepreneurship. Win for the workers because they have the freedom to break the bonds of wage labour through self-reliant entrepreneurship; win for the state because having self-reliant entrepreneurs is less expensive to govern. By creating the self-reliant entrepreneur, the state is able to separate workers from lifetime employment, to make them mobile subjects that can provide for themselves wherever they are needed. Thus, the state celebrates entrepreneurialism as a method of job creation to help absorb displaced workers (Guiheux 2013). This type of entrepreneurship which creates self-reliant subjects, the self-reliant replicative entrepreneur, is the type of entrepreneurs many industrial workers in China seek to become.

Conclusion

Precarity reduction for industrial workers in Guangdong has plateaued. Lack of security during retirement and wage stagnation during a period of tremendous growth are both signs that industrial workers in Guangdong are entering a new phase of precarity. This is because institutional instability is failing to act as an effective mediating relationship, especially during a worker's later years. Additionally, market mechanisms that are supposed to reduce precarity as the supply of labour decreases are not working because the mediating relationships necessary to pressure business owners are severely restricted by the state. Gone are the days of extreme poverty but in their stead new forms of precarity seem to be much more persistent. Workers are looking for solutions to overcome this precarity. Entrepreneurship is ostensibly one way to solve this problem, achieving the dual objective of the individual realizing the Chinese Dream and the government having one less group disturbing internal security. In reality this type of entrepreneurship is itself quite precarious. This is especially the case if the labour shortage eases and businesses start failing; workers will no longer have the security of easily returning to wage labour and do not possess strong mediating relationships to assist them with starting or maintaining their businesses. Regardless, entrepreneurship is one of the few avenues that industrial workers have to overcome the precarity plateau. Serious questions remain about how successful entrepreneurship will be for industrial workers and what is sacrificed by individualizing responsibility for precarity reduction. Are workers themselves undermining their best interests by focusing on entrepreneurship instead of collectivization? What are the political consequences of this choice? We certainly cannot ignore the compelling nature of owning one's own business, but how are the possibilities for labour mobilization minimized when, rather than seeing being a worker as something that one is proud of, wage work is seen as one stop on the way to something better? The Chinese Dream may be simultaneously forcing Chinese industrial workers deeper into precarity while further minimizing the role of the Chinese labour movement, a strategy that may seriously restrict precarity reduction in the long-term.

Notes

1 Fieldwork took place in the summer of 2014 when there were acute labour shortages. This situation has changed since mid-to-late 2015 which has resulted in an increased frequency of layoffs due to the economic slowdown.

2 Under the socialist Iron Rice Bowl system, the *danwei* was the main connection between industrial workers and the state. *Danwei* is the term used to refer to the place of work in China. The *danwei* provided all of the essential responsibilities of the social safety net which included housing, healthcare, schools, shops, as well as bureaucratic and administrative functions like permission to marry, have a child or travel.

3 Fieldwork was conducted with Dr Stefan Schmalz. Funding for the fieldwork came from my SSHRC Masters-CGS as well as the Friedrich-Schiller-Universität Jena and especially the DFG research group for fieldwork funding that was obtained by my co-investigator Dr Stefan Schmalz.

4 Low-wage service workers were interviewed to understand why choices were made about working in manufacturing or services and what the benefits of each was in relation to reducing precarity.

5 The SER was not the norm in China under the Iron Rice Bowl, but rather it was reserved for formal industrial workers; the majority of people were in fact peasants, strictly excluded from the system.

6 Workers described in this group are overwhelmingly fully proletarianized. Semi-proletarianized workers are able to rely more extensively on the security and some transfers afforded to them in rural areas and if necessary using their farmland for subsistence (Zhan 2011). Yue *et al.* (2010) evaluate the perspective of workers and the choices they make regarding whether they want to move back to the countryside after retirement. They find that an older generation of workers (those born before 1970) want to move back to the countryside and younger workers are less inclined to do that. Pun and Lu (2010) suggest that because first generation workers more easily consider retiring in the countryside they are less politically active then the second generation of migrant workers who are better educated and either grew up in the city or were left-behind children, growing up in the countryside while their parents had migrated for work. Although I suspect that the choice to move back is a moving target as workers get older and realize that they are increasingly precarious in the cities as the retirement support is minimal, they will more consciously consider moving back to the countryside, suggesting incomplete proletarianization.

7 This refers to the 2011 Social Insurance Law which attempts to universalize coverage for all workers. This law details provisions for pension, health insurance, maternity insurance, work accident insurance and unemployment insurance.

8 The number refers to the chronological order of the interviews, and the letter refers to w=worker, o=factory owner, a=employment agency, 0=other supporting interviews including academics, lawyers, teachers, or other interested parties.
9 Based on the answers of 24 respondents.
10 The high GINI may be one indicator to support his argument but the GINI is a highly contested figure in China for fear that it will increase social unrest. So commentators using independent surveys estimate that China's current GINI is between 0.47 and 0.52 and growing and considered very high, risking social instability (Yue *et al.* 2013). For a discussion on the problems of the GINI in China see (Yue *et al.* 2013; Kanbur *et al.* 2005; Sen 2005).
11 An agreement permitting collective bargaining was finally approved in Guangdong on 1 January 2015.
12 Other new opportunities include staying in the countryside due to increased funding for rural activities (Zhan and Huang 2012), and possibilities of moving to the service sector, although interviews with service workers showed less remuneration than in factory work.

References

Ahlstrom, D. and Ding, Z. (2014) Entrepreneurship in China: An overview. *International Small Business Journal* 32(6): 610–18.

Arnold, D. and Bongiovi, J.R. (2013) Precarious, informalizing, and flexible work: Transforming concepts and understandings. *American Behavioral Scientist* 57(3): 289–308.

Baumol, W.J., Litan, R.E. and Schramm, C.J. (2007) *Good Capitalism, Bad Capitalism, and the Economics of Growth and Prosperity*. New Haven, CT: Yale University Press.

Berner, E., Gomez, G. and Knorringa, P. (2012) 'Helping a large number of people become a little less poor': The logic of survival entrepreneurs. *European Journal of Development Research* 24(3): 382–96.

Blecher, M. (2009) *China Against the Tides,* 3rd ed. London: Bloomsbury Publishing.

Boltanski, L. and Chiapello, E. (2006) The new spirit of capitalism. *International Journal of Politics, Culture, and Society* 18(3–4): 161–88.

Butollo, F. (2013) *The End of Cheap Labour in China?* Frankfurt am Main: Johann-Wolfgang-Goethe Universität zu Frankfurt am Main.

Castel, R. (1996) Work and usefulness to the world. *Int'l Lab Rev* 135(6): 615–22.

Castel, R. (2002) *From Manual Workers to Wage Laborers*. New Brunswick: Transaction Publishers.

Chan, A. and Siu, K. (2012) Chinese migrant workers: Factors constraining the emergence of class consciousness. In Carrillo, B. and Goodman, D. S. G. (eds), *China's Peasants and Workers: Changing Class Identitites*. Cheltenham: Edward Elgar Publishing.

Chan, C.K.- C. (2012a) Class or citizenship? Debating workplace conflict in China. *Journal of Contemporary Asia* 42(2): 308–27.

Chan, C.K.- C. (2012b) *The Challenge of Labour in China*. New York: Routledge.

Chan, K.W. (2010) A China paradox: Migrant labor shortage amidst rural labor supply abundance. *Eurasian Geography and Economics* 51(4): 513–30.

Chen, A. (2002) Capitalist development, entrepreneurial class, and democratization in China. *Political Science Quarterly* 117(3): 401–22.

Dörre, K. (2014) Precarity and social disintegration: A relational concept. *Journal Für Entwicklungspolitik* 30(4): 69–89.

Friedman, E. (2014) Alienated politics: Labour insurgency and the paternalistic state in China. *Development and Change* 45(5): 1001–18.

Gallagher, M.E. (2005) *Contagious Capitalism: Globalization and the Politics of Labor in China*. Princeton: Princeton University Press.

Gibb, A. and Li, J. (2003) Organizing for enterprise in China: What can we learn from the Chinese micro, small, and medium enterprise development experience. *Futures* 35(4): 403–21.

Guiheux, G. (2007) The promotion of a new calculating Chinese subject: The case of laid-off workers turning into entrepreneurs. *Journal of Contemporary China* 16(50): 149–71.

Guiheux, G. (2013) Chinese socialist heroes: From workers to entrepreneurs. In Florence, E. and Defraigne, P., *Towards a New Development Paradigm in Twenty-First Century China. Economy, Society and Politics*. New York: Routledge, pp. 115–26.

Kaiming, L. (2013) The shortage of peasant workers and the dilemma facing Chinese industry. In P. Defraigne, P. and Florence, E. (eds), *Towards a New Development Paradigm in Twenty-First Century China*. New York: Routledge.

Kalleberg, A.L. and Hewison, K. (2013) Precarious work and the challenge for Asia. *American Behavioral Scientist* 57(3): 271–88.

Kanbur, R., Wan, G. and Zhang, X. (2005) Introduction: Growing inequality in China. *Journal of the Asia Pacific Economy* 10(4): 405–7.

Lee, C.K. (2007) *Against the Law. Labor Protests in China's Rustbelt and Sunbelt*. Berkeley: University of California Press.

Lee, C.K. and Kofman, Y. (2012) The politics of precarity: Views beyond the United States. *Work and Occupations* 39(4): 388–408.

Lee, C.K. and Zhang, Y. (2013) The power of instability: Unraveling the microfoundations of bargained authoritarianism in China. *American Journal of Sociology* 118(6): 1475–508.

Merk, J. (2008) Restructuring and conflict in the global athletic footwear industry: Nike, Yue Yuen and labour codes of conduct. In M. Taylor (ed.), *Global Economy Contested: Power and Conflict Across the International Division of Labour. Rethinking Globalizations*. New York: Routledge, pp. 79–97.

Moore, M. (1997) Societies, polities and capitalists in developing countries: A literature survey. *Journal of Development Studies* 33(3): 287–363.

Pun, N. (2007) Gendering the dormitory labor system: Production, reproduction, and migrant labor in south China. *Feminist Economics* 13(3–4): 239–58.

Pun, N. and Lu, H. (2010) Unfinished proletarianization: Self, anger, and class action among the second generation of peasant-workers in present-day China. *Modern China* 35(5): 493–519.

Schmalz, S. and Weinmann, N. (2014) 'Two crises, two cycles of contention. Workers' protests in Western Europe in comparison'. Paper presented at ISA World Congress of Sociology. Yokohama.

Schmalz, S., Sommer, B. and Xu, H. (2017) The Yue Yuen strike: Industrial transformation and labor unrest in the Pearl River Delta. *Globalizations* 14(3).

Sen, A. (2005) Conceptualizing and measuring poverty. In D. B. Grusky and R. Kanbur (eds), *Poverty and Inequality*. Stanford: Stanford Univ Press, pp. 30–46.

Sina News (2015) The State Council issued a document to encourage entrepreneurship to promote employment. *Sina News*. Available from: http://news.sina.com.cn/c/2015-05-03/082931787668.shtml [Accessed January 25, 2016].

So, A.Y. (2009) Rethinking the Chinese developmental miracle. In H.-F. Hung (ed.), *China and the Transformation of Global Capitalism*. Baltimore: The Johns Hopkins University Press.

Sweeney, P. (2015) China is promoting college grads to startup CEOs. Available from: http://uk.businessinsider.com/r-beijing-promotes-low-paid-college-grads-to-startup-ceos-2015-10 [Accessed January 28 th, 2016].

The Economist (2013a). Chasing the Chinese dream. *The Economist*, 4 May 2013. Available from: www.economist.com/news/briefing/21577063-chinas-new-leader-has-been-quick-consolidate-his-power-what-does-he-now-want-his [Accessed 28 June 2015].

The Economist (2013b) China's Future: Xi Jinping and the Chinese dream. *The Economist*. 3 May 2013. Available from: China's Future: Xi Jinping and the Chinese dream. Available from: www.economist.com/news/leaders/21577070-vision-chinas-new-president-should-serve-his-people-not-nationalist-state-xi-jinping [Accessed 28 June 2015].

Vosko, L.F. (2009) *Managing the Margins: Gender, Citizenship, and the International Regulation of Precarious Employment*. Oxford: OUP.

Wright, E.O. (2000) Working-class power, capitalist-class interests, and class compromise. *American Journal of Sociology* 105(4): 957–1002.

Xu, F. (2014) *Looking for Work in Post-Socialist China: Governance, Active Job Seekers and the New Chinese Labor Market*. New York: Routledge.

Yang, C. (2012) Restructuring the export-oriented industrialization in the Pearl River Delta, China. *Applied Geography* 32(1): 143–57.

Yang, D.T., Chen, V.W. and Monarch, R. (2010) Rising wages: Has China lost its global labor advantage? *Pacific Economic Review* 15(4): 482–504.

Yu, X. and Hu, X. (2013) China's reform of the migrant labour regime and the rural migrants' industrial citizenship. In Florence, E. and Defraigne, P. (eds), *Towards a New Development Paradigm in Twenty-First Century China*. New York: Routledge, 89–104.

Yue, X. Li, S. and Gao, X. (2013) How large is income inequality in China: Assessment on different estimates of Gini coefficient. *China Economic Journal* 6(2–3): 113–22.

Yue, Z., Li, S., Feldman, M.W. and Du, H. (2010) Floating choices: A generational perspective on intentions of rural–urban migrants in China. *Environment and Planning A* 42(3): 545–62.

Zhan, S. (2011) What determines migrant workers' life chances in contemporary China? Hukou, social exclusion, and the market. *Modern China* 37(3): 243–85.

Zhan, S. and Huang, L. (2012) Rural roots of current migrant labor shortage in China: Development and labor empowerment in a situation of incomplete proletarianization. *St Comp Int Dev* 48(1): 81–111.

3 Hybrid areas of work in Italy

Hypotheses to interpret the transformations of precariousness and subjectivity

Emiliana Armano and Annalisa Murgia

Introduction

In this period of late-capitalism and austerity, new areas of work are emerging outside the current system of regulations, and they seem to be expanding out of all proportion. Our contribution proposes the concept of 'hybrid areas of work' as an alternative to the more common one of 'grey zones' (Supiot 1999; Freedland 2003). The intention is to supersede the polarisation which counterpoises a 'black' and a 'white', and to question the historical binary opposition between standard and non-standard work arrangements, and between employment and self-employment. Moreover, while the adjective 'grey' evokes the idea of being undefined and undistinguishable, with 'hybrid' we refer to the co-existence of features usually attributed to categories that have been traditionally kept sharply distinct, by acknowledging the kaleidoscopic and complex character of contemporary work. In our understanding, a renewed interpretation of work is also needed in order to rethink the concepts of inequality and precariousness as they emerge from subjective experiences. Indeed, the emerging areas of work are no longer – or at least not only – mere containers of the growing forms of 'non-standard' employment; they also concern the ideology, expectations, and social imagery that permeate forms of work that, though organised around neoliberal rules, can create zones of experimentation and withdrawal from the dominant model (Corsani 2012).

In light of the Italian case, and twenty years after the introduction of so-called 'project work' into labour law, the questions that we address are these: How is the social world populated by freelancers structured? How is precariousness perceived in hybrid areas of work? And above all, what are the devices of subjectivity that invest experiences and representations poised between growing inequalities and growing margins of autonomy?

Querying the concept of hybrid areas of work for a renewed understanding of social inequalities

The case of precarious freelancers and project workers

The aim of this chapter is to conduct a discussion that is wide-ranging but starts from a specific context, that of Italy. In terms of employment relations, the Italian system has undergone profound changes in labour law. They began in 1995 – the year when the National Social Security Institute (INPS) established a special fund for freelancers and 'project workers' – and continued with the reforms of 1997, 2003, and 2012, and then the more recent 'Jobs Act' of 2015. These reforms have substantially altered contractual work arrangements by fostering the rapid and extensive spread of employment relations impossible to classify in terms of the classic dichotomy between salaried employment and self-employment. In this chapter, we focus on a hybrid area of work which falls formally under the heading of 'self-employment' (Bologna and Banfi 2011; Armano and Murgia 2013), but which is extremely heterogeneous in its composition. Indeed, so-called 'project workers' comprise both 'dependent self-employed workers', hired on a self-employed contract only because this was the cheapest option for the employer (Muehlberger and Bertolini 2008; Eichhorst *et al.* 2013), and highly skilled professionals, who work project by project in a mode of work organisation typical of freelancers (Rapelli 2012).

Therefore, at the core of this study are the experiences of different subjects comprised in the heterogeneous category of self-employed workers, who possibly represent themselves differently, and who work in different sectors and with different pay levels, but all of whom were hired on the same self-employed contract. In particular, we shall analyse some key dimensions around which social inequalities have been traditionally articulated – a precarious status, a low pay level and a lack of rights and social protection – and then re-interpret these inequalities in light of the transformations of subjectivities.

As discussed in previous works (Armano and Murgia 2013), in our view, the process of making people precarious, or social precarisation, is a mode of subjectivation. In other words, it is a process essential for shaping contemporary forms of subjectivity as a whole. Therefore, while we recognise that precarity is particularly evident in temporary, discontinuous, and uncertain employment relations, our interest is not restricted to 'employment precarity', which characterises a structural condition tied to the employment contract; rather, our concern is with 'precariousness', a term which better describes an experiential state that permeates the entire lives of individuals (Murgia 2010; Armano and Murgia 2013), a quality inherent to a person's specific position. In these terms, the concept of precariousness concerns experiences that are partial and situated, so that the different, manifold, and dynamic positions differ not only among individuals – in this case independent professionals or dependent self-employed workers – but also for the same individual over time.

In regard to inequalities connected to the economic dimension, it has been emphasised that the recent economic crisis has exacerbated the polarisation of incomes by widening the range of income distribution (Piketty 2013). A recent study on project workers and freelancers in Italy (Di Nunzio and Toscano 2015) has highlighted the situation of these 'new working poor': 57.8 per cent of a sample of 2,210 subjects, in fact, declared that they earned less than 15 thousand euro gross per year. However, according to neoliberal doctrine, this condition of impoverishment does not necessarily lead to the emergence of new inequalities, since it is often perceived as normal performance-related pay and therefore not as unfair. Income inequalities, which according to the logic of Fordism were generally represented as such, are now not even recognised as inequalities, but rather as the consequence of different remunerations for differing capacities. Thus as incomes diminish, there is a growing sense of inadequacy with respect to social expectations, goals, and self-perception in the socially dominant model of the neoliberal culture.

Finally, a last dimension usually analysed in order to understand social inequalities in the emerging areas of work regards the forms of social protection. In fact, the changes in the socio-productive system have come about in a context of deregulation of the Fordist welfare system, which selectively protected key actors in the production cycle, but today is out of joint and increasingly distant from a social structure no longer founded on salaried and permanent employment. Thus, in recent years, inequalities in terms of access to social rights and welfare have been exacerbated by several factors: the precarisation of work, which has become normal for a large part of society (Lorey 2015), the related growth of hybrid areas of work characterised by unprotected or weakly protected contractual forms, and the simultaneous existence of a welfare system still excessively patterned on a Fordist model. In this regard, while recent studies on freelancers and project workers in Italy (Di Nunzio and Toscano 2015) stress that these workers should have access to social security (e.g. maternity, paternity and parental leave, sickness leave, unemployment benefits, etc.), they also report a marked propensity for associative commitment (grassroots and auto-organised groups, co-working spaces, freelancers' cooperatives, etc.). Therefore, the apparently non-organisable character of precarious workers – especially in the hybrid area composed of different kinds of self-employment – seems to require new forms of collective action outside the traditional trade union system, in order to address the issue of precariousness by alternative forms of representation based on shared knowledge and on the network as the organisational form.

Interpretive hypotheses: Re-reading inequalities in light of the transformations of subjectivities

Inequalities and precariousness do not refer merely to the polarisation which has occurred in past decades in the distribution of good and bad jobs, levels of income, access to rights and social protection (Kalleberg 2009; Vosko 2010); they also refer to how they are represented and legitimised in the current social imagery and dominant culture. These changes have led to the emergence of unprecedented social inequalities which reconfigure the perimeters of the risk zones drawn by the above-mentioned structural factors. Indeed, in contemporary knowledge societies, the wide and multiple senses of precariousness and inequality experienced by people can no longer be read within the narrow confines of employment relations; rather, they should be considered as intertwined with the subjectivities of individuals and with their different positions.

We maintain that, in order to conceptualise the phenomenon, it is necessary to analyse the dominant cultural representations by adopting a critical approach (Deleuze 1990). In this regard, we hypothesise that representations are socially constructed into an order of ideas based on principles of individualisation and meritocracy different from those of the past. In this scenario – based on a systematic evaluation of individuals with respect to performance on the job and their 'potential for development' – the ways in which 'merit' and individual performance or 'excellence' are interpreted by those concerned differ according to their adherence to that order. Cultural representations are therefore themselves social processes and products. They are constructs consisting of interactions among different social actors; interactions whose outcomes are open and not at all predetermined. In fact, while on the one hand the current forms of freelance and project work are increasing economic self-precarisation and thereby sustaining neoliberal capitalism (Puar 2012), on the other, the construction of innovative and creative formats also leaves space for the invention of new subjectivities able to face the emerging inequalities collectively (Lorey 2015) within the hybrid areas of work.

To contextualise the discussion on forms of inequality in highly tertiarised economies, we refer to the transformations of subjectivity that have fashioned the new spirit of capitalism (Boltanski and Chiapello 1999). We therefore assume as our interpretative framework that there are now broad processes where human activities tend to come about according to the typical logic of business. We are witnessing a process in which the subject becomes an enterprise (Gorz 2001), in particular self-employed workers; in other words, the dynamic of neoliberalism foresees the capitalisation of the self – that is, making oneself into competitive human capital (Dardot and Laval 2009).

In this chapter we concentrate in particular on the case of project workers and precarious freelancers in Italy, who engage in different activities and professions, regardless of the skills level. The theoretical-interpretative approach adopted explores the subjective, existential, as well as work-related condition of precarious self-employed workers, conceptualised as a broad and composite social group. This positioning is in fact connected to employment conditions – which are usually considered to classify workers as 'dependent self-employed' or as 'independent professional' – but it is primarily and variously characterised by the individual assumptions of risk by social actors and by the cultural representations to which they adhere.

Case studies and research design

The discussion that follows is based on two different research projects focused on precariousness and knowledge work, and carried out in Northern Italy between 2006 and 2012. In the first project, we conducted 39 in-depth interviews with knowledge workers employed in different sectors: information technology, digital production, the Web, new media, multimedia arts, publishing, training, and research (Armano 2010). The second project was carried out in Milan, Bologna and Trento in 2011–2012. Thirty interviews were conducted with highly educated precarious workers who had at least five years of work experience (Murgia and Poggio 2014).

As mentioned above, the precariousness of knowledge workers in the hybrid areas of work is highly heterogeneous. On the one hand, there are those who choose to work as freelancers, managing the discontinuity of income and the transitions between one job and another. On the other hand, there are those who are also self-employed, but who perceive themselves as fake self-employed, since they would opt for salaried employment if they had an opportunity to make decisions on their contract. Nonetheless, our research identified some common and recurrent aspects that point to a phenomenology of subjectivity that cuts across these different positionings. In what follows we discuss four devices that, in our view, transform subjectivities according to the new spirit of capitalism and generate new inequalities and a sense of precariousness in subjects' trajectories within the hybrid areas of work. In order to shed light on the main devices that characterise the transformation of subjectivity, we shall outline some exemplary subjective characteristics; that is, devices that we assume to be common to the various experiences considered.

Research findings

The task-oriented logic and the contingency of employment relations

The first device that we consider consists in the task-oriented logic, and in the sense of the contingent which is the core of the imagery that can be constructed around that logic. The Fordist model of industrial production, which used to be based on the system that the British historian of industry Edward Thompson termed 'clock-work' – work regulated by the criterion of time as measured by the clock – has shifted to work regulated by tasks, projects, and objectives, and measured by results. This task-oriented logic grounded on performance-based criteria is a *modus operandi* that shapes the new organisational form of capitalist production and the positioning of the self in relation to others typical of knowledge work.

> I have various project jobs … on or off the books. […] I don't know if they'll pay me, plus other projects and other things that are more or less always … I try to stay within the area for which I've been trained.
>
> [32 years old, Milan]

> These work times are tied to project deadlines [...] with ever shorter schedules and more and more standardised products, a lot of copying and pasting, and especially processing times reduced to the minimum, with heavy mental stress. Until a few years ago I saw only the advantages, today after a few more years ... there's a downside. I don't know anyone who's never spent a weekend working or stayed up all night because the next day they have to deliver and they're late.
>
> [39 years old, Turin]

In the experiences of the interviewees, self-employment and freelancing exhibit new forms of precariousness and subordination which depend more directly on the internalisation of market logic and certainly less on an external disciplinary authority as in the age of the clocking-on machine in industrial society. In this sense, the interviewees appreciate the supposed freedom that derives from the absence of the forms of external control typical of industrial work (fixed schedules and clocking on and off machines). But they feel the strain of having to balance different projects in order to maintain work consistent with their training, and of respecting the increasingly tight deadlines that must be met to obtain payment. What at first glance seems to be a choice and a form of freedom thus shows its dark side: the difficulty of self-imposing limits to engagement in productive activity. To cite the thought of Foucault and Deleuze, we may say that with the expansion of forms of work based on the accomplishment of tasks, we have moved from a form of external disciplinary control to control internalised in the social body of work.

Identification, 'passion trap' and free work

The second subjective feature – closely related to the previous one – is the identification of the self with working activities, which is connected in two ways with precariousness to become a source of self-exploitation and a vehicle for the subsumption of personal qualities and emotions whose value is exploited, as well as professional competences and skills (Morini and Fumagalli 2010). It is a part of the process defined as self-precarisation, which has become a normal way of living and working in neoliberal societies (Lorey 2006). In this logic of valuing passion and the most intimate and emotional aspects, passions and desires may become traps. In fact, when a person's passion for a certain job acts as a driver of his/her action based on intimate and emotional involvement, then this involvement may become an outright trap (Ballatore *et al.* 2014; Murgia and Poggio 2014) which induces that person to accept even unbearable working and contractual conditions. Moreover, this dynamic leads to a qualitative amplification of the phenomenon that years ago Sergio Bologna and Andrea Fumagalli (1997) termed 'domestication', i.e. the non-distinction between life and work, which does not simply consist in a lack of distinction between the times (and places) of life and work; indeed, they are so profoundly fused in the person's identity that s/he can no longer distinguish between being a worker and being a person.

> I believe that my work and life are the same things. I mean, I'd like my work to be my everyday life, in the sense that my work is very dynamic. I have so many different things to do. I'm in contact with lots of people, so I don't have one day like any other. I devote most of my free time to my work. In the end, I don't have any free time, even if my excuse for being self-employed is to say 'I manage my free time as I want' …
>
> [39 years old, Trento]

> Personally, I live with these materials in my everyday life as well … even the films that I go to see at the cinema … a DVD … a magazine that I buy. There's no discontinuity among my personal life, hobbies, and job.
>
> [35 years old, Turin]

This ambivalence translates into a device that leads even to the possibility of working for free (Chicchi *et al.* 2014), beyond contractual obligations and fixed working hours; and it breaks down the distinction between life time and work time. Emblematic in this regard are the concepts of 'free work' (Beverungen *et al.* 2013; de Peuter *et al.* 2015) and 'free labour' (Ross 2016) that identify working activities which are free but also unpaid, and act as devices to maintain precarisation in a process of normalisation. In this regard, it is crucial to understand the difference between the meaning that individuals attach to their practices – a sense of achievement and remuneration in terms of identity – and the function performed at a systemic level by gratuitous participation in the production of value. In fact, the way in which people represent social inequalities, and whether or not they perceive having suffered them, is closely bound up with their level of emotional involvement in their work, which may change – even with the same income and contractual conditions – from one individual to another, but also for the same individual over time. In a sense, we may argue that the system of social inequality is more pervasive, the more it is not identified as such. Indeed, the model of contemporary capitalism seems to set up an invisible chain sustained by the same people that it alienates. While exploitation has been defined as the extortion of surplus value, today it more closely resembles 'voluntary servitude' (Durand 2004).

The promise of (material and symbolic) recognition

The device of the promise – which is closely connected with the above-described mechanism of a person's identification with his/her work – consists mainly in the repositioning of the person within a debtor–creditor relationship that overlaps with and replaces the relationship between the worker and the employer. The specific moral of promise (like the power of debt, as argued by Lazzarato 2012) is not exercised with repression, but rather with the internalisation of those values and desires that induce the subject voluntarily to assume commitments. In exchange for a promise, the person therefore renounces and self-divests his/her rights, and his/her capacity as a choice-maker. The logic of the promise, far from concerning the employment relation alone, impacts on public and social life. In fact, it is not exclusively a form of economic compensation by the company – a new (paid) job or the renewal of a contract – but a (personal) relationship between the employee and the employer in which symbolic value plays a crucial role.

> They told me 'Two years, then we'll see ... there's a two-year project, then we'll probably give you a one-year contract.' […] So you make sacrifices, give up having a family, hope that things will soon get better. But you say … I can hack it till the end of the month and continue to do something that I enjoy. […] But you always have to live with compromises.
>
> [37 years old, Bologna]

> The main worry at work is that they promise you, they promise you, and then … you're still waiting, and you continue to work like crazy. My fear is … but not so much at the economic level, more at the personal one, in the sense that I really believe in the project that I'm doing. […] And I'm afraid of getting caught up in this thing … which might then disappoint me … my worry is that I'll switch off.
>
> [34 years old, Trento]

Among the various studies that have investigated the device of the promise in recent years (e.g. Bascetta 2015), of particular interest is the one by Carrot Workers Brigade (2012), which has declined the concept of promise as the 'syndrome of free labour' by discussing the results of a self-inquiry – a critical collective practice, therefore – conducted among interns and precarious workers in creative jobs in the UK. The analysis concerns workers' expectations and the unpaid work performed by virtue of an explicit or implicit promise. More specifically, it focuses on the lives of a generation of young people ready and willing to stake their subjectivity, their relationships, and more generally their lives, on a process that leads to an overlap between new inequalities and subjectivation processes.

Network and relationality

This fourth feature, which subjectively characterises self-employed knowledge workers, is relationality, i.e. embeddedness in a relational network. The jobs of project workers and freelancers typically take place within a dense network of contacts extending beyond the formal boundaries of the workplace as a physical and regulated space. In fact, thanks also to mobile technology, working activities re-territorialise themselves in a space of connectivity in which trust, work, and learning relationships are constructed and need to be constantly reproduced and maintained.

> Then there began another recent trend […], free work, right? All very free, 'Look, come in only when it's necessary.' Bloody cell phone, it makes you almost always contactable. It's gone from being a very free job, where I could

> be somewhere in Italy and say I was in Turin, which nobody bothered about, to being a job with two cell phones constantly ringing…
>
> [30 years old, Turin]

> We're constantly in contact with customers, we're asked to be ... there's always someone who's working and has to get results, so ... they ask us to keep our cell phones switched on even when we're on holiday ... you're always connected, and in any case friendship starts with the customers. They've got your personal contacts; it's difficult not to answer. But you can still find ways to disappear; you have to have imagination [*laughs*] ...
>
> [31 years old, Trento]

The interview excerpts show that the jobs of the project workers and freelancers interviewed took place within a network that was reterritorialised in an intermediate space, neither public nor private, which constituted a veritable transcorporate network. While in the Fordist period, the physical locus was the office or the factory, in knowledge work the physical place extends to other spaces (often elsewhere in the metropolis) where the various projects on which people work are located. The main feature of these networks is the relational dimension: interpersonal relationships are essential for survival, but at the same time they discipline work relations. In fact, while on the one hand the workers acquire degrees of freedom in terms of mobility and time management, on the other, they must be constantly available, precisely because of the 'subjective' nature of their work contacts. Moreover, the importance of interpersonal relationships and friendships does not replace that of formal relations, which instead flank and intertwine with them. Hence the rules of employment contracts continue to exist formally; but predominant are practices which are apparently more fluid but in fact substantially more rigid and binding. It is in this type of professional network – in which the more it becomes personal, the more it functions professionally – that the new inequalities in hybrid areas of work are constructed. Nevertheless, the person still has margins of freedom to self-organise in the looser mesh of the networks and the creative interweaving of their threads.

Discussion: Devices of subjectivity and of value extraction – emerging inequalities and the precariousness of trajectories

The above-described devices transform contemporary neoliberal subjectivities and generate new inequalities and a sense of precariousness in people's trajectories. The combined effect of the four devices is to produce a Darwinian mechanism of social selection between those with the resources to manage transitions from one project to another and those who do not possess those resources. This, therefore, is a systematic mechanism implicit in the system, although it is invisible, which transfers the weight of social, as well as business, risks to single individuals.

In order to define how such subjectivity devices engender new inequalities in employment relations, we have focused on what we have termed the 'emerging hybrid areas of work' in Italy. These are populated by workers who, although they have formally independent contracts, cannot necessarily enjoy wide margins of freedom and autonomy. Our intention, however, has been not so much to take part in the debate that seeks to distinguish between 'real' and 'bogus' self-employed workers (Eichhorst *et al.* 2013) as to give account of a complex, polysemic, and sometimes highly contradictory area of work where inequalities between individuals assume unprecedented and constantly changing forms. The fact that job precariousness has extended to all professions and social classes does not mean that inequalities have been eliminated or that individuals have become equal in insecurity. In fact, as efficaciously highlighted by several inspiring authors: 'the logic of neoliberalism thrives on inequality, because it plays with hierarchised differences and governs on this basis' (Puar 2012: 172).

In our opinion, the hybrid areas of work make up a category emblematic of the changes taking place in the world of work and the new inequalities that characterise it. Freelancers and self-employed workers – but to an increasing extent all categories of workers – are required to have skills different from those of the past. They must first demonstrate cooperative and interpersonal skills, which translate into both new expectations of corporate loyalty by the employee and informal norms related to the 'affective work' inherent in large parts of the emerging forms of work (Hardt 1999; Morini 2010). This is especially evident in knowledge-based production and the service sector – where deregulation and individualisation are the norm and adaptability a core requirement – as well as in the new media and training industries, in which cultural representations of 'creativity' and self-promotion fuel and circumscribe the imaginations of individuals (Dardot and Laval 2009; Corsani 2012; Cingolani 2014). Common to many of these areas is an ethic of work and self-activation that accompanies an unprecedented intensification of work and a process of self-precarisation.

Consequently, the hybrid, ambivalent and contradictory nature of this condition cannot be investigated by means of linear and simplificatory analyses. If we adopt this perspective, we can no longer be content with counterposing self-employment and dependent employment, or (supposed) standard work and (not further defined) 'non-standard' work. Beyond reductive and simplifying labels, what is crucial, we believe, is understanding how experiences of subjectivity are varyingly patterned by economic/contractual and symbolic issues. Therefore, to speak of hybrid areas of work is to speak of free work, identity, lifestyle, and how the devices of subjectivity and value extraction are activated. Moving in this direction, moreover, would also mean acknowledging that the acquisition of new rights is also a matter of subjectivity management. From this perspective, analysis of the fabrication of the neoliberal subject loses the semblance of abstract theorisation to become pragmatically oriented and crucial for interpretation of the changes taking place.

Conclusions

To conclude the argument of this chapter, we shall discuss the relationship among emerging hybrid areas of work, new inequalities, and social and political action:

that is, what Standing (2014) in one of his latest works has called the transition between the 'class-in-becoming' (composed of temporary workers) and 'citizenship-in-becoming'. In this scenario – characterised by the dynamics described in the previous sections – the challenge is to combat inequalities while bearing in mind that – at least potentially – people in the hybrid areas of work are already opposed to both the neoliberal agenda (scant social protection, vulnerability to blackmail, loss of control over personal time) and the social-democratic tradition based on monolithic professional identities and wage labour as providing access to welfare.

This can be done on the one hand by embracing the 'beyond employment' approach (Supiot 1999; Vosko 2010), which pursues a vision of labour and social protection inclusive of all people, regardless of their labour-force status, in periods of training, employment, self-employment, and work outside the labour force, including voluntary work, unpaid caregiving and civic engagement (Lee and Kofman 2012). On the other hand, however, it should also theoretically address the issue of the managerialisation of subjectivity to understand how it can be reappropriated by withdrawal from commodification and valorisation. It is therefore not just a matter of determining what, or how much more, workers in the hybrid areas of work should be paid, and the benefits and forms of social protection to which they should be entitled. It is also necessary to understand how to mobilise collective social action when the value-extraction device merges with expression of passions, when free work is self-gratifying, when the wage itself becomes a promise, and when professional relationships become intimate and personal. How can these devices of subjugation and subjectivity be removed? The tradition of industrial work was based on respect for promises and agreements, which then became employment contracts. But today the contracts that really matter are the informal, 'psychological' ones in a Faustian dimension where life-time now is given in exchange for a future that is expected but utterly uncertain.

In an attempt to answer these questions, some theorists have talked of micropolitical practices of resistance to inequality; others have envisaged a return to mutualism through the invention of new forms of social cooperation and a bottom-up welfare state. These experiences involve embryonic, but important situations, especially at a time when traditional forms of collective representation have progressively lost their efficacy. At the same time, however, they do not currently have the necessary impetus to change the balance of power in society and to alter national and international agendas. The underlying problem is that, in the age of precariousness, models of social coalition and (self)representation should primarily foresee and include recognition of subjects with such differently positioned expectations and demands. The prospect to be hoped for is the creation of affirmative and recompositive practices, so as to hold together social cooperation and new institutions, autonomy and neo-mutualism, also on the basis of demands for a minimum income as a social equality which takes into account and respects differences, and a new project for social change.

References

Armano, E. (2010) *Precarietà e innovazione nel postfordismo. Una ricerca qualitativa sui lavoratori della conoscenza a Torino*. Bologna: Odoya.

Armano, E. and Murgia, A. (2013) The precariousnesses of young knowledge workers. A subject oriented approach. *Global Discourse* 3(3–4): 486–501.

Ballatore, M., Del Rio Carral, M. and Murgia, A. (eds) (2014) Quand 'passion' du métier et précarité se rencontrent dans les professions du savoir. Special Issue of *Recherches Sociologiques et Anthropologiques* 45(2).

Bascetta, M. (ed.) (2015) *L'economa della promessa*. Roma: Manifestolibri.

Beverungen, A., Otto, B., Spoelstra, S. and Kenny, K. (eds) (2013) Special Issue on Free work. *Ephemera: Theory & Politics in Organization* 13(1).

Bologna, S. and Banfi, D. (2011) *Vita da freelance. I lavoratori della conoscenza e il loro futuro*. Milano: Feltrinelli.

Bologna, S. and Fumagalli, A. (1997) *Il lavoro autonomo di seconda generazione*. Milano: Feltrinelli.

Boltanski, L. and Chiapello, E. (1999) *Le nouvel esprit du capitalisme*. Paris: Gallimard.

Carrot Workers Brigade. (2012) Free labour syndrome. Volunteer work or unpaid overtime in the creative and cultural sector. In Armano, E. and Murgia, A. (eds), *Mappe della Precarietà, vol. II, Knowledge workers, creatività, saperi e dispositivi di soggettivazione*. Bologna: Odoya, pp. 51–65.

Chicchi, F., Risi, E., Fisher, E. and Armano, E. (eds) (2014) Free and unpaid work, gratuity, collaborative activity and precariousness. Processes of subjectivity in the age of digital production. Special Issue of *Sociologia del lavoro* 133.

Cingolani, P. (2014) *Révolutions précaires. Essai sur l'avenir de l'émancipation*. Paris: La Découverte.

Corsani, A. (2012) Autonomie et hétéronomie dans les marges du salariat. Les journalistes pigistes et les intermittents du spectacle porteurs de projets. *Sociologie du travail* 54(4): 495–510.

Dardot, P. and Laval, C. (2009) *La Nouvelle Raison du monde. Essai sur la société néolibérale*. Paris: La Découverte.

de Peuter, G., Cohen, N.S. and Brophy, E. (eds) (2015) Special Issue on Interrogating Internships: Unpaid work, creative industries, and higher education. *Triple-C* 13(2): 329–602.

Deleuze, G. (1990) Post-scriptum sur les sociétés de contrôle. *Pourparlers*. Paris: Éditions de Minuit.

Di Nunzio, D. and Toscano, E. (2015) *Vita da professionisti*. Roma: Associazione Bruno Trentin.

Durand, J.P. (2004) *La chaîne invisible. Travailler aujourd'hui: flux tendu et servitude volontaire*. Paris: Seuil.

Eichhorst, W., Braga, M., Famira-Mühlberger, U., Gerard, M., Horvath, T., Kahancová, M., Kendzia, M.J., Martišková, M., Monti, P., Pedersen, J.L., Stanley, J., Vandeweghe, B., Wehner, C. and White, C. (2013) Social protection rights of economically dependent self-employed workers. *IZA Research Report* 54. Available from: www.iza.org/en/webcontent/publications/reports/report_pdfs/iza_report_54.pdf [Accessed: 27 July 2016].

Freedland, M. (2003) *The Personal Employment Contract*. Oxford: Oxford University Press.

Gorz, A. (2001) La personne devient une entreprise. Note sur le travail de production de soi. *Revue du MAUSS*, 18(2): 61–6.

Hardt, M. (1999) Affective Labor. *Boundary* 26(2): 89–100.

Kalleberg, A.L. (2009) Precarious work, insecure workers: Employment relations in transition. *American Sociological Review* 74(1): 1–22.

Lazzarato, M. (2012) *La fabbrica dell'uomo indebitato.* Saggio sulla condizione neoliberista. Roma: DeriveApprodi.

Lee, C.K and Kofman, E. (2012) The politics of precarity: Views beyond the United States. *Work and Occupations* 39(4): 388–408.

Lorey, I. (2006) Governmentality and self-precarization: On the normalization of cultural producers. *Transversal.* Available from: http://eipcp.net/transversal/1106/lorey/en [Accessed 27 July 2016].

Lorey, I. (2015) *State of Insecurity: Government of the Precarious.* London: Verso.

Morini, C. (2010) *Per amore o per forza. Femmilizzazione del lavoro e biopolitiche del corpo.* Verona: Ombrecorte.

Morini, C. and Fumagalli, A. (2010) Life put to work: Towards a theory of life-value. *Ephemera: Theory & Politics in Organization* 10(3–4): 234–52.

Muehlberger, U. and Bertolini, S. (2008) The organizational governance of work relationships between employment and self-employment. *Socio-Economic Review* 6(3): 449–72.

Murgia, A. (2010) *Dalla precarietà lavorativa alla precarietà sociale. Biografie in transito tra lavoro e non lavoro.* Bologna: Odoya.

Murgia, A. and Poggio, B. (2014) At risk of deskilling and trapped by passion: A picture of precarious highly educated young workers in Italy, Spain and the United Kingdom. In Antonucci, L., Hamilton, M. and Roberts, S. (eds), *Young People and Social Policy in Europe: Dealing with Risk, Inequality and Precariousness in Times of Crisis.* London: Palgrave, pp. 62–86.

Piketty, T. (2013) *Le capital au XXIe siècle.* Paris: Éditions du Seuil.

Puar, J. (2012) Precarity talk: A virtual roundtable with Lauren Berlant, Judith Butler, Bojana Cvejić, Isabell Lorey, Jasbir Puar, and Ana Vujanović. *TDR/The Drama Review,* 56(4): 163–77.

Rapelli, S. (2012) *European I-Pros: A Study.* London: Professional Contractors Group (PCG).

Ross, A. (2016) Working for nothing – The latest high-growth sector. In Armano, E., Bove, A. and Murgia, A. (eds), *Mapping Precariousness, Labour Insecurity and Uncertain Livelihoods: Subjectivities and Resistance.* London: Routledge.

Standing, G. (2014) *A Precariat Charter: From Denizens to Citizens.* London: Bloomsbury.

Supiot, A. (1999) *Au delà de l'emploi: transformation du travail et l'avenir du droit du travail en Europe.* Paris: Flammarion.

Vosko, L.F. (2010) *Managing the Margins: Gender, Citizenship, and the International Regulation of Precarious Employment.* Oxford: Oxford University Press.

4 The French Business and Employment Cooperative

An autonomy factory?

Marie-Christine Bureau and Antonella Corsani

In the mid-1990s, a new concept of cooperative was developed in France, the Business and Employment Cooperative (BEC). Every project leader, entrepreneur and creator of their own job, is entitled to apply for membership in a BEC; in that way, they can be supported by the cooperative during the launch period. As soon as the business generates revenues, the project leader signs an employment contract with the cooperative; he becomes an employee of the BEC. The cooperative invoices clients for the services provided by the salaried entrepreneur, and pays wages, social contributions and taxes. For every salaried entrepreneur, the salary is indexed to his own turnover and the BEC collects a percentage to cover the costs related to management and shared services (administration, accounting, taxation, etc.). Thanks to this non-standard form of employment, the project leader benefits from employee status, while retaining autonomy in his work. He thus enjoys control over his business activity and his working time.

In some ways the BEC sounds like an umbrella company, but there are major differences. First, the nature of the contract: salaried entrepreneurs are mostly recruited on permanent contracts, while the short-term contract is a standard in most umbrella companies. More significantly, individual and collective support is an essential function of BECs. Continuing education (business, profession, trade, cooperation) constitutes their *core business*. Furthermore, its cooperative status sets BECs apart from umbrella companies: the salaried entrepreneur is destined to become a member of the cooperative. We could say, using the titles of two books written by Elisabeth Bost (2011) and Béatrice Poncin (2004), two major actors in the BEC movement, that a BEC is constituted by 'entrepreneurs – employees without a boss – cooperative members'.

Nevertheless, for a large number of salaried entrepreneurs, the salary conditions remain of low quality, since they depend on the business revenue; in many cases they do not meet the eligibility criteria for social rights (unemployment insurance, retirement coverage, etc.). Therefore, the 'entrepreneur – employee without boss – cooperative member' quite often experiences the precarious condition characteristic of the neoliberal era. Are BECs not extending precariousness? Are they not the Trojan Horse of neoliberalism? (Darbus 2006). We aim to provide some answers to these questions, but first we have to specify what we mean by neoliberalism.

According to Michel Foucault (2004), neoliberalism must not be understood as a political philosophy, a theory, or an economic policy, but as a political rationality, an art of governance. As a technique of government, neoliberalism produces subjectivities or, more precisely, a kind of subjectivity. From this point of view, the prefix 'neo' may hide a rupture in the story of liberalism (Jeanpierre 2006): new techniques of government and new forms of subjectivities. The subject of the Fordist era was a good worker and a family head; for him, the consumption of goods and leisure was a compensation for workplace alienation. But the subject of the neoliberal era is a new subject, free at work and acting in a world of widespread competition.

Looking back at the history of the BECs, we will see, in the first part of the chapter, how these structures have been teetering on a razor's edge from the outset. They are developing in the wake of neoliberal employment policies and contribute to a new form of government, but they also constitute a political laboratory for experimentation and institutional innovation so as to prefigure a new horizon of emancipation beyond salaried work and individual entrepreneurship. Studying the story of Coopaname, the largest BEC in France, we will try to develop this point in the second part. As a political laboratory, BECs also hijack neoliberal techniques and produce other collective subjectivities, against the mainstream logic of individualization. This will be the focus of the third part of this chapter.

Teetering on the razor's edge

The first BEC was created in 1995 against an economic and social backdrop of high unemployment (around 8.5 per cent). Nevertheless, the extent of unemployment is only one part of a global transformation that affects the organizational models of large companies, labour relations and employment policies.

Nowadays the overarching aim of the capitalist enterprise is to 'go lean', with few workers and machines, by outsourcing low value-added production and focusing control on strategic tasks. This had already been the case in the textile industry in Lyon since the 1960s. The response of the silk workers, in fact, inspired the formation of the BEC. In the 1960s, the silk industry began to outsource part of its production. The silk workers, subcontractors for textile firms, decided then to organize themselves into a cooperative, the COOPTIS company, in order to increase their bargaining power with their principal contractors. This experience nurtured the seeds of the BEC concept.

As the industrial enterprise goes lean, it also becomes finance-oriented. This entails two interrelated processes: a growing prominence of financial assets and intellectual property rights – in this way, the enterprise becomes a product (Hannoun 2010) rather than a production-oriented organization; the financialization of remuneration – stock options and forms of incentives aim to involve employees in the company plan, especially at the very top level. The process of financialization also concerns indirect wages (funded pension schemes). This is a major subjectivation device that produces the hybrid figure of the 'salaried-rentier' (Corsani 2013), at the opposite end of the precarious-indebted worker, who is often *self-employed.*

The emergence of a grey zone between salaried work and self-employment is the result of a double and contradictory process of flexibilization and stabilization of workers. The new management encourages employees to behave like autonomous workers, whereas the new self-employed are heteronomous (Supiot 2000; Corsani 2012) without enjoying the social rights of salaried workers. In other words, we observe a process of formal 'de-salarization' and precarization (Bologna and Fumagalli 1999).

This grey zone consists in part of self-employed and/or intermittently unemployed workers. It is a zone 'without rights' because it remains in the blind spot of labour protections that are based on the Fordist model and rely on the binary distinctions between salaried work and self-employment, as well as employment and unemployment. This grey zone, whence the concept of the BEC is emerging, expands gradually, depending on new employment policies. The increasing number of self-employed in developed countries (ILO 2015) is a valuable indicator of the potential development of the grey zone, impelled by workforce management policies as well as public employment policies.[1]

The guidance provided to the unemployed as part of the latest employment policies can be described as a political involvement of subjectivity (Cantelli and Genard 2007) in a global project geared to the transformation of every individual into a 'self-entrepreneurial' subject (Foucault 2004). But as early as the 1970s, social workers developed a critical reflection on the practices established by their profession in the implementation of public policies. At the end of the 1970s, these reflections led to the creation of associative and cooperative projects with craftsmen, workers and artists outside institutions. This is the case of the company SMTS (Société de Manutention de Travaux et Service), a maintenance company, created in Grenoble, which tried hard to reconcile an objective of economic integration with the perspective of developing collective entrepreneurship (Poncin 2004). SMTS was based on a certain pooling of business revenues: in that system, everyone in turn could owe a debt to the others, or become a creditor. This form of sharing requires mutual trust and long-term involvement. The SMTS experience prefigures the BEC concept.

In the 1980s the figure of 'project initiator' or 'business developer' (*porteur de projet*) was perceived negatively as an answer to the employment crisis, and positively as an opportunity to develop autonomous work. In 1985, Elisabeth Bost created an association in order to provide an institutional framework for project initiators. At the same time, she was recruited by a business developer with the task of supporting unemployed workers in the creation of businesses. In this context she found a way of combining these two tasks and founded the first BEC, CAP Services, in 1996 in Lyon. According to Elisabeth Bost, project initiators wish to create their own activity, rather than become entrepreneurs (2011). This distinction is very important in understanding the 'core business' of BEC and its sidestepping of the neoliberal logic: it is less a matter of creating individual businesses or transforming every worker into a self-entrepreneur, than of rethinking work and enterprise in a pragmatic way (Veyer 2010).

BECs developed rapidly in France from 1995, with further acceleration from 2001 onward, when a decree from the Ministry of Employment allowed people to experiment with salaried entrepreneurship. They organized two networks, COPEA (Association nationale des Coopératives d'Activité et d'Entrepreneurs) and 'Coopérer pour entreprendre', which differ in their legal status and in their philosophy. The first focuses on the creation of businesses, the second on the task of implementation. These two aspects are indicative of the tension between two logics. COPEA is a national association of cooperatives, whereas 'Coopérer pour entreprendre' looks like a cooperative of cooperatives. COPEA focuses on the development of long-term viable businesses – justifying a selection process for entry – whereas the BECs in 'Coopérer pour entreprendre' focus on a public service mission, to make use of public funding and welcome any project. Béatrice Poncin stresses this point:

> The concept is twofold and its naming reflects the duality: a BEC has a goal of inclusion in the labour market through economic integration – the name of 'business cooperative' is used to mean the opportunity to test a project – but also a goal of mutually supportive development of activities – the name of 'employment cooperative' means the sustainable pooling of employments.
>
> (Poncin 2004: 73)

The BECs developed thus on a razor's edge, between the implementation of neoliberal policies and criticism by cooperative practice, at the crossroads of two different perspectives. Nevertheless, over time the BEC project has evolved and both networks interact, as is shown in the recent history of the two largest cooperatives, Coopaname and Oxalis, linked together now in two significant projects: 'Bigre!' (Boy! Good Lord!) and 'Manufacture cooperative' (Coopaname 2013; Bodet 2016). The story of Coopaname exemplifies the common process of evolving towards a 'mutual work cooperative'.

Coopaname: a permanent political laboratory

In 2003, the BECs had developed on a national level but they still had no presence in the Paris region. An experiment was then launched in Paris, on the initiative of the network 'Coopérer pour entreprendre'. The network entrusted the mission to one of its members from Grenoble with several years of experience in the field, and two more people were recruited some time later. This was the beginning of Coopaname in 2004: the BEC concept was exported from the provinces to the capital, in the opposite direction to the processes usually observed in France. According to the account by J. Sangiorgio, who was co-managing director of Coopaname with Stéphane Veyer until 2014, the pilot team agreed on a common task: turn Coopaname into a 'permanent laboratory' and foster, in this way, a dynamic for all the BECs. Coopaname's story is thus a 'work in progress' at every moment. While the first generation of BECs aimed overall to secure career paths for project initiators, the BEC subsequently evolved towards a more ambitious goal, to become a shared company: 'the second-generation BEC no longer aims to secure the creation of individual businesses, but to sketch out an alternative through a project of collective entrepreneurship' (Sangiorgio and Veyer 2009).

The tensions running through the BECs from the outset between support for neoliberal employment policies and social innovation tend to diminish under this common horizon: to become shared enterprises, and furthermore, mutual work cooperatives. Coopaname, which is an outstanding BEC in size and evolution, now works like a cooperative group, without acting as a parent company: smaller cooperatives were created as legally independent entities although they can benefit from the mutualisation of tools inside the group (such as administration and human resource management). By 2014, with a legal status of SCOP-SA, Coopaname brought together more than 750 people, which included 445 salaried entrepreneurs, 228 accompanied people and 26 permanent employees. Twenty-five per cent of the employees were shareholders, and this share is growing. The cooperative has a majority of women (more than 60 per cent) and is characterized by the high level of education of its employees: more than 60 per cent have a level greater than or equal to high school + 3 more years (Bac+3). Qualified service providers are over-represented. In 2014, the turnover was more than 6 million euros, after doubling in five years. Although the per-person public funding has decreased, the average per-person revenue is increasing.

Nevertheless, the salaried entrepreneurs who succeed in generating sufficient revenues remain a minority. As a matter of fact, a third of the employees work on short-term contracts and 82 per cent are part-time workers. The average number of working hours per month is around 55.[2] These poor working conditions explain a significant turnover: in 2014, 107 salaried entrepreneurs left the cooperative[3] and 129 new contracts were signed. The precariousness of salaried entrepreneurs affects the whole company, through the volatility of the work collective. On the basis of this fact, Coopaname decided to conduct research, in order to imagine its future, beyond the principles of the BEC, with a view to ensuring more regular income streams for its members and increasing their standard of living.

The founding document of the project 'Mutual Work Cooperative' is ambitious. It aims to innovate globally, through principles of mutuality, both work and employment. This document emphasizes the notion of 'security' and proposes several possible interpretations of the mutual work cooperative, noting the fact that we can pursue various aims, according to our vision of work itself and the importance we wish to grant it in our life. So, according to the authors, the mutual work cooperative can be imagined in various ways: as a support for emancipation, in order to resist the various forms of subordination and heteronomy; as a vector to facilitate professional transitions and multiple activities; as a means to allow everyone 'to live as well as possible by working less'.

When we became interested in this kind of cooperative company, we soon started meeting members of Coopaname. We were requested by the Research

Commission to contribute to the collective reflection on the mutual work cooperative project and invited to attend some of the BEC events to observe its functioning. We gradually decided, in agreement with the cooperative's members, to conduct a long-term sociological survey.[4] The design of the survey is inspired by two influences: the early phase of Italian workerism (*Operaismo*) which conceived the methodology of 'co-research' (Alquati 1993), gathering researchers and non-researchers in order to produce common knowledge; and the works of John Dewey (1993). According to Dewey, a survey does not aim to attain knowledge of reality for its own sake, but in order to change this reality. The survey is precisely the endeavour to solve a problem, in this case the precariousness that undermines individual careers and collective life inside the BEC. It requires a long time-span for transformation. The validation of results is linked to the validity of the solutions presented. This perspective leads us to a sequential approach: the results of each sequence constitute the starting point for further sequences, while the process of objectivation allows shifting of the initial problem. In a way, Coopaname's story is a story of shifting problems by democratic practices of solution finding.

Autonomy as collective enterprise

The absence of hierarchical relationships represents both the anomaly and the power of the BEC concept. Far beyond formal and institutional aspects, the refusal of hierarchical relationships, as well as the refusal of individual self-employment, seems to be a core value of Coopaname. The rejection of a relationship of subordination, which Coopaname's members have experienced during their career as salaried workers, constitutes for many of them one of the strongest motivations to join the cooperative, as the following excerpts from interviews we conducted with Coopaname's members attest:

> Coopaname is a tool for my freedom and my flexibility. It allows me to invoice who I want, when I want, to say yes to some clients, and to say no to others. It grants the possibility to remain free, independent, autonomous, but still benefit from social protection.
>
> (Economics journalist and writer, employee of Coopaname for more than 5 years)

> I wanted to make a living from my activity, without having to refer to anybody. I didn't want to be put into a salaried status. Coopaname allowed me to achieve this.
>
> (Webdesigner in Coopaname for more than 5 years)

> If I have no other choice than to face commercial pressures, the pressure might as well be mine!
>
> (Clinical psychologist, former employee in human resources management)

If the relationship of subordination that characterizes the employee status is rejected, that does not necessarily mean that the formal aspect of the employment contract disappears, and employee rights may be activated. But how can we account for a salaried status without a relationship of subordination, or a salaried worker without a boss, who is nevertheless entitled to benefit from social rights that are usually the counterpart to subordination? At the beginning of the BEC, this anomaly was accepted by public authorities, in the name of the right to experimentation. A relationship of subordination was later acknowledged by public powers, due to the form of compensation: entrepreneurs don't issue invoices in their own name, but in the name of the cooperative, and they don't collect fees directly. That is a formal solution, which nevertheless makes it possible to conceive social rights as a pooling of risk, rather than as the counterpart for accepting subjugation. In the BEC concept, there is no boss, but when the project initiator applies for membership in a BEC, it is, in a certain way, an act of wilful subordination, a way to acknowledge his dependency on the collective. At the same time, his autonomy is limited by the contractor's power. In fact, a major issue is how to increase the bargaining power of entrepreneurs with their contractors.

Since 2005, in view of the number of its employees, Coopaname has been legally obliged to have representative bodies for its staff. BEC members have begun thinking about the role of representative bodies, in this particular context where everyone is at the same time his own employer and his own employee. Nathalie Delvolvé and Stéphane Veyer tell this story:

> Rather than elect puppet representative bodies, in order to comply with the letter of the law, we decided to get into the spirit of the law and to imagine a staff representation, adapted to the challenges of the cooperative, even if that meant taking the necessary time and taking some liberties with the letter of the law.
>
> (Delvolvé and Veyer 2010)

Conceiving the employment contract as a voluntary subordination to the collective, they define employee representation as:

1. a means to collectively protect employees and employers, where the self-employed are both the boss and the employee;
2. the linchpin in a 'pedagogy of resistance' against the abusive or even irregular practices of contractors who tend to impose social dumping;
3. a counter-power against the moral authority of the cooperative's management over its members.

BEC members highlight the importance of promoting law, social dialogue and social protection in independent work, where there is usually none of these things. In this way, the representation of salaried entrepreneurs can be understood as an institutional innovation: indeed, it adapts a major device of industrial relations, against a background where psychosocial risks do not arise from the relationship of subordination, but from other forms of economic and moral dependency, as well as from an unreasonable involvement of salaried entrepreneurs in their own business. On a wider scale, power relationships are constantly questioned in Coopaname; this characterizes a political laboratory. In that perspective, what holds the members together is less the adherence to a common concept than the involvement in its invention. To this end, meeting opportunities are numerous: monthly meetings, General Assemblies, Autumn University, commissions, etc. If pooling and sharing are a basis of the BEC, their development is at stake, in order to increase the project initiators' autonomy. The establishment of groups within the cooperative, as well as the endeavour to create shared spaces, marks a change in focus towards a future of the mutual work cooperative. Against income inequalities and precariousness, the creation of groups is a tool, used to increase the capability of everyone to generate a sufficient volume of activity and earn his own living.

Today, Coopaname appears as a laboratory for the experimental formation of multiform collectives, offering a vast range of possibilities, in order to articulate individual activity and collective commitment. The concept of a collective taking shape through these dynamics is not one of a group with defined borders that everyone must either belong to or not, but rather that of a process directed to develop the possibilities for a common future. In other words, collective formation is the process by which individuals share their 'becoming as future' (Simondon 1989). This vision dovetails, in a way, with Charles Fourier's utopia of 'passionate series', by offering to all the possibility of choosing their level of cooperation as well as its duration, the possibility of circulating between various levels of commitment, between several forms of 'independence in the plural' (Bureau and Corsani 2012). So conceived, commitment does not turn into a moral duty but rather into a passion and a search for pleasure.

This collective dynamic does not affect every salaried entrepreneur. Motivations for joining BECs are heterogeneous: some salaried entrepreneurs are only looking for access to social rights, whereas others aim to experiment with new work relationships. Nevertheless, if joining the BEC can be due to chance rather than result from adherence to common values, the whole dynamic of the cooperative and interactions in different groups produce a transformation of subjectivity. Autonomy is no longer an individual situation but a collective project, based on mutual knowledge and learning cooperation. In that sense, Coopaname constitutes a resistance zone within the neoliberal fabric of subjectivity.

Conclusions

Coopaname is a political enterprise, in the sense that it is an institutional fabric. By 'institutional fabric' we mean the long-term work done by the members involved, in order to change mental categories, imagine some alternatives and gain acknowledgement at different levels of legitimacy: charters, partnership agreements, social security and labour law, etc. This endeavour is part of the process of 'permanent self-institution of society' (Castoriadis 1975): according to Castoriadis, the institution is a symbolic network where functional and imaginary dimensions are combined in a variable relation and varying proportions. The institutional fabric requires both an imaginary and a means of action. It is an intense work of language and thought, as well as a struggle for new rights.[5]

Analysing Coopaname's experience, we can see that BECs, though harbouring some forms of precariousness, prefigure at the same time a path of emancipation in the grey zone between salaried work and independent work: from that perspective, the autonomy of each person is guaranteed by the balancing out of independence and cooperation. The cooperation that we are discussing here does not refer to the legal status, but to the interactions inside the structure and the collective experience that contribute to nourishing the individual and collective imaginary.

Notes

1 According to the European Employment Observatory, the increasing number of independent workers in Europe attests the success of policies that incentivised and encouraged the unemployed to start their own business. Moreover, the Europe 2020 Strategy underlines incentive devices for the support of independent work.
2 The importance of part-time work must be understood in reference with arrangements in determining working time and remuneration level. The latter is determined in order to secure income by the smoothing of wages.
3 Twenty-five per cent gave up on the idea of developing their own business, 18 per cent returned to salaried work, 11 per cent created an individual company or a cooperative outside Coopaname.
4 The survey was conducted as part of a project financed by the National Research Agency (ANR): 2011–2015 ANR 2011 SHS (Human and Social Sciences) Programme: 'Changing societies. Inequality-Inequalities;' Project: 'Evolving Employment Norms and Emerging Forms of Inequality Towards a Comparison of Grey Zones', coordinated by Donna Kesselman.
5 Finally, the struggle for institutional recognition of BEC was won on 20 May 2014, by a vote in the National Assembly.

References

Alquati, R. (1993) *Per fare conricerca*. Padua: Calusca Edizioni.

Bodet, C. (2016) *La manufacture coopérative*. Available from: http://manufacture.coop/. [Accessed: 24 July 2016].

Bologna, S. and Fumagalli, A. (1997) *Il lavoro autonomo di seconda generazione*. Milan: Feltrinelli.

Bost, E. (2011) *Aux Entreprenants Associés. La coopérative d'activités et d'emploi*. Valence: REPAS.

Bureau, M.C. and Corsani, A. (2012) *Un salariat au delà du salariat?* Nantes: PUN.

Cantelli, F. and Genard, J.-L.(eds) (2007) *Action publique et subjectivité*, tome 46. LGDJ.

Coopaname (2013) *Bigre! Une coopération de 7.000 personnes!* Available from: www.coopaname.coop/actualite/bigre-cooperation-7000-personnes. [Accessed: 24 July 2016].

Castoriadis, C. (1975) *L'institution imaginaire de la société*. Paris: Seuil.

Corsani, A. (2012) Autonomie et hétéronomie dans les marges du salariat. Les journalistes pigistes et les intermittents du spectacle porteurs de projets. *Sociologie du travail* 54(4): 495–510.

Corsani, A. (2013) Rent and subjectivity in neoliberal cognitive capitalism. *Knowledge Cultures* 1(4): 67–83.

Darbus, F. (2006) Reconversions professionnelles et statutaires. Le cas des coopératives d'emploi et d'activités. *Regards sociologiques* 32: 23–35.

Delvolvé, N. and Veyer, S. (2010) La quête du droit : approche de l'instauration d'une représentation du personnel dans une coopérative d'activités et d'emploi. *Actes du 23ème colloque de l'ADDES.* Paris. Available from: www.coopaname.coop/sites/www.coopaname.coop/files/file_fields/2015/07/06/2011-recma-delvolveveyer-laquetedudroit.pdf. [Accessed: 24 July 2016].

Dewey, J. (1993) *Logique. La théorie de l'enquête*. Paris: PUF.

Foucault, M. (2004) *Naissance de la biopolitique. Cours de 1978-1979.* Paris: Gallimard-Seuil.

Hannoun, C. (ed.) (2010) *La dématérialisation de l'entreprise*. Paris: L'Harmattan.

Jeanpierre, L. (2006) La mort du libéralisme. *In* Alizart, M. and Kihm, C. (eds), *Fresh Théorie II.* Paris: Léo Scheer, pp. 405–29.

International Labour Organization (ILO) (2015) *World Employment and Social Outlook: The Changing Nature of Jobs*. Available from: www.ilo.org/global/research/global-reports/weso/2015-changing-nature-of-jobs/WCMS_368626/lang--en/index.htm. [Accessed: 24 July 2016].

Poncin, B. (2004) *Salariés sans patron?* Bellecombe-en-Bauges: Éditions du croquant.

Sangiorgio, J. and Veyer, S. (2006) L'entrepreneuriat collectif comme produit et projet d'entreprises épistémiques : le cas des coopératives d'activité et d'emploi. *Revue de l'entrepreneuriat* 5(2): 89–102.

Simondon, G. (1989) *L'individuation psychique et collective*. Paris: Aubier.

Supiot, A. (2000) Les nouveaux visages de la subordination. *Droit Social* 2: 131–45.

Veyer, S. (2010) Cessons de créer des entreprises. *Impertinences 2010: huit contributions pour penser et agir autrement*. Editions de la documentation Française. Available from: www.coopaname.coop/sites/www.coopaname.coop/files/file_fields/2015/07/13/2010-stephane-veyer-impertinence-2010-cessons-de-creer-des-entreprises.pdf. [Accessed 24 July 2016].

5 Against precarity, against employability

Ivor Southwood

The discourse of employability

A key ideological instrument for normalising precarious work is the contemporary discourse of employability and the vast industry to which it has given rise. The capitalist state uses this discourse to project a position of flexibility and fungibility onto its subjects, who are assigned the duties of endlessly advertising themselves and competing for episodes of work, and made to feel responsible for bringing about their own insecurity or poverty, regardless of the economic conditions imposed upon them. This chapter explores how the language of employability has expanded into an orientation towards work and a relation with the self and others that has superseded the traditional compartmentalised model of employment and is rapidly colonising welfare provision and educational curricula. The discussion focuses specifically on the situation in the United Kingdom, and refers to examples from British institutions.

The official discourse of employability can be traced back at least as far as 1998, when the UK government's Department for Education and Employment commissioned a think-tank to write a report documenting the significance of this emerging term. Employability is defined here, within the context of the end of job security, as 'the capability to move self-sufficiently within the labour market to realise potential through sustainable employment' (Hillage and Pollard 1999: x–xi). In the new environment of flexible work, the report suggests, individuals should be ready to move regularly between jobs and roles, and be able to manage their own 'transitions' by using their 'employability assets' effectively.

This definition of employability is framed by a corporate/governmental duty to institutionalise and formalise insecurity as a positive development and as the only possible way forward. Stable employment, the report implies, is simply a thing of the past, as obsolete as the age of steam, incompatible with the realities of a globalised and virtualised economy. Years later this story is wearily familiar. Precarious working conditions are conflated with technological progress and must be embraced, like it or not. Objections to these conditions are viewed as nostalgic weakness or intransigence, an inability or unwillingness to move with the times.

The power of capitalism is inextricably linked to this need for the business-owning and political class to maintain its own security by engineering insecurity in its proletarian labourers, through an economic system in which survival is reliant upon the indefinite surrender of one's 'assets'. After industrialisation and post-Fordism, the emphasis upon employability as a form of empowerment and self-management, signifying both personal responsibility and individual fulfilment, is the latest configuration of the ruling ideology. Self-employment and entrepreneurship have filled the void left by the hollowing out of occupational or union identity. Connectivity, epitomised by the mobile phone, has replaced collectivity; the personal narrative has replaced history. Class conflict is displaced onto individual anxiety and peer competition, enabling a relation of frictionless exploitation.

Whereas in the past workers would identify themselves as a group and the employer would stand out as a singular focus of hostility, now this arrangement has been mystified or even reversed. While the worker is isolated, with co-workers positioned as rivals rather than colleagues, the boss is dispersed across a whole network of abstract institutions: not just employer but recruitment agency, welfare advisor, landlord, credit card company, all of which are combined in an internalised virtual authority which oversees and audits one's attempts to act as a responsible, hard-working, 'employable' citizen. Under such conditions, workplace resistance becomes impossible. Complaints bounce back off sealed administrative entities onto the individual; dissent is fatal; industrial action is merely self-destructive.

The actual attributes required of the employable candidate in this environment are 24/7 flexibility and unquestioning positivity, and the rise of employability might be viewed as crucial in the legitimising not only of precarity but also of emotional labour as a form of social control. The UK government report mentioned above identifies three types of assets needed by the employable individual: 'knowledge, skills and attitudes'; and then goes on to explicitly compare the development and presentation of these assets to the process of 'production, marketing and sales'. Simple possession of knowledge and skills is no longer enough: self-sufficient individuals also need to promote these qualities competitively, to 'exploit their assets, to market them and sell them' (Hillage and Pollard 1999: x–xi).

So, the key to employability is self-exploitation. Knowledge and skills have been separated from the old, obsolete model of work and redefined as human capital. The third asset, 'attitude', is perhaps the most significant in engineering this change, as it dissolves the boundary between the internal and external or work and non-work areas of the employable worker/candidate's life. Attitude can no longer be held back by the worker but must now be brought to market and sold to the capitalist, in manual as well as service jobs. The employee has a duty to show enthusiasm, to express personal interest in the success of the business and suppress signs of boredom, to convey a positive outlook regardless of the actual conditions of work, because the attitude (or a convincing performance of that attitude) is part of the job description and often indistinguishable from other core duties. In terms of selling oneself in competition with other equally qualified/desperate candidates and effecting smooth 'transitions' between roles, this attitudinal packaging attracts continual scrutiny: a moment's hesitation, the slightest glitch in the performative display, can turn an asset into a liability.

After stepping to the side of the process of production in order to operate the machines, as Karl Marx would say, today's worker/'jobseeker' is required to jump onto the assembly line and arrange her own 'personal assets' into a saleable form. The language of employability provides both an operating manual for this human assembly line and a catalogue of its products, models of what Michel Foucault, in his study of the origins of neoliberalism, calls *homo oeconomicus*: the human defined not as a partner in an exchange but as a living commodity, an entrepreneur of oneself (Foucault 2010: 226; Moore 2009: 246, 265).

Scholarly employability

Since the 1990s the employability industry has undergone its own period of expansion due to the growing need to teach people how to adapt to and prepare for this new quasi-objective reality of work. As part of its 'employability framework', the Department for Education and Employment report recommended that education programmes for 16–17-year-olds should incorporate work experience and mock interviews to help students 'present their assets to employers' (Hillage and Pollard 1999: 27–9). Similarly, between 2002 and 2006 the newly formed Higher Education Academy, regulator of standards in higher education, published a series of reports under the heading 'Learning and Employability' (Moreland 2006; Yorke and Knight 2004). While mostly consisting of jargon, these papers nevertheless functioned as ideological nudges to institutions seeking to satisfy the HEA's official criteria.

The bureaucratic pressure has brought results, and universities have become highly efficient human factories. Students are required to attend lectures on employability, and interview techniques and social networking are now regarded as legitimate fields of academic knowledge. The amnesic and individualising effect of this curricular innovation is illustrated by the case of a history lecturer being ordered to use a seminar to instruct degree students in CV-writing (Sarson 2013). While some academics are cajoled into delivering such material, others make it their life's work: employability has its own gurus and specialists and has become a profession and scholarly subject in its own right.

As ever more physical and mental space is invaded by work-related duties and anxieties, it seems at times that life itself has become a compulsory game of employability, an endless, banal quest to find and keep work. As Phoebe Moore puts it, employability 'requires people to use every waking minute for preparation for entering into an unpredictable job market, or for management and education of the self once a person is in work, meaning that everyday life is subordinated to these preparations and activities' (Moore 2009: 245). Higher education is increasingly seen as providing the map for this personal journey into employability, and the student who does not enter into the spirit of this interactive adventure will fail, maybe not academically but almost certainly economically and socially. The parallel cultural curriculum which students were once encouraged to pursue alongside a degree, giving a training in how to critique and resist structures of power, has been turned into its opposite, a handbook for subordination filled with shortcuts to management and tips on how to out-conform your peers by standing out (i.e. blending in) in the graduate job market (Trought 2011). Unprecedented levels of student debt and anxiety about finding work after graduation have of course contributed greatly to this transformation.

Having been incubated in government policy and higher education, employability has now, like its shadow term 'jobseeking', become part of the vocabulary of everyday life, obscuring the reality of work through an endlessly spun narrative of aspiration and personal responsibility. The most deadening wage labour has been rebranded as a unique and life-changing 'opportunity' which transcends such earthly concerns as food or rent. Having successfully buried the power relation between capitalist and worker, neoliberalism has now set about detaching wage labour itself from the old (again obsolete, nostalgic, unrealistic) need to make a living.[1] This has opened up previously undreamt-of possibilities for employers. The Department for Work and Pensions now exhorts companies to 'try before you hire',[2] liberating them from the responsibility to provide even the legal minimum wage. The rise of employability has brought with it the normalisation of unpaid work, regarded as an inevitable or even desirable state of affairs. The resourceful candidate has become a travelling sales rep, hawking episodes of unpaid labour: the manager merely waits by the revolving door and collects sufficient free samples to upholster his entire office.

The supposedly win-win game of employability therefore appears to have been rigged from the start against the interests of its involuntary players, whose aspirational journeys usually lead no further than concrete mausoleums and open-plan prisons (a futile circuit of dozens of short-term jobs, each requiring huge effort to get and keep, replacing the Fordist scenario of one just about bearable dead-end job for life) and whose 'personal assets', when brought to market, turn out to be worthless, of only sentimental value. To spirit away these inconvenient outcomes, the pedagogues and proselytisers of employability draw on the narratives of self-help and positive psychology which insist that regardless of actual economic conditions anything is possible if you try hard enough.

By attaching the neoliberal model of human capital and entrepreneurship to the magical belief system of positive thinking, employability becomes a powerful and dangerous ideological vehicle. The message is sent down from the 'self-made' business leaders and gurus who profit from this system, via the administrators and team leaders who have to believe in it to maintain their own careers, to the workers and 'jobseekers' on the receiving end: you are the creator of your own openings and obstacles. Think positive and you will succeed. You are not depressed because you are unemployed; you are unemployed because you are depressed. Change your 'mind-set' and get a job.[3] Similarly, if you are depressed by your job this is a personal issue, rather than a problem of the job itself: make an effort to feel more positive about it, and this positivity will then bring its own reward, enabling you to move on to something better (don't worry about the person stepping into your miserable shoes). If your job does not pay enough to live on, this is a personal issue… and so on.

Its use as an instrument of workplace and welfare discipline in an era of declining wages and rising insecurity means that positive psychology, like employability, has moved out of the pages of self-help manuals and into the public sphere. As Barbara Ehrenreich puts it in *Smile or Die*, a study of the positive thinking industry in the United States, in recent years the pressure to 'act in a positive way has taken on a harsher edge' (Ehrenreich 2010: 55). Behind the smiling mask is a sneer: just as success is down to the individual, so is failure. Just as self-belief and hard work will allow you to miraculously achieve that dream career (Not there yet? Work harder! Believe more!), so unemployment is viewed as a self-created predicament, not a structural inevitability but a lifestyle choice, brought about not by a lack of jobs in society but by a lack of aspiration in the individual. Welfare provision therefore becomes a matter not of economic support but of motivational coaching (which, according to the 'welfare dependency' narrative, can actually be impeded by economic support). If you really want to work, the sneer-smile says, you will find a job.

This doctrine is a key ingredient in schemes imposed on benefit claimants in the UK. For instance, a training course run by welfare-to-work company A4E (its name stands for 'Action for Employment') included speeches on positive thinking as a solution to unemployment and a display of posters bearing inspirational quotes from motivational gurus (Koksal 2012). In 2014 the DWP offered private contractors £165,000 to run a one-year course supposedly tackling 'Entrenched Worklessness'; according to the DWP specification, the course should aim to 'change the "hearts and minds" of claimants by empowering them to take responsibility for improving their lives' (DWP 2014) The winning bidder proposed sitting claimants in front of 'life coaches' and subjecting them to neuro-linguistic programming and 'law of attraction' exercises (DWP 2014).[4]

While their relations to economic reality might be non-existent, these kinds of privately run and often mandatory schemes swallow vast sums of public money and are routinely approved by politicians. Preaching the neoliberal gospel of self-help and entrepreneurship, these politicians, like the programmes they endorse, are more concerned with 'hearts and minds' than the material conditions of welfare or employment.

Disciplinary employability

For the 'jobseeker' held hostage by such welfare-to-work schemes the law of attraction and the commandments of positive thinking must be seen to be obeyed, regardless of their patent absurdity. For where employability in higher education is presented as a form of knowledge, in the sphere of welfare it functions as exactly that: a rule of law. Where the first is a pastiche of learning, the second is a parody, a cynical re-packaging of drudgery as opportunity. The power relation which remains unspoken in higher education – perhaps partly because students are led to believe that they could, if they perform well, become partners in the elite which wields that supposedly benign power – is here formalised through the signing of 'claimant commitments' and the disciplinary language of 'conditionality' and compliance. Burdened with arbitrary bureaucratic tasks, the un-employee is expected to provide evidence of job searches and ordered to attend courses ostensibly designed to teach lessons about correct conduct. Whereas the university student is an apparently self-directed scholar of employability, the recipient of Jobseeker's Allowance (who might be a graduate or a school leaver, a parent or someone made redundant in middle-age) is required to recite its buzzwords like a sort of remedial literacy. A 'failure' to find work is viewed as a failure of personal or moral hygiene. It is not coincidental that welfare-to-work 'training' programmes often include lectures on bodily matters such as washing and grooming as part of their regimes of humiliation.

These two versions of employability – the scholarly and the disciplinary, or the liberating and the incarcerating – have a shared history and a symbiotic relationship. The second is evoked, if not spelt out, as a warning by the first: if you do not follow the aspirational script you risk becoming an unemployed 'other'. The first is used as an alibi by the second to lend a false legitimacy to exploitative and stigmatising programmes, as if lecturing claimants in positive thinking and threatening them with unpaid work and benefit sanctions is a form of education which will help them overcome their personal 'barriers to employment'.

It is notable that alongside the need to facilitate smooth 'transitions' for students and those already in work, the New Deal welfare-to-work scheme also featured heavily in the 1998 government-commissioned report on employability (Hillage and Pollard 1999: 7, 25–6, 30–31). The personalisation of welfare imposed through this and subsequent schemes is an ideological cornerstone of neoliberal policy, using the language of empowerment and choice as a cover for an entire scapegoating and stigmatising rhetoric of 'strivers' versus 'skivers' and 'hard-working families' versus a 'something-for-nothing' culture. This rhetoric has been keenly adopted by both government and opposition politicians and amplified by sensational media stories (Coote and Lyall 2013). Jettisoning all ethical considerations about work itself, and at the same time harking back to a Calvinist 'work ethic' conspicuously exempt from the purging of the old world of employment – perhaps because of its connections to positive thinking and self-help (Ehrenreich 2010: 74-96) – this elevation of all work, no matter how poorly paid, socially destructive or environmentally damaging, to the status of spiritual vocation, alongside the recasting of unemployment as moral weakness, has been crucial in engineering an environment in which maintaining one's employability has become a duty and work a virtual religion.

The ultimate correctional intervention for those deemed to have strayed from the righteous path is workfare, meaning forced unpaid labour, portrayed as a tough but necessary moral lesson granted by employers whose financial interests are secondary to their generosity in giving hope to these wayward souls. In February 2012, in a speech defending the government's workfare programmes, the Prime Minister David Cameron explicitly referred to supermarkets as places of learning: 'Put a young person into a college for a month for learning unpaid and it's hailed as a good thing. Put a young person into a supermarket for a month learning unpaid and it's slammed as slave labour' (Cameron 2012). A supermarket, then, is not just a workplace but a learning environment, even though the learning activity – for instance putting products on shelves so they can be bought by customers – might appear indistinguishable from actual work. The supermarket is under no obligation to pay its learners, any more than a student of English should expect to be paid by a university for writing an essay. If the supermarket profits from this activity this is a mere by-product, a happy accident. The real learning experience, according to the gospel of employability, is the acceptance of the discipline and subordination of work, the process of becoming an *employable subject*. This is the lesson which the employer provides on behalf of the state, and for which the trainee should be grateful.

Resolving the contradictory status of these schemes as both work (for ideological reasons) and not-work (for legal reasons) requires immense amounts of political sophistry. Hence the arbitrary language of 'welfare reform', in which work becomes 'work-related activity', workers become 'participants', employment becomes an 'employment programme', and a wage becomes Jobseeker's Allowance.[5]

One of the many ever-changing workfare programmes is the 'traineeship' scheme, targeting 16–24 year olds and consisting of up to six months of unpaid work alongside attendance at an educational institution. On the one hand it is emphasised that a traineeship is a real job – hard work, not a soft alternative – and these positions are advertised accordingly as vacancies, with an employer, duties and set hours. However, their status as 'training' means the jobs – which might be in retail outlets, factories, offices or the public sector – are paid not in wages but in welfare benefits. In lieu of remuneration traineeships and work experience schemes offer 'employability skills', by which employers can present themselves innocently as partners in learning. For instance, in 2014 footwear retail chain Shoe Zone claimed that its unpaid eight-week work experience programme offered a 'stepping stone', helping people to gain 'valuable retailing skills and core English and Maths qualifications' (Shoe Zone 2014). Here Shoe Zone was following the government script, styling itself not as a retail chain but as an educational placement, at which a paid job was a possible destination, rather than a starting point. Even as they stood in the shop and shifted the products, for the unpaid recruits who would 'like to work' for Shoe Zone an actual job remained elusive, an unfulfilled but still cherished aspiration.

The government's priority in pushing these programmes is to artificially reduce the official unemployment rate, as people on workfare, along with those who are entitled to benefit but dare not claim for fear of such schemes, are not counted in the figures. However, the material advantages for employers of using workfare labour in place of paid work and on-the-job training are also undeniable. While television viewers have been distracted by lurid tales of welfare dependency, chief executives and politicians have been busily building their own something-for-nothing culture. Working for free, either as an intern or as a workfare conscript, is no longer seen as problematic but merely as a fact of life, and those who object are labelled as unreasonable extremists.

Mainstream news coverage contributes to this mystification, reducing arguments against workfare to easily deflectable soundbites such as the 'slave labour' cliché beloved of David Cameron, rather than addressing the conversion of welfare into a state-sponsored poverty wage. Similarly, debates about whether various workfare schemes are voluntary or compulsory neglect to unpick the coercive thread running through all of them. In a grim, penal version of the graduate self-help manuals, offering oneself unpaid on one's own initiative before being ordered to do so by the Jobcentre is regarded as the gold standard of employability.

Another emerging trend is forced self-employment, whereby Jobcentres coerce claimants into becoming 'entrepreneurs' by monetising non-work activities, usually with negligible and unsustainable results (Andreou 2014). Enforced entrepreneurship represents a kind of terminal employability, again a dark parody of the bright language of the think-tank documents: far from liberating untapped skills, those reserves of the self which might previously have been a refuge from the demands of capital – hobbies, crafts, online trading – are commandeered by an institution keen to shift social pressure onto the individual. On this rickety platform the neoliberal cheerleaders then celebrate 'a golden age for entrepreneurship' (Heath 2014), rather than what is in reality the cynical reduction of people to *homo oeconomicus* action figures.

From employability to unemployability, from aspiration to desire

The discourse of employability concentrates distant institutional power on the individual, like heat through a magnifying glass, while ensuring that none of that heat can be directed back. The ruling authorities and conglomerates convey their power through countless media and face-to-face interactions, and in the same moment that they enforce this power, they disguise it, denying that such a concentration of interests exists. The exertion of power is disguised as empowerment. This virtual barcoding of the individual with the bodily signs of flexible conformity is the true meaning of that most intimate of all duties of employability, 'personal branding'. Whether in the marketing and selling of the individual-as-commodity, or as an echo of that violent signification of otherness whereby a person is physically labelled as criminal or deviant, the branding of the un/employable subject is crucial in the internalisation of conflict, the narrowing of social problems into personal issues and the reduction of politics to a drop-down menu of lifestyle choices.

It is not surprising then that employability appears to be a post-political matter, as its narrative of generic personalisation creates career politicians who are themselves the beneficiaries of that branding process, and in many cases, including in so-called opposition, the brand is all that remains of them. This political force-field around employability is proof of its ideological content. Employability is a matter not of party politics but of biopolitics, of 'the subjugation of bodies and the control of populations' (Foucault 1998: 14), and it cannot be opposed by politicians who are themselves embodiments of this ideology, but only through the development of new forms of collective resistance within those everyday spaces and interactions which it has colonised.

In an insightful critique of the psychodynamics of employability, Colin Cremin suggests that its demands are the result of a never-fulfilled desire which must be reclaimed from the tyranny of the internalised boss (Cremin 2009). His analysis however also raises problems in terms of how the ideological grip of employability might be broken. Cremin concludes by suggesting that the never-ending quest for employability, representing a 'desire for the thing that is lost or lacking', should not be rejected but instead collectively pushed forward, overcoming the alienation built into capitalist labour, closing the distance between the worker-subject and the mythic boss and finally wresting the impossible object of desire away from capital, presumably in the form of self-determination (Cremin 2010: 146). As seductive as this idea sounds, it perhaps underestimates those conditions – the atomised, precarious worker and remote, abstract network of capitalist authorities – which have been engineered precisely to prevent such an overthrow. An alternative reading therefore envisages the same goal but proposes exactly the opposite means of achieving it. As subjectivity and desire have been increasingly subsumed into the role-playing game of employability, a starting point for resistance would be to refuse to play: to recover a critical distance and interpose a sense of estrangement from the aspirational/entrepreneurial subject position; in short, to disconnect desire from employability.

As an instrument of neoliberal power, employability neutralises desire and channels it into a passive and profitable form – aspiration – which drives the human production line of capital. An unemployable desire will no longer serve to reproduce an endlessly aspiring subject, but instead aim to destroy and transcend the conditions of that subjugation. Such a desire will be insubordinate and disruptive, defined not by contrived competition with peers and identification with corporate interests but by active and collective conflict with those interests, fought on the terrain once held by unions, as well as in the interstices of work-discipline. Rejecting the constrictions of the branded persona, this desire will also be truly anonymous, contemptuous of the neoliberal model of generic personalisation and the milestones of the personal journey. Where the aspirational, employable subject is always available and apparently happy to go the extra mile, the subject driven by unmanageable, unemployable desire will recite the gospel of employability under duress, through gritted teeth, renouncing this discourse even as it is spoken and making explicit its nudged coercions. This negative desire will be articulated through new forms of what Foucault has termed 'counter-conduct' (Foucault 2009: 200–214, 355–7): non-productive interactions, withholding of emotional labour, indifference as sabotage. The compulsion to manufacture and market oneself as a must-have commodity will be opposed by the desire to bring the human assembly line to a halt.

For a regime shaped by the amnesic and passive language of employability with its frictionless, copy-and-paste interactions, the smallest signs of such negative energy are regarded as inexplicably hostile, almost as a form of violence (whereas pressurising the individual to the point of despair or death is regarded simply as 'the way things are'). Employers and educational institutions are now so well versed in the discourse of employability that its language of friendly oppression has become second nature; but, just as direct industrial action is impossible for most workers/non-workers, the fact that most organisations are as ill-equipped to reply to the smallest challenge to this discourse as they would be to a message from an alien species betrays their complacency and vulnerability. The terror for the engineers and guardians of employability is the prospect of its repressive apparatus being made visible, allowing a return to conscious awareness of a long-buried collective opposition to the 'labour market;' an opposition which would threaten the security of this state of managed insecurity.

In an environment where outright refusal is impossible, it is the duty of socially responsible employees, 'jobseekers' and students to enact the compulsory script of employability without passion or feeling, while directing all their assets against its ruling mechanisms, in order to turn this prospect of collective opposition into a reality.

Notes

1 'As wages bear less and less relation to the cost of living, it seems as good a time as any to ask if the underlying fantasy is that employers will one day be able to pay their workers nothing at all, because all those issues like housing, food, clothing, childcare will somehow be dealt with in another, mysterious, way' (Power 2013).

2 A DWP banner in a Jobcentre invited employers to 'Try before you hire – try out a potential employee for free.' The location of this notice however suggests that it was aimed primarily at claimants, as a reminder of their disposable status. Image at https://twitter.com/boycottworkfare/status/395177932773392385, 29 October 2013.

3 James Reed, boss of employment agency Reed, co-wrote a book called *Put Your Mindset to Work: The One Asset You Really Need to Win and Keep the Job You Love* (Reed and Stoltz 2011). Reed has been involved in delivering welfare-to-work programmes, and the book has reportedly been given to trainees as an educational text.

4 This proposal came from a company called Vedas Recruitment and Training. There is no information as yet on the experience of the course itself. For details of this and similar schemes, see Refuted (2015) and Friedli and Stearn (2015). The 'law of attraction' was popularised by Rhonda Byrne's self-help DVD/book *The Secret* (2006); see also Ehrenreich (2010: 59–73).

5 See the DWP response to a Freedom of Information request asking why people on work placements are not paid the minimum wage (DWP Central Freedom of Information Team 2014).

References

Andreou, A. (2014) *The unemployment figures expose the philosophy behind our economic recovery*. Available from: www.theguardian.com/commentisfree/2014/aug/13/unemployment-figures-economic-recovery-uk-government-neoliberal-philosophy [Accessed: 28 June 2016].

Byrne, R. (2006) *The Secret*. London: Simon & Schuster.

Cameron, D. (2012) Cabinet Office, Prime Minister's Office, 10 Downing Street and The Rt Hon David Cameron. *Business in the community speech*. Available from: www.gov.uk/government/speeches/business-in-the-community-speech--2 [Accessed: 28 June 2016].

Coote, A. and Lyall, S. (2013) Strivers v. skivers: The workless are worthless, *New Economics Foundation*, April 2013. Available from: https://libcom.org/files/Strivers_vs._skivers_full-publication.pdf [Accessed: 28 June 2016].

Cremin, C. (2010) Never employable enough: The (im)possibility of satisfying the boss's desire. *Organization* 17(2): 131–49.

Department of Work and Pensions (2014) 'Entrenched Worklessness' *Contracts finder archive* (no date). Available from: https://data.gov.uk/data/contracts-finder-archive/contract/1649703/ [Accessed: 28 June 2016].

DWP Central Freedom of Information Team, (2014) Why people on unpaid workfare-style programmes are not paid National Minimum wage, 11 March 2014. Available from: www.whatdotheyknow.com/request/188492/response/491936/attach/3/Internal%20review%20WDTK%20response%202013%20IR910%20and%202014%20IR51.pdf [Accessed: 28 June 2016].

Ehrenreich, B. (2010) *Smile or Die: How Positive Thinking Fooled America and the World*. London: Granta Books.

Foucault, M. (1998) *The History of Sexuality: The Will to Knowledge: V. 1*. Translation by R. Hurley. London: Penguin Books.

Foucault, M. (2009) *Security, Territory, Population: Lectures at the Collège de France, 1977–1978*. In Senellart, M. and Ewald, F. Translated by Graham Burchell. New York: Picador/Palgrave Macmillan.

Foucault, M. (2010) *The Birth of Biopolitics: Lectures at the Collège de France, 1978–1979*. In Senellart, M. and Ewald, F. Translated by Graham Burchell. United States: St Martin's Press.

Friedli, L. and Stearn, R. (2015) Positive affect as coercive strategy: Conditionality, activation and the role of psychology in UK government workfare programmes. *Medical Humanities* 41(1): 40–47.

Heath, A. (2014) The recovery is being driven by a revolution in the jobs market, *City AM*. Available from: www.cityam.com/article/1397452896/recovery-being-driven-revolution-jobs-market [Accessed: 28 June 2016].

Hillage, J. and Pollard, E. (1999) *Employability: Developing a Framework for Policy Analysis (Research Report RR85)*. London: Her Majesty's Stationery Office: Institute for Employment Studies / Department for Education and Employment.

Koksal, I. (2012) Adventures at A4E, 13 April 2012, Available from: http://izzykoksal.wordpress.com/2012/04/13/adventures-at-a4e/ [Accessed: 28 June 2016].

Moore, P. (2009) UK education, employability, and everyday life. *Journal for Critical Education Policy Studies* 7(1): 242.

Moreland, N. (2006) *Entrepreneurship And Higher Education: An Employability Perspective*. HEA, Available at: www.heacademy.ac.uk/sites/default/files/id461_entrepreneurship_and_higher_education_341.pdf [Accessed: 28 June 2016].

Power, N. (2013) What would a world without work look like. *The Guardian*, 3 January 2013. Available from: www.theguardian.com/commentisfree/2013/jan/03/world-without-work [Accessed: 28 June 2016].

Reed, J. and Stoltz, P.G. (2011) *Put Your Mindset to Work: The One Asset You Really Need To Win and Keep the Job You Love*. New York: Penguin Group (USA).

Refuted, (2015) PsychoCrat Welfare, 19 March 2015. Available from: https://wwwrefuteddotorgdotuk.wordpress.com/workfare/psychocrats/ [Accessed: 28 June 2016].

Sarson, S. (2013) Employability agenda isn't working, *Times Higher Education*, 21 March 2013. Available from: www.timeshighereducation.co.uk/comment/opinion/employability-agenda-isnt-working/2002639.article [Accessed: 28 June 2016].

Shoe Zone (2014) We'd like to take the opportunity to clarify our position on our voluntary work experience programme for young adults, *Twitter*, 14 March. Available from: https://twitter.com/Shoezone/status/444489197190017024 [Accessed: 28 June 2016].

Trought, F. (2011) *Brilliant Employability Skills: How to Stand Out From the Crowd in the Graduate Job Market*. Harlow, England: Pearson Education.

Yorke, M. and Knight, P.T. (2004) *Embedding Employability into the Curriculum: Learning & Employability Series*. York: Learning and Teaching Support Network.

6 The 'academic career' in the era of flexploitation

George Morgan and Julian Wood

Some years ago we conducted a research interview with a man who taught sound production at a college in Sydney, Australia. We asked him whether he had any ethical misgivings about training young people to enter a career in which he had himself had been unable to make a living. Not surprisingly, the question elicited a soul-searching response. When George recounted this conversation to a friend recently, the friend asked: 'Isn't it the same when you supervise graduate students?' This is a reasonable question, but one that few of us who supervise doctoral candidates face up to. A PhD is a more general qualification than a diploma in sound production, of course, and it qualifies graduates for various careers outside academia. However, many, perhaps most, doctoral students aspire to work in universities even though the shortage of academic jobs means their prospects are increasingly remote. Those in this situation of post-doctoral limbo often continue to rely on the guidance of their supervisors/advisors/mentors. But the rise of managerialism means that scholarly communities have a declining ability to replenish their numbers, to recruit aspirants into tenured jobs.

This chapter will explore the reasons for this, with particular reference to the example of higher education in Australia, where most universities have grown enormously in recent decades, both economically and in terms of enrolments. Yet the number of full-time academic staff has failed to keep pace with this growth. The same period has seen a rise in the corporate model for running higher education and of the intensification of competition between universities for students and research funding. Staff have endured the turbulence of organizational restructuring, undertaken ostensibly to modernize and streamline the universities, the effect of which is to undermine scholarly communities and the leverage that scholars can exert over university affairs. They become the end point of the chain of line management, increasingly remote from the processes that determine budgets and staffing. Their work is measured with the blunt instruments of key performance indicators and they are subject to various forms of speed-up and ever increasing bureaucratic demands.

At the same time universities have come to rely on sessional staff to cover classes that would once have been taught by full-time staff. Casualization has sandbagged the conditions of tenured academic staff against the rising tide of neoliberalism: underwriting the costs of research, mitigating the time-consuming effects of 'administrivia', and ensuring that staff are able to meet the expectations imposed upon them by managerial forms of measurement and assessment. Thus despite the nominal solidarity between full time and the sessional 'academic precariat', there has been an attenuation of prospects that the latter group can obtain full-time work. In making sense of this process, we will consider two key concepts by which we conventionally understand the pattern, values and progress of working life: those of *career* and *vocation* or *calling* (terms we will use interchangeably). While the former is based on the pursuit of experience, credentials and rewards within stable institutional settings (private companies, public bureaucracies, education institutions etc.), the latter implies loyalty to a particular calling that transcends the specific social and structural conditions through which that calling is given public expression. Career structures may well correspond with particular callings, but not necessarily.

Taylorism in the new university

Originally vocation referred to a particular gift or passion that could be put to do God's work in the world, before assuming more a secular connotation of work as an expression of inner-self.[1] Cohen states:

> Vocation unfolds as an inner directed quest or drive for an authentic self, primarily through the realisation of a special gift, talent, or calling. It is associated with the mastery of artistic or spiritual disciplines and with various forms of service.
>
> (Cohen 2015)

For Cohen, vocation operates largely within a sort of moral economy. The worth of the person and the value of the work they perform are intimately bound together. The satisfactions of such work are supposedly related to being in the position of the apprentice in the first place. The touchstone of such labour is thus a kind of authenticity.

By contrast, a career is shaped more pragmatically around structures and opportunities. Career in this construction implies at the same time structures of inter-worker competitiveness of which outward recognized success is the benchmark. This modern rational way of working assumes a ladder of success with graded increments of status and higher income as its common features. Professional qualifications matter and the worker is often subject to reviews and managed according to so-called performance indicators. Within this market economy model, which is structured competitively within a segmented labour market, every promotion is both a proof of worth and a reminder of the competition that has been beaten off or overcome.

Much of what brings us to scholarship is the passion for an intellectual field and the desire to work within it, by conducting original research, reading, writing, and teaching, sharing our enthusiasms with others. Many who pursue the scholarly calling might have pursued more lucrative, and possibly prestigious employment but chose not to do so. In analysing a major qualitative research survey on academic life, Bexley *et al.* (2011) found that:

> A deep commitment to scholarship draws people to academic work and lies at the core of their professional values. The opportunity for intellectually stimulating work, a genuine passion for a field of study and the opportunity to contribute to new knowledge are the aspects of academic work most prized.
>
> (Bexley *et al.* 2011: xi)

Traditionally the scholarly vocation has been nested in collegial communities, that are, in ideal terms, sites of intellectual ferment and enduring social bonds, of mentorship and collaboration. In their purest form they are also akin to mediaeval guilds, introspective, parochial and inscrutable. Their members place much more store on peer esteem than on outside/bureaucratic assessment. But in their clannishness, they are also vulnerable to paternalism, and the exercise of informal and arbitrary power, lacking the structures to ensure equitable decision-making. Indeed, the proponents of traditional scholarly groups see them as the indivisible elements of the university, defined as nothing more than a 'federation of self-governing academic communities' (Spence 2008) a benign carapace harbouring disinterested scholarship under the principles of academic freedom.

Such communities have long been vulnerable in the neoliberal university where managers measure scholarly performance with standardized instruments – e.g. the number of citations of published work, student evaluation of teaching, external research income. In many cases Key Performance Indicators (KPIs) are false proxies for quality and can sometimes undermine scholarly integrity. For example, the ability to achieve grant success may not correspond with the value of the research but with its modishness, or the applicants' ability to play the system. Citations may not be a particularly good measure of the quality or impact of published research: systems can be gamed and corrupted; notoriously poor research may be roundly criticized but also highly cited. Nor is an academic's popularity with students a *sufficient* indicator that they are good teachers – although it may be evidence of such. The new university's quest to maximize student ('consumer') satisfaction might actually compromise pedagogical rigour. These KPIs are the stock-in-trade of the modern academic career but are often incompatible with vocational integrity. Many in the profession resent the replacement of peer-based discipline-specific qualitative criteria of scholarly worth with tables, charts and ratings, but feel powerless to resist these incursions and obliged to organize their work around the imperatives that they generate.

More important perhaps is the way that restructuring – herding academics into larger and larger organizational units, agglomerating departments into schools or colleges – undermines the scholarly vocation. Universities undertake restructuring under the pretext that it generates economies of scale, allows for the modernization of the curriculum and encourages interdisciplinary research. Crusading managers challenge the old scholarly borders as being ossified and out-of-date, incapable of providing the flexibility required in the new university, attacking what Collini summarizes as 'their archaic structures of self-government, their gentry-professional ethos and their blinkered devotion to useless knowledge' (Collini 2016). But the hidden political agenda is to break down the academic guild system and deprive scholars of any leverage over university affairs. Primarily this means rejecting the notion that scholarly leaders – heads of departments, deans etc. – are in any sense representatives of, and accountable to, their disciplinary colleagues. This corporate model demands that such people become part of a line-management chain charged with implementing the policies and directives issued from above. So restructuring provides the opportunity to achieve obedience to this system by appointing new heads of organizational units, usually outsiders, through managerially-controlled selection processes.

We can see this process as representing the Taylorist moment for higher education, the point at which scientific management came to dominate, one hundred years after it became the central organizing creed of industrial capitalism. Based on the ideas of Frederick Taylor, it emerged in the service of Fordism and sought to achieve greatest efficiency by breaking down production processes to their smallest components: a highly refined division of labour where workers perform specialized repetitive tasks (Braverman 1974). But Taylorism was also an industrial-political project to undermine the power of blue-collar trades, their skills and solidarity, and the last vestiges of craft satisfaction in work. It located the scientific manager at the centre of the productive universe. In Fordist enterprises, white-collar workers grew in number and power at the expense of those on the production line and the blue-collar resentment towards those who imposed the ruthless division mental and manual labour runs very deep in class memory (Watson 2015). So the managerial revolution in the universities is a belated attack on the guild system, akin to the onslaught on skilled trades in the early and mid-twentieth century. In its most evolved dystopian form this management approach constructs the new university as a factory of atomized scholars who are allowed to collaborate only where it provides the institution with a competitive advantage, such as in applying for research grants. They are beholden to performance indicators, and must pledge absolute obedience to managerial diktat. Any stubborn vestiges of collegiality can only frustrate this vision of the university as a well-oiled bureaucratic machine.

The rise of managerialism has also estranged those who run university finances and affairs from the beleaguered communities of scholarship. To move into a management role in the Taylorised university is then, to some extent, to burn your collegial bridges: the managerial career is incompatible with many aspects of the scholarly vocation. Such a career is particularly unpalatable to most who were trained in the humanities, social sciences or pure sciences. Unlike members of the newer disciplines they lack alternative, non-academic career paths and generally have more invested in the idea of the scholarly vocation.

By contrast with the universities of the sixties and seventies, when radical scholars would confront officialdom and treat campus struggles as a microcosm of the larger revolutionary project, contemporary managerialism generally elicits cautious obedience and pragmatic accommodation. The managerial machine appears too formidable and impervious to challenge such that even the scholars whose values are most offended by managerialism will at most engage in passive resistance and non-compliance. Rarely will they openly challenge the discourses and processes that trammel them. Besides, the managerial university has evolved procedures to funnel dissent into formal grievance processes – to smother conflict with paperwork and dispute resolution sessions – rather than meeting it head-on. The price of this strategy is tacitly to consent to the managerial domination of the new university, allowing managers to steer the institutional ship and drain the resources available to do good work. As the walls of the hidden academy close in, tenured scholars allow their numbers to be eroded by the process of casualization, effectively sacrificing their children at the altar of neoliberalism, banishing the next generation of scholars to the vocational margins.

Academic precarity in Australia

Numerous commentators (Furlong and Cartmel 1997; Burgess and Campbell 1998; Standing 2011; Antonucci *et al.* 2014) have demonstrated the growing precariousness in working life and there is now evidence that this pattern is not confined to low skill areas, but has been extended into professional fields that require years of study to obtain requisite qualifications (Chan and Tweedie 2015). Academia provides a case in point. Those seeking to enter the profession are likely to be employed on short term, sessional or casual arrangements rather than in tenured jobs (Junor 2004; May 2011). The optimistic and functionalist account of precarious academic work suggests that it forms a bridge to more secure employment, but universities across the world are growing the casual workforce to the point where the prospects of a stable academic career are becoming more and more remote.[2] This points to the increasing use of casual or sessional staff 'as a buffer against the vagaries and oscillations in the global higher education market, and in government policy and funding' (Ryan *et al.* 2013: 163) particularly in disciplines like those of the humanities and social sciences, where there is an oversupply of labour and fewer job options outside the academy. In this section we will examine the structural and political causes of the precarization of the academic labour force with particular reference to Australia, where university participation rates have increased spectacularly over the last fifteen years, but where the numbers of staff in secure employment have failed to keep pace with the growth in student numbers.

Throughout the western world, the rise in unemployment has forced governments to use post-school education as a way of alleviating the structural problems associated with youth transitions, by delaying the entry of young people into the full-time labour market. The extension of the period of compulsory education (or *de facto* compulsory education) has been spectacular. An average of 80 per cent of young adults (18–22) were enrolled in some form of post-school education in OECD countries in 2010, up from 75 per cent in 2000 (by contrast with 6.8 per cent in sub-Saharan Africa, OECD 2014). Policy makers generally describe this expansion of higher education as part of the process of economic modernization, of providing the workforce with skills to promote national prosperity, however, in many societies public funding has not kept pace with the prodigious growth in undergraduate enrolments. In Australia, in the decade from 1995, expenditure on higher education, as a proportion of GDP, fell by 4 per cent while student numbers increased by 45 per cent (May *et al.* 2011) making it the only OECD country in this period that underwent a reduction in public resources in real terms (Tiffen 2015). There has been a growing dependence on private resources, including fees paid by domestic and overseas students. In 2011 54 per cent of university funding came from public sources (OECD 2014) where in 1986 this figure was 87 per cent (May *et al.* 2011). Private funding includes 'Higher Education Contribution Charges' paid by domestic students and full fees paid by the rapidly increasing numbers of overseas students. Tiffen (2015) observed that only one of the thirty-four OECD countries spends a smaller proportion of GDP on funding universities than Australia.

Australian universities have responded to this attrition of public resources through two central strategies: first, by undermining the conditions of learning and teaching and second, by increasing the employment of low-cost sessional staff rather at the expense of those in secure jobs. In an environment of increased competition, where government funding follows student choice, universities have huge budgets to market their offerings and attract enrolments. They extol the virtues of the student experience – the campus environment, the quality of teaching – and the benefits their degrees will confer in future. At the same time, however, they have implemented programmes that can only be seen as compromising the quality of education: reducing full-time staff numbers and face-to-face teaching hours and increasing class sizes.[3] Such moves are often referred to euphemistically as productivity or efficiency gains, but clearly there are few benefits for students.

The second response to declining marginal public funding is to undermine job security, in particular by employing sessional staff when tenured staff resign or retire. Those who are paid by the hour can perform the labour of teaching and research at much lower cost than full-time staff. The ostensible rationale for casualization is to give universities the ability to maximize workforce flexibility. University managers frequently speak of market risk, of increased competition for students and volatile enrolments, in seeking to justify employing more and more workers on precarious contracts. They seek a flexible staffing profile in order to be more 'agile' in their curriculum offerings and point to the threat posed by Massive Open Online Courses (MOOCs) and competition from private and overseas institutions entering the deregulated 'higher education market'. They argue that institutions need the ability to restructure degrees and curricula in response to rapidly changing demands for skills in the quicksilver conditions of the new economy and that it is irrational to hire long term staff in particular areas. Yet, for all this, enrolment numbers continue to grow inexorably, and in the period 2000–2011 the academic workforce grew by barely half of the 70 per cent increase in student enrolments (Larkins 2011).

The full dimensions of academic precarity in Australia are unclear. Given that universities report the levels of employment of sessional staff in notoriously cryptic ways (Bexley *et al.* 2011), in 2004 Junor estimated that by head count, 40 per cent of academic staff were sessional employees (Junor 2004). However, May *et al.* (2011) suggested that by 2010 this figure had reached 60 per cent with 67,000 academic staff employed on a sessional basis. They found that between 1990 and 2008 the numbers of such staff grew by 180 per cent, compared with a 41 per cent growth in non-sessional academic staff numbers during the same period (2012). According to official figures only 20 per cent of all jobs created in Australian universities have been continuing, relatively secure, positions (DET 2014). Bentley *et al.* (2013) calculated that sessional academics undertake half the teaching load but 80 per cent of first-year teaching in Australian universities.

A class of jobbing academics 'tramp their trade' – much as the travelling artisan workers of the nineteenth century (Hobsbawm 1951) – around the campuses on what Edwards *et al.* (2009) refer to as the 'post-doctoral treadmill'. They have little time to pursue their research careers and thus are condemned to trying to survive in the increasingly crowded pool of the secondary academic labour market. They cannot plan for long-term adult life – relationships, family, home ownership – and are stuck in a poverty trap. In addition, they suffer a lack of professional recognition, condemned to be academic outsiders, even where they work for many years at a single institution. Watson (2013) observes the paradox that for full-time secure workers age and duration in the workforce confers career recognition and esteem, but to be employed long term on a casual basis can be a source of stigma. This means that academics can become less competitive for tenured jobs over time, despite their accumulated experience.

They are also treated as the institutional underclass, the ghosts who walk the corridors of the universities: not included in staff discussions, curriculum planning, rarely provided with their own office space, unable to supervise graduate students or to follow undergraduates through a teaching programme. They are usually appointed to teach courses at very short notice and so have little time for preparation, and will often teach those courses only once and so, unlike tenured staff, do not have the opportunity to develop and fine-tune curricula over time. Many work across two or more institutions and most are not paid to consult with students outside of teaching hours. They also suffer a deficit of professional recognition. Although some tenured staff endeavour to treat sessional staff as colleagues, the structural/ institutional situation means the latter can experience such gestures as being hollow and disingenuous. While many spend years trying to obtain more secure employment, other brilliant academic aspirants abandon their career ambitions for jobs where their prospects are more secure. In discussing the rapidly ageing profile of the academic workforce, Hugo wrote of the 'lost generation' of academics (Hugo 2005).

It is important to understand the industrial reasons for the erosion of job security. In Australia the trade union covering academics, the National Tertiary Education Union (NTEU), has been relatively successful in securing pay rises and protecting the jobs of staff with 'continuing employment' (i.e. not subject to regular review/contract renewal). Such workers dominate the membership and the policy and industrial priorities of the NTEU. Although the organization is formally committed to converting sessional and short-contract staff into ongoing positions, it has failed to prevent the erosion of employment security in the higher education sector.

From an industrial relations perspective, we might lay the blame for this process at the feet of academic managers, but the picture is much more complicated. It is important to consider the latent divisions within the academic profession, and acknowledge that in Australian universities the line between management and workers is not particularly clear: many staff who would not consider themselves managers perform managerial functions – for example in recruiting sessional staff to teach with them. While the industrial model operates with a putative horizontal solidarity between academic staff across the board there are clearly structured power relations between those whose employment is not subject to regular review and those employed on various forms of insecure contracts. The latter have to rely on the support of the former in order for their employment contracts to be renewed.

Much of the process of casualization emerges from capillary-level decisions that benefit those in relatively secure positions, such as, for example, allowing staff members to 'buy out' their teaching, by employing sessional staff, so that they have more time for the research that is more important for career advancement. The effect of the declining real funding has been to use resources provided to universities for teaching in order to cross-subsidize research and administration. Norton estimates that $A2 billion dollars of public money that is provided to universities each year to teach students annually, is redirected to research, a levy of around 20 per cent (Norton 2015). These fiscal trends are symptomatic of a structured power relation that drives the process of casualization: this process of siphoning resources from teaching revenues has been used to sandbag the conditions of research-active tenured staff.

However, it is, of course, not just research that is being subsidized from teaching revenues but also the burgeoning university administrative costs, including the cost of the growing number of middle and senior managers. A report by Ernst and Young (2012) entitled *Universities of the Future* analysed a sample of fifteen Australian universities and found that only one, an elite university, had more academic staff than administrative staff.[4] In their estimation, four of the fifteen universities considered had as much as half their staff in support or administration roles. Further, half of their sample comprised universities that had 20 per cent more support staff than academics. In comparative terms the report also made the point that

> Organisations in other knowledge-based industries … typically operate with ratios of support staff to front-line staff of 0.3 to 0.5. That is, 2–3 times as many front-line staff as support staff. Universities … are unlikely to survive with ratios of 1.3, 1.4, 1.5 and beyond.
>
> (Ernst and Young 2012)

The effect of this growth in non-academic staff ironically has been to increase the time that academics spend on administration. The over-managed university develops an obsession with auditing performance, record-keeping, and policies and processes that seem to grow inexorably and drain the time available for 'core-business' of teaching and research (Graeber 2015).

Two case studies: Di and Marian

The case studies presented below come from a sample of nine doctoral graduates interviewed over the past two years for a small, unfunded research project on the personal effects of casualization. Both Di and Marian work in universities in inner Sydney, and participated in one-on-one semi-structured interviews. The ability of casual workers to draw on alternative sources of income support may influence their ability to remain in the academic labour market and our two case studies illustrate contrasting pressures. Both accounts can be read as narratives of forced adaptation, of careers shaped pragmatically and individualistically. The adaptations that the respondents speak of are in relation to their mostly limited view of university reforms and the general drift under neoliberalism to the reduction of fixed costs and the (re)disciplining of labour. They are less concerned, for example, with labour market trends and the context-shaping pressures of universities re-positioning themselves and being rationalized or reformed as businesses.

Di is 32 and has worked as a casual tutor in her faculty since joining it as a PhD student seven years ago. She was born and raised in the United States, in a non-academic but professional middle class family. Di did her undergraduate degree in psychology in the United States. Upon meeting and marrying an Australian musician who was travelling the United States, she accompanied him back to Australia where she completed a PhD in educational psychology over four years on a scholarship. She has not yet managed to convert much of it to published articles nor obtain a post-doctoral grant or secure position. Sometimes she seems to regret the effort it took. '*I look at it, sitting in the drawer and think 'why did I bother'?*' Her parents are proud of Di's achievements and have supported her decision to study overseas, both financially and emotionally. Having split with her Australian partner after several years, she lacks someone who can help cover joint expenses. She considered going home to the States but felt that this would carry elements of a defeat. '*I don't want to just go back to mum and dad, cap in hand.*'

Di's testimony is peppered with contradictory feelings. On the one hand she is sceptical of the honesty and compassion of the senior staff, blaming them for failing to mentor her and just using her to fill gaps in their tutoring workforce. On the other, she speculates that 'they' (the tenured academics) have a 'nice life' and feels keenly the loss of that idealized life of the academy, the stable communities of practice. Di has not been involved in collaborative researching or writing, nor the joint effort of getting research published, and observing at close quarters how seasoned academics organize their time and accumulated knowledge. In a sense she is hyper individualist, and conflates 'standing on her two feet' with working in deliberate isolation from other academics. She refuses to join the union on campus because of the 'exorbitant' fees ($55 per annum). Despite herself Di is forced back onto questions of status and self-worth and she returns to these throughout the interview. Sometimes she feels she has 'done well' to get where she is but a sense of not receiving validation from her academic peers continues to bother her. The lack of attention she has received from others can morph into anger and self-doubt.

Di is a 'hyphenated worker': academia is not her only source of precarious income as she also works in the arts. There are three aspects to this. She is a collagist, who very occasionally sells her pictures. She teaches fine arts, although does so without formal training, tutoring teenagers studying art at school wishing to brush up their skills. She is also a talented pianist and she supplements her irregular academic income by giving private piano lessons. She considered going into the arts full time, but realizes the field is even more precarious than academia. However, she is more successful in networking to source work in this sphere than at the university and music accounts for as much income generation as her university tutoring. In the end, like many precarious workers she ends up with periods where she takes on too much rather than risk losing a potential student. Di wishes she could keep the customers on hold long term, but at least she has a revenue stream. '*I have got more pupils than I can handle most of the time.*' She resists seeing this work as constituting her core vocational identity precisely because of the years she has invested in the scholarly calling.

Marian is 35. She was born in Australian in a working-class area. Neither Marian nor her parents expected her to gain entry to university, but she progressed all the way to doctoral level completing a thesis on the university experiences of working-class 'first in family' students like herself. She is single and, like Di, lives in rented accommodation. Neither can afford to buy a house in Sydney, and in any event with irregular incomes they would not be good candidates for a home loan.

Marian lacks Di's confidence and has not penetrated the informal circuit that distributes the leftover teaching from the permanent academics. She has done a little tutoring but her longer-term goal was to be a research academic. If she could get post-doctoral grant money she would like to continue her research exploring how working-class students relate to the university. In the absence of such a path opening up, and desperately needing a steady income, Marian has worked her contacts to get some casual administrative work. It is not well paid and will likely last for six months. University administration is an increasingly common pathway for doctoral graduates who face the difficulties of oversubscribed academic labour markets. It allows them to remain in a familiar environment, although with neither the level of remuneration nor the job satisfaction that their qualifications merit. More than Di, Marion relies on the university for income and work identity.

Unlike Di, Marian is a unionist. Her job gives her some insight into how the casual conditions are viewed within the administrative hierarchy and what plans the faculty management have in this direction. There is a level of nuance here. The increased management of staff (including ever-increasing mechanisms to benchmark and force productivity as noted) is part of a university-wide accommodation with conservative government policy. Marian reserves most of her anger for the more abstract target of 'neoliberalism', as she struggles to complete her administrative tasks in the face of a declining administrative workforce and the consequential speed-up.

The two case studies set out here display a common set of attitudes and strategies. It is perhaps not surprising in that they share common challenges to do with their chosen path at this conjuncture for the higher education sector.

Let us revisit the common features. Neither has much control over their workflow or job continuity. Both seem dependent upon working their connections and being 'work ready' as members of a reserve army. Casual work in universities means metaphorically lining up at the factory gates in front of the foreman and waving as visibly as possible. Both have to rely upon networking, upon nurturing relationships with secure workers. They need to put in the emotional labour by keeping superiors 'sweet' and by managing upwards. Di is more angered by this in one sense. She thinks her years of study should more or less automatically put her on an escalator of promotion/consolidation. More than once in her interview she returns to this notion: '*I have a PhD for god's sake!*' Marian's skills as an administrator are under more time management and potential scrutiny but the work is neither particularly challenging nor satisfying. Di is both more mobile and erratic. Her main strategy is to keep close with the permanent academic that convenes one of the biggest courses in the faculty. '*I stick very close to [staff member] as he always has more teaching than he can manage.*' This illustrates how important patronage is in the allocation of teaching work. Similarly, those seeking employment as research assistants must know and befriend academics with research grants. This climate encourages individualism rather than solidarity among members of the academic 'precariat'.

The other factor is pay and security of income. Both respondents have low and irregular income streams. Di is more proactive in organizing a supplementary source of income. In terms of the rhythms of the years she is faced with the classic 'casuals' dilemma'. She has to eke out any savings as she faces the long wage-less semester breaks with the anxiety of not knowing if she will get enough to carry on next time. Di confesses how ashamed and angry she was to be made to go back to her parents in her thirties and ask for a loan for the summer.

There are other emotional social–psychological issues again here. For example, there is the process of identity management. When you are not teaching and you do not even have a firm commitment from the university that they will use you again (how long before zero hour contracts come to academe?), can you honestly say that you are actually still an academic? Both Di and Marian have thought about this question. Marian is more diffident but she can easily cover up her situation by saying that she works in 'university admin'. Di takes a more compartmentalized approach. '*I never tell my outside uni friends what I do here. It is just easier that way.*'

Both Marian and Di have feelings of self-doubt and alienation and reserves of anger too. Di feels that she was implicitly promised a pathway into academia proper by dint of her hard-won PhD. Marian perhaps understands more why this entry path is increasingly blocked. She feels the pressure to become a competent administrator but, as noted, she never intended to 'end up in admin'. The more that she stays in that role the more it becomes an opportunity cost as she fears that she cannot keep up her research knowledge for her desired return to research.

Both suffer periods of isolation, with just enough 'reward' to make them feel that it is worth going on. Though one has an eye on the (embattled) union, neither of them really looks like part of a Guy Standing's 'dangerous' class (2011). Militancy and academia are perhaps not temperamentally allied. Whether that will happen is still an open empirical question perhaps.

The self-assembled academic career

The condition of long-term precariousness has produced a new kind of post-modern career in late modernity. Large corporations have reduced the size of their core workforces and rely more and more on precarious secondary workers and subcontractors/freelancers. Fewer now have access to employment rights that full-time workers accrue in most western societies, for example, sickness and recreation leave. Post-Fordism has liberated workers from Fordism's repetitive routine and manual toil but has thrown them into a state of perpetual insecurity.

Traditionally the idea of the career was based on the presence of stable employers, solid institutional structures, credentialing processes and relatively durable skills. Under these conditions modern workers could feel a sense of objective momentum in working life. For the white-collar workers in the mid-twentieth century, Whyte's 'organisational men' (1956), the modern career was housed in a relatively stable corporate hierarchy (see also Wright Mills 1951). By contrast, the contemporary worker is, in Beck's term (1992), 'disembedded' from such structures. The idea of 'boundaryless career' (Arthur *et al.* 1999) was coined to capture the fluid situation of economic and institutional restructuring – downsizing, flattening of structures, outsourcing – in which 'the stable internal labour markets that served as platform for the traditional career ceased to be the norm' (Baruch and Bozionelos 2010).

There has been much sociological reflection on the rootless worker, some of which extols the virtues of the turbulence and uncertainty. Charles Handy (1990) coined the term 'portfolio worker' to capture the condition of structural instability generated by the turbulence of contemporary labour markets. In conditions of radical uncertainty workers are forced to improvise.

Seeking to recast precarity as a virtue of neoliberalism encourages new forms of worker subjectivity. The quest for security – coveting the job for life – is a sign of weakness or lack of motivation or ambition. The 'post-modern worker' is the idealized figure of the new economy, capable of embracing flexibility and instability, the infinitely labile vocational subject (Morgan and Nelligan 2015), with a manic eagerness for serendipitous opportunity, a capacity for self-reinvention, and a readiness to shed relationships with co-workers and to embrace the porous networks that are central to flexible capitalism. Charles Handy wrote:

> The real social revolution of the last thirty years, one we are still living through, is the switch from a life that is largely organised for us, once we

> have opted into it, to a world in which we are all forced to be in charge of our own destiny.
>
> (Handy 1997: 67)

Furlong and Cartmel (1997) observed that the 'new worker', no longer guided by the fatalism associated with Fordism, now faces a challenge to articulate 'choice biographies' parlaying diverse experiences into coherent career accounts (Wyn and Dwyer 2000; Morgan 2006). Young people are told that credentials are essential to vocational success but that even the best education provides no guarantees. We are required to adopt dispositions of individualism, calculation and tactical wisdom in everyday life.

In many ways the rhythms of the new academic career mirror the larger trends of late modernity, towards individualization and social fragmentation, as university managers encourage academics to embrace a mindset of restlessness rather than of calm stability. As Berg *et al.* (forthcoming) argue

> under neoliberalism precarity is purposely created to operate on minds and bodies as a disciplinary and disciplining practice. Ironically, it is often constructed in public discourse as a form of freedom, whereby academic faculty members get to 'choose' the form that their careers will take.
>
> (Berg *et al.* forthcoming)

Yet, as Murgia (2015) argues, few scholars see the virtue of turbulence and insecurity. Instead they seek stable environments in which to work because the post-modern career, with its innervated individualism, its encouragement of self-exploitation, is the antithesis of what draws most scholars to the academic vocation in the first place. Many yearn for the values and environments that characterized their doctoral studies – of careful scholarship, with the slow accretion of knowledge and skills, in stable communities of practice – rather than the shallow, questing individualism of the managerial version of the academic career. The diminution of secure academic employment makes such environments increasingly scarce and available only to the privileged few, while the others who choose to remain in the profession are forced to dance on the hot coals of the new university.

Conclusion

The implication of our argument is that those who enjoy the relative security of employment – the shrinking vestiges of the salaried intellectual class – have an ethical obligation to re-engage with the politics of the university, in a way and to an extent that has not been seen since the 1970s. This involves challenging managerial privilege and prerogative, and (in Hall's terms, 1990:18) 'alienating that advantage' in relation to the academic precariat. In this chapter we have used the example of Australian higher education to demonstrate that the neoliberal managerial university has overseen the growth of a class of freelance 'teaching-only' academic staff: the galley slaves of higher education. Di falls into this category but Marian is typical of a recent trend for doctoral graduates to work in university administration, when the academic career opportunities dry up, rather than abandoning the university completely. The predicament of the academic precariat is the product of a tacit compact between tenured staff and university managers under which the former's working conditions – in particular research time – enjoy some degree of protection while the administrative empires of the latter expand inexorably. But the price that academics pay for their submission is to allow their performance to be subject to the metrics and measurements that form a central part of the neoliberal academic career. This undermines the values that are central to the scholarly vocation and erodes the social forms within which scholarship was traditionally nurtured. By 'pulling up the ladder' those in the primary labour market have cut themselves adrift from the next generation, including those whom they have mentored, and consented to a process of intellectual and political fragmentation. The challenge then is to find the political forms – both collegial and industrial – within which the interests of the academic precariat can be represented and to reconstitute some of the ethical core of the calling of scholarship.

Notes

1 In *The Protestant Ethic and the Spirit of Capitalism* Max Weber demonstrated that Protestant theology encouraged people to pursue a calling. Through hard work, thrift and abstemiousness, they could show they were worthy to enter heaven, though they would never know in this world whether they were among the elect. Such a moral philosophy, Weber argued, provided the conditions for the emergence of capitalism.
2 See Burgess and Campbell (1998) for a refutation of the 'bridge' idea for precarious work in general.
3 Australian university student to staff ratios were around 8:1 in the early 1960s (Bebbington 2012: 12) but by the beginning of the current decade they were 20:1, even when casual staff are taken into consideration (Larkins 2011).
4 This is supported by current data, see www.education.gov.au/staff-data.

References

Antonucci, L., Hamilton, M. G., Roberts, S. (eds) (2014) *Young People and Social Policy in Europe: Dealing with Risk, Inequality and Precarity in Times of Crisis*. London: Palgrave Macmillan.

Arthur, M., *Inkson*, K. and Pringle, J. K. (1999) *The New Careers: Individual Action and Economic Change*. London: Sage.

Baruch, Y. and Bozionelos, N. (2010) Career issues. In Zedeck, S., *APA Handbook of Industrial and Organizational Psychology, Selecting & Developing Members of the Organization*. Washington DC: American Psychological Association. v. 2, pp. 67–113.

Bebbington, W. (2012) Déjà vu all over again: What next for universities? *Australian Universities Review* 54(2): 73–7.

Beck, U. (1992) *Risk Society: Towards a New Modernity*. London: Sage.

Bentley, P.J., Coates, H., Dobson, I.R., Goedegebuure, L. and Meek, V.L. (2013). Factors associated with job satisfaction amongst Australian university academics and future workforce implications, Volume 7 of the series *The Changing Academy – The Changing*

Academic Profession in International Comparative Perspective. Netherlands: Springer, pp. 29–53.

Berg, L.D., Huijbens, E.H. and Larsen, H.G. (forthcoming) Producing anxiety in the neoliberal university. *The Canadian Geographer.* Available from: www.academia.edu/19714927/Producing_Anxiety_in_the_Neoliberal_University [Accessed 22 May 2016].

Bexley, E., James, R. and Arkoudis, S. (2011) *The Australian Academic Profession in Transition.* Commissioned report prepared for the Department of Education, Employment and Workplace Relations. Melbourne: Centre for Study of Higher Education, University of Melbourne.

Braverman, H. (1974) *Labour and Monopoly Capital, the Degradation of Work in the Twentieth Century*. New York: Monthly Review Press.

Burgess, J. and Campbell, I. (1998) Casual employment in Australia: Growth characteristics, a bridge or a trap? *Economic and Labour Relations Review* 9(1): 31–54.

Chan, S. and Tweedie, D. (2015) Precarious work and reproductive insecurity. *Social Alternatives* 34 (4): 5–13.

Cohen, P. (2015) To vote, perchance to dream, Ay there's the rub. In *Lawrence and Wishart Publishing Blog 9th September.* Available from: www.lwbooks.co.uk/blog/vote-perchance-dream-ay-theres-rub [Accessed 22 July 2016].

Collini, S. (2016) Who are the spongers now. *London Review of Books* 38(2) (online). Available from: www.lrb.co.uk/v38/n02/stefan-collini/who-are-the-spongers-now [Accessed 22 May 2016].

(DET) Department of Education and Training (2014) *Selected Higher Education Statistics – Student Data.* Available from https://education.gov.au/student-data [Accessed 5 July 2015]

Edwards, D., Radloff, A. and Coates, H. (2009) *Supply, Demand and Characteristics of the Higher Degree by Research Population in Australia.* Canberra: Department of Innovation, Industry, Science and Research, Commonwealth of Australia.

Ernst and Young (2012) *University of the Future.* Available from www.ey.com/Publication/vwLUAssets/University_of_the_future/$FILE/University_of_the_future_2012.pdf [Accessed 5 July 2016]

Furlong, A. and Cartmel, F. (1997) *Young People and Social Change: Individualisation and Risk in Late Modernity*. Buckingham: Open University Press.

Graeber, D. (2015) *The Utopia of Rules. On Technology, Stupidity and the Secret Joys of Bureaucracy*. Brooklyn: Melville House.

Hall, S. (1990) The emergence of cultural studies and the crisis of the humanities. *October* 53 (Summer):11–23.

Handy, C. (1990) *The Age of Unreason*. London: Arrow Books.

Handy, C. (1997) *The Hungry Spirit*. London: Hutchinson.

Hobsbawm, E. (1951) The tramping artisan. *Economic History Review* 3(3): 299–320.

Hugo, G. (2005) Some emerging demographic issues on Australia's teaching academic workforce. *Higher Education Policy* 18(3): 207–30.

Junor, A. (2004) Casual university work: Choice, risk, inequity and the case for regulation. *The Economic and Labour Relations Review* 14(2): 276–304.

Larkins, F. (2011) *Academic staffing trends: At what cost to teaching and learning excellence?* LH Martin Institute for Higher Education Leadership and Management. Available from: www.lhmartininstitute.edu.au/insights-blog/2011/10/65-academic-staffing-trends-at-whatcost-to-teaching-and-learning-excellence [Accessed 5 July 2016]

May, R. (2011) Casualisation; here to stay? The modern university and its divided workforce. In R. Markey (ed.), *AIRAANZ 2011*. Auckland New Zealand: City AUT.

May, R., Strachan, G., Broadbent, K. and Peetz, D. (2011) The casual approach to university teaching: Time for a re-think? In Krause, K., Buckridge, M., Grimmer, C. and Purbrick-Illek, S. (eds) *Research and Development in Higher Education: Reshaping Higher Education Conference Proceedings*, 34: 188–97.

Morgan, G. (2006) Work in progress: Narratives of aspiration from the new economy. *Journal of Education and Work* 19(2): 141–51.

Morgan, G. and Nelligan, P. (2015) Labile labour – gender, flexibility and creative work. *Sociological Review* 63(1): 66–83.

Murgia, A. (2015) The obverse and reverse sides of precariousness: Young highly educated workers between passions and skill mismatch. *Social Alternatives 34(4): 14–21.*

Norton, A. (2015) The cash nexus: How teaching funds research in Australian universities. Grattan Institute. Available at: http://grattan.edu.au/wp-content/uploads/2015/10/831-Cash-nexus-report.pdf [Accessed 5 July 2016]

OECD (2014) *Education at a Glance - Country Note: Australia.* Available at: www.oecd.org/edu/Australia-EAG2014-Country-Note.pdf. [Accessed 20 June 2015]

Ryan, S., Burgess, J., Connell, J. and Groen, E. (2013) Casual academic staff in an Australian university: Marginalised and excluded. *Tertiary Education and Management* 19(2): 161–75.

Spence, M. (2008) Essential questions for flourishing universities. *Sydney Morning Herald* 23 (July): 11.

Standing, G. (2011) *The Precariat: The New Dangerous Class*. London: Bloomsbury.

Tiffen, R. (2015) The university rankings no government wants to talk about. Inside Story 24 March. Available from: http://insidestory.org.au/the-university-rankings-no-government-wants-to-talk-about [Accessed 27 May 2015].

Watson, I. (2013) Bridges or traps? Casualisation and labour market transitions in Australia. *The Journal of Industrial Relations* 55(1): 6–37.

Watson, I. (2015) *A Disappearing World: Studies in Class, Gender & Memory*. Melbourne: Australian Scholarly Publishing.

Whyte, W. (1956) *Organization Man*. New York: Simon & Schuster.

Wright Mills, C. (1951) *White Collar: The American Middle Classes*. Oxford: Oxford University Press.

Weber, M., Parsons, T. and Giddens, A. (1992) *The Protestant Ethic and the Spirit of Capitalism*. London; New York: Routledge.

Wyn, J., Dwyer, P. (2000) New patterns of youth transition in education. *International Social Science Journal* 164:147–59.

7 Coping with uncertainty

Precarious workers in the Greek media sector

Manos Spyridakis

Precariousness is currently very much on the agenda. Although it increasingly used to refer to vulnerable conditions of employment and eroded labour relations affecting large segments of the global population, its precise notion is still vague. Originally used by French sociologists, its most global definition concerns the objective and subjective features of uncertainty and insecurity that operate as an instrument used by employers to shift risks and responsibilities onto workers in the formal or informal economy (Barbier 2004; I.L.O. 2012). This process effectively makes economies rely on their supply side only.

Precarious employment takes a variety of forms essentially re-regulating the relationship between labour and capital to the advantage of the latter. Thus, although questions remain as to the scientific use of the term, statistical measurements, the extent to which non-standard forms of employment are precarious or not, and the cross-national differences of its significance, evidence suggests that a status of precariousness affects large and growing segments of economically active people. Hence empirical data based on cross-national comparisons from selected European countries and specific sectors of the economy, such as call centre companies, the performing arts, care for the elderly and the multimedia industry, have documented worrying trends. In most cases, in these sectors one finds no guarantee of continuing employment, hard working conditions with unpredictable work locations, unsocial working hours, constantly changing work times, low and very low earnings, and, finally, little to no access to social protection (ESOPE 2004). In addition, recent surveys show a dramatic expansion of mini-jobs in Germany and zero-hour contracts in Britain, where the figure has been estimated to exceed one million. The accuracy of this figure is debatable, and it is thought to be very conservative, but these contracts do not occur in the informal economy: they are essential features of business strategy (Lavery 2014). This suggests that precariousness is turning into an institutionalization of employment insecurity. Precariousness relies on the pool of dispensable workers with no security, low wages, poor benefits and few chances of professional advancement, who must choose between work in increasingly adverse conditions and unemployment.

In this context, according to Guy Standing, the people who form the precariat are those with no access to the advantages of the standard employment regime of industrial citizenship, such as labour market security, employment security, job security, work security, skill reproduction security, income security and representation security (Standing 2011: 10). Far from being a homogeneous category, the precariat can be seen as a second-class citizenry denied a range of rights, the main being equal access to forms of protection and an equal opportunity to live with dignity. Hence, as Standing puts it, the precariat experiences the four 'A's, that is, anger, anomie, anxiety and alienation. This process owes much to the way the global market works and is backed by political decisions made by neoliberal governments; it commodifies fully and intensively every aspect of human life, eroding regulated safety nets and legalizing the reproduction of labour power as pure commodity disembedded from society. The 'precarious experience' is endemic to the mechanism of capitalist profit making, rendering large segments of the workforce vulnerable and flexibly exploited and creating a new defenceless reserve army. The distinctiveness of today's precarity is related to the spatial restructuring of work on a global scale, the increasing centrality of the service sector, the use of layoffs as a foundation of employers' restructuring strategies, the rhetoric of the end of ideologies that defended workers' rights, and the spread of unstable and uncertain jobs in all sectors of the economy that essentially cancels the dividing line between primary and secondary labour market (Kalleberg 2009: 5). Hence, despite the postmodern glamorousness and rhetoric about the dynamics of the new economy and the democratization of work, the often forgotten and disguised feature of the capitalist labour market is its constant effort to subject workers to the disciplinary tenets of market (de-) and/or (re-)regulation. Increasing unemployment rates along with the emergence of a heterogeneous workforce constituted on the basis of diverse ethnicity, age and employment status in a deregulated working context bring anew to the fore the old issues of social inequality and unequal distribution of wealth and power.

The following ethnographic data converge to capture a situation where insecurity, operating as the scarecrow of the future, transcends the wills, wishes and efforts of downward, displaced and employable workers, no matter how hard they try to rely on their own efforts to define their work trajectories. In this light I focus on workers whose employment and life status are characterized by non-permanent, temporary, casual, insecure and contingent working arrangements. As a matter of fact, since the protagonists of this study are informants and respondents who do not own any means of production, in what follows, I attempt to empirically explore the extent to which they accept the unequal allocation of resources as well as the degree of their sense of belonging in the same boat.

Especially after 2010, through various experimental versions of the neoliberal memorandum, precariousness started to be felt more intensively in Greek society as the result of the panoptical economic austerity, internal devaluation and reductions of public deficits and spending imposed in exchange for financial support from the International Monetary Fund and the European Central Bank, despite these measures accentuating and reproducing an already problematic economic structure. This complex situation led to a series of deregulations of the

Greek labour market that ended up in significant wage cuts, the introduction of lower minimum income scales, and greater ease was granted to employers wanting to cut labour costs via layoffs by means of a reduction of compensation payments and a relaxing of the justifications required when making redundancies (Kretsos 2014). As a consequence, precarious employment is rising in the context of a dramatic increase of unemployment levels and the diminished role of collective bargaining. Precarious workers do not get more than the 60 per cent of the respective median, in terms of income. It is difficult to define them accurately, due to their cloudy employment status and the significant weakness of the tools of the state to monitor the labour market. They include mainly those employed in temps' agencies being underpaid, working under adverse collective agreements used to save costs by tweaking staff requirements and increasing management power. Their number is roughly estimated to be between 10,000 and 30,000. Additionally, they include self-employed workers who are actually employed in consecutive fixed-term contracts adding up to a total of about 270,000 people. Temporary workers (about 40,000), part-time day labourers and those employed in subsidized jobs – such as those in training programmes – expand the grey zone of precariousness as they are low paid in low quality posts. To this, one should add unregistered labour, which thrives and spreads in small enterprises, a phenomenon intensified by the current economic crisis where available jobs are low paid and require low skills (Mouriki 2010). It is indicative that between 2010 and 2014, formal employment decreased to 21.3 per cent in the private and public sector, part-time employment doubled, employment levels decreased from 60 per cent in 2009 to 50 per cent in 2014, and almost one million jobs were lost during the crisis hitting mainly the long-term unemployed, the young and women (I.N.E. 2014). Also, according to Eurostat, Greece currently has the highest rate of unemployment among the EU-27, at 25.2 per cent.

It is in this adverse context that I will address, in ethnographic terms, the ways in which ex-workers from a TV channel tried to cope with precarious employment conditions, how they conceived of their involvement in the struggles resisting management's power, how they tried to make a living, and the quality of social relations that emerged from these conditions. It must be noted that precariousness in the media sector first appeared in Greece during the crisis and in this particular station; afterwards, it spread to other media, such as newspapers, culminating in the notorious dismissal of employees of the public broadcast company ERT (6 Nov 2013).

The ethnographic context

The TV channel was a private broadcasting corporation with nationwide coverage. Founded in 1994, it was one of the first sectors where workers felt the adverse effects of the current ongoing economic recession in Greece.[1] From November 2011, after a decision by the general assembly, it was occupied by its workers who had carried on working after declaring strike action, waiting to receive the wages the employer owed to them, according to Greek law.

Between 2002 and 2011 the channel offered a versatile programme schedule including news and entertainment. In April 2011, due to chronic mismanagement and financial problems the channel announced that it would temporarily suspend its news reports and live programmes until a strategic investor was found. The sum total of its debt was estimated to exceed €500,000,000. In the following months there was a new effort to reopen the channel by broadcasting live programmes again. This lasted until November 2011, when the workers, still unpaid, went back on strike because they regarded the consolidation plans presented by the owner to be unrealistic: they seized the live broadcast to display cards with their own occupational demands.

From January to February 2012, while the terrestrial and satellite broadcast had stopped, the workers created and broadcast their own programmes through analogue transmitters throughout Greece, calling on a considerable number of workers from different professions representing the unemployed, laid-off and other unpaid colleagues, to join in their struggles. During these programmes, the presenters were appointed by the workers themselves, and several uncensored documentaries that focused on the economic crisis in Europe and in Greece were shown. In addition, workers formed a kind of self-provisioning structure for medical and food assistance on a voluntary basis while the management kept trying to end their fight through unconvincing proposals. The channel remained active, broadcasting messages from workers, until 9 February 2012, when the transmission signal was cut off by the management. This happened right after workers had expressed their intention to broadcast a multi-camera coverage of the protest in Syntagma Square on the occasion of the memorandum debate in the Greek Parliament. This is how the three-month period of workers' station management ended. However, the strike, occupation and workers' use of the station's facilities and equipment continued until October 2013, shortly after the judicial certification of bankruptcy of the company requested by the workers. Currently, workers are still demanding their unpaid wages while experiencing liminal employment status (Spyridakis 2013), in a permanent position oscillating from precariousness to unemployment. Thus, the data refer to a transitional stage, a time when the workers' occupation of the station was waning, not only due to fatigue caused by their long-term presence there, but mainly out of the frustration caused by their loss of control over the broadcasting and the stagnant status of their negotiations with management.

Facing job deprivation

Confronted with this condition, workers developed a number of survival strategies exploiting new market information or resorting to established past practices, such as activating old and new social networks. Some of them maintained a second job. Although 'station work' had been their main source of income, sometimes, either through station channels or independently, opportunities for a secondary job of a temporary or even permanent nature presented themselves. For a significant proportion of the workers who were carrying on their strike action, this practice was, even temporarily, a way to survive.

However, for others the loss of a fixed income became a drive towards a 're-invention' of agriculture, especially those with a rural background. Although the connection between urban and rural settings in terms of kin networks had never been completely severed over the past decades, it seems to have taken on a new meaning in the context of the economic crisis, facilitating a positive reconceptualization of the countryside and its value. As one informant stressed:

> You know, we have a small farm in the village and we can make our living there … When it comes to clothing, we usually wear what we can get from friends and relatives – and I am not ashamed to admit it – with the exception of children's shoes which we need to buy anyway … My daughter, her godfather provides for her, other people provide for her … those that care to … Us too, we always give to our friends, when they come to us. We have our lemons, our olive oil. If my husband loses his job, we will certainly move there. We can make our own detergents; we never have to buy anything … Soap from olive oil, also suitable for clothes' washing, for dish washing, shower, hand washing … Of course, I modify it, I can't use it raw. We also make our own cosmetics … Our summer fruits, we got all of those, also at the village … So, all in all, we have drastically limited our financial needs. If this story ends here, I'll see what I can do … It has to end here, so this cycle might close and I can focus and see what I could do to add up to my income. This is what I miss …

This informant shows that, while entrapped in the revolving door of precariousness, even before the crisis all the means at her disposal were flexibly combined for the purpose of making a living. This shows that the debate on 'downward occupational mobility' present in some of the literature (Edgell 2006) may not be analytically useful, because it perceives employment narrowly in terms of profession and not in terms of overall social activity leading to social reproduction, which is how informants seem to understand it instead. In this sense, the crisis could be a proper background for the production of new theoretical tools that are more tailored to the logic agents apply when formulating their own strategies and using a wide range of responses to it, as has already been shown in anthropological research (Pardo 1996; Procoli 2004).

Aside from the purely material aspect of survival, one of the most burning issues emerging during fieldwork was the extent to which journalism was a 'lost' cause for the workers, and whether or not they felt they had to adjust to a new condition of flexible labour relations at the expense of their true expression. Their representations were normally vague as the 'new media' context demanded a degree of self-financing, multiple jobs, competitiveness and little or no union coverage. As one informant stated:

> For me, journalism is over, and it has been for many years now. The reason I stayed in the first place was because the money was good – of course not anything more than what's specified in our collective agreement … The

> agreement was really good, journalists working for TV stations. And this wasn't the only reason; sometimes I covered stories that I really wanted ... sometimes ... maybe one story out of ten was of the kind that I really like in journalism [...] But I am not giving up. Once it was the pen, now it is the computer. I am not giving up. Me and 50 others have created a blog ... I am involved in this process, roughly 40 of us and another 10 or 15 coming from other 'shops'. We put some money on the site as well, trying to make it commercially viable, to compete with other sites, to make some money ... To be entrepreneurs with shares, partners, participants ... you can call it whatever you like. We just say things as they are, our own view, properly signed ...

During fieldwork the possibility of re-opening the station on a cooperative basis in the context of the so-called social economy was frequently discussed. Despite workers' enthusiasm from the three-months experience of self-management, they argued in favour of restoring the television model and employment relationship they had experienced before. In other words, they were suspicious and even fearful of taking over management, which showed a sort of distrust towards organized struggle. No doubt this was due to their lack of experience in collective demands for labour rights as well as their indifference towards existing political parties. This inexperience, however, did not prevent them from mobilizing a number of fixed social networks, such as their family and friends initially, or creating new ones to manage the need for survival or give maximum exposure to their demands. But above all, they recognize as their most important experience the fact that they managed to introduce an experimental logic into the TV scene, an 'alternative TV' during the short period of self-management. In this case the alternative character was not only related to a 'militant journalism' that 'dares to reveal what systemic stations conceal', but also a socially sensitive attitude towards colleagues and disadvantaged citizens. This was during the famous period of free broadcasting, or 'free air' as informants named it, when they turned themselves from TV station workers into a social network. So, even though they failed to establish permanent self-management, for a long time they succeeded in collectively managing extremely pressing needs, such as those of psychological survival and mutual support.

Re-discovering collectivity

By November 2011, after voting in their general assemblies, all channel workers decided to proceed with the strike action because management had been delaying their payments throughout the previous year. As was made clear after some time, the company could never really pay its workers, and the financial mismanagement and the unaffordable loans it had secured throughout the years of its operations as a TV channel came into public view. The leading shareholders conceived of the company as a convenient medium to expand their economic activities to other sectors alongside show business, lifestyle magazines and tabloids. In due course the TV channel was used as a kind of money box for the expanding financial investments of the leading shareholders in the stock market. The economic recession that occurred in Greece by 2010 brought to the fore the bubble-like economic structure of the company and too many debts remained unpaid. By mid-2010 a minority of workers, mainly technicians, started the legal process of strike action to demand their wages, while the rest of the personnel waited patiently and hopelessly to be paid, not willing to believe that their workplace was about to shut down. In due course, however, they were convinced that the only means to get their money was a collective struggle and, for this reason, they decided to follow the technicians' struggle by 2011. Of the 700 workers involved in the struggle, some found employment, mainly the well-known journalists, some of whom adopted an opportunistic stance towards the collective cause, while others continued to actively take part in the forms of struggle decided by the general assemblies. As another informant said:

> Everybody knew, all of us knew very well what was going on, you know. It is almost impossible to walk around the workplace, talking to people and being in certain cliques not knowing persons and things. We knew about the huge loans, the big salaries, the unfair competitiveness with other mass media companies and the thoughtless spending, but so long as the wages were paid, nobody really cared, we thought that we would be here forever doing simply our jobs no matter what was going on in the outside world; we had this petit-bourgeois blindness, we refused to really see, we considered ourselves as being a kind of civil servant, unmovable.

During the fieldwork, workers experienced a highly volatile situation, having been on strike for about 16 months. Moreover, they had occupied the workplace, day and night, in order to protect their struggle and the premises. The workplace was the physical domain where they carried out their general assemblies, slept, ate and got to know each other better. In a way, the channel's premises were turned into their second home, acquiring a new identity and life content. Those who had agreed to proceed with the strike action were the vast majority of all the workers at the channel; they passed by the premises to get information about the ongoing struggle, to exchange ideas and to lend their hand to several emerging needs of their cause.

What these workers appeared to be re-discovering was a kind of egalitarian culture, different from that imposed by management aspirations. They came to the conclusion that management tactics privileged those who were able to get whatever they wished for in individualistic terms. Although this gradual awareness would not in itself lead to a class-based understanding of the cause, it made them think in terms of a democratic egalitarian solidarity, mediated by respectfulness and openness to other people's ideas, sharing a common but non-homogenizing morality with respect to the ethical rightfulness of their struggle, and making decisions based on democratic and transparent processes. In a way, this strike action radically reformed the pre-existing social and cultural relations in the workplace, and imposed the workers' understanding of some aspects of a possible and more lasting collectivity.

The point here is not that these precarious workers suddenly discovered a kind of collective egalitarianism but that they made their own way towards conceiving anew their personal identity in relation to others, and learning through daily struggle that ideals such as openness to other ways of life, true democratic co-existence and equal participation are but dead dogma when not followed in practice. In fact, the interesting element in this reframing process was that workers had in due course found out the immanent possibility of realizing what had previously seemed to be an unrealized utopia. Irrespectively of their full awareness of the situation, the TV channel workers created a spontaneous social space that arose out of contested actions and modes of cognition. Therefore, their ideas about the effort they undertook stemmed from within a critical evaluation of their lives as citizens with rights, obligations and a chance to imagine a better future. As another informant puts it:

> I don't mean to say that now we live in paradise, of course people looked first at the material side of the problem and no doubt there are colleagues who don't truly believe in the cause they have taken on. But the important thing for us now is that we learn to listen to each other and even most important is that we don't blame a different opinion. I often feel that there is a real 'we' and you know this is a painful process to make it happen. I remember the 'good' days when I simply was doing my job, without really caring about the others around me. Now I see my situation differently.

As this kind of collectivity arose out of a condition of emergency, it pointed to the fact of the social condition of its origin. Indeed, without this aspect collective action is but an academic exercise and a meaningless term for, as the ethnography in the TV channel's workplace revealed, the constant dialogues and ideas exchanges required a new demotic collectivity at odds with the cannibalistic culture currently diffuse in the mass media market. As one informant put it:

> Oh, yes, I must add that we aren't very popular among media big heads. They don't really want us in their companies now because we are experienced, we know how to claim our working rights and they are afraid of 'contaminating' their employees. We are stigmatized you know, we know that, but it is better that way than being docile. Once you are docile, you lose your dignity, you lose yourself.

Implied in this condition among struggling workers was the development of an understanding that their material deprivation makes their fortunes overlap, requiring at the same time collective practices, ideas and solutions to exist and to resist the marginalization process that precariousness engenders. Throughout the fieldwork period, this collectivity was evidently based on the hybridity of different selves rather than on the suppression of difference. Struggling workers had to be certain of every step they had to take, rather than uncritically follow decisions from the top of syndicalist unions. It is for this reason that, through constant interaction in the workplace, there existed a kind of permanent general assembly that installed a sense of belonging in a community open and receptive to critical debate and reflexivity. Games, discussions, personal problems, love affairs, law interpretation and understanding, syndicalist decisions, all were part of a process where the social was conceived of as an emergent reality, formed out of re-interpretations of experience. In fact, the understanding was that if this community of co-existence was to succeed, it would have to respect unconditional participation, contrary to the pseudo-egalitarian aspects of the vulgar lifestyle culture that management had promoted in the past.

This kind of participation reframed the way of belonging to a collectivity of colleagues who valued certain principles and standards, such as political transparency, democratic decision making, equal participation, respect of individuality, different human ways of being and justice. In this light I would argue that these precarious workers defined their belonging through a kind of membership in a morally and emotionally important and significant community, where one is 'taking pleasure from the presence of other, different places that are home to other, different people' (Appiah 1998: 22). Undoubtedly, one could object that this community is but an imagination of sameness and nothing more (Rapport 2012: 49). The ethnographic experience, however, revealed that these workers, compelled by the force of need and management's unfairness, have discovered, even ephemerally, a special mode of becoming a constantly struggling community. One informant explained:

> None of us could ever imagine we could communicate with all our differences, misunderstandings and interests, you know. Well we made it, the motive was getting our money in the beginning but then things changed. I have spent a life's routine here, I used to hate this place inside me because it was just that, a workplace. Now I can really understand the role of this fucking state and of all those who supposedly work for my own good. Now I feel that my true family is here, I am more confident and to be honest I don't really care about getting all my money for I earned my life again.

This view was very present throughout the period of fieldwork among the workers who either passed by or stayed in the workplace. No doubt there were casualties in due course; trying to struggle and establish a new sort of concept of work and personal life was not an easy effort, especially among people who were used to following a seemingly mono-dimensional employment career. Nevertheless, either due to forced choices or to side effects of unconscious drives, these decisions have been made on the basis of an imaginative realism through a reconceptualization of belonging and a meaningful attachment to elementary forms of sociality, beyond stereotypical unionized organization, which created the preconditions of an egalitarian path towards a collective freedom.

Conclusions

This ethnographically informed account of the case of the TV channel workers provides us with a snapshot of the deregulated Greek labour market and how the nastier side of the business cycle generates unemployment and insecurity, the main route to the formation of a precariat. Within a context of minimal social protection these workers experienced employment precariousness as a standard working condition. This is an emphatic reminder that, in the so-called post-industrial period of employment tertiarization, the relations of exploitation and inequality that characterize the labour process have essentially not changed, and that the Marxian notion of real subsumption of workers under capital is still an inexorable reality. Neoliberalism has become the dominant policy paradigm; its main philosophy is guided by a theological faith in the assumption that unfettered markets distribute goods, services and happiness more efficiently. In this context, not only do workers find themselves in the middle of the complex relation between the local and the global levels of production, they also experience the devastating effects of structural adjustment programmes, including growing poverty and greater restrictions on public spending. From an anthropological perspective, several studies demonstrate that the first victims of this philosophy are social services and the more vulnerable social categories, such as women and children, while the main beneficiaries are multi-national corporations looking for a flexible, docile and cheap labour supply (Durrenberger and Martí 2006). Although the rhetoric of these corporations is that they are doing workers a favour by hiring them, in reality, as ethnographies reveal, the people concerned have been deprived of all the alternatives that would have made their lives possible and independently sustainable. This, ironically, recalls the situation of the eighteenth-century Enclosure Acts in England.

Yet, the ethnography also revealed that workers refused to be passively adjusted to the asymmetrical conditions created by the capitalist accumulation process; instead, they tried to make a living through the rediscovery of family networks, the alternative option of agricultural production, and mainly through the reconceptualization of journalism as a profession. Hence by using their past know-how, their imaginative resourcefulness and empirically informed flexibility, they struggled to deal with uncomfortable processes and showed a strong commitment to the work ethic, not only as a means for survival but as a source of personal identity and self-worth. For this reason, they can be thought of as a 'community of practice': as such, they were formed through the process of sharing information and experiences with their colleagues, creating an opportunity to develop themselves personally and professionally.

This case also showed that making a living is no longer a straightforward process, but demands collective action and struggle. TV workers tried their own social 'experiment', rejecting traditional unionism and old-fashioned political rhetoric, and re-signifying the social in a period of extreme individuality. This was a bottom-up effort to demand material and social rights. But they did not succeed, in the end. Workers did not expect to get their jobs back – that would have been an unrealistic utopia – but they certainly wanted to make the most out of this struggle and, in particular, receive the salaries they were due from management, not for purely materialistic reasons, but for moral ones in the first place. Besides, this was their main objective when they decided to go on with their struggle even after realizing that they would not be re-employed again in the same workplace. Hence, although on the basis of legal decisions made by the Greek courts, their compensations are still due and their struggle has stopped, they created a new paradigm in terms of politics and morality. These workers, now communicating through the social and cultural network they built during their struggle, have shown a different moral and political awareness because their employment precariousness was simultaneous with the moral collapse and discrediting of the old-fashioned political regime, which liberated them from the illusions of party politics or state protection. In this context, they now tend to build new social networks of controlled size, focusing on specific goals and managing their needs on a new ethical basis. They also have shown that it is possible for a political community to discover on its own terms a way of being in the world and demand the means of its social and cultural existence. The outcome of this possibility is still open to the extent that precarious workers, increasingly aware of their power, may indeed become 'the new dangerous class' (Standing 2011).

Note

1 The ethnographic data come from fieldwork that took place between August 2012 and October 2013. The ethnographic research was conducted with Dr Vassilis Dalkavoukis, anthropologist at the Democritus University of Thrace.

References

Appiah, K.A. (1998) Cosmopolitan Patriots. In Cheah, P. and Robbins, B., *Cosmopolitics: Thinking and Feeling Beyond the Nation.* Minneapolis: University of Minnesota Press.

Barbier, J.C. (2004) A comparative analysis of employment precariousness in Europe. In Letablier, M.T., *Learning from Employment and Welfare Policies in Europe.* E.S.R.C. Cross-National Research Papers. Available from: www.xnat.org.uk/PDFs/SeventhSeries/Seminar%203%20Learning%20from%20Employment%20and%20Welfare%20Policies%20in%20Europe.pdf. [Accessed 28 June 2015]

Durrenberger, P. E. and Martí, J. (2006) Introduction. In Durrenberger, E. P. and Martí, J., *Labor in Cross-Cultural Perspective*. New York: Altamira Press, pp. 1–27.

Edgell, S. (2009) *The Sociology of Work. Continuity and Change in Paid and Unpaid Work.* London: Sage.

ESOPE (2004) *Precarious Employment in Europe: A Comparative Study of Labour Market Related Risks in Flexible Economies*. European Commission.

I.N.E./G.S.E.E.-ADEDY (2015) *The Greek Economy and Employment. Annual Review.* Athens: INE/GSEE.-ADEDY.

I.L.O. (2012) *From Precarious Work to Decent Work.* Geneva: I.L.O.

Kalleberg, A.L. (2009) Precarious work, insecure workers: Employment relations in transition. *American Sociological Review* 74, February: 1–22.

Kretsos, L. (2014) Youth policy in austerity Europe: The case of Greece. *International Journal of Adolescence and Youth* 19(S1): 35–47.

Lavery, S. (2014) The politics of precarious employment in Europe: Zero-hour contracts and the commodification of work. In Cardoso, P.M., Erdinc, I., Horemans, J. and Lavery, S., *Precarious Employment in Europe*. Brussels: FEPS.

Mouriki, A. (2010) The new proletariat: Precarious workers – the outcasts of contemporary labour market. In Naoumi, M., Papapetrou, G., Spyropoulou, N., Fronimou, E. and Chrisakis, M., *The Social Portrait of Greece 2010*. Athens: National Centre for Social Research.

Pardo, I. (1996) *Managing Existence in Naples: Morality, Action and Structure*. Cambridge: Cambridge University Press.

Procoli, A. (ed.) (2004) *Workers and Narratives of Survival in Europe. The Management of Precariousness at the End of the Twentieth Century*. Albany: State University of New York Press.

Rapport, N. (2012) *Anyone. The Cosmopolitan Subject of Anthropology*. Oxford: Berghahn Books.

Spyridakis, M. (2013) *The Liminal Worker. An Ethnography of Work, Unemployment and Precariousness in Contemporary Greece*. Farnham: Ashgate.

Standing, G. (2011) *The Precariat. The New Dangerous Class*. London: Bloomsbury Academic.

8 Stories of precarious lives

Joanne Richardson

Precarious Lives is a feminist documentary from 2007–2008 that mixes archival footage of women's labour over the past century with ten portraits of Romanian women working in 2007 in different countries. The idea for the video arose after a previous collaboration (*Made in Italy*, 2005–2005) with Candida TV from Italy, in which we began with the intention to research and document precarious work in Romania, but found that the concept of precarity, which had been imported from Western Europe, didn't find a genuine corresponding reality. When we started the research in 2005, our first interview was with a highly educated 26-year-old woman who was working at a call centre (a relatively new phenomenon in Romania), and who was earning 250 Euro per month for a part-time job. This was precarious, by Western definitions, but she told us she felt very lucky to find this job, which offered her a lot of free time and flexibility and was twice the salary of 8-hour jobs with permanent contracts. At one point in the interview she said, if you really want to see precarity, go look in the factories. In the end, for our collaborative project, we decided to shift our focus to the delocalization of Italian shoe and textile factories to Romania. Two years later, *Precarious Lives* took up the unanswered question about precarity, at a time when theories of precarity were becoming fashionable in Romanian intellectual discourse, but there was still a significant disconnect between the theoretical concept and the practical reality. *Precarious Lives* sought to challenge the dominant Western discourse about precarity and its disregard of gender and economic inequalities that still divided the first and third worlds of Europe. Although the economic situation in Romania has changed during the seven years since the video was made, the stories of the ten women in the documentary still offer compelling insights into both the differences and the similarities that exist across European borders.

Script of the film

[voiceover]

Precarity arrived in Romania a few years ago. As discourse.

Before, precarious meant anything insecure or unstable. In economic terms, it meant poverty.

Now there are articles and blogs, with a new definition, matching its European context.

Precarity, noun: the condition of flexible, intermittent, short-term and part-time work under post-Fordist capitalism. Armed with the theory, we set out to investigate the reality. Starting with the immediate.

Brighi, 22, law student/salesperson

My first job was at Arta Graf, where I worked as a salesperson.

I stayed for a year. I had no time for my personal life or school or anything else.

I quit this job because the salary was minimum wage and because I wanted something better.

My second job was at Praktiker, I was initially recruited as a cashier, then I advanced to customer service and later to the sales office.

The salary was low and I stayed only four months.

My third job was as a sales assistant for Urania, which distributed Nestle products.

It was my best job till now, and the salary was OK but I had to quit due to health problems.

I had to arrange products, and also to carry weights from the warehouse to the shelves.

I injured my back, and this means no effort for an extended period of time.

Now I'm searching for a better job, I'd prefer an office job because of the health problems.

Oana, 30 artist/librarian

After college I started teaching. I endured it for three years.

It was hard, I had too many students and couldn't get to know them or build a relation with them.

And if I had an idea that was closer to their own interests, my bosses didn't agree to it.

Then I heard about this job as a painter, it was painting oil reproductions for an Italian firm.

But I had problems there as well. The bosses forced us to resign, for a month I was in limbo, then they called some of us back, but at a much lower salary, and with all sorts of strange rules.

It felt like being on a conveyor belt. We had to wear lab coats and tags with numbers.

The frustrations piled up. Our new boss asked us to grade our colleagues, from best to worst.

The aim was to plant discord among us. Of course, we all refused to do it.

But over time more seeds were planted to divide us. And sometimes it worked, conflicts appeared.

Now I work at the library. It's not like I imagined, that I'd sit and read all day.

It's more demanding than the job as a painter. Working with people usually is.

But they have a different mentality than my old bosses. Here I work for another type of people.

It's a state job, so I could have it for life. But I don't want to stay here all my life.

Laura, 27, business developer

My first job was a shop assistant or salesperson in a store for mobile telephones and accessories.

After two months there, I quit to have time to finish my Master's thesis.

Then I worked as a substitute teacher in a somewhat untraditional high-school.

After this there was a period, it wasn't really a job, when I tutored former twelfth-grade students in Romanian and English for their graduation exams.

After the exams I started to work again with a proper contract for the commerce trade union in a 4-hour part-time job.

Working for the union, I entered a field that was unknown to me but seemed very exciting, I liked the idea of working for a trade union, an organization with power to change things.

A large part of my job consisted of campaigns, and I saw the reaction of workers: 'nothing will change, we are powerless to do anything'.

Things didn't really happen there, it was more of a job for appearances, and the financial benefits were equal to zero, so I started to look for something better paid.

And for the past two years, I've been working for a company that sells construction materials, in a job that was invented for me, 'business developer', or someone who does everything.

Being a worker for this company now, I see that the attitudes of workers who preferred to solve problems with bosses by themselves without complicating things, were justified.

I don't know how other jobs are, but mine leaves me very little free space for myself, and using my free time to get involved in a trade union is something I wouldn't do.

Dora, 28, transport coordinator

In my second year of college, I started working at an orphanage. I stayed there for three years.

I was someone who did everything. I worked as a volunteer at first, later they started paying me.

When I finished college, my dad owned an auto parts shop, and he decided to start a transport company in which I would work. I was still at the orphanage.

I had to weigh the two and choose. And in the end I chose the company because dad got sick.

It's a risk to open a company, you can make a profit or lose everything you invested.

The first big problem was when the value of the Euro dropped.

As an international transport company, all of our income was in Euro, but all the major expenses – salaries, bills, taxes – were in Romanian Lei.
And you realize your profit has decreased by a sufficient percentage to have real problems.
The end came last year, in 2006, when all the bank accounts were frozen for debts we still had to the leasing company. The leasing problems forced me to close down.
That's why I had to get a new job urgently, as a transport coordinator for a factory.
What's good here is that I have no stress, I get a stable income every month, on the same day.
With your own company things are never sure ... will I make money this month?
Do I need to work harder; do I need to ask for a loan?
You're constantly stressed, you think about it day and night.

A.I., 24, activist/therapist
In college I began working as a volunteer in several projects for handicapped children.
After graduating I got a job in the same field, social services for the handicapped. I stayed for one year.
I decided to quit because I couldn't live on the salary.
And it was a hard job, it didn't end in the workplace, I had to do research and prepare at home.
In my private life, all my passion went on activist projects on feminism, anti-fascism, animal rights.
Since my job took 90 per cent of my time, I couldn't even manage a double life like I did before, split between my profession and my activism.
At the beginning of last year, I decided to move to a city in the west where I found an MA in my field, and in the summer I went there to register, but the tuition had tripled, so I decided to give up.
It was a point of no return, I couldn't go back to Bucharest or move to the other city, and a friend who was visiting proposed that I move to Berlin, or at least try it.
It took a long time to find a job in Berlin. I would have liked to work in my field, but after realizing I can't work in my profession, I got a job as a babysitter.
I have a one-year contract. I'll stay till the end of the contract and then I'll probably leave.
I still hope to go back to do the MA, but I'll have to raise the money here.

[voiceover]
After staring at the obvious, doubts emerge ... Is precarity new?
Hasn't instability been the constant experience of workers under capitalism?
And also of capital itself?
Doesn't the focus on instability blur the distinction between labour and capital?

Do the proposed solutions – job security and a guaranteed income – sound like utopian ideals?
Even for workers who once experienced the stability guaranteed by state socialism?

Viorica, 42, gardener/salesperson
I started working in 1981 in the city's greenhouses.
We grew flowers for beautifying the city.
We also did patriotic service that we weren't paid for.
When a new construction was finished we were taken there to do the landscaping.
Often they would drive us back home late in the evening after we were done.
We were happy to stay because we knew we had a secure job and income.
Things were very good back then. A huge difference from what followed the revolution.
There were 100 people when I started in 1981. In 2002 there were only 7 people left.
After the revolution many private companies opened and took our projects.
We were so insecure, we thought we'd close.
I went home scared every day because I'd hear that more people were losing their job.
It feels bad to be anxious, wondering if you still have a job tomorrow, and for how long.
This is no way to live.
After the greenhouse, I got a job at a fruit and vegetable kiosk.
Now being in the EU, this job isn't stable either.
They could close down the kiosk, as the law demands.

Doina, 47, civil servant
During the time of the dead one (Ceausescu) you could only find strange jobs.
One summer I picked raspberries. Another summer I worked at a pastry shop.
Then I went to college, but it wasn't what I wanted. I wanted to become a French teacher.
But I went on to chemistry.
I want to stress that those who claim there was no unemployment during Ceausescu are lying.
I looked for a job in Baia Mare for several months.
The jobs I was offered by the employment agency, or its equivalent back then, were selling lottery tickets, or picking apples in an orchard.
I tried factories, chemical plants, I even tried the mines …
I graduated from chemistry high-school and had nearly two years of college.
I also tried a chemistry lab, but didn't find anything. These were the only two offers I had.
Selling lottery tickets in restaurants wasn't a way to earn a living for me,
I don't want to say it wasn't a decent way since it's impolite to those who did this job.
But it wasn't the job I wanted or that represented me.

Eniko, 47, professor of gender

I graduated in philosophy in 1984.

I went through different schools, as a substitute teacher of Romanian history, universal history, social sciences, political economy, and occasionally philosophy.

It was a very strange period, I thought I was preparing myself for a different kind of job, not that I knew for what exactly, in the 1980s people couldn't really plan their future.

Our dreams were determined for us. And I could not see past the limits of the system.

The system offered security and stability, the promise of a job for life, a pension, a flat, etc.

These were secure and stable for everyone, which made planning your life easier than it is today, when there are obstacles and constant changes.

But personal freedom was restricted, so in this sense there was no room for subjective projection.

Ulrike, 41, artist/unemployed

I graduated from art high-school in Timisoara in 1985.

Then I went to Petrosani because my parents lived there and I could only get residency there.

In Timisoara I wouldn't have found a job because I didn't have the right connections.

In Petrosani my step-father used his connections to find me a job – decorating shop windows.

I didn't last long there. I left because a friend offered to find me a job in Sibiu, in an enterprise with many workshops, including a ceramics workshop.

But many problems appeared. Our bosses expected all sorts of favours from us.

The worst problems were with people who abused the power the regime gave them.

I felt the system offered me very few opportunities.

I applied twice to the art academy, in Bucharest and again in Cluj.

I knew daughters of party members who became students while I could not.

At that time, no one in Romania believed anything would change.

I escaped in 1988 through Hungary, knowing it wasn't sending Romanian refugees back.

My father was for a long time in Germany with his new family, and I stayed with him for a year.

Afterwards I applied to art schools and became a student in Kiel, north Germany.

Mioara, 48, chemical engineer

In 1982 after I finished college in chemical engineering, I was assigned a job at PetroMidia.

After 1990, when we became independent, when the state gave up control of the refinery, it functioned for two months until crude oil ran out, then stopped for two to three months to get more oil.
It was a constant stress since salaries were dependent on production.
In 2001 PetroMidia was privatized by Dinu Patriciu and was renamed Rompetrol.
There was massive restructuring, and in 2002 I was restructured.
It was very hard for me. I kept asking myself, 'why me?'
I think age was a main factor. I and another female colleague who was fired were the oldest.
I went through a very difficult time. I cried all day, reminisced about the past, and cried again.
Dinu Patriciu's team told us it's not good to stay at the same job more than five years.
At first we didn't realize that they were right.
Now I realize it's better to change jobs and companies often.
Afterwards, I took two courses. One was for starting your own business.
But to start a business you need money, which I didn't have.
If I couldn't start my own business, I considered going to cosmetic school.
After all you have to do something to survive.
I also took a course in selling insurance, which I tried out for 3–4 months.
I had about 14 customers who insured themselves.
I had to have contracts every month, and I kept doing sales pitches but had no new customers.
After three months with no results, they sort of push you aside.
Meanwhile I found a job as an engineer at the Cernavoda plant.
It was paid around 4 million (€100), plus meal coupons.
I woke up at 5am, left at 5:40am, came home at 7:30pm; it was more than 12 hours a day.
In November 2003, I started working at SAPARD, a programme for EU agricultural development.
The programme is funded by the EU community and will last until 2013.
So there are five more years. Afterwards we don't know what will happen.
Probably other programmes will follow, but anyway there are five more years.

[voiceover]

We began with the stories of ten women, in post-communist Romania. Why post-communist?
Because it is our context, and we wanted to see how a foreign theory could explain it.
In 2005, the Romanian government tried to change the labour code to favour flexible, short-term contracts.
After many strikes, the unions claimed victory: most jobs remain stable, with permanent contracts.

And Romanians are still leaving to find unstable, short-term, illegal work in other countries.

Laura

I started with 3 million Lei (€75) in 2003 at the mobile phone shop.
In the union, since it was part-time, I had 2.5 million (€62) per month.
In the two months as a substitute teacher I got 800,000 (€20).
Now I have a salary of 12 million (€325), plus meal coupons.

[voiceover]

In 2007, the average salary rose to 12 million (€325). In real terms – of purchasing power – it caught up to the 1989 level, after 18 years.

Brighi

It's hard to live alone, paying college, bills, rent; with a small salary, you can't survive on your own.
But living with my boyfriend, we try together to get by.
There are days when we crave the sun but we can't afford it.
We make a pact not to buy certain things, we limit ourselves, otherwise we can't...

[voiceover]

The minimum wage is set by estimating minimum consumption. In 2007, amounts estimated for food were 1/2 of the rations under Ceausescu.

Oana

Four years ago when I quit teaching I had 3 million (€75), and I started with 1 million (€25) in 2000.
Now, I also don't have a high salary in the library; it just went up to 6.8 million (€180).
As far as money goes, my situation is not so bad because I still live with my parents, and what I give them is only symbolic, I don't really pay my full expenses.
I couldn't live alone on my salary.

[voiceover]

The EU defines poverty as any income below 30 per cent of the average salary per country. That means half the population in Romania.

A.I.

My first salary was 5.5 million (€140) per month, for 40 hours a week, 8 hours a day.
4–5 months ago they raised it to 8.8 million (€230), but I really couldn't live on it.
In Berlin I make €600 a month.

In Romania although I had a good profession, here I earn three times more, and it's not more expensive than Bucharest, some things are even cheaper in Berlin, like housing.

Here I pay €130 for my room, including utilities in the flat, but in Romania I wouldn't have found as nice a place for €130.

[voiceover]

More than 3 million Romanians are working in other countries. Italy and Spain are the leading destinations for Romanian migrants.

Viorica

I went to Spain in 2003. I left on February 21st and came back on June 18th.

There were 37 Romanian women, 10 Polish women and 17 Spanish.

We were paid €31 for 6 hours (€700 a month).

We worked a lot, they made us work fast. It was very difficult.

Every day in the same bent-over position, it was hard.

After four hours you can't bear the pain anymore. But you stand up and go on, there's no choice.

I still feel the pain when the weather changes … and four years have passed.

I'm lucky that my in-laws lived near and took care of my small child.

I wouldn't have gone if my in-laws couldn't care for him.

It was worth it. You make an effort for your family.

I couldn't earn that money here. In three years I couldn't make what I made there in three months.

[voiceover]

The money sent back by migrants working in other countries is equal to 30 per cent of Romania's GDP. Without it, the economy would collapse.

Ulrike

I started working bad jobs when I was a student, and I was convinced it was a temporary phase.

They were diverse: babysitting, caring for old people, cleaning lady, cafeteria helper, waitressing, measuring land, restoring buildings.

I did a one-year course in media design because I hoped to escape from these unqualified jobs.

Afterwards, I had a year-long internship at an advertising agency, and then they hired me.

But I realized it wasn't what I wanted because it left me no free time for my art projects, and we were all badly paid. I made 1,000 DM (€500) per month.

In 2004, I applied for the first time for social assistance.

When you apply, you have to prove that you have no resources from which to live.

The amount is €345 (plus rent).

At first I was ashamed, I told few people I was on social assistance and tried to avoid the issue.

Until I realized how many people in Berlin in the cultural field live on social assistance.

I can't say I've accomplished myself in any way. I can't live from my art works or artistic projects.

[voiceover]

We began with the stories of ten women. Why women? Because every theory has its blind spot.

The cultural worker has become the model precariat, the new subject of history, while others are invisible.

Many university-educated experts now work in conditions common to women across time: at home, with unpredictable hours, with periods of inactivity, without contract, without rights.

The idea of a common precarity ignores inequalities that place some workers in positions of disadvantage.

Eniko

Communist ideology presupposed that women and men were equal, that gender didn't matter, it mattered only how you contributed to the production that sustained socialist society.

On the other hand, it's well-known that Romania had a demographics policy that criminalized abortion and the use of modern contraception.

This obviously put a huge burden on the shoulders of women.

On the one hand to be a heroic worker, equal to male workers, and on the other hand to be the heroic mother of four, five, six children.

The fact that the division of labour at home, in the family, didn't change, meant that many women experienced the right to paid work as an obligation, an extra burden.

Doina

The rights given to women by the state are mostly tied to maternity.

So much is done for women with children, there are 7–8 types of benefits for mothers.

[voiceover]

Under Ceausescu, women were 'encouraged' to have four children – to ensure the reproduction of the workforce. The state's aim is not so different now. Maternity pay is twice the minimum wage.

A.I.

My current job places me in a role I don't like, taking care of a child.

My previous job, as a therapist, also framed me in this stereotype of a woman caring for a child.

In my field, most therapists, psycho- and kineto-therapists, are women, but the project leader is most often a man.

Laura

I started as a secretary at my current job. After three months, I became assistant business developer.

I suggested hiring a man as secretary, but they were outraged and wouldn't hear of it.

My boss felt that a secretary should look a certain way to attract the attention of clients.

This created a culture of ridiculing the secretary.

Eniko

Of course it's necessary to have a division of labour because no one can do everything.

The problem is not that women, due to how they have been socialized, tend to work certain jobs.

We see that jobs in education and healthcare are tied to the idea that women take care of others.

Of course, this can also be changed.

But the real problem appears when these jobs are compared, valorized differently, and hierarchized.

The issue is not that some jobs are done by women and some by men, but that women's work is valued less, has less social prestige and is paid less.

[voiceover]

The income of all women in Romania is 50 per cent of the income of men. The gap is largely due to a division of professions that are paid differently.

Doina

We can speak of discrimination in the context of institutions, but on a general level, discrimination begins in the family, from what's expected of women in Romania.

You always hear, a woman's duty is to: have a clean home, take care of her kids, help them with homework, make preserves and sweets, to care for the elderly and sick in the family, to take care of her husband, to be available at all times, not to gossip … What else? Oh yes! To have a job and perform her professional duties there as well.

This is the main discrimination, in the way girls are brought up.

[voiceover]

We began with ten stories. In retrospect, the number seems inadequately small.

But it allowed us to glimpse differences, singular realities behind the concept.

As a noun, precarity does not exist. It is an adjective, modifying subjects, changing through circumstance.

To understand what it means to be precarious, we must invert the theory, starting from our own lives.
To walk the streets that bring us together, and the routes that sometimes divide us.
And while walking, ask questions...

End credits
Precarious Lives, 43 min, 2008
A D Media Production
Concept, texts, montage: Joanne Richardson
Camera: Nita Mocanu, Joanne Richardson, Andreea Carnu
Animations: Andreea Carnu
Voiceover: Ramona Dumitrean
Translations: Joanne Richardson, Andreea Carnu, Ruxandra Costescu
Many thanks to Ruxandra Costescu and Doina Sulea for help with the research
Inspiration from the texts and practices of: Precarias a la Deriva in Spain
Image and sound fragments recycled from:
Prelinger Archives (occupational films), CC Mixter, Mum, Photek, Paul Schutze, Migrant, Subdued
CopyLeft, 2008

9 Precarious Japan[1]

Steffi Richter
Translated by Kelly Mulvaney

A Manifesto

> A spectre is haunting Japan, the spectre called 'Lost Generation'. We, in our late 20s, early 30s, released into society at a moment when there was nearly no prospect of finding a job (the 'lost decade' of the 1990s) – we work, live and die every day as existences that still cannot be named ... 20 million in number.
>
> 'Working poor,' 'freeter,' 'hikikomori,' 'NEET,' 'depressive generation,' 'the generation that drew the lot of poverty,' 'losers,' 'low-stream (*karyū*),' 'lost generation.' Labels like these lump us together. But we don't want the problems and contradictions we face to be covered up by such labelling. And we don't want to treat our anguish and worries with the term 'self-responsibility.' We have been suppressing all these feelings and not spoken of them, but now we finally know: 'It is time to be indignant!'
>
> (*Rosu jene* 2008: 5)

These are the opening lines of the 'Manifesto of the *rosu jene*', a kind of credo of the journal of the same name, *Rosu Jene*, first published in May 2008 with over 10,000 copies. At this moment, worldwide, the historically specific constellation of a multiple crisis became exacerbated by the outbreak of the financial crisis, and this was also the case in Japan. It led to a further intensification of the situation of the labour market and increased insecurity for those working under regular jobs, but much more for those on atypical (non-regular) work contracts, such as the cited 'working poor' or 'freeter' (a German–English combination of 'free' and 'Arbeiter' [*worker*]). These people have since been called '*rosu jene*' – the Japanese abbreviation of *lost generation*, which has become the familiar term for every generation that has pushed its way into the labour market since the mid-1990s, the so-called 'lost decade'. After the abrupt end of the economic bubble, it became increasingly hard in the labour market to find a permanent position that would promise a 'normal life' with life-long security. For this reason, the talk at that time was of an 'employment ice age for graduate job seekers' (*shūshoku hyōga-ki*). In 2008 the expression 'rosu gene' was entered into the annual publication 'Basic Knowledge of Current Terminology' (*Gendai yōgo no kiso chishiki* 2008) – a kind of seismograph of sensibilities in Japanese society. And in the August issue of the renowned literary journal *Subaru*, 'My Dream: I wish I had never been born' (*Umarete konakatta koto o yume miru*) was the title of the first instalment of a five-part series, 'Literary Considerations of *rosu jene*' (*Rosu jene bungeiron*), written by the precarious publicist and activist Sugita Shunsuke (born 1975) (Sugita 2008). Evidently, the crisis year of 2008 catalysed the *lost generation* into an event: it 'revealed' itself in a sudden manner, which not only raises the question of what led to its emergence, but also marked an opportunity to problematize the perception and systems under which similar phenomena had been framed (Žižek 2014: 11).

'Lost generation' and all the other labels used to try to articulate the vaguely sensed upheavals currently underway in post-industrial societies are also discussed in and with reference to Japan with the concept of the precarious, the precariat, and precarization. This is by no means self-explanatory. In this sense, for example, in her book *State of Insecurity: Government of the Precarious*, Isabell Lorey characterizes the process of precarization as a mode of subjectivation that becomes hegemonic explicitly in 'leading neoliberal Western industrial nations' ('Western' in the sense of Occidental-European). This limit is certainly to be welcomed, insofar as it marks a recognition that Europe can no longer function in academic knowledge production as the Archimedean point from which the world is measured. And this caution is *apparently* confirmed by sociological studies of Japan guided by conventional models of society, where the rising social inequalities and poverty caused by the increase of precarious employment are quantitatively determined. But when considering society as a whole, for these studies, Japan would 'surely not count as precarious [...] Even the (discursive) creation of a new 'class' of the precariat blurs [...] large, actually-existing differences between individual life circumstances' (Obinger 2016: 345).[2]

What is lost on this kind of sceptical academic investigation, however, is that activists in Japan, too, were taking part in the developments of Western initiatives, where activities of precarious activists and research on precarity were interlaced from the outset. They communicated with like-minded counterparts in Italy, Spain, and other Western countries and grappled with their texts, symbols, and movement practices with a view to the circumstances in Japan. Evidence of this can be seen as early as 2006, when the bimonthly journal *Impaction*, which understands itself as an organ of left-wing theory, published two issues containing: 'Precariat of the world! Conspire! (*Bankoku no purekariāto! Kyōbō' seyo!*) in April, and 'Connect! Research Machines' (*Setsuzoku seyo! Kenkyū kikai*) in October. Both issues contributed to the entry of the language of the precariat into the language of movement and protest in Japan, including in the journal *Rosu jene* referenced above, as well as in the institutionalized academy. The introductory words to the first thematic issue *Precariat of the world! Conspire! For a new politics of the class of the insecure (the precariat)* read:

> Who is the precariat? Simply put, it is those who, in globalizing market-centrism, find themselves in insecure relations (in precarity) both in terms of

> their working lives as well as with respect to their daily lives, especially the young generation. Typical examples of this are the chain-workers who work in the *konbini* (convenience stores, S.R.) and fast food restaurants, or the part-time teachers who do not find stable employment after finishing their doctorate, and the irregular brainworkers. In Japan, furthermore, the young generation referred to as 'NEET' and 'freeter' can be considered as a reserve army of the precariat (in potentia). Of course, they are called precariat not only for their insecure situation, but also because this word contains an aspect of being conceived as a new 'movement subject.' While raging capital ensures for one that the stratum of the insecure expands more and more, it appears as if it would also want to suppress the danger of a crisis of social dismantlement that would start from the precarious through surveillance and control. If we allow things to continue in this manner, we will probably face a 'world' of global totalitarianism in the 21st century. In order to work against totalitarianism and to create a global world of 'freedom' and 'democracy' and 'justice', a route/course/possibility is needed to sound the voices of the minority of societally disadvantaged in society (in the world). For precisely this reason, it is necessary that the precarious of all countries 'conspire.' Online, through print media, and by actually meeting face-to-face, a 'common voice' must be generated that guarantees difference and diversity (meaning, which does not reduce these to 'a whole').
>
> (*Impaction* 2006a: 9)

In the same year, the demonstration 'May Day for Freedom and Survival' (*Jiyū to seizon no mēdē*) (which had occurred since 2005, following the Euro Mayday movement) took place for the first time with the slogan 'For the Conspiracy of the Precariat'. In this context, an activist of the Part-Time, Worker, Freeter and Foreign Workers' Union (PAFF; *Furītā zenpan rōdō kumiai*, founded in 2004), co-organizer of the demonstration, emphasized that the word 'precariat' had emerged from popular parlance. This made it different from, for example, 'multitude', which

> was not created as an academic word, but first saw the light of day as anonymous graffiti. [...] Thus, the word precariat does not have scientific precision. How should 'insecurity' even be statistically and empirically defined [...]. Instead, we should depart from [...] the lack of protection that we sense on a daily basis.
>
> (Dialogue on Precariat 2006)

What is articulated here is a new kind of precarization and its analysis, one that Mario Candeias once accurately described as 'underdetermined and over-differentiated' (2005) and until now has barely been taken up in social scientific research regarding Japan. This relates, among other things, to the fact that the movement and activists themselves are increasingly also the experts with the knowledge necessary to examine the circumstances by which they are directly affected: 'We are the ones this is about.' Precarity became a mass phenomenon in the academic sphere some time ago – considered in the second *Impaction* issue mentioned above. Author, translator, and activist Sabu Kohso explains this in a 2006 text as follows. The majority of universities are

> no longer institutions for producing middle-class, white collar workers, to say nothing of Japan's future elites, but temporary camps for chronically jobless youth. [...] Thus it is high time to re-categorize students [...] and organize them according to this concept [of jobless young workers, S.R.] [...] In this sense, universities themselves might become stages for the struggle again, but in a totally unprecedented way.
>
> (Kohso 2006: 416–34)

Given what has been argued so far, we can present the following hypothesis: moods as well as uprisings – however minoritarian – can no longer be explained away as a simply marginal or populist phenomena in Japan, or elsewhere. In Japan, too, all social spheres and a growing part of the population are becoming pervaded and affected by precarization. At the same time, highlighting the commonalities demands that we do not lose sight of the differences. The latter result, diachronically, from the historical path dependency of the capitalist modernization of individual societies, and synchronically from various social and/or geopolitical constellations they are embedded in. This cautious proceeding is an empirically and theoretically based mode of thinking commonalities and differences with respect to the young concept of 'precarization society', which is still at an early stage. From a macro perspective that considers structural changes, it would be important to examine more closely the inflections precarization assumes in Japan starting from the fact that the 'Post-Fordist accumulation regime' developed there as 'Toyotism', flanked by policies of privatization, de-regulation and a shrinking welfare state that started in the 1980s and accelerated since 2000. The relation between this model of production, implemented beyond the automobile and assembly factories to include the service sector, and Fordism remains disputed. There are also controversies surrounding the experience of those who must now bring their labour-power to market under new conditions of media technology (Berndt 2009: 99–106; Elis 2016: 70–78). This model is simultaneously shaped by the informationalization and computerization of production and communication processes, facing workers with new challenges that paradoxically take the semblance of both impositions (intensification of work and control) and opportunities (autonomy, creativity, self-responsibility, flexibility).

'Nomen est omen': from the outset, the social figure 'freeter' was discussed ambivalently. To free oneself from the 'lifestyle regime' of the middle class and especially of the salaried employee (*sararīman*), to craft one's own life plans, was initially perceived in the quite positive terms conveyed by the word 'free'. For young people, it became necessary to earn a livelihood with 'flexible' jobs; these rapidly increased in number and were needed by (male) workers 'freed' from stable positions of employment with guaranteed promotion. Since the mid-1990s, however, both the image and the actual situation of the 'junior baby boomer generation' (born in the 1970s) increasingly became recognizable as 'working poor' or the 'lost generation'. Their numbers grew, as did the numbers of those

> who cease to be ashamed for their wealth, cease to be humble or to derive a sense of responsibility for others from it. Especially the young rich want to demonstrate success and wealth, to perform much more [...] The upper and lower stratums are growing at the cost of the middle stratum, the difference between above and below becomes larger.
>
> (Berndt 2008: 76)

These developments are discussed in Japan as 'low-stream society' and 'gap society' (*karyū shakai* and *kakusa shakai*).

It is worthwhile to consider them using Oliver Marchart's encompassing concept of precarization. Marchart does not reduce the phenomenon to poverty or the lower social stratum, or to a set of social spheres linked to certain work relations, but rather depicts it in terms of its relevance to all of society, which is why he speaks of a 'precarization society'. In this society, 'the social assemblage is subject to a process in which nearly all work and living relations become insecure, that is, the diffusion of precarity into the whole space of the social' (Marchart 2013: 7).

Three are the crucial axes along which precarization 'cuts through' social spaces and spheres that were previously separated from one another (Marchart 2013: 7–20). Precarization runs transversally along the first axis crossing all social strata. As traditional social standards are eroded and subverted, precarization reacts and threatens also those with regular employment contracts. On a second axis, according to Marchart, insecurity and precarization affect countless spheres not only of work, but also of the reproduction of life in its biological, social and cultural dimensions. The main reason for this is the spreading of work from the factory onto the entire social sphere, not least through the transformation of more and more (immaterial) goods into commodities and the marketization of all labour potential and capacities. 'Even when one doesn't seem to be working, one is working' (Marchart 2013: 12). This is the case for the 'creatives', while many of the 'working poor' need to work two or three jobs to make ends meet. On the third axis, Marchart looks at the unbounded nature of objective and subjective processes of precarization. Objectively, widespread deregulation leads to increased risks of loss of social status. Subjectively, fear spreads among not only the poor and unemployed. As a threat, the reserve army of the precariat ensures that precarity remains constantly present in *everyone's* heads. At the same time, however, the growing responsibility individuals must assume for their own risk management in their careers and lives leads to strategies of subjectivation that make it possible for this risk and precarious conditions to be experienced as an enrichment and the freedom of self-realization. Established mechanisms of domination support the 'potential of autonomy of freely acting subjects who think in entrepreneurial terms', in order to 'tap into it as a resource for productivity', and in so doing draw on certain 'technologies of governmentality' (Marchart 2013: 13). These technologies, however, are always subjective to individuals, so they also become an integral element of new subject cultures with ambivalent potential. It is significant that Marchart does not understand precarity as a 'logic of economic fatality', according to which 'larger and larger parts of the population [fall into] poverty, exclusion and deprivation'. Rather, he states, 'because it is driven by political action [it] also [opens] new perspectives for political action' (Marchart 2013: 16).

With reference to the ambivalence of the technologies of self-government of precarious subjects, Marchart's work is linked to the studies of governmentality by the late Michel Foucault. These are also central to Lorey's analyses of the ambivalence of precarization mechanisms, developed in the context of her own academic precarity and self-reflexive participation in the movements of the precarious. Lorey's analyses are close to my own take on precarity and precarization, which I apply to the Japanese context. Thus, I will briefly present a few of her core ideas. I will also draw on the excellent study by Carl Cassegård, *Youth Movements, Trauma and Alternative Space*, published in 2014, that introduces countless actors who were also relevant to the two issues of *Impaction* mentioned at the beginning of this text.

Exodus as self-empowerment[3]

The concept of governmentality, influenced by Foucault, is the focal point of analysis of the ways individuals are made governable and simultaneously make themselves and each other governable. At the heart of this double perspective – of being governed by others and self-governing – Foucault places the question of its hidden potential for critique: 'how not to be governed *like that*, by that, in the name of those principles, with such and such an objective in mind and by means of such procedures, not like that, not for that, not by them' (Foucault 2007: 44). Lorey takes up this question to address not only 'the ambivalence between being governed by others and self-government', but also and above all 'the ambivalence *in* self-government – between servile making-governable and refusals that aim to be no longer governed in this way' (Lorey 2015: 4). First is the servile side of (precarious) self-government, where modern citizens, 'believing in collective, and thus implicitly their own, sovereignty, autonomy and freedom,' (Lorey 2015: 4) voluntarily submit to societal relations, which ultimately follow the social and political logic of threat, protection and security historically traceable back to Thomas Hobbes' conception of the security state. To no longer be governed like that, 'and to even be governed less and less', in contrast, orients itself around a logic of care. '[T]he term 'reproduction', and the multiplicity of care activities associated with it, [are situated] in the context of post-Fordist production conditions, and tak[e] into consideration the new forms of communicative knowledge and affect work' (Lorey 2015: 94).

In order to understand what this means for Lorey's studies of precarity – and what it could mean for other cases – the three dimensions of her concept of the precarious should be introduced: precariousness, precarity and governmental precarization (Lorey 2015: 17–22). None of these concepts is isolated; they are in a historical relation to one another.

When using the term 'precariousness', Lorey follows Judith Butler's notion, which points to the fact that life and the bodies of all humans are contingent, thus they are social, that is, dependent on others and therefore ineluctably endangered, the counterpart of which is a need for protection. This precarious being-together that is shared by all, however, does not make humans existentially equal, for from the beginning, 'precarity' involves a political dimension, which locates the insecurity of individuals in societally distinct positions. Through processes of political or legal regulations, precariousness manifests itself in unequal relations and hierarchies. 'This dimension of precariousness covers naturalized relations of domination, through which belonging to a group is attributed or denied to individuals' (Lorey 2015: 12). Here, domination (*Herrschaft*) means 'the attempt to safeguard some people from existential precariousness, while at the same time this privilege of protection is based on a differential distribution of the precarity of all those who are perceived as other and considered less worthy of protection' (Lorey 2015: 37). Finally, the third dimension, 'governmental precarization', refers to the historically specific modes of governing that emerged with the development of wage labour and capitalist industrial relations. In their Western-liberal phase, forms of precarity emerge that, according to bourgeois norms, are excluded as abnormal, foreign and poor, in the societal and colonial peripheries. Under the neoliberal regime of flexibilization, deregulation and insecurity, however, precarization undergoes a process of normalization, which 'enables governing through insecurity'. In neoliberalism precarization becomes 'democratized' Lorey 2015: 11).

Contingent, uncertain, risk-laden working and living conditions are thus no longer only decisive for those at the 'margins', who through applicable laws, rules and regimentation are to be integrated as much as possible into secure zones. 'Worry about loss of social status and fears of exclusion' creep into the everyday life of those considered normal and regular, crossing through all of society, which makes it impossible to suggest or establish a unification of the precarious in politically and culturally identitarian terms, among other things (Hommerich 2016).[4] 'There are no lobbies of forms of representation for the diverse precarious' (Lorey 2015: 9). Yet Lorey deplores this not only as a lack, as already mentioned above with reference to the second 'ambivalence *in* self-governing'. There are 'competencies' that the precarious attain in their respective situations: competencies that they need to instrumentalize to 'add value', but they can also turn into capacities that become the new starting point for the search of new communities that overcome isolation. The *Precarias a la Deriva* initiative in Spain, for example, calls itself 'care community' (Precarias a la Deriva, 2014).

Can comparable initiatives and movements be found in the Japanese context? In Japan-related studies of precarity[5] there is talk of a 'precarity boom' in academic, pop culture and literary circles (which they also in part 'fuel'). This attention is directed mostly at the undoubtedly significant victim aspect and psychological strain of the impositions of precariousness (and rather rarely at a resigned-happy setup in the here and now). Herein lies 'the great potential to influence the perception of an entire society in a sustainable and one-sided manner' (Obinger 2016: 342), as this boom also means that a veritable market has grown where those who are really and perceptibly affected allow their stories to circulate and be valued in various forms of media. Such representations led to the impression that:

> in particular the middle classes and their abstract fears of losing social status and feelings of crisis should be served, in brief the disparity discourse there revolves around the perceived threat of the 'not-yet-precarized' and not around a search for concrete approaches to finding solutions, for a real debate about the situations of poverty that have existed for decades and become fixed, as we would conclude, for example, with respect to day-workers, homeless persons or (illegal) immigrants, is broadly ignored.
>
> (Obinger 2016: 343)

This finding can be confirmed if one shares its analytical 'framing' and the dichotomizing model of society, which follows the abovementioned logic of the (Hobbesian) security state, to which it is linked: perceived vs. real, limiting precarization to certain zones of insecurity and threatened social strata, in other words, a construction of precarity with an exclusively negative connotation. Lorey and Marchart, however, take a stance against this yet hegemonic model with their approaches (which certainly does not mean to dispute all of its analytical and explanatory potential). They are concerned, as mentioned, with the equally important perspective of empowerment and the potential for action immanent in this form of subjectivation. As a currently '[apparently] marginal and [yet] obvious phenomenon that subverts the stability of the whole,' therefore, this potential, the 'not like that!' actors, should be given voice, which is also the intention of the mentioned study by Cassegård.

'Just let us be!'

A figure that is mentioned in several studies and usually promoted as a kind of symbol of the precariat movement makes a frequent appearance in Cassegård's research: Amamiya Karin (born 1975). 'The term precariat encompasses both irregularly employed, as they are represented by freeters, as well as those with fixed employment contracts in the service industry with many overtime hours, self-employed or freelance authors like myself' (Amamiya 2008: 44). This is how Amamiya defined this then largely unknown term in her contribution to the *Rosu Jene*, helping it spread beyond the *Impaction* circle. Amamiya is a former right-wing punk singer, often characterized as a disputable figure, also involved in the mentioned boom and marketing processes via her writing. But she played a considerable role in making atypical (non-regular) work and living no longer understood as 'one's own fault' both in the public sphere and among those affected, who thus no longer see themselves as mere victims or 'losers' and who, with the help of newly founded organizations such as the Part-Timer, Workers, Freeter & Foreign Workers' Union, defend themselves against wrongdoing and injustice. This is also the case for Amamiya, who transformed her own contingent, fearful and once self-deprecating precariousness into empowerment to care for herself and others, as she demonstrates in her publications and elsewhere.[6]

Unlike other investigations of precarity, however, Cassegård's study embeds Amamiya in an entire continuum of a movement, of which she surely is a prominent node, but without stylizing her as a 'champion' (Field 2009: 3), 'opinion maker' or 'spearhead' (Obinger 2016: 342, 344).[7] In contrast, rather than strict ethnographic analysis, Cassegård's approach is more informed by an engaged and empathetic being-with these actors. 'During my stay in Kyoto 2009–2010 I visited the [Kubikubi] café or attended events arranged by the union several times a month. Not only was it a pleasant hangout. It was also a convenient hub for getting to know activism in Kansai – the area around Kyoto and Osaka' (Cassegård 2014: 2). This direct communication is accompanied by analyses of texts 'produced by activists – books, articles, pamphlets, leaflets, homepages, discussion forums, newsletters and blogs' (Cassegård 2014: 7), to map basic ideas and forms of action of freeter activism.[8] In addition, Cassegård uses concepts of 'alternative space' and 'empowerment' to investigate events and processes where the precarious manage to question and redirect hegemonic discourses that attribute certain modes of subjectivation and identities to them. In the case of activists like Amamiya, this entails publicly rejecting neoliberal impositions that are ideologically embellished as 'self-responsibility' (*jikosekinin*) and self-confidently demanding the right to an adequate and cultivated life, as warranted in Paragraph 25 of the Japanese Constitution. Cassegård's study also features a further group of freeter activists that has become prominent, 'Amateur's Revolt' (Shirōto no ran) (Cassegård 2014: 104–11). Their best-known protagonist, Matsumoto Hajime (born 1974) is now also active in the wider East Asian context and has become an object of academic investigation beyond Japan.[9] I will cite one passage here that can be understood as the credo of 'Amateur's Revolt:'

> **They** are demanding the improvement of working conditions and social welfare by making appeals to the government and corporations, while **I** am instead trying to **exit** that world as completely as I can.
>
> (Matsumoto in Cassegård 2014: 106)

'Exit' in this case means 'revolution', and this, in turn, is 'the idea of building a post-revolutionary world in advance and then just telling everyone: 'Come, it's more fun over here!' (Matsumoto in Cassegård 2014: 106). The struggle of the precarious for *survival* ('Let us live!') is here inseparable from the demand for a *good life* in common here and now, in the sense of pre-figurative politics (Obinger 2015: 100–10). In a crisis-stricken shopping street in Western Tokyo, these activists created an alternative space for themselves where they live primarily from 'recycling, repairing and reshaping' things that the 'rip-off economy' (*bottakuri keizai*) disposed of in order to uphold the endless flow of new goods to the market (Matsumoto 2008: 63). The refusal of a mainstream society driven by the desire to endlessly consume is accompanied by an ironic self-awareness that they are somehow nevertheless dependent on the 'trash' it throws away. This recalls Lorey's apparently paradoxical statement that the refusal of neoliberal impositions is by no means a victorious liberation from these, 'but rather the beginning of engagements and struggles to no longer be governed and no longer govern oneself in this way, at this price. A non-servile virtuosity is immanent to a servile one, just as the potential to flee from present servile virtuosities emerges, not least of all, in precarious modes of subjectivation themselves' (Lorey 2015: 102).

It should be highlighted once again that actors such as Amamiya or Matsumoto are for Cassegård neither particularly exposed figures nor 'opinion leaders' (Obinger 2015). Their individuation occurs in the actor-networks that constitute themselves in this process. These networks are not free of conflict and involve risks of failure, as evidenced in another form of freeter activism portrayed in a study based on artistic actions (*artivism*) in tent villages for the homeless. The rapid rise of such 'villages' in public places with nearby sanitary facilities (parks, river promenades, train station districts) is another outcome of the crisis of the 1990s. Since then it has been much more difficult for day labourers to find jobs and this frequently results in homelessness. At the same time, more and more young people flocked to take on irregular jobs, in competition with the day labourers, but also in increasingly 'precarious proximity' to them. This development has found symbolic expression since the 2000s in the phenomenon of 'net café refugees': 'young homeless people, often working in short-term jobs, who spend their nights in cheap individual boxes provided in places like 24-hour internet cafes or so-called *manga kissa*' (Cassegård 2014: 124).

The term 'café' brings me to a final consideration regarding freeter activism, with which I return to the double ambivalence of (self-)government discussed by Lorey: the ambivalence of governing by others and self-government, and the ambivalence *within* self-government. The café, which in modernizing and modern societies was and is generally a place shifting between the public and private that can be used in multiple ways, proves here in many ways to be an open space, depending on who does what there and how. While the internet café is a place guaranteeing mere survival to its working poor users (where the use of the internet is a means to getting the order for the next job), who are precarious in the narrow sense and largely governed by others, the café is in fact ambivalent in the context of 'self-government'. The spectrum of cafés that have been established in larger and smaller cities around the world since the turn of the millennium is broad. At one end, there is the lifestyle-store type, led by creatives 'between economic compulsion and artistic pressure' (Manske 2016).[10] At the other, for example, the Kubikubi Café Cassegård so frequently visited, on the campus of Kyoto University: 'a place for pleasant talk and cheap coffee [...], serving as a gathering place, as a centre for disseminating information and, for a time, as a temporary residence of one of the union members' (Cassegård 2014: 1); the Nantoka (Somehow) Bar of the people of Amateur's Revolt, for whose operations volunteers are constantly needed to take care of orders and run the place for special events that raise money to support actions and projects; or Café Enoaru in Yoyogi Park, run by the artists and homeless village residents Ogawa Tetsuo (born 1970) and Ichimura Misako (born 1971), who organize painting circles for the homeless and other events there. The list could go on not only for Japan, but also for other cities in South Korea, Hong Kong, Taiwan, Beijing, Shanghai. Thanks to digital media, the actors of these various projects know each other directly or indirectly. They also discuss and learn with and from one another in 'analogue' forms and via direct communication, which, for example, produced the Chinese-language publication *Creative Space: Art and Spatial Resistance in East Asia* in 2014 (Yuk Hui and DOXA). This kind of encounter of artistic, social and political action has been given expression for some time with the coined term 'artivism'. The artivist Wong Ah-Kok from the independent art group 'Hidden Agenda' in Hong Kong summarized it on the occasion of a visit to Amateur's Revolt in December 2012 as follows: 'We are not activists who are fighting against the government, the state. We just want them to give us space, scope, where we can create our own life. Just let us be!' [My notes, SR]. This 'Just let us be!' must also be understood as a claim to want to live now in such a way as if large-scale societal change had already taken place, that is, in a 'realized utopia'.

Notes

1 The following text is a shortened and elaborated version of Richter (2016).
2 Translator's note: this and other citations of German-language publications are my own, unless otherwise specified (KM).
3 A discussion of exodus, a practical and theoretical concept of movement, can be found in the work of Paolo Virno (2010) and most recently in Daniel Loick (2014).
4 Hommerich presents a data survey conducted by the German Institute for Japanese Studies (DIJ) in Tokyo in 2009 on 'Worry about loss of social status and fears of exclusion' (= 'perceived precarity'), on the basis of which she argues that perceived precarity is pronounced, but that further studies are needed in order to evaluate the effects of experiences of precarity in a differentiated manner (2016: 173).
5 In addition to Hommerich and Oberinger, the studies of Gebhardt (2010), Allison (2013), Iwata-Weickgennant and Rosenbaum (2015) and recently Köhn and Unkel (2016) deserve a mention.
6 See, for example, the book *Melancholia of the Precariat*, composed of 18 reports of very different precarious (Amamiya 2009).
7 The latter occurs not least as a result of the circular mode by which conventional academic research relies on the sources and investigative techniques that it trusts, under which trained participant observation and the reading of texts most closely embodying academic standards are favoured – with which the 'commercial appetite' complained about (Field 2009) gets 'fed'. Aspects of this include, for example, a clear 'authorship' of contributions in publications, whose lack is complained about (see for instance Obinger 2015: 152) or which 'complicates' the creation of lists of works cited.
8 He uses the term 'freeter' in a broad sense, 'to refer to young people characterized by precarity, i.e. a lack of secure employment resulting in a precarious existence. To be a freeter is not to have a particular type of employment, but to belong to a stratum of people who may drift in and out of studies, unemployment, dispatch work or other forms of irregular work or states of withdrawal. Students, young academics, artists, and

young homeless people can all be part of this stratum, as well as dispatch workers, part-time working housewives and social withdrawers' (Cassegård 2014: 4).

9 For more detail on these actors, see Obinger (2014) and Richter (2012: 118–23).

10 The field of the precarious in the cultural and creative economic sphere is not considered in this text not only for reasons of length, but also because it remains, in my opinion, a desideratum, at least in Japanese studies.

References

Allison, A. (2013) *Precarious Japan.* Durham/London: Duke University Press.

Amamiya K. (2008) Ikizurasa ga koesaseru 'sayū' no kakine. *Rosu jene.* Tōkyō: Kamogawa shuppan, 1: 44–53.

Amamiya K. (2009) *Purekariāto no yūtsū.* Tōkyō: Kōdansha.

Berndt, E. (2008) J-Society. Wieviel Unterschied verträgt das Land? In Richter, S. and Berndt, J. (eds), *J-Culture. Japan Lesebuch IV*, konkursbuchverlag Claudia Gehrke: pp. 74–85.

Berndt, E. (2009) *Toyota in der Krise von den Widersprüchen und Grenzen des Status quo.* Leipzig: Leipziger Universitätsverlag.

Candeias, M. (2005) Prekarisierung: unterbestimmt und überdifferenziert. *arranca! Für eine linke Strömung* 32: 4–7.

Cassegård, C. (2014) *Youth Movements, Trauma and Alternative Space in Contemporary Japan.* Leiden/Boston: Global Oriental.

Elis, V. (2016) Japan und die postfordistische Prekarisierungsgesellschaft. In Köhn, S. and Unkel. M. (eds), *Prekarisierungsgesellschaften in Ostasien? Aspekte der sozialen Ungleichheit in China und Japan.* Wiesbaden: Harrassowitz Verlag: pp. 61–82.

Field, N. (2009) Commercial appetite and human need: The accidental and fated revival of Kobayashi Takiji's *Cannery Ship.* Available from: http://apjjf.org/-Norma-Field/3058/article.pdf. [Accessed: 24 July 2016].

Foucault, M. (2007) *The Politics of Truth.* Cambridge: MIT Press.

Gebhardt, L. (2010) *Nach Einbruch der Dunkelheit.* Berlin: EB Verlag.

Gendai yōgo no kiso chishiki (2008) *Gendai yōgo no kiso chishiki.* Tōkyō: Jiyūkokuminsha.

Hommerich, C. (2016) Die Wahrnehmung der Differenzgesellschaft – Abstiegssorgen und Ausschlussängste in Japan. In Köhn, S. and Unkel, M. (eds), *Prekarisierungsgesellschaften in Ostasien? Aspekte der sozialen Ungleichheit in China und Japan.* Wiesbaden: Harrassowitz Verlag: pp. 155–76.

Hui, Y. and DOXA (2014) 創意空間 - 東亞的藝術與空間抗爭. *Creative Space: Art and Spatial Resistance in East Asia.* Hong Kong: Roundtable Synergy Books.

Impaction (2006a) Special Issue on 'Bankoku no purekariāto! 'Kyōbō' seyo!' *Impaction* 151.

Impaction (2006b) Special Issue on 'Setsuzoku seyo! Kenkyū kikai.' *Impaction* 153.

Iwata-Weickgenannt, K. and Rosenbaum, R. (eds) (2015) *Visions of Precarity in Japanese Popular Culture and Literature.* London/New York: Routledge.

Köhn, S. and Unkel, M. (eds) (2016) *Prekarisierungsgesellschaften in Ostasien? Aspekte der sozialen Ungleichheit in China und Japan.* Wiesbaden: Harrassowitz Verlag.

Kohso, S. (2006) Angelus Novus in Millennial Japan. In Yoda, T. and Harootunian, H. (eds), *Japan after Japan.* Durham and London: Duke University Press: pp. 415–38.

Loick, D. (2014) Stichwort: Exodus. Leben jenseits von Staat und Konsum? *WestEnd. Neue Zeitschrift für Sozialforschung* 1: 61–6.

Lorey, I. (2015) *State of Insecurity. Government of the Precarious.* London: Verso.

Manske, A. (2016) *Kapitalistische Geister in der Kultur- und Kreativwirtschaft. Kreative zwischen wirtschaftlichem Zwang und künstlerischem Drang*. Bielefeld: Transcript Verlag.

Marchart, O. (2013) Auf dem Weg in die Prekarisierungsgesellschaft. In Marchart, O. (ed.), *Facetten der Prekarisierungsgesellschaft. Prekäre Verhältnisse. Sozialwissenschaftliche Perspektiven auf die Prekarisierung von Arbeit und Leben*. Bielefeld: Transcript Verlag: 7–20.

Matsumoto, H. (2008) *Binbōnin no gyakushū! Tada de ikiru hōhō*. Tōkyō: Chikuma Shobō.

Obinger, J. (2015) *Alternative Lebensstile und Aktivismus in Japan. Der Aufstand der Amateure in Tokyo*. Wiesbaden: Springer VS.

Obinger, J. (2016) Megatrend Prekarisierung? Eine sozialwissenschaftliche Annäherung an den 'Prekarisierungsdiskurs' in und über Japan. In Köhn, S. and Unkel, M. (eds), *Prekarisierungsgesellschaften in Ostasien? Aspekte der sozialen Ungleichheit in China und Japan*. Wiesbaden: Harrassowitz Verlag: pp. 329–50.

Precarias a la Deriva (2014) *Was ist Dein Streik? Militante Streifzüge durch die Kreisläufe der Prekarität*. Available from: http://transversal.at/books/precarias-de. [Accessed: 24 July 2016].

Richter, S. (2012) Das Ende des 'endlosen Alltags?' Post-Fukushima als Japan-Diskurs. In Richter, S. and Gebhardt, L. (eds), *Japan nach Fukushima. Ein System in der Krise*. Leipzig: Leipziger Universitätsverlag: pp. 91–133.

Richter, S. (2016) 'Prekarisierungsgesellschaft': Der Fall Japan. In Köhn, S. and Unkel, M. (eds), *Prekarisierungsgesellschaften in Ostasien? Aspekte der sozialen Ungleichheit in China und Japan*. Wiesbaden: Harrassowitz Verlag: pp. 351–77.

Rosu jene (2008) Rosu jene sengen. Ima 'ware ware' no kotoba wa rearu darōka. In *Rosu jene*. Tōkyō: Kamogawa shuppan 1: 5–7.

Settsu, T. (2006) Dialogue on Precariat "Purekariato" nitsuite. Available from: http://blog.goo.ne.jp/harumi-s_2005/e/3a5c227572637222ce248d2849da85b6 [Accessed: 24 July 2016].

Sugita, S. (2008) Rosu jene no bungei-ron. *Subaru*. Tōkyō: Shūeisha 8: 265–76.

Virno, P. (2010) *Exodus*. Wien/Berlin: Verlag Turia + Kant.

Žižek, S. (2014) *Was ist ein Ereignis?* Frankfurt am Main: S. Fischer Verlag.

Part II

Resistance

Social movements against precariousness

10 The two endings of the precarious movement

Dimitris Papadopoulos

The trans-European precarious movement at 15

2000 was the year of the precarious movement. The actions of *Stop précarité* and *AC! Agir ensemble contre le chômage et la précarité* in Paris, the initiatives of the group *Chainworkers Crew* in Italy and then the first *MayDay* parade in Milan in 2001 kickstarted the trans-European movement of the precarious, a movement of movements, an ecology of events autonomously organised outside the traditional trade unions and the established radical left (Precarias 2004; Cosse 2008; Fumagalli 2015; Hamm 2011; Mattoni 2008; Mattoni and Doerr 2007; Murgia and Selmi 2012; Shukaitis *et al.* 2007; Tarì and Vanni 2005). And so the term 'precarity' entered our vocabulary. For several years the movement was growing, putting pressure both on trade unions as well as political parties and public opinion to recognise the proliferation of precarity, and to act. Simultaneously organised in many European cities, Euro May Day parades were powerful actors within this wide ecology of campaigns, direct actions, small and large self-organised events, militant research and media interventions.[1]

This was a transnational and transversal ecology connecting precarity to other divergent social movements and mobilisations across many different locations in Europe. The precarious movement was never just a protest campaign against precarity and the dismantling of welfare provision. Nor was it only a voice against the new configuration of exploitation with the proliferation of atypical, casual and insecure employment. The precarisation of work was the starting point for the movement. But precarity was not just about work. It was about the precarisation of life along many different fields: housing, women's rights, education, health, social rights, culture, mobility and migration. And then in addition to this expanded understanding of precarisation, precarity had another, even more important, affective and imaginary connotation within the movement: the hope that the exit from the old system of employment and welfare provision could open the search for a better life. Precarity was considered simultaneously a new system of exploitation and a practice of liberation from the previous system of exploitation.[2] The energy and ingenuity of the precarious movement have their source in this ambivalent and multi-layered understanding of precarity.[3]

In a moment when the movement seemed to win one battle after the next, the 'war against precarisation' was suddenly lost. This was probably in 2008. The cycle of struggles of the precarious that had started, at least formally, in 2000 had come to an end. Ironically the moment the 'war' was lost is also the moment popular media as well as academia discovered the term precarity and turned it into a synonym for insecurity or a sociological category and a social theory concept.[4] What happened in 2008? I will only try to sketch some preliminary thoughts, as a sustained reflection on the history of the movement and its political as well as organisational legacy is not possible at this moment; there is no account and interpretation of this period produced through militant research and coming from inside the movement itself.

The year 2008 seems to be a turning point in many respects. There is the eruption of the economic crisis and there is also the beginning of a new cycle of social movement struggles. Each one of these events takes place on various scales and involves a multiplicity of actors making it almost impossible to discern a direct impact on the precarious movement. But there is affectively as well as conceptually something happening in 2008 that did not allow the mobilisations of the precarious to continue as before. There is a sense in the air that something has radically changed. One would expect that the economic crisis would strengthen the movement of the precarious. This was not the case: the thrust of the movement was not enough to confront the effects of the economic crisis and the response of the European elites to financial collapse.

The December 2008 uprising in Athens was an event that absorbed the energy of the previous autonomous precarious movement to create an actor that was positioned vis-à-vis social order at large, not just precarity. As the economic crisis was engulfing the whole of European society so also it engulfed the social movements. The wave of events that followed – from the Arab Spring and Spain's 15M to Gezi Park in Istanbul – was hailed as a revolt of the precarious generation. Unlike the previous mobilisations of the precarious though, these events where addressing much broader issues than precarity itself. This second cycle of struggles that started in 2008 seems to have come to an end in 2014. It may have propelled a wave of extraordinary transformations that I will discuss later in this chapter, but as a social movement it is unclear whether it will continue.

Embodying value production

Current social movements have their roots in the ways social and political power was reorganised as a response to the contentious mobilisations of the working classes and subaltern populations of the 1960s and 1970s. These struggles transformed gradually and diversified through the 1980s and 1990s into a multiplicity of social conflicts: from migrant mobilisations, feminist struggles and social rights campaigns to ecological movements and global justice initiatives. We see two main transformations unfolding as a response to these mobilisations: stagnant wages, underemployment and the flexibilisation of labour markets as well as finance-led accumulation with the introduction of securitisation and increased consumer, corporate and sovereign lending. Let's start with labour.

One of the key components of these transformations is the externalisation of production from the workplace to the social sphere. This does not mean that the site of value production is transferred 'outside' living labour. Activities that people perform as part of their non-work life or secondary activities of their work life become directly productive. More importantly though it also means that working people mobilise multiple social and personal investments in order to be able to remain in the labour market (e.g. social relations, general skills, making personal debts, informal networks, ideas, their subjectivity, their mobility, their health, their self-organised structures for cooperation, their potential for development).[5] The epicentre of value production is the workplace, but it is only the epicentre. If we were to focus on the workplace only we would miss the important and sometimes defining broader conditions in which work and employment take place. And these broader conditions together with the precarisation of work were the focus of the precarious movement.

The extended mode of value production does not mean that work becomes simply dispersed and socialised, that it moves outside the singular worker. It rather means that value production becomes embodied: it becomes an indissoluble characteristic of the whole situated social existence of each singular worker (Papadopoulos *et al.* 2008). The situated and embodied quality of work includes all things and artefacts that constitute the worlds in which we exist, our social relations as well as the broader networks of the commons that we rely on to maintain everyday life. In order to be able to survive precarious work one has to rely on and mobilise a wide array of relations, tricks, people and infrastructures that are only indirectly connected to the actual labour process.

Control over embodied production (Lorey 2015) is taking place along several lines that attempt to cut across and appropriate this existential continuum of people: first, the attempt to measure labour-power and to quantify it despite the fact that it mobilises the whole embodied conditions of life (De Angelis and Harvie 2009); second, the expropriation of the infrastructures of cooperation through property rights, patents and the re-privatisation of access to and circulation of information (Boyle 2010; Bollier 2008; Brophy and Peuter 2007); third, the individualisation of the costs of social reproduction and privatisation of those forms of social reproduction that cannot be taken up by the individual (Weeks 2011; Barbagallo and Federici 2012); fourth, the transformation of citizenship into a tool for creating various tiers of working people whose degree of exploitation depends on their varied access to citizenship rights (Alberti 2011; Anderson 2010). One could say that all these lines break the horizontal and continuous lived experience of working people and create some form of separate vertical segments that are the productive motor of current precarious work and life conditions.

Biofinancialisation

The other side to the responses to the crisis of the 1970s is the financialisation of the economy.[6] Financialisation is not just an economic strategy; it is culture. Not only because it came to pervade the everyday (Martin 2002; Bryan and Rafferty 2006; Langley 2008) but also because it contributed to the consolidation of an ever expanding culture of translating disparate judgements about value to financial measurements. The underlying logic of this culture is that the worth of goods, things, activities and spaces can be essentially translated into financial evaluations. Although different scales of evaluation are by definition incommensurable (Barbier and Hawkins 2012; Beckert and Aspers 2011; Karpik 2010; Moeran and Pedersen 2011; Stark 2009; Zelizer 1979), the predominance of the culture of valuation in Global North societies presupposes and promotes that the worth of almost everything – including the present and future appreciation of assets, goods, services, intangibles, the health and subjective capacities of individuals, the physical environment, human artefacts, other species, urban space – is in principle transferable into one single logic of financial value that is potentially tradeable in the market. This is biofinancialisation: the financialisation of everyday life, subjectivity, ecology and materiality.[7]

Financial value is here used to express the primacy of investment value over other values (aesthetic, use, moral, ecological, material, cultural) that predominantly assess the future monetary profit to be gained from potentially any field of life or the environment.[8] The principle of investment value hinges upon the belief that the future is exploitable. Future value is by definition unpredictable and in order to be realised the actors involved need to experiment, to manage conflicting information and to create knowledge in action (Smith 1999; Stark 2009). Future value and investment value are recombining other forms of value into a process of uncertainty.[9]

One can see for example how this logic shapes the role time plays in precarious workers' subjectivities: how these workers 'invest' in 'themselves' by shaping their current activities according to the possible future gains in unstable labour markets (Papadopoulos *et al.* 2008). At the core of this temporal form of regulation of precarity is the increase of precarious contracts. That is, non-standard contract forms based on different configurations between the length and stability of the working contract (from permanent contracts, to fixed-term contracts, to informal or free/unpaid labour) and the working-time arrangements (from full-time employment, to part-time employment, to irregular working patterns) (McKay *et al.* 2012). The less stable and regular the working contract, the higher the degree of atypicality and the intensity of precarity. As contracts become increasingly insecure, exploitation is maintained through the break of the bond of the contract, rather than through the contract itself. This results in an amplification of dependency and the 'exploitation of the self' (Ehrenstein 2006): one is under increased pressure to ensure that one's future capacity to be 'productive' will be compatible with the demands of the market (lifelong learning, continuous acquisition of skills and entrepreneurial innovation are keywords in this process).

One is not only exploited in the present but also one's future is exploited: one's own potentials, what one might become.

But beyond this immediate point of contact between precarity and the uncertainty of the underlying culture of valuation there is an even stronger link between the regulation of precarity and the financialisation of life. Uncertainty is managed by speculating on almost all aspects of everyday life: openly and commonly used infrastructures (information channels, collaboratively produced knowledge, cultural networks), the material commons as well as structures of cooperation, everyday sociality and exchange between producers and consumers. Biofinancialisation traverses the whole continuum of everyday life. Precarious life and work are regulated through an infinite array of devices that evaluate and provide tools for managing precarious existence.

The first ending

The main political response[10] to this situation circulating in the precarious movement was some kind of revival of the autonomous politics[11] of the 1970s and 1980s, in particular the refusal of work and the self-organisation of social reproduction: an exit from work and the subtraction from labour towards activities that lie outside capitalist valorisation and the organisation of immediate social life outside of formal public services or private provision.[12] But when biofinancialised value production becomes literally embodied in the very existence of working people, as argued earlier, these political alternatives seem almost impossible. Production no longer operates through an externality between the subject and her work, but through accumulation of the embodied totality of one's own existence. Equally, large scale self-organised social reproduction in the sense that has been described in places outside the metropolises of the Global North seems an untenable political scenario simply because it is impossible to give up work in its embodied configuration in order to free space for a complete self-organisation of social reproduction.

Franco Bifo Berardi (known as Bifo) delivers an intriguing description of the mixture of everyday life and the biofinancial regime, but his vision that 'autonomy is the independence of social time from the temporality of capitalism' (2009: 75) does not seem to hold against the carnal orgy of contemporary biofinancialisation's feasting on the everyday life and the commons. One cannot say as an expression of autonomy today 'I don't *want* to go to work because I *prefer* to sleep'. The refusal of work is impossible, not only de facto – that is, because work is indissoluble from the body of working people, animals and things – but also because it is not desired: verticalised value production has become the condition for maintaining everyday existence within the social order.

We can exist and make a life only through the biofinancialised bodies we have. One can only say 'I no longer *can* work' and be punished, as Bifo (2011) so aptly describes, with stigma, panic, depression and the deactivation of one's own capacity for empathy. But neither can empathy be infused to the social body nor panic and stigma just simply extracted from it, as if they are external to it; neither

Prozac nor poetry, neither Ritalin nor mindfulness are enough to do this – they inhabit the social body and when they move from one individual body to the next, they leave their traces on them, they mark life for ever.

Biofinancialisation, or rather the realisation of its unstoppable pervasiveness, put a halt to the possibility of freedom and justice that was so crucial for the success of the precarious movement. I have mentioned in the beginning of this chapter that the precarious movement embodied not only a cry against precarity (that is, both the precarisation of work and the precarisation of life) but also a vision for a better life outside the instituted social provision and the Fordist labour arrangement. Precarity for the precarious movement was not just a new configuration of exploitation but also a political project of justice and liberation. Biofinancialisation directly attacked the feasibility of this political project and simultaneously consolidated the first dimension of precarity as a new spreading configuration of exploitation. The economic crisis and the response to it in 2008 made this tenacious grip more obvious than ever. The precarious movement lost its ground.

Financialisation is culture because it came to dominate our imaginary to such an extent that wide segments of society believe that even social justice can be fought for with financial means. Financialisation is not ideology; it is as real as something can be: engrained in the everyday ontology of life.

This made apparent that precarity could not be considered as something that can be addressed as a single separate issue. Rather it should be considered as something that is embedded in the broader system of biofinancialised societies. A precarious movement focussing primarily on precarious issues was not only not possible but it was also not enough. In order for the movement to exist it had to scale up its politics. It had to target the political-financial system as such. But the movement that created the 2000–2008 cycle of struggles was not theoretically, practically and organisationally prepared for this kind of conflict. This was the first ending of the precarious movement that saw precarity as both its main target and a source of imagination and freedom.

The second ending

But a new cycle of struggles had begun. Starting from the Athens uprising in 2008 (Papadopoulos *et al.* 2011), the unexpected cycle of struggles that followed in the next five years addressed the totality of a new situation: widespread university occupations and the so-called 'anomalous wave' in Italy and other countries in 2008–09, the Arab Spring, 15M movement in Spain, Syntagma 2011 in Athens, the Occupy movement, the 'stop evictions' and housing campaigns such as the Plataforma de Afectados por la Hipoteca (PAH) in Spain, Gezi Park in Istanbul, and so forth. Perhaps there are also some links between the London riots of 2011 and these mobilisations. The precarious stepped up their game. The movements of this second cycle of struggles developed an understanding of themselves as able to create an alternative form of life that had the capacity to articulate a full-scale negation of power: 'They do not represent us' is the central motto of this cycle of struggles. The critique of representationalism was always at the heart of the precarious movement since its beginning and throughout the first cycle of struggles. Now it becomes something more than a theoretical assumption and an organisational principle: it becomes a widespread everyday perception.

The long-term effects of this cycle of struggles are probably still unknown but their immediate impact was very different from what the movements intended. Instead of creating a situation that would force instituted power to reconstitute itself and respond to the pressures of the movement, power consolidated the role of financialisation as the main way of managing conflict in European societies. This caught us by surprise. While biofinancialisation was considered up to this point as the heart of the problem now it turned to be the instrument deployed to solve or ameliorate problems. It became obvious that the instability of biofinancial societies 'has nothing to do with any presumed instability per se of the mechanisms of the financial system; quite the contrary, the ambition of those mechanisms is precisely to absorb shocks and to smooth out discontinuities in the economic cycle,' as Moulier Boutang put it (2012: 152). Thus the instability and the conflicts that emanate from the precarious organisation of life and labour are not intensified by the indeterminacy of the culture of valuation – rather the opposite is the case: cultures of valuation become the main tool through which conflict in value production is regulated (and potentially also contested). The pervasiveness of the culture of valuation with the crucial indeterminacy of value that lies at the core of this culture is the main way to control the outputs of work in the extended mode of production and, simultaneously, also serves as the vehicle which working people themselves deploy to modify and change their position in the social nexus.

The effect of biofinancialisation is not only that it created the ground for a new phase of expansion (and crisis) but also that along with the culture of valuation it created a tool for managing the conflicts that traverse embodied value production. It is through biofinancialisation and more broadly the culture of valuation that specific segments of the working classes as well as the elites and the middle classes maintain and strengthen their position in the social order. The lack of significant opposition to austerity and the meagre responses to the crisis is not only imposed by the elites but also desired by segments of the working and middle classes. The effect of this is double: first, a turn to the right and a conservative social, political and cultural backlash in many European countries; second, the annihilation of many social democratic parties and of social democratic ideology.

Paradoxically the movements of this second cycle of struggles that have been operating against representation as an organising practice and as a political maxim found themselves in the vortex of the formation of a new wave of political representation in many European contexts. As the motto 'They do not represent us' was echoing across the squares and the net, a demand for political representation was forming. One possible reason that allowed such a demand for formal political representation to emerge was that the vacuum left behind by the demise of the European centre ground and of the social democratic parties was increasingly filled by the voice of the movements. Generational issues also might have played a role: the generation that grew up within the first and second cycle of struggles felt they should have a say in this new situation characterised by the consolidation of conservativism on the one hand and the absence of any progressive or left politics on the other. New forms of organisation (Nunes 2012; Free Association 2011) and in particular the convergence of technology and politics (Ghelfi 2015) facilitated the expression of this collective demand for entering into representational politics. The year 2015 saw Syriza in Greece, Barcelona en Comú, Ganemos Madrid, Podemos in Spain, the popularity of Jeremy Corbyn in Britain, the success of the Scottish National Party – these are all scattered indications of how this second cycle of struggles has fuelled a very different political change than it had originally intended. The close contact of the precarious to instituted power in 2015 signalled the second ending of the precarious movement. The cycle of struggles that started in 2008 has come to an end; the movement disappears again. And the issue it addressed is still with us.

Notes

1 For an extended collection of many voices on the precarious movement see Murgia and Armano (2012a, 2012b).
2 For an in depth discussion of many of these issues see Precarias a la deriva (2004).
3 This is the reason why reductionist definitions of precarity as a structural feature of labour markets in the current regime of production and accumulation – however topical they might be, see for example Standing (2011) and McKay *et al.* (2012) – miss the point of the precarious movement and strip precarity of its real social and political transformative potentials. Already in Tsianos and Papadopoulos (2006) we have discussed these appropriations of the idea of precarity and its transformation into a sociological and governmental category for managing insecure employment. For a discussion of some of these issues see also van der Linden (2014), Waterman *et al.* (2012) and Raunig (2007).
4 For example, in social and cultural theory see Gill and Pratt (2008), in industrial relations see Milkman and Ott (2014), in work and employment see Simms (2015). Probably the most problematic of all is the work of Savage *et al.* (2013) who took the concept without any attention to its situated history within social struggles and local experiences and emptied it from all its meaning.
5 The mobilisation of various aspects of one's own life in order to be able to work has been explored in many different settings, see for example Ehrenstein (2012), Ross (2009), Brophy and Peuter (2007), Hesmondhalgh and Baker (2011).
6 The ideas on biofinancialisation presented here are based on Lilley and Papadopoulos (2014).
7 For different understandings of biofiancialisaton that have influenced the position presented in this paper see French and Kneale (2012), Fumagalli (2011), Marazzi (2010), Martin (2002), Murphy (2013).
8 See for example the insightful research of Kortright (2012) on transgenic rice and how the promise of a high yielding crop shapes geopolitics, agro-food investments, research and experimental labour. In earlier work we called this the 'formation of emergent life, that is the attempt to develop means for the maximum control of life and to exploit life's emergent qualities in highly uncertain conditions' (Papadopoulos *et al.* 2008: 107ff.).
9 On the political implications of the regulation of uncertainty see Lorey (2015).
10 The other one is labour organising. Trade Unions have been for too long obsessed with full-time employment and it was only the pressure of precarious movement in its various expressions (and of course the dramatic decline of the influence of trade unions) that made them more sensible to precarity (Milkman and Ott, 2014). The effect of this

focus on full time employment is the segregation between different types of workers (which also involves a segregation between migrant workers and indigenous workers, see Alberti *et al.* (2013).

11 Autonomy refers to the idea that social conflicts and social movements drive social transformation instead of just being a mere response to (economic and social) power. This position primarily reversed the idea that capital is the driving force of change; instead workers' refusal and insubordination force capital to reorganise itself (Cleaver 1992; Dyer-Witheford 1999; Negri 1988). This perspective on autonomy is of course limited to the relation between capital and labour but the question of autonomous politics exceeds this relation. In the wake of the new social movements that emerged from the Zapatista *encuentros* and the Seattle mobilisations in the mid/end of the 1990s, autonomy is explored in relation to technoscience, culture, feminist politics, and the struggles for the commons (Bifo Berardi 2009; Böhm *et al.* 2010; Dinerstein 2010; Papadopoulos 2012, 2014). Autonomy in this sense produces an excess of practices and social spaces that 'opens up frontiers of resistance and change towards radical practices, an equal society and self-organization' (Böhm *et al.* 2010: 28). On the idea of excess see Free Association (2011) and Papadopoulos *et al.* (2008).

12 Regarding autonomous politics see originally Tronti (1965), also Bowring (2002), Cleaver (1992), Weeks (2011: 96ff.), Fleming (2012). Regarding subtraction, see for example Hardt and Negri (2009), who call for a subtraction of labour power from capital or Holloway (2010), who tries to make the case that our alternative doing can be outside and *against* abstract labour (that is labour that produces capitalist value) and a discussion in Bowring (2004).

References

Alberti, G. (2011) *Transient Working Lives: Migrant Women's Everyday Politics in London's Hospitality Industry. School of Social Sciences.* Cardiff University, Cardiff: Unpublished PhD dissertation.

Alberti, G., Holgate, J., and Tapia, M. (2013) Organising migrants as workers or as migrant workers? Intersectionality, trade unions and precarious work. *The International Journal of Human Resource Management* 24(22): 4132–48.

Anderson, B. (2010) Migration, immigration controls and the fashioning of precarious workers. *Work, Employment & Society* 24(2): 300–317.

Barbagallo, C. and Federici, S. (2012) 'Care Work' and the Commons [Special Issue]. *The Commoner* 15: 1–431.

Barbier, J.-C. and Hawkins, P. (eds) (2012) *Evaluation Cultures : Sense-Making in Complex Times.* New Brunswick: Transaction Publishers.

Beckert, J. and Aspers, P. (eds) (2011) *The Worth of Goods : Valuation and Pricing in the Economy.* Oxford: Oxford University Press.

Bifo Berardi, F. (2009) *Precarious Rhapsody. Semiocapitalism and the Pathologies of Post-Alpha Generation.* London: Minor Compositions.

Bifo Berardi, F. (2011) Cognitarian subjectivation. In Aranda, J., Wood, B. K. and Vidokle, A. (eds), *Are You Working Too Much? Post-Fordism, Precarity, and the Labor of Art.* Berlin: Sternberg Press.

Böhm, S., Dinerstein, A. C. and Spicer, A. (2010) (Im)possibilities of Autonomy: Social Movements in and beyond Capital, the State and Development. *Social Movement Studies* 9(1): 17–32.

Bollier, D. (2008) *Viral Spiral : How the Commoners Built a Digital Republic of their Own.* New York: New Press.

Bowring, F. (2002) Post-Fordism and the end of work. *Futures* 34: 159–172.

Bowring, F. (2004) From the mass worker to the multitude: A theoretical contextualisation of Hardt and Negri's *Empire*. *Capital & Class* 83: 101–32.

Boyle, J. (2010) *The Public Domain : Enclosing the Commons of the Mind*. New Haven: Yale University Press.

Brophy, E. and Peuter, G. d. (2007) Immaterial labour, precarity, and recomposition. In C. McKercher and Mosco, V. (eds), *Knowledge Workers in the Information Society*. Lanham, MD: Lexington Books.

Bryan, D. and Rafferty, M. (2006) *Capitalism with Derivatives. A Political Economy of Financial Derivatives, Capital and Class*. New York: Palgrave Macmillan.

Cleaver, H. (1992) The inversion of class perspective in Marxian theory: From valorisation to self-valorisation. In Bonefeld, W., Gunn, R. and Psychopedis, K. (eds), *Open Marxism. Volume II: Theory and Practice*. London: Pluto Press.

Cosse, E. (2008) The precarious go marching. *In the Middle of a Whirlwind*. Available from: http://inthemiddleofthewhirlwind.wordpress.com/2008/10/03/the-precarious-go-marching/ [Accessed 23 October 2008].

De Angelis, M. and Harvie, D. (2009) 'Cognitive capitalism' and the rat-race: How capital measures immaterial labour in British universities. *Historical Materialism* 17(3): 3–30.

Dinerstein, A. C. (2010) Autonomy in Latin America: Between resistance and integration. Echoes from the Piqueteros experience. *Community Development Journal* 45(3): 356–66. doi:10.1093/cdj/bsq029

Dyer-Witheford, N. (1999) *Cyber-Marx : Cycles and Circuits of Struggle in High-Technology Capitalism*. Urbana: University of Illinois Press.

Ehrenstein, A. (2006) *Social relationality and affective experience in precarious labour conditions. A study of young immaterial workers in the arts industries in Cardiff*. School of Social Sciences, Cardiff University, Cardiff: Unpublished dissertation.

Ehrenstein, A. (2012) *Precarity and the Crisis of Social Care. Everyday Pollitics and Experiences of Work in Women's Voluntary Organisations*. Cardiff University.

Fleming, P. (2012) The birth of biocracy and its discontents at work. *Research in the Sociology of Organizations* 35: 177–99.

Free Association. (2011) *Moments of Excess : Movements, Protest and Everyday Life*. Oakland, CA: PM Press.

French, S. and Kneale, J. (2012) Speculating on Careless Lives. *Journal of Cultural Economy* 5(4): 391–406. doi:10.1080/17530350.2012.703619

Fumagalli, A. (2011) Twenty theses on cognitive capitalism (cognitive biocapitalism). *Angelaki* 16(3): 7–17. doi:10.1080/0969725x.2011.626555

Fumagalli, A. (2015) Cognitive, relational (creative) labor and the precarious movement for 'Commonfare': 'San Precario' and EuroMayDay. In B. S. Giuseppe Cocco (ed.), *Creative Capitalism, Multitudinous Creativity: Radicalities and Alterities*. Lanham, MA: Lexington Books: pp. 3–24.

Ghelfi, A. (2015) *Worlding Politics. Justice, the Commons and Technoscience*. University of Leicester: PhD dissertation.

Gill, R. and Pratt, A. (2008) In the social factory?: Immaterial labour, precariousness and cultural work. *Theory, Culture & Society* 25(7–8): 1–30. doi:10.1177/0263276408097794

Hamm, M. (2011) *Performing Protest. Media Practices in the Trans-Urban Euromayday Movement of the Precarious*. University of Lucerne, Lucerne.

Hardt, M. and Negri, A. (2009) *Commonwealth*. Cambridge, Mass.: Belknap Press of Harvard University Press.

Hesmondhalgh, D. and Baker, S. (2011) *Creative Labour: Media Work in Three Cultural Industries*. London: Routledge.

Holloway, J. (2010) Cracks and the crisis of abstract labour. *Antipode* 42(4): 909–923.

Karpik, L. (2010) *Valuing the Unique : The Economics of Singularities*. Princeton: Princeton University Press.

Kortright, C. (2012) *C4 Rice and Hoping the Sun Can End Hunger: Tales of Plants, Evolution, Transgenics and Crisis*. PhD thesis, University of California Davis.

Langley, P. (2008) *The Everyday Life of Global Finance : Saving and Borrowing in Anglo-America*. Oxford: Oxford University Press.

Lilley, S. and Papadopoulos, D. (2014) Material returns: Cultures of valuation, biofinancialisation and the autonomy of politics. *Sociology* 48(5): 972–88.

Lorey, I. (2015) *State of Insecurity: Government of the Precarious*. London: Verso.

Marazzi, C. (2010) *The Violence of Financial Capitalism*. Los Angeles: Semiotext(e).

Martin, R. (2002) *Financialization of Daily Life*. Philadelphia: Temple University Press.

Mattoni, A. (2008) Serpica Naro and the others. The Media Sociali experience in Italian struggles against precarity. *PORTAL Journal of Multidisciplinary International Studies* 5(2): 1–24. Available at: http://epress.lib.uts.edu.au/ojs/index.php/portal/article/viewArticle/706 [Accessed: 01 Dec 2016].

Mattoni, A. and Doerr, N. (2007) Images within the precarity movement in Italy. *Feminist Review* (87): 130–35.

McKay, S., Jefferys, S., Paraksevopoulou, A. and Keles, J. (2012) *Final Report: Study on Precarious Work and Social Rights*. London: Working Lives Research Institute, London Metropolitan University.

Milkman, R. and Ott, E. (eds) (2014) *New Labor in New York: Precarious Workers and the Future of the Labor Movement*. Ithaca: ILR Press.

Moeran, B. and Pedersen, J. S. (eds.) (2011) *Negotiating Values in the Creative Industries: Fairs, Festivals and Competitive Events*. Cambridge: Cambridge University Press.

Moulier Boutang, Y. (2012) *Cognitive Capitalism*. Cambridge: Polity Press.

Murgia, A. and Armano, E. (2012a) *Mappe della precarietà. Vol. I: Spazi, rappresentazioni, esperienze e critica delle politiche del lavoro che cambia*. Bologna: I Libri di Emil.

Murgia, A. and Armano, E. (2012b) *Mappe della precarietà. Vol. II: Knowledge workers, creatività, saperi e dispositivi di soggettivazione*. Bologna: I Libri di Emil.

Murgia, A. and Selmi, G. (2012) 'Inspire and conspire': Italian precarious workers between self-organization and self-advocacy. *Interface: A Journal For and About Social Movements*. 4(2): 181–96.

Murphy, M. (2013) Economization of life: Calculative infrastructures of population and economy. In P. Rawes (ed.), *Relational Architectural Ecologies: Architecture, Nature and Subjectivity*. London: Routledge.

Negri, A. (1988) *Revolution Retrieved : Writings on Marx, Keynes, Capitalist Crisis, and New Social Subjects (1967–83)*. London: Red Notes.

Nunes, R. (2012) The Lessons of 2011: Three theses on organisation. Available from: www.minorcompositions.info/wp-content/uploads/2012/03/Nunes-LessonsOf2011.pdf. [Accessed 3 August 2016].

Papadopoulos, D. (2012) Worlding justice/Commoning matter. *Occasion: Interdisciplinary Studies in the Humanities*. 3 (March 15). Available from: http://arcade.stanford.edu/sites/default/files/article_pdfs/OCCASION_v03_Papadopoulos_03152_0.pdf [Accessed 3 August 2016].

Papadopoulos, D. (2014) Politics of matter: Justice and organisation in technoscience. *Social Epistemology* 28(1): 70–85.

Papadopoulos, D., Stephenson, N., and Tsianos, V. (2008) *Escape Routes. Control and Subversion in the 21st Century*. London: Pluto Press.

Papadopoulos, D., Tsianos, V., and Tsomou, M. (2011) Athens: Metropolitan blockade – real democracy. *Transversal - European Institute for Progressive Cultural Policies Journal, Special issue: Occupy and Assemble.* (October). Available from: http://eipcp.net/transversal/1011. [Accessed 3 August 2016].

Precarias a la deriva. (2004) *A la deriva por los circuitos de la precariedad feminina.* Madrid: Traficantes de Suenos.

Raunig, G. (2007) The monster precariat. *Transversal - European Institute for Progressive Cultural Policies Journal* (March). Available from: http://translate.eipcp.net/strands/02/raunig-strands02en#redir. [Accessed 3 August 2016].

Ross, A. (2009) *Nice Work If You Can Get It. Life and Labor in Precarious Times.* New York: New York University Press.

Savage, M., Devine, F., Cunningham, N., Taylor, M., Li, Y., Hjellbrekke, J., Miles, A. (2013) A new model of social class? Findings from the BBC's Great British Class Survey experiment. *Sociology* 47(2): 219–50.

Shukaitis, S., Graeber, D., and Biddle, E. (2007) *Constituent Imagination: Militant Investigations, Collective Theorization.* Oakland, CA: AK Press.

Simms, M. (2015) *Report on Sectoral Regulation of Precarious Work in Four Sectors: Industrial Cleaning, Health, Construction and Temporary Agency Work. The UK Situation.* Leicester: University of Leicester.

Smith, C. W. (1999) *Success and Survival on Wall Street : Understanding the Mind of the Market.* Lanham, Md.; Oxford: Rowman and Littlefield.

Standing, G. (2011) *The Precariat: The New Dangerous Class.* London: Bloomsbury Academic.

Stark, D. (2009) *The Sense of Dissonance : Accounts of Worth in Economic Life.* Princeton, N.J.: Princeton University Press.

Tarì, M., and Vanni, I. (2005) On the life and deeds of San Precario, patron saint of precarious workers and lives. *The Fibreculture Journal* 5. Available at: http://five.fibreculturejournal.org/fcj-023-on-the-life-and-deeds-of-san-precario-patron-saint-of-precarious-workers-and-lives/ [Accessed 1 December 2016].

Tronti, M. (1965) *The Strategy of Refusal.* Available from https://libcom.org/book/export/html/439. [Accessed 3 August 2016].

Tsianos, V. and Papadopoulos, D. (2006) Precarity: A savage journey to the heart of embodied capitalism. *Transversal – European Institute for Progressive Cultural Policies Journal.* 11. Available from: http://transform.eipcp.net/transversal/1106. [Accessed 3 August 2016].

van der Linden, M. (2014) San Precario: a new inspiration for labor historians. *Labor: Studies in Working-Class History of the Americas* 10(1): 9–21.

Waterman, P., Mattoni, A., Humphrys, E., Cox, L., and Esteves, A. M. (2012) For the global emancipation of labour: New movements and struggles around work, workers and precarity [Special Issue]. *Interface: A Journal For and About Social Movements.* 4(2): 1–368.

Weeks, K. (2011) *The Problem with Work. Feminism, Marxism, Antiwork Politics, and Postwork Imaginaries.* Durham: Duke University Press.

Zelizer, V. A. R. (1979) *Morals and Markets : The Development of Life Insurance in the United States.* New York: Columbia University Press.

11 The precariat for itself

Euro May Day and precarious workers' movements

Alex Foti

A decade before Guy Standing wrote *The Precariat*, the precariat had already named itself. In the Autumn of 2004 in London, anti-globalization activists drafted 'The Middlesex Declaration of Europe's Precariat', a manifesto that set forth a call for a Pan-European May Day and listed a set of basic demands.[1] It called for an international May Day across Europe focusing on precarity and reclaiming labour, welfare, and the social rights denied to the precarious youth by neoliberal governments and corporations. As ChainWorkers had (in)famously written in 2001, the service sector precariat is to the industrial proletariat what informationalism is to Fordism.[2] From its inception, the Euro May Day was intended as a First of May for the precariat and by the precariat, the class composed of young/queer/female/migrant precarious workers temping and toiling in the large cities transformed by the transnational flows of capital, knowledge, culture, information. The precariat was first mobilized by media and union activists in Milan, then in Barcelona, and then Hamburg, Berlin, Helsinki, Paris, Liège, Malaga, Seville, Lisbon, Ljubljana, Maribor, Stockholm, Copenhagen (to name just some of the Euro May Day hotspots).[3]

At the origin of this dynamic was a creative collective of Milanese subvertisers that started networking social spaces in the city in 2001–2003, and began to interact with the rest of Italy and Europe, with the aim of reinterpreting, in terms of discourse and communication, the meaning and purpose of International Workers' Day, in light of the radical transformations in the economy and the workplace that had occurred due to the combined effects of neoliberal deregulation and the information revolution. Our first ally was the Roman autonomous movement, which to this day has produced an interesting string of theoretical reflections on the precarious question.[4]

All this would have been unthinkable without the hopes and energies raised by the Seattle-Genoa movement. With respect to the revolutionary movement of 2011, a successor that inherited some of its characteristics, the global justice movement of the late 1990s and early 2000s involved fewer people but greatly extended its reach across borders to create a strongly motivated transnational community of activists, united by anarcho/autonomous ideology and willing to create a common style of struggle and set of demands (no borders, no discriminations, yes to minimum wage, yes to basic income), all this on a

European scale, in the momentous years when euro bills were making their way into people's wallets and the EU enlarged towards the East. Anti-globalization activists were fewer than those mobilized by Indignado-style radical populism, but managed to cover a wider range of issues – they never ceased to mobilize onto the next cause: from Zapatismo to veganism, from queer rights to bicycle activism, from food sovereignty to financial transactions, from state repression to climate justice, and finally from international solidarity to global precarity, there was no issue that the motley coalition of black, pink, red, green activists (and hacktivists!) left unturned.[5]

It was in this heady atmosphere of peer-to-peer collaboration and social innovation that San Precario and its collective were born on 29 February 2004 with an action in a Milanese supermarket open that Sunday (in spite of the then existing prohibition on holiday work). The day was chosen because leap years are intermittent, like the incomes of precarious workers.[6] At its peak in 2004–2006, the movement of San Precario attracted media and labour collectives from all Italian large cities (Milan, Rome, Turin, Bologna, L'Aquila, Palermo and many others), with several of them featuring their own MayDay Parades. What turned San Precario into a social meme was the prayer card that had been designed by a trio of ChainWorkers: it became wildly popular and could be seen on all desks of precarious workers in Milan, to signal their condition (although they performed the same work as others, they had no right to the wages and benefits of permanent employment) and their complicity in the so-called 'precarious conspiracy'.

What ultimately projected Euro May Day and its discourse on precarity onto the international stage was San Precario with its subversive inventiveness: precarious superheroes collection cards, elaborate fashion hoaxes like that of Serpica Naro, anagram of San Precario, full sets of precariat tarot cards, and a lot more marked the first few years of Euro May Day. But what was really crucial was the early attention given to the ferments of the Italian precarious' movement first by *Brumaria* and *Greenpepper Magazine*, then by *Mute*, *Adbusters*, and a host of other publications (Foti and Romano 2004; Adbusters Editors 2005; Kruglanski 2005; Mute Editors 2005). It also helped that Michael Hardt and Antonio Negri had included precarious labour in their treatment of the multitude in the second volume of their *Empire* trilogy (Hardt and Negri 2004).

In 2004, the whole Italian anti-globalization movement came to Milan in one of the biggest MayDay Parades ever. In 2005 and 2006, the whole of radical Europe joined the Euro May Day network. In the years between 2007 and 2009, interest in sabotaging EU governance grew and then waned, after the successful stunts pulled against the Eurocracy in Brussels on Good Friday 2006, and in Aix-la-Chapelle on May Day 2008.[7] The latter coincided with Ascension Day that year, when European elites traditionally award themselves the Charlemagne Prize. Euro May Day spoiled the public event held by Nicolas Sarkozy in honour of Angela Merkel, with Barroso and Trichet in attendance. In those same years the Milano MayDay parade became increasingly queer and eco-active, concerned with LGBT rights and climate justice. The parade also progressively turned into a daytime open-air rave with masses of very young people high and out of their minds. In 2009, it was shocking to discover that a rape occurred on the lawns around the Sforza Castle, where the parade traditionally ended. After that, MayDay lost its festive joviality forever, but never ceased to attract thousands of people, with San Precario's mighty, dazzlingly decorated truck always at the parade's front.

In the mid-2010s, as the Milan World Expo approached, the protest against the upcoming world fair and its exploitation of young interns, temps, and volunteers became the dominant theme, until the 2015 showdown, when May Day coincided with the official inauguration of EXPO Milano, and the government forced a suspension of the legal day of rest during International Workers' Day, which had never really been violated since 1945. The smugness or blindness with which local and central authorities abolished *Primo Maggio* occurred in a context of rampant youth unemployment (at 40 per cent in Italy in 2016) and months of mobilization by Milan's social centres against what they saw as the Expo Triad: concrete, debt, precariousness. It didn't take a fortune-teller to forecast a massive riot instead of the fifteenth May Day Parade. This occurred in the bourgeois streets of Milan and therefore louder than usual calls for the criminalization of the movement were heard across the media. Several Milanese activists were jailed and some were dealt harsh prison sentences. The powerful mix of rage and frustration expressed in Milan was also fuelled by the energies unleashed by the Blockupy siege of the European Central Bank in Frankfurt a few months earlier, which saw burning barricades all around the financial district.

Looking back a decade after the Euro May Day was first conceived, what needs to be done is to rescue its theoretical legacy which is being jumbled by academics with little hands-on experience of social movements, as well as assess the trajectory of one of Europe's – with sister May Days in Tokyo, Osaka, and Toronto as well – most interesting experiments in social radicalism in the 2000s. Let me start addressing the issue, so that academics can stop referring to just one 2004 interview, when they cite the theory behind the movement of the precarious. In 2001, the Milano May Day Parade for the precarious youth was born in direct opposition to mainstream unions who were doing nothing to defend their rights. In 2003, it had become the city's most important May Day demonstration, surpassing in participation the traditional morning march. By then, ChainWorkers had started talking of '*il precariato sociale*' (the social precariat) as the key actor in the post-industrial economy which was destined to radicalize and fight for its rights (Chainworkers 2006). By doing this, activists turned a stigma into a sign of pride and combativeness, because in Italy *precariato* tends to be considered a condition you have to suffer without complaining, rather than a subject composed of people capable of self-organization and empowerment.

It is fundamental to stress this point: we saw the social precariat as the successor of the industrial proletariat, plain and simple. Unlike social-democrats and communists, we harboured no illusions about working-class commitment to the Left, and were adamant about the fact that the political and economic arrangements that had revolved around the industrial factory were being supplanted by those of the network economy. Industry was no longer the central site for class conflict: its place had been taken by the City, the Mall, the Web. We saw a new class emerging, the precariat, composed of women and immigrants, working-class and middle-class youth, cleaners and hackers,[8] and we thought this would soon eclipse the political priorities of an aging generation of blue and white collars. We thought that the precariat was destined to be the gravedigger of neoliberalism.

So what is the precariat? It is the mass of people who are temporary, part-time and/or freelance workers under advanced capitalism. This is my simplest definition. I would also throw NEETs and the temporarily/permanently unemployed into the mix. The precariat is a class and it is a generation. It is the new class of workers, and it is the younger cohort of the labour force. But the logic of precarity pervades the whole of society.

Anyway the May Day movement went into decline after 2008 in Italy, due to the destructive effects of the Great Recession on social solidarity, and the unwillingness/inability by the now aged San Precario collective to adopt a clear local/national strategy to unionize the precariat. The same occurred with the Euro May Day network. Slowly but surely, traditional leftist hostility against the idea of Europe, which was at the heart of the whole process, resurfaced in many countries. After all, both the French and the Dutch had voted against an EU Constitution in 2005. In 2010, Geneva held its first May Day. It also hosted the last Euro May Day assembly. In the previous years, first Berlin, then Liège had tried to revive the enthusiasm of the mid-2000s, but the anti-globalization movement was in decline after Rostock (Foti 2007): probably the huge Strasbourg riots of 2009, and the 1 April protest in front of the Bank of England will come to be seen as the ending moments of that cycle of struggle. After that, the Euro May Day legacy has partly survived in Belgium, where experienced stop-precarity activists are presently collaborating with JOC (*Jeunes Organisés et Combatifs*), an anti-racist youth federation that gathers students and precarious workers of mixed descent and is quite active in Brussels and its movements (such as D1920 against the TTIP).

The Euro May Day network no longer exists, although some of its fragments were reconstituted as the Precarious of Europe United and participated in Climate Justice Action in Copenhagen (December 2009) and organized with no-border networks a 'Fuck Austerity!' demo in Brussels during the European Union Confederation march, in protest against the summit of EU finance ministers that was deciding for austerity. It ended up in mass arrests, with union officials helping police officials locate troublemakers (Foti 2009b, 2009c).

Since 2011, individuals of the Euro May Day collective have participated in the Spanish, Tunisian, and Egyptian revolutions, some playing prominent roles in the Indignado movement and in the recent wave of progressive populism in Barcelona and Madrid: in charge of Ada Colau's social media campaign, Javier Toret was Euro May Day organizer in Malaga, Sevilla and Tarragona, while the co-founder of the Euro May Day network, Marcelo Expósito, has just been elected to the Cortes for En Comú Podem.

When the Arab Spring came and turned the world alight for two brief but incredible years, it was clear who the prime-movers behind the revolutions of

Tahir and Plaza del Sol were: the precarious youth, i.e. the vanguard of the precariat, organizing protests via social media and setting up the logistics for huge occupations and assemblies asserting people power against corrupt elites. What Gerbaudo calls the anarcho-populist ideology was the combination of the often anarchist outlook of activists (students, temps, freelancers, the unemployed) with popular needs in terms of real democracy and the end of austerity and inequality (Gerbaudo 2016). To end precarity means to end inequality. To end precarity you need to put austerity in reverse and redistribute wealth away from the digital and financial oligarchy toward the precariat, starting with the setting of a $15/€15/¥2000 minimum wage per hour of work. In fact, the movement 'Fight for 15' in America is the first labour movement organizing a major section of the precariat, that of part-time workers in retail industries.

In Italy, there has been a movement to organize freelancers, who are considered *The Fifth Estate*, to quote the title of a recent essay by two Roman intellectuals directly involved in the precarious' movement. Allegri and Ciccarelli find new forms of association and reciprocity in the world of freelance work, as welfare and labour rights are slowly being extended to them, but one could argue that the same is also true of the much larger ranks of temporary workers (Allegri and Ciccarelli 2013).

I consider the temp the ideal type of precarious worker. No matter the industry or the company s/he is employed in, if s/he is on a short-term contract, her/his leverage on the boss is lower than if she were a permanent worker. The problem is that the demand for permanent employees dropped thirty years ago, when neoliberalism came to power. Those who, against the odds, manage to get permanent employment tend to look down on the precarious workers who are legion. Today, a little more than 15 per cent of employees work under temporary contracts in the Eurozone, according to Eurostat data and definitions. For example, short-time employees constituted 15 per cent of all employees in France and Germany in 2013. The same figures apply for Finland and, outside the Eurozone, Sweden (Eurostat 2013). In North America, the share of temporary employment had climbed to 14.5 per cent of the total working population at the end of 2012, according to the OECD's *Employment Outlook*. Looking at the generational cross-section, in Europe short-term employees account for about 25 per cent of people in dependent employment aged 15–39. In Mediterranean Europe, the numbers are higher: in Spain and Portugal about a third of workers under 40 have an expiration date written on their foreheads, while in France and Italy, 23 per cent and 21 per cent respectively of young(ish) workers are permatemps without hope of permanent employment. In Holland, the corresponding percentage stands at a high 31 per cent, but unlike most Eurozone countries, this is matched by high, rather than low, employment rates for people under 40. Looking at people under 25 years of age, the OECD reported that in Europe more than 39 per cent of employees were temps (up from 36 per cent in 2000). Since the precarity rate is around 15 per cent and there were a total number of European employees in excess of 115,000,000 in early 2013, we can say that today there are over 17 million precarious workers in the Eurozone). These numbers translate into a stark fact:

when we talk about the gig economy, we are really talking about labour crucially performed by the precariat. The profits of the sharing economy and social media empires would be unthinkable without the flexibility and knowledge of the precariat.

Although Standing does not acknowledge his intellectual debt to the movement, he is right in arguing that the precariat is making the leap from class in itself to class for itself (Shukaitis 2013). Although these are Marxian categories, Marxist nostalgia is having none of this: don't touch the centrality of the working class! But the fact is that the precarization of the middle class and the pauperization of the service class brought by the Great Recession have turned precariousness (or precarity, the distinction is not important here) into a mainstream issue, and the precariat into an item for discussion in the in op-ed columns of major newspapers around the world. Never has the word 'precarious' been written with more frequency, and applied to a larger variety of contexts. Standing thinks the precariat will veer to the right. Conversely, I think it is veering to the left and is behind the political renewal occurring in Spain, Greece, Portugal. It is the petty bourgeoisie and parts of the old working class that are voting in increasing numbers for Wilders in Holland or the DPP in Denmark, to name just two of the despicable xenophobic parties threatening Europe today.

I suggest we take another approach to study the precarious question.

1 A new precarious class has superseded the old working class: the service precariat of the twenty-first century, which is the analogue of the industrial proletariat in the twentieth century;
2 The precariat is the revolutionary subject that opposes and will ultimately undermine the economic and political elites that caused the crisis.

In fact, I have long been persuaded that only the precariat has the energy and urgency to dismantle neoliberalism, defeat political reaction, and end the dying rule of fossil capitalism. Prove me wrong, but do not misappropriate what social movements have been working on, both in theory and practice, for years and years, particularly in France (AC!, Stop Précarité, Intermittents), Spain (Precarias a la Deriva, Oficina Precaria, PAH), Germany (FeLS, Interventionistische Linke), and of course Italy (many collectives that were part of Euro May Day are now part of Sciopero Sociale, which has engendered the European Social Strike Network).

In order to describe the precariat, academic researchers should do well to rely on the self-description made by the movements of the precariat themselves, rather than their own theoretical tropes. Unlike what is argued by the Great British Class Survey,[9] the precariat is not the poorest of social classes (there is the underclass of the *banlieues*, for instance) and has considerable relational and cultural capital, in contrast with the traditional working class. From the point of view of the technical division of labour, the precariat is made up of young people working in information, culture, knowledge, and service industries, who have unsteady jobs and suffer from the twin evils of oligopoly and oligarchy. Let's start from there, if we really want to map precariousness.

Notes

1 This can still be viewed here: 'The Middlesex declaration of Europe's Precariat' (2004) Available at: www.euromayday.org/2005/middle.php (Accessed: 17 July 2016).
2 See ChainCrew (2001). The Crew was started in early 2000 after I read *No Logo*. I am forever intellectually indebted to Naomi Klein, whom I regard as a fundamental influence in progressive thinking and global activism, from *No Logo* to *The Shock Doctrine* and *This Changes Everything*.
3 For an idea of its diversity, consider the www.euromayday.org website and the contents of the DVD *Precarity* (2004).
4 See for instance the Italian movement journal *Posse* or the Roman social centers' magazine *Infoxoa*. The latter has long been active in the movement for the right to basic income.
5 For a taxonomy of the movement(s) and materials from my personal trajectory across Europe, see Alex Foti (2009a).
6 It just celebrated its 'third' birthday in a subdued party co-sponsored by *MilanoX*, an alternative news website, in a squatted space in Northern Milan.
7 See article in Autonomedia (Foti 2009d).
8 A fundamental source of inspiration was the Justice for Janitors (J4J) movement, the US labour movement famously portrayed in *Bread and Roses* by Ken Loach. The EuroMayDay movement was greatly helped by the J4J European coordinator, Valerie Alzaga. As for hackers, the Autistici/Inventati collective was part of ChainWorkers from day one.
9 Commissioned and reported by the BBC in 2013, the 'class calculator' has proved wildly popular with users (BBC 2013).

References

Adbusters Editors (2005) The precarity issue. A crack in the façade. *Adbusters*. #62, 13(6) (November/December).

Allegri, G. and Ciccarelli, R. (2013) *Il quinto stato: perché il lavoro indipendente è il nostro futuro: precari, autonomi, free lance per una nuova società*. Milan: Ponte alle Grazie.

BBC (2013) *The great British class calculator*. Available from: www.bbc.com/news/magazine-22000973. [Accessed: 24 July 2016].

ChainCrew (ed.) (2001) *ChainWorkers: Lavorare nelle cattedrali del consumo*. Rome: DeriveApprodi.

ChainWorkers (2006) *MayDay 003: Il Precariato Si Ribella* Available from: www.ecn.org/chainworkers/chainw/mayday003/autonomo.htm. [Accessed: 24 July 2016].

Euro May Day (2004) *The Middlesex Declaration of Europe's Precariat*. Available from: www.EuroMayDay.org/2005/middle.php. [Accessed: 24 July 2016].

Eurostat (2013) Employment and unemployment (Labour Force Survey) Available from: http://ec.europa.eu/eurostat/web/lfs/data/database. [Accessed: 17 July 2016].

Foti, A. (2007) Pink, black, pirate: Taking stock of Rostock. Rostock: A new start for the European antiglobalization movement. Available from: http://transform.eipcp.net/correspondence/1182944688#redir#redir. [Accessed: 24 July 2016].

Foti, A. (2009a) *Anarchy in the EU: Movimenti pink, black, green e Grande Recessione*. Bologna: Agenzia X.

Foti, A. (2009b) Climate anarchists vs green capitalists. *ZNet The Spirit of Resistant Lives*. Available from: http://ruby.fgcu.edu/courses/twimberley/EnviroPhilo/Foti1.pdf. [Accessed: 24 July 2016].

Foti, A. (2009c) The precariat and climate justice in the great recession. Available from: www.academia.edu/9343608/The_Precariat_and_Climate_Justice_in_the_Great_Recession. [Accessed: 24 July 2016].

Foti, A. (2009d) From precarity to unemployment: The Great Recession and EuroMayDay. Available at: http://dev.autonomedia.org/node/12334 [Accessed 1 December 2016].

Foti, A. and Romano, Z. (eds) (2004) Precarity. Special Issue of *Greenpepper Magazine*. London: AK Press.

Gerbaudo, P. (2016) *The Mask and the Flag: The Rise of Anarchopopulism in Global Protest*. Oxford: Oxford University Press.

Hardt, M. and Negri, A. (2004) *Multitude: War and Democracy in the Age of Empire*. New York: The Penguin Press.

Kruglanski, A. (2005) Precarity explained to kids (a medley). *Journal of Aesthetics and Protest* 4 (February). Available from: http://joaap.org/4/aviv.html. [Accessed: 24 July 2016].

Mute Editors (2005) Precarious reader. *Mute Magazine* 2(0). Available from: www.metamute.org/editorial/magazine/mute-vol-2-no.-0-%E2%88%92-precarious-reader. [Accessed: 24 July 2016].

Precarity (2004) Documentary. Concept and realization by Francesca Bria, Tora Krogh and Lize De Clercq. [DVD] Vienna: P2P Fightsharing Crew. Available from: http://republicart.net/cal/precarity_contents.htm. [Accessed: 24 July 2016].

Shukaitis, S. (2013) Recomposing precarity: Notes on the laboured politics of class composition. *Ephemera. Theory and Politics in Organization* 13(3): 641-658. Available from: www.ephemerajournal.org/sites/default/files/pdfs/contribution/13-3shukaitis.pdf. [Accessed: 17 July 2016].

12 Fake it until you make it

Prefigurative practices and the extrospection of precarity

Valeria Graziano

After twenty years of struggles around precarity, the question of whether this category can produce a collective subjectivity capable of political action remains open. Thus, in a recent article on precarity and art workers, Andrew Ross wondered: 'does it make sense to imagine cross-class coalitions of the precarious capable of developing a unity of consciousness and action on an international scale?' (Ross 2013:7). More recently, Alessandro Delfanti returned to this issue while commenting on the Milan Mayday Parade, an important symbolic event within European movements against precarity for having first introduced this theme as the focus of a public demonstration since its first edition in 2001. Delfanti noted how for the first time Mayday 2015 'has abandoned the centrality of the problem of welfare and of work' (Delfanti 2015, my translation), and wondered whether this should be read as a failure of what the movement has 'bet on and worked on head down for fifteen years: precisely, the emergence of a precarious political subjectivity' (Delfanti 2015).

This chapter puts forward a reflection around this apparent stalling in the processes of composition of a broad precarious political class, considering specifically the allure of finding individual satisfaction through work as one of the most pressing challenges in this respect. By examining the contemporary widespread reliance upon a series of prefigurative techniques for re-orienting subjective desires and managing the self, I want to call attention to the pragmatic mechanisms that could be hacked strategically as part of the struggles against the precarization of life.

Dimensions of struggle: prefigurations

The concept of 'prefiguration' was first used in the late 1970s by theorists who were inventing a new vocabulary to narrate the novel kinds of political practices initiated in black, student and women's movements at the time (Boggs 1977; Rowbotham 1979; Breines 1980). These authors observed how new social movements were producing a qualitatively different kind of political experience from traditional left wing organizations, decentring some of their traditional goals such as the conception of politics as a matter of strategy to seize central power, while at the same time challenging their authoritarianism and avant-gardist aspirations. Carl Boggs, who coined the term 'prefigurative politics', defined it as 'within the ongoing political practice of the movement […] those forms of social relations, decision making, culture, and human experience that are the ultimate goal' (Boggs 1977:100).

It is worth noting that the discourse around prefigurative politics emerged at the same time as neoliberalism, a phase of capitalism that also inaugurated an unprecedented interest towards the most intimate behaviours of the general population and that begins to increasingly rely on so called 'soft' techniques of governmentality to exercise its power. To put it in another way, the late 1970s can be taken as marking a moment when everyday social practices became a terrain of struggles between dominant and counter-powers.

There is undoubtedly an element of utopianism in prefigurative practices, and the extent to which such element can be part of an effective political strategy or remain an impediment to more pragmatic achievements has recently re-emerged in the commentary that accompanied the latest mobilizations of social justice movements across the world, including the alter-globalization struggles of the early 2000s (Maeckelbergh 2011); the Egyptian uprising (van de Sande 2013); the Spanish *acampadas* (della Porta and Mattoni 2014); the Gezi Park occupation (Kaya 2014); and Occupy Wall Street (Smucker 2014). The concept appears an essential component of debates around the successes and failures of such movements, embedded in discussions of their political orientation vis-à-vis strategies of direct action and open, egalitarian decision-making processes. Rather than articulating a clear set of demands, the protestors of the international occupations focused on setting up common kitchens, libraries, classes, performances, investigations, debt-relief initiatives, etc. In this context, the meaning of prefigurative politics has come to be at the centre of a lively debate.

In some cases, the prefigurative elements of the protests have been celebrated as the expression of the collective intelligence of the multitudes composing the movement, and as a sign of their ability to self-organize autonomously and democratically, without the need for a vertical leadership.

For instance, David Graeber wrote that activists were 'creating a vision of the sort of society you want to have in miniature' (Graeber 2011).

As the occupation movements began to wane, however, other commentators saw this as a failure due to an excessive focus on prefiguration. For some, this meant an excessive investment in the formal procedures and methodologies of collective decision making. As one Occupy activist put it:

> Debate continuously raged over whether the General Assembly was adequately democratic and inclusive, whether the spokescouncil was being controlled by a secret cadre of activists, and whether such a council or assembly could ever adequately realize the pure image of democracy and consensus to which we aspired.
>
> (Murray 2014)

For others, the insistence on prefiguration was called into question as an emotional relation to the politics of the camps at the expense of more rational effort to subvert broader social dynamics. The comments of another Occupy activist express this concern clearly, reflecting on the time spent in Zuccotti Park:

> I began to wonder if the heightened sense of an integrated identity was 'the utopia' that many of my fellow participants were seeking. What if the thing we were missing, the thing we were lacking [...] was a sense of an integrated existence in a cohesive community, i.e., an intact lifeworld?
>
> (Smucker 2014)

In response to both the enthusiasts and the critics of the role of prefiguration in recent movements, a third position is emerging that argues for a reframing of the debate away from the binaries strategy/community or rational/affective politics, in favour of a strategic understanding of prefiguration itself. From this perspective, true prefigurative politics is precisely found when a congruence and a resonance are maintained between broader long term political goals and everyday practices (Yates 2015).

In a recent speech in Venice calling for an 'abstract strike', Antonio Negri explained:

> Today it is clear that these two levels of struggle are not identical, but are highly connected to each other. The first one is *horizontal*; the second is *vertical*. The first is a struggle for the emancipation *of* labour; the second for liberation *from* labour.
>
> (Negri 2015)

For Negri, precarity has to be fought on two levels, one fighting against capital's abstract extraction of value from life, and the other inventing alternative modes of valorization of life. In this perspective, the political question is not so much between strategy/prefiguration nor between rational/emotional experiences of struggles (della Porta and Mattoni 2014: 49), but between what we could call, after the Occupy activist mentioned earlier, movements that stage 'prefigurative spectacles' (Smucker 2014) and struggles which are able to produce actual prefigurative practices viable in the long term.

Bringing this argument back to the theme of struggles against precarity, it must be noted how most mobilizations that tackled this issue specifically in relation to the conditions and quality of working lives, such as the Mayday parade, were typical of the early 2000s, as they really invested in the invention of playful and carnivalesque ways of making the issue tangible in public discourse so that a precarious subjectivity could emerge.

It might be tempting to dismiss the performative and symbolic mode of organizing of earlier movements from fifteen years ago as a failed prefigurative politics. After all, it can be argued, when we come back from the utopian space of the struggle we still need to embrace our neoliberal condition. However, it would be equally possible to trace an arch of consistency connecting the organizational practices of movements during the early 2000s, focused on alter-globalization (Seattle protests, Social Forum), right to the city (Reclaim the Streets, Critical mass) and precarity (Euro Mayday), who engaged with prefiguration by constructing temporary miniature societies in which processes of commoning took place mainly on the performative level; to the occupation movements of the late 2000s (Spanish *acampadas*; Gezi park; Tahrir square; Occupy Wall Street, etc.), who expanded their range of prefigurative politics, engaging with practices that had a longer duration and also implicated participants more materially in the reproduction of a common sustenance (but that were still confined to a specific time-place and therefore partially performative in nature); to the most recent organizational processes of movements such as Black Lives Matter, PAH or the anti-austerity movements in Greece and the migrant and refugee solidarity mobilizations, which seem finally able to invent prefigurative practices beyond the limits of the symbolic and the performative. Perhaps this arch can attest to a specific pedagogical capacity found in prefiguration: the impact of symbolic and performative practices on the collective processes of subjectivation taking place in connection with social movements might be indeed propaedeutic to more complex breakages comparable to what in psychology is referred to as a positive feedback loop, or in layman terms, the 'fake it until you make it' motto of self-help/mutual aid culture (more on this later).

What about precarity?

In suggesting that an expansive prefigurative tendency has characterized the modes of organizations of the recent struggles, my intent is not to ignore the important differences between each context and experience, but to offer a framework to qualify the texture of the experimentations taking place in these different autonomous contexts as they resonate and affect each other. If the most effective prefigurative politics of the present seem to be focused on social reproduction, this begs the question of whether the fatigue felt in the struggles against labour precarity can also be taken in a similar direction, building upon the challenges to the dominant representation of the working life launched in previous phases such as the one inaugurated by Euro May Day.

How would a prefigurative practice of subversion of the regime of precarity that goes beyond the logic of the prefigurative spectacle look?

Answering this question could be key to reigniting the political subjectivity of the precariat as an active presence in solidarity with the current struggles focused on migration, racism, welfare provisions and housing. This prefigurative focus would be complementary to and in resonance with the goal of a universal basic income, but it would approach the question of the impact of labour in life from the point of view of its intrinsic dynamics. Some interesting experiences and militant research have already looked in this direction, including the more politicized segments of the makers' movement; the nascent international network of occupied and re-purposed factories; radical areas of the cooperative movement; the recent wave of occupied theatres in Italy, alongside an array of other radical social enterprises across a variety of fields of production (among which the agricultural and food sectors are particularly important) that are creating alternative labour relations. In the second part of this chapter however I will leave these aside to focus on exploring the role of prefigurative practices within precarious labour understood as a condition that demands, in many, less sympathetic sectors of employment, a high degree of introjection of the capitalist command within subjectivity.

Struggles of the soul

'Who is the worker and who is the boss today?' – Negri asks, only to answer: 'In the context of cognitive labour, the boss is financial capital who extracts social value' (Negri 2015). Indeed, the boss might be financial capital, but the reason why Negri even needs to raise this question is that the two roles are often blurred in the everyday experience of the precariat. The class struggles that were once palpably perceivable and visible in the factory and at the office, now often play out as a silent, ferocious internal monologue. The experience of precarity incentivizes the adoption of a cynical and opportunistic repertoire to deal with the violence of working relations (Virno 1996). Such repertoires of behaviours are not spontaneous or innate however. They need to be learned, rehearsed, and perfected through techniques of the self. A burgeoning number of organizations and infrastructures are assisting the precariat through this endless training process by offering an array of reactionary prefigurative practices to those who need to fend off the sting of anxiety from within their souls. For Michel Foucault,

> It would be wrong to say that the soul is an illusion, or an ideological effect. On the contrary, it exists, it has a reality, it is produced permanently around, on, within the body by the functioning of a power that is exercised on those punished – and [...] on those one supervises, trains and corrects.
>
> (Foucault 1979: 29)

Over the course of modernity power became more and more interested in the soul of its subjects, making it a legitimate terrain of struggle within the process of fighting capital's most recent mutations. This struggle is not a matter of individual discomforts; as Franco Bifo Berardi reminded us, the soul is a collective affair. He distinctively contributed to further the discussion of precarity as a specific relation of the self with labour which calls for prefigurative tactics. In his book *The Soul at Work*, he writes:

> Politics is weakened, since all that is given in the politically visible has no value, it is pure 'spectacle' [...]. Domination [...] shifts from the domain of bodily, mechanical and political disciplining to that of logical and psychological, or logical and biogenic automatisms. Not the body but the soul becomes the subject of techno-social domination.
>
> (Berardi 2009: 200).

For Franco Bifo Berardi (often known as Bifo), the social psyche is trapped in a state of panic produced by an overload of semiotic stimuli disseminated via the ubiquitously pervasive info-sphere that the brain is simply not able to process. Caught in an endless injunction of connectivity, the singular psyche loses the possibility of processing an autonomous sense of the world.

Psychopathologies as labour

In this light, Bifo has described depression and burn-outs due to existential, performative exhaustion of the precarious as forms of resistance to the brutal injunctions of power, a defence mechanism that the soul triggers in order to subtract its energies to the enforced participation in the relentless chatter of semio-capitalism. The idea that 'the new form of action of social protest in the last period is desperation' (Berardi 2014, my translation) has found a certain resonance in the discourse around precarity. For instance, in her contribution to *The Psychopathologies of Cognitive Capitalism* (De Boever and Neidich 2013), Tiziana Terranova states that attention-deficit disorders and anhedonia (the inability to experience pleasure) 'read as a constituent strategy of resistance of the social brain to exploitation and subsumption' (Terranova 2013: 59).

But what if, rather than being expressive of the resistance of the 'soul on strike' (Smith 2013: 33), the widespread psychic suffering of the precariat is signalling a fatal vulnerability and a capitulation to the injunction of capitalist power that 'you are not enough'? What if depression, anxiety and other psychopathologies are a price that the precariat subjectivity is willing to pay in order to cling on to what we could call, after Gilbert Simondon, the capitalist system of individuation'? (Simondon 1989)

The above proposition does not mean to favour this more pessimistic possibility over the resistance hypothesis, but to introduce a more nuanced understanding of what phenomena such as mass depression and diffused psychic suffering might tell us about the present. The interpretation of contemporary cognitive psychopathologies as tentative forms of exodus or withdrawal echoes the classic psychoanalytic idea that the patient has to experience as breakdown before she can have a breakthrough. However, even in such classic (contestable) framework, breakthrough is just one of the possible outcomes of a breakdown (Field 1996). If we can agree with Laurent Berlant as she suggested that 'the benefits of bad work are soul-making, not soul-killing' (Berlant 2007: 275), then the psychopathologies experienced by the labour force of cognitive capitalism can also signal the soul's refusal to strike, to persist, no matter at what costs, in discarding the other kinds of meaningful, joyful relations with the world and the self, in favour of the rewards promised by power? What if there is a specific kind of suffering that is indeed accepted and embraced as the cost of the pleasure of becoming our own cadres, that is, of 'symbolically cross[ing] over on the side of capital?' (Duménil and Lévy 2003, cited in Lordon 2014: 80) These would be symptomatic not of a subjective resistance, but as an existential strategy for escaping the misery of work by reinvesting it with our re-aligned desires (Lordon 2014), in the hope of partaking in the delirium of omnipotence that is capitalism.

As the pressure for the soul to cross over on the side of power rises, we are witnessing a parallel proliferation of reactionary prefigurative practices that offer a relief from the pain of entertaining desires that are out of tune with the majority of bodies one encounters in capitalist relations. I am referring here to the new social formations and knowledges offered by coaching; neuro-linguistic programming; cognitive behavioural psychology, self-help methods; mutual aid groups and the various incarnations of prosperity gospel. It is important to note that these techniques are specifically interested in the habits of their constituents in relation to labour, not in their inner life as more traditional therapeutic approaches; they understand very well that the soul is not within but in between, a compound of quotidian practices and refrains that shape the patterns of encounter with others and the world, and accordingly, they provide templates for exercises that through repetition can forge new habits. Some of these reactionary prefigurative practices are emerging as part of governmental policies dealing with the now chronic rise of employment. An exemplary instance of this approach would be the rising phenomenon of 'practice firms' in Europe. These virtual companies, often supported through public schemes, are organized to provide a fake job routine for the unemployed, who are expected to go to work every day in a mock office, where everyone needs to act 'in character' to produce and trade fake goods in a make-believe market in exchange for a virtual salary. The benefits of practice firms are seen to be psychological and social as well as pedagogical, and the model is expanding fast, with over 5,000 practice firms currently operating in Europe and an extra 2,500 internationally, according to a recent article which appeared in the *New York Times* (Alderman 2015). Another example of a governmental prefigurative intervention could be seen in the recent proposal of the UK government to introduce mandatory psychotherapeutic consultations to people on benefits to help them improve their personality traits for employment, fixing issues such as shyness or low self-esteem (Friedli and Stearn 2015).

The disquieting element of these policies is not only found in their measure of coercion, but also and more paradoxically in the fact that they could actually 'work', successfully supporting precariat subjects in embracing their condition of disposability with less sadness. And the urgency of finding pragmatic techniques to keep such sadness of work at bay emerges as a transversal urgency of the precariat in all those contexts where the materiality of social reproduction is not immediately under threat. The relevance of this matter can be grasped even further by looking more closely to another example of a reactive prefigurative practice that rather than being offered as a private service or a public provision is being organized voluntarily through a volunteer network: this is the case of Underearners Anonymous.

Underearners Anonymous

Underearners Anonymous (UA)1 is a mutual aid group providing a 12-step programme of rehabilitation for people unable to entertain a healthy relationship with their working lives. It was founded in New York as an offshoot of Debtors Anonymous (first established in 1976) in 2005, only a few years before the first subprime crisis exploded in Wall Street, and at a time that saw the massive increase, in the global north, of the phenomenon of the 'working poor' (Andreß and Lohmann 2008; Shipler 2008). It has since spread internationally, with meetings taking place in Canada, Colombia, Denmark, Israel, the United Kingdom, and 11 other states across the US.

Rather than focusing on overspending like its sister organization, UA reformulated the issue of poverty as a form of compulsion affecting 'poor-aholics' (Kadet 2010). It functions as a classic 12-step programme (such as the one used by Alcoholics Anonymous) comprising of time management techniques to help fight procrastination, visualization tools to strategize priorities, peer-support and sponsorship sessions to help stick to plans, and weekly meetings where participants can anonymously elaborate on one's sense of shame and failure in the face of the unlimited promise of capital's *realization*, both in the economic and in the spiritual sense of the term.

UA's definition of 'underearning' is not qualified only as a matter of income, but it explicitly caters to those people who are unhappy about the kind of jobs they do and the satisfaction they can derive from them. Being dependent on others to meet one's needs, keeping possessions that are broken or no longer useful rather than buying new ones, and failing to keep in touch with people who might be beneficial to one's career prospect are all signs of underearning revealing a fear of success. Based on this blurred formulation, people of any income level can identify as being affected by underearning. Indeed, it appears that many among those attending meetings have a professional, educated, and artistic background, or in other words belong to the 'cognitariat', and their motivations for joining were more about improving the quality of their work life rather than simply about income.2 UA addresses the problem of precarity from the locus of subjectivity, but unlike its sister organization Debtors Anonymous, it cannot provide a clear name for the source of the 'addiction' it seeks to combat, underearning being just an expression, or a consequence, of a refusal of work that is recast as an addiction to something else: a certain relation with the passage of time, a certain carefree rhythm of life, an intolerance towards the drudgery and boredom of meaningless employment.

Leaving aside the debates around the efficacy of 12-step programmes in general, the success and rapid growth of UA signals that this network is meeting a widespread need to alleviate the pain caused by the failure to successfully adopt techniques of the self and orient one's desires in the preferred direction of capital. When the attempt to escape labour is carried out in the private space of individual biographies, the cost is often unbearable in the long run. UA offers a response to this pain by naming it and providing a space for socializing individual anxieties around one's relation with capital and labour, breaking it down in manageable components addressing how this relation pervades and shapes many aspects of life beyond income, from personal relations to relationships with time and education.

UA can be seen as being effective as it collectivizes and makes explicit the techniques of the self that are required to bear living in the precarious condition of work today. It does alleviate pain, but it does so encouraging a realignment of the existential repertoire of the individual (reconfirming the subject as an *individual*) on the side of the 'boss', at the expenses of all tropisms and elective affinities (Benasayag 2013) that cannot be adapted.

Folks who identify themselves as underearners might have strong feelings against capitalist society, which might be a factor that contributes to their difficulties in fitting in it in the first place, and yet UA offers them a collective practice that is conspicuously absent from much critique and activism: mutual and non-judgemental support in transforming their habits, which they understand, perhaps instinctually, as being directly constitutive, and not merely expressive, of their subjectivities (Deleuze and Guattari 1987). Unfortunately, the reactive techniques of UA might actually 'work' for them, but the price they pay is the transformation of their dangerous disquiet into regular unhappiness.

UA and prosperity gospel coaching exercises can all be seen as reactive prefigurative practices in the sense that while they make no full commitment to a therapeutic process, they offer exercises that transform the self to match its future aspirations of feeling less sadness or even find joy in relation to work. They are however reactive because they act by reducing the range of life's possible refrains, rearranging commitments, interests and relations to become more narrowly focused, that is, less diverse. In the construction of a career, the multiplicity of conflicting desires becomes a lack of focus to be sorted out. In his own reading of Spinoza, Frederic Lordon explains well how this loss of experiential variety might be the key to re-interpret the Marxist idea of alienation without having to evoke the problematic notion of a lost authentic experience: alienation would then be not some kind of transcendental 'loss of one's autonomy as subject' nor is it a mysterious 'separation from one's powers', but, immanently, alienation is 'the contraction of the scope of one's effectuations' (Lordon 2014:79).

Christian Laval and Pierre Dardot push this line of reasoning even further in their concept of 'subjective subsumption' (Laval and Dardot 2015: 161, my translation). This hypothesis extends the realm of what different Marxist traditions have termed a 'total subsumption' of labour under capital to the sphere of subjectivation, especially of the idealized 'worker-artist-inventor', reconfigured to submit to the unlimited 'injunction of the surplus' (Endnotes 2010). Laval and Dardot emphasize subjective subsumption as a partial corrective to the political expectations placed by post-operaist thought on the role of the cognitariat. According to this line of enquiry, contemporary capitalism has a tendency of becoming rent, as opposite to profit, describing a methodology of extraction of surplus value from 'a position of exteriority in relation to production' (Vercellone 2008). For Laval and Dardot however, more conceptual tools are needed to differentiate between the autonomous capacity of self-organization of the multitudes and the symptoms of the 'ultrasubjectivation' elicited by capitalist command (Laval and Dardot 2015: 161).

The (ironic) Clinic

The diffused and toxic reliance of the precariat upon the growing bulk of reactive and reactionary prefigurative practices is one of the serious obstacles that stands in the way of the composition of the elusive precarious subjectivity capable of solidarity beyond sector-specific struggles. An autonomous politics in this sense might experiment with different provisions of opportunities to learn, exercise, invent and refine a range of 'counter-conducts' (Foucault 2009: 201) to counter the subjective subsumption of the precariat's soul.

For instance, a straightforward attempt in this direction has been the Clinic initiated by the Radical Education Forum, an open collective of 'people working in a wide range of educational settings who meet monthly to discuss radical pedagogical theories and techniques, and contemporary issues of interest to those involved in education' (Radical Education Forum) who have been meeting in London since 2010. The Clinic was the ironic title the group gave to a series of 'free flow discussion meetings' (Radical Education Forum 2013) held monthly since 2012. During these encounters, participants would introduce specific episodes and micropolitical situations impacting their pedagogical practices. This exchange of anecdotes would then constitute the basis for a group discussion of alternative ways to tackle the issue at hand in both pragmatic ways ('have you tried doing this…?') and in theoretical ones ('have you thought of it in this way…?'). What is interesting is that the focus of conversations remains geared towards the generation of collective practical application of political and ethical principles in actual situations. To put it in a sentence used repeatedly by several participants, the ideas for the meeting is to host 'the kind of conversations that we wish we could have in our staff room'. The Clinic offers a safe and non-judgemental space of reflection around one's practices and struggles in an increasingly coercive and precarious sector of employment that is pressuring educators to become 'behaviour managers' (Radical Education Forum 2013).

Extrospective practices

Without forcing the comparison between the two instances too far, as they differ in many respects, it can be said that UA and the Clinic produce diametrically opposed technologies of the self (Martin *et al.* 1988) vis-à-vis the injunctions of capitalism. As in the UA programme, the Clinic's focus is on habits, reflex responses and behaviours and how to change them. Here, too, participants come looking for collective support in their quest to reduce the painful affects experienced in their relation with work. However, while UA's approach encourages individual self-reliance and fosters self-critique in accordance with the dominant requirement of introspection, the Clinic stimulates what Lordon calls a 'movement of extrospection' (Lordon 2014: 56), a shift of attention towards the exterior forces that shape singular responses and behaviours.

The Clinic is just one among several initiatives that are contributing to the 'affective struggles' (Institute for Precarious Consciousness 2014) within social justice movements. These 'critical reflective practices' (Finlay 2008) conjure up a connection between the soul, everyday practices and the broader institutional formations that organize the social sphere. Opposing dominant introspective practices on their own terrain, such practices of extrospection can de-privatize and de-personalize the toxic inter-individual affective states of precarity. In connection with the horizontal struggles for the emancipation of labour and the vertical ones that seek liberation from it, to go back to Negri's formulation quoted earlier, they might provide just the right 'transversal field of experience' (Brunner and Rhoades 2010) able to kick-start the abstract strike we are all looking forward to.

Notes

1 See the Underearners Anonymous website: http://underearnersanonymous.org [Accessed 24 July 2016].
2 Statistical data confirming this are not available, due to the anonymous nature of the organization, however ethnographic accounts of meetings in New York (Anderson 2013; Kadet 2010) and London (personal interviews with two attendees) point to these conclusions.

References

Alderman, L. (2015) In Europe, fake jobs can have real benefits. *The New York Times*. 29 May 2015. Available from: www.nytimes.com/2015/05/31/business/international/in-europe-fake-jobs-can-have-real-benefits.html?_r=0. [Accessed 24 July 2016].

Anderson, T. (2013) 12 steps to making more money: My stint at Underearners Anonymous. *Forbes*. 13 June 2013. Available from: www.forbes.com/sites/learnvest/2013/06/13/12-steps-to-making-more-money-my-stint-at-underearners-anonymous/. [Accessed 24 July 2016].

Andreß, H.-J. and Lohmann, H. (2008) *The Working Poor in Europe*. Cheltenham: Edward Elgar.

Benasayag, M. (2013) Vers une hybridation du vivant. Presentation at Ethique de la terre: arts, littérature, philosophie, environnement. Centre de Recherche LLACS. Université Paul Valéry, Montpellier. Available from: www.youtube.com/watch?v=hEP-G2vtXYk. [Accessed 24 July 2016].

Berardi, F. (2009) *The Soul at Work. From Alienation to Autonomy*. Los Angeles: Semiotext(e).

Berardi, F. (2014) *La nuova forma della protesta sociale? La disperazione*. Interview with Davide Turrini, 31 December 2014, IlFattoQuotidiano.it / Emilia Romagna. Available from: www.ilfattoquotidiano.it/2014/12/31/franco-bifo-berardi-nuova-forma-dazione-protesta-sociale-disperazione/1307634/. [Accessed 24 July 2016].

Berlant, L. (2007) Nearly utopian, nearly normal: Post-Fordist affect in *La Promesse* and *Rosetta*. *Public Culture* 19(2): 273–301.

Boggs, C. (1977) Marxism, prefigurative communism, and the problem of workers' control. *Radical America* 11(6): 99–122. Available from: http://library.brown.edu/pdfs/1125404123276662.pdf. [Accessed 24 July 2016].

Breines, W. (1980) Community and organization: The New Left and Michels' 'Iron Law'. *Social Problems* 27(4): 419–29.

Brunner, C. and Rhoades, T. (2010) Transversal fields of experience. *Inflexions.* 4. Available at: www.inflexions.org/n4_Introduction-by-Rhoades-and-Brunner.pdf. [Accessed 24 July 2016].

De Boever, A. and Neidich, W. (eds) (2013) *The Psychopathologies of Cognitive Capitalism.* Part I and II. Berlin: Archive Books.

Deleuze, G. and Guattari, F. (1987) 1837: of the Refrain. In Deleuze, G. and Guattari, F. (eds), *A Thousand Plateaus: Capitalism and Schizophrenia.* London: Athlone Press: pp. 310–50.

Delfanti, A. (2015) La Potenza e la disfatta. *Effimera. Critica e sovversioni del presente.* Available from: http://effimera.org/la-potenza-e-la-disfatta-di-alessandro-delfanti/. [Accessed 24 July 2016].

della Porta, D. and Mattoni, A. (2014) *Spreading Protest: Social Movements in Times of Crisis.* Colchester: ECPR Press.

Endnotes (2010) The History of Subsumption. *Endnotes 2, Misery and the Value Form.* Accessible from: http://endnotes.org.uk/issues/2. [Accessed 24 July 2016].

Field, N. (1996) *Breakdown and Breakthrough: Psychotherapy in a New Dimension.* New York: Routledge.

Finlay, L. (2008) Reflecting on reflective practice. Practice-based professional learning center. Paper 52. The Open University. Available from: www.open.ac.uk/opencetl/resources/pbpl-resources/finlay-l-2008-reflecting-reflective-practice-pbpl-paper-52. [Accessed 24 July 2016].

Foucault, M. (1979) *Discipline and Punish.* London: Penguin.

Foucault, M. (2009) *Security, Territory, Population: Lectures at the Collège de France 1977–1978.* Edited by Davidson, A.I. Basingstoke: Palgrave Macmillan.

Friedli, L. and Stearn, R. (2015) Positive affect as coercive strategy: Conditionality, activation and the role of psychology in UK government workfare programmes. *Medical Humanities* 41(1): 40–47.

Graeber, D. (2011) Origins of Occupy Wall Street and prefigurative politics. *Daily Kos.* 3 October 2011. Available from: www.dailykos.com/story/2011/10/04/1022528/Origins-of-Occupy-Wall-Street-and-Prefigurative-Politics# . [Accessed 24 July 2016].

Institute for Precarious Consciousness, The (2014) Anxiety, affective struggle, and precarity consciousness-raising. *Interface: A Journal for and about Social Movements* 6(2): 271–300.

Kadet, A. (2010). A program for poor-aholics. *The Wall Street Journal.* 20 November 2010. Available from: www.wsj.com/articles/SB10001424052748704170404575624641909709202. [Accessed 24 July 2016].

Kaya, A. (2014) Right to the city: Insurgent citizens of the Occupy Gezi movement. *Political Studies Association Annual Conference.* Manchester, UK, 14–16 April 2014.

Laval, C. and Dardot, P. (2015) *Del comune o della rivoluzione nel XXI secolo.* Roma: DeriveApprodi.

Lordon, F. (2014) *Willing Slaves of Capital. Spinoza and Marx on Desire.* Translated by Gabriel Ash. London and New York: Verso.

Maeckelbergh, M. (2011). Doing is believing: Prefiguration as strategic practice in the alterglobalization movement. *Social Movement Studies* 10(1): 1–20.

Martin, L.H., Gutman, H. and Hutton, P.H. (eds) (1988). *Technologies of the Self: A Seminar with Michel Foucault.* Amherst: University of Massachusetts Press.

Murray, D. (2014) Prefiguration or actualization? Radical democracy and counter-institution in the Occupy movement. *Berkeley Journal of Sociology*. November 3. Available from: http://berkeleyjournal.org/2014/11/prefiguration-or-actualization-radical-democracy-and-counter-institution-in-the-occupy-movement/. [Accessed 24 July 2016].

Negri, A. (2015) Notes on the abstract strike. *Euronomade. Inventare il commune sovvertire il presente*. Translated by Phillip Stephen Twilley. Available from: www.euronomade.info/?p=5624. [Accessed 24 July 2016].

Radical Education Forum (2013) *Radical Education Forum Clinic*. Available from: www.commonhouse.org.uk/event/radical-education-forum-clinic/. [Accessed 24 July 2016].

Ross, A. (2013) The new geography of work: Power to the precarious?. *On Curating* 16: 5–12. Available from: www.on-curating.org/files/oc/dateiverwaltung/old%20Issues/ONCURATING_Issue16.pdf. [Accessed 24 July 2016].

Rowbotham, S. (1979) The women's movement and organizing for socialism. In Rowbotham, S., Segal, L. and Wainwright, H. (eds.) *Beyond The Fragments: Feminism and the Making of Socialism*. London: Merlin Press: 21–155.

Shipler, D.K. (2008) *The Working Poor: Invisible in America*. New York: Vintage.

Simondon, G. (1989) *L'individuation psychique et collective*. Paris: Aubier.

Smith, J. (2013) Soul on strike. In De Boever, A. and Neidich, W. (eds), *The Psychopathologies of Cognitive Capitalism, Part One*. Berlin: Archive Books: 33–44.

Smucker, J. (2014) Can prefigurative politics replace political strategy? *Berkeley Journal of Sociology*. 58. Available from: http://berkeleyjournal.org/2014/10/can-prefigurative-politics-replace-political-strategy/. [Accessed 24 July 2016].

Terranova, T. (2013) Ordinary psychopathologies of cognitive capitalism. In De Boever, A. and Neidich, W. (eds), *The Psychopathologies of Cognitive Capitalism, Part One*. Berlin: Archive Books: 1–17.

Van de Sande, M. (2013) The prefigurative politics of Tahrir Square – an alternative perspective on the 2011 revolutions. *Res Publica* 19(3): 223–39.

Vercellone, C. (2008) Wages rent and profit: The new articulation of wages, rent and profit in cognitive capitalism. Translated by Arianna Bove. Available from: www.generation-online.org/c/fc_rent2.htm. [Accessed 24 July 2016].

Virno, P. (1996). The ambivalence of disenchantment. In Hardt, M. and Virno, P. (eds), *Radical thought in Italy: A potential politics*. Amherst: University of Minnesota Press: pp. 13–36.

Yates, L. (2015) Rethinking prefiguration: Alternatives, micropolitics and goals in social movements. *Social Movement Studies* 14(1): 1–21.

13 'Precariedad everywhere?!'

Rethinking precarity and emigration in Spain

Maribel Casas-Cortés and Sebastian Cobarrubias

Introduction

Due to the recent austerity crisis in the Eurozone, Spain is no longer a top receiving country in terms of international immigration. In 2006/7, Spain was recorded as the number two immigrant receiving country in the world (OECD 2014), but this unexpected record was reversed after 2008. While government officials dismiss or reframe this wave of emigration as 'opportunities abroad for our adventurous youth', social movements are pointing to precarity as both the root for 'economic exile' as well as the condition of arrival in destination countries. This chapter explores the challenges and potentials of the current politicization of Spanish emigration from the standpoint of precarity.

Over the past thirty years in Spain, *precarity* has served to articulate a series of critiques to current social transformations and make alternative forms of politicization possible. Starting as a critique of worsening job conditions, temporary contracts and unemployment, struggles over precarity became a way to understand *and* invigorate emerging sites of conflict. The context for this was a fragmented social landscape made up of knowledge workers, undocumented migrants, reproductive labourers, and open-source advocates among other actors and interrelated issues. Since the cuts in public services and rising unemployment ensuing from the recent crisis have caused large numbers of people to leave, precarity is now seen as a sort of 'push factor' for emigration, but it could also be understood as a potential common ground between local precarious youths leaving Spain and other mobile or migrant populations from EU and non-EU countries. Three basic questions guide our reflections in this chapter: what are the dynamics, struggles and challenges of Spanish emigrant mobilizing; what uses and contributions are they making to the concept of precarity as a political tool; and as a result, how do emigrant movements articulate the connections between precarity and mobility?

Recent European movements have addressed the intersections of precarity and migration. For instance, '*Precarious and Migrants Unite*' was a provocative slogan used to evoke the growing commonalities between local precarious youth and non-EU migrants to Spain and the EU. Overtime, this call for a symmetrical alliance – one based not on compassion from an affluent European citizen towards an undocumented foreigner, but on an understanding of shared precarious conditions – came to be known among activist collectives as the 'prec-mig hypothesis' (*Chainworkers* in Oudenampsen and Sullivan 2004; *Frassanito* 2006; *Observatorio Tecnológico del Estrecho* 2006; *Asamblea Ninguna Persona es Ilegal* 2006). In the meantime, scholars pointed out how migration regimes are indeed producers of domestic labour policies leading to a further precarization of migrants through instruments such as visas (Mezzadra 2011; Papadopoulos *et al.* 2008; Anderson 2010; De Genova and Peutz 2010; Avila 2012; Schierup *et al.* 2015).

In what follows we first outline the 'prec-mig hypothesis' and how the themes of precarity and immigration intertwined before the 2008 crisis. Then, we contextualize the recent coordination and struggles of emigrant collectives in the movement against austerity in Spain, paying special attention to their work on defining emigration as a result of precarity, and on considering recent emigration as a form of economic migration. Finally, we ask how incipient experiments are being developed that articulate immigration, emigration and precarity in social movements?

To analyse these events, we discuss how social movements are pointing to precarity as a common ground that may overcome the limits and the divisive effects of 'citizenship' (both as a legal category and a lived identity). We look at scholarly contributions such as Bridget Anderson's use of 'precarity' to overcome the 'migrant' vs. 'citizen' divide (2013; 2010), Standing's use of 'denizenship' (2014; 2011) or Mezzadra and Neilson's idea of 'differential inclusion' (2013) as ways of making precarity a common ground to move forward. We conclude with remarks on how further political and research work might encourage the intersections of mobility and precarity.

Prec-Mig: precarious and migrants. A common struggle?

The prec-mig hypothesis posited that 'working conditions suffered by migrants today (such as informality of contracts, vulnerability in the workplace, intense links between territory and employment, low salaries, lack of union rights, temporality, demand of total availability, etc.) are spreading to the rest of the population, including natives from the EU' (Toret and Sguiglia 2006: 108). These shared conditions could be the basis for a horizontal struggle that creates connections between precarious local youth and non-EU migrants (Paratcha 2009). For instance, the *EuroMayDay* mobilizations against precarity across the EU[1] began to include a strong migrants' contingent. In Spain, the *Offices of Social Rights*, which evolved out of precarity movements, had explicit goals of mingling the two populations, starting Spanish lessons for new speakers, establishing lawyers' consultancies for temp workers and migrants as well as campaigns on informal employment and domestic work (Arribas Lozano 2012).

While the prec-mig argument was appealing, the efforts to work on joint demands to benefit both locals and migrants have been considered by some to be 'a failure' (Arribas Lozano, 2011 email communication). While activists recognized the asymmetries between the two groups, these were difficult to overcome, and in some cases were reproduced in movements with certain post-colonial resonances and possibly racialized overtones. The solidarity organizing in support of non-EU migrants was particularly burgeoning when international migration in Spain was high, mainly during the economic 'boom' of the late 1990s and early 2000s. Taking the prec-mig call to its conclusion as a transversal space for organizing could seem unrealistic in practice. There was a necessary but also divisive focus on working *for* migrants without papers. This left the local precarious youth on another (privileged) plane, without articulating in first person how exactly these 'precarities' intersected. While the goal was a horizontal platform that would include a multitude of precarious experiences, the reality of fighting practices such as deportation and detention could make the ambition for a common struggle sound unrealistic.[2] As a member of the *Red de Apoyo a Sin Papeles* (an Office of Social Rights in Zaragoza that the authors were part of) expressed:

> While we're working on all this really important stuff: like documents for undocumented members of the collective; police brutality; getting people out of detention; or even just orienting people in a place with different language, culture and way of doing politics… I feel like I can't even focus on my precarity, it's not like my situation is stable and I feel in creating this joint space/mestizo alliance we're also creating dependencies … the 'chicos' [a term used to refer to undocumented members of the collective] look to us to help solve their problems, and this means even less time on working on things that affect us all.

This difficulty identified by movements in their practice is prescient of observations made by Anderson in her work *Us & Them*:

> Considering immigration and employment regimes in parallel, one cannot help but be struck by the extent to which they seem to be moving in opposite directions. Migration is increasingly onerously regulated and overseen at the same time as employment is de-regulated. […] Immigration is to be excessively regulated but working conditions, not.
>
> (Anderson 2013: 79)

Anderson explains how this seemingly opposite movement of migration and labour policy are both simultaneously producing precarity. Yet, these joint mechanisms of 'precarity-production' as a shared condition operate through enforcing what Anderson refers to as the 'community of value' and the perceived 'Good Citizen' (2013). Thus the line between 'Migrant' and 'Citizen', via processes such as nationality, visas, legality, becomes more distinct even as precarity increases on both fronts.[3]

Precarities on the move?

With the current reversal of migration flows in and out of Spain, with more people emigrating per year than immigrating (Izquierdo *et al.* 2015; INE 2014; Banco de Espana 2014), could a revisiting of the prec-mig hypothesis that social movements posed more than ten years ago prove fruitful in understanding and shaping different political alliances and proposals? Could these multiple precarities *on the move* destabilize the idea of a 'native' 'national' precarious youth and an 'extra-communitarian' as two easily distinguished blocks? Can this bridging of mobile precarities occur in the midst of the levels of discrimination experienced in receiving EU countries by differently labelled mobile populations (i.e. 'Southern Europeans', 'Africans', 'refugees', etc.)?

Made in Spain: precarization of labour and migration

The number of unemployed and/or on temporary contracts has risen to alarming numbers in recent years.[4] According to a *New York Times* August 2015 article on the Spanish 'recovery', 'a new figure has emerged in Spain: the employed person who is below the poverty threshold' (Daley 2015). Debates on the 'working poor' have entered the Spanish mainstream media; but despite the role of the crisis, these numbers result from a long trajectory of unemployment and temporary work, involving youth, in the 'black box' of the Spanish labour market.[5]

The context of unemployment had spurred various forms of collective action since the late 1980s: first the move towards labour flexibilization and austerity measures was critically named 'precariedad'; then, the ambivalent identity of a 'precarious generation' was embraced (Alba Rico 1992). Sector-based struggles over contracts, initially led by traditional unions, circulated to influence a series of discussions among disparate sets of actors in social movements. The notion of 'precarity' was useful to question and politicize transformations in the knowledge economy, the emergence of a workfare regime, the growing recognition of the importance of the care economy and, as a question related to all of the above, migration. The experience of precarity and its reconceptualization beyond labour reforms *strictu sensu* was exacerbated and encouraged by increasing cuts on welfare state provisions and intensified by the growth of undocumented migration (Martinez Veiga 1999, 2006).

During Spain's recent property boom, in 2001, just as immigration was at its peak,[6] there were intense mobilizations by migrants to demand rights, documentation and the repeal of the new Organic Law on the Rights and Freedoms of Foreigners in Spain and their Social Integration signed in 2000. Marches, hunger strikes and occupations of sympathetic parishes occurred over many days and became a top news item (Suarez-Naval *et al.* 2007). The 'migrant' had entered the landscape of the Spanish state as a political actor. These immigrants' self-organized efforts became increasingly interesting to social movements, especially to those working on precarity. Solidarity with the figure of the 'irregular' migrant focused on issues such as migrant-detention centres and the increasingly securitized southern border (there were many initiatives, i.e. *Caravana a la Valla*, *Ferrocarril Clandestino*, and *Red de Sin Papeles*).

Gradually, common points of struggle between 'migrants' and 'locals' and new organizing experiments emerged. The efforts at politicizing migration were many, the most productive being actions such as *EuroMayDay*[7] and campaigns such as 'Cities without Borders'.[8] These experiences aimed at creating non-hierarchical forms of solidarity and spaces where 'immigrants' and 'locals' could find common grounds and organize together, each against his or her own precarity. As such, those efforts led to different analyses and formulations of the precarity + migration equation, trying to articulate a common form and understanding of struggles that did not ignore important hierarchies and privileges. This developed a rich political lexicon among activists that established a tighter link between precarity and mobility (Casas-Cortés, forthcoming).

The eruption of indignation: #Occupy in Spain

Before the social unrest of 2011, there had been numerous protests against the loss of labour rights, which organized experiences of disparate issues through the prism of precarity (such as housing, health, education, knowledge economy, and migration). The financial crisis, bank bailouts and high unemployment rates engendered a generalized sense of discontent, particularly among young people.[9] The younger generation, with their parents having fought Franco's dictatorship, many organizing autonomous struggles during the Transition period,[10] felt deeply defrauded by the 'new democratic regime'. On the eve of the Spanish general elections on 15 May 2011, people organized through social media and swarmed the main streets. The media named them 'Indignados', and their main organizing platforms were Democracia Real Ya (Real Democracy Now) and Juventud Sin Futuro (Futureless Youth).

The 15M movement started with this gesture: an unexpected number of people overflowing public spaces and *camping* for extended periods of time (going from hours of open microphone assemblies to weeks of elaborate encampments as cities in miniatures) (Corsín and Estalella 2011). The revolts of the Arab Spring which started in January 2011, especially the encampment in Tahir Square in Egypt, were an immediate source of inspiration for the 15M movement. In turn the 15M movement was an inspiration for others, such as Occupy Wall Street in the USA and Syntagma Square in Greece (Sitrin and Azzellini 2014).

By 2012 the political energy had spread, and while there were no longer visible camps, new waves of mobilization grew, focusing on cuts to public services. Public sector employees joined service recipients to protest against cuts: they formed the '*mareas*' (tides or waves), pushing for access to decent public services and fighting austerity measures.

The precarious generation abroad: the contested politics of emigration

A growing and unexpected emigration was particularly notable by 2011 (Banco de Espana 2014), which was also the peak of anti-crisis social movements in Spain. The politicization of Spanish emigration occurred in this context: some of the earliest nodes of emigrant activism consisted of Spaniards abroad who had been organizing as international nodes of the 15M or the Juventud sin Futuro collective. Shortly thereafter an emigrant *marea/tide* was created:

> The *Maroon Wave* is a transnational movement of Spanish immigrants who fight from abroad against the causes that originated the economic and social crisis that forced us to flee our country; [...] born in the light of other recent social movements [...] maroon like the *colour of our passports*, the symbol of our forced migration.[11]

Campaigns on emigrants' rights raised the issues of voting from abroad, access to the Spanish healthcare system, and labour rights. The campaigns of *Marea Granate* tactically focused on demanding that the precarious situation that many members feel 'pushed' them to emigrate and the loss of 'rights' they experienced as 'immigrants' did not result in a loss of rights back in Spain. For instance, with the campaign *voto rogado/voto robado* (begged vote/stolen vote), emigrants' collectives demanded a reform to the old system of absentee ballots based on stable emigrant communities with easy access to consulates and embassies. The *Marea* argued for a more fluid system of voting from abroad adapted to the newer generations of emigrants who often cannot pay to travel and register in official consular offices.

Another example is the *Vuelve sin Sanidad* ('return without healthcare') campaign. As part of the austerity measures of the Spanish government, a law was passed in 2012 that stipulated the loss of regular access to Spanish health care for people who had left the country for extended periods (90 days in a 12-month period under current legislation). Emigrant organizations fought this measure, pointing out that many emigrants have limited access to the healthcare of their countries of destination, and that even emigrants to other EU countries are prevented from accessing the European Health Card due to the temporary nature of the employment they find. Thus return visits to Spain are often used for medical consultations. For this campaign, the *Marea Granate* joined the *Yo si Sanidad universal* campaign that struggles not only against cuts to healthcare but specifically against the exclusion of immigrants from it (especially 'undocumented') in Spain. Thus a specific and explicit organizational link was made between immigrants' and emigrants' access to healthcare:

> Marea Granate Sanidad began with the goal to demand and struggle for the rights of all people to public, universal and free at moment of use healthcare, making no distinction based upon place of birth, skin colour or maternal

> language, always placing people's welfare before economic interests. (*Grupo de Trabajo Sanidad, Marea Granate*[12])

Given the dispersed nature of the collective across many countries of destination and their different geopolitical relations to Spain (for example, EU, Morocco, Latin American countries, etc.), most of the coordination work takes place via Mumble, email, text messaging platforms and social media. Actions often consist of demonstrations at consulates and embassies and online, and media advocacy and meetings with or demands made to particular institutions (the European Parliament and political parties such as *Podemos*, for instance). Cities with larger groups often engage in labour organizing of emigrants in local contexts as well as coordination with other local social movements (such as the *Oficinas de Derechos Sociales* discussed later).[13]

In addition to specific campaigns on issues affecting emigrants, one of the central ongoing goals has been making emigration visible as a political question.[14] This is particularly challenging, since emigration was thought to be a ghost of Spain's 'past'.[15]

Politicizing emigration: the cultural battle over 'adventurers' or 'economic exiles'

As the numbers of emigrants grew, government authorities either ignored or underestimated the phenomenon as the 'adventurous spirit of the Spanish youth' (Europa Press 2012). The Minister of Employment renamed emigration as 'external mobility' (*El País* 2013*)*, and the President of the Supreme Council of Scientific Research in Spain defined concerns about a brain drain from Spain as an 'exaggerated urban legend' (*El País* 2014).

A form of competition emerges in the debates around emigration. This has been one of the primary terrains of struggle for the nascent emigrant movement. On the one hand, official declarations from politicians and public officers relate the phenomenon of emigration to that of an 'adventure or experience abroad', akin to the idea of studying abroad, a sort of luxury and investment in the future. On the other hand, this emigration is politicized as being, rather than a trip to improve one's foreign language skills, a response to questions of unemployment, underemployment, and consistent precarious employment. The latter position has found expression in social media campaigns (*Yo tambien soy leyenda urbana*),[16] documentaries (*En Tierra Extraña* 2014), [17] and films (*Perdiendo el Norte* 2015). Graphics by the *Marea Granate* also explicitly relate current emigration to historic emigration patterns. 'Moving' abroad is not framed as a celebration of modern Spain, but as a return to the past social and economic exclusion experienced by the grandparents of many of these activists.

'I am also an economic migrant': campaigns, icons and slogans

Juventud sin Futuro (JSF), one of the collectives that formed part of the initial Spanish 15M/Occupy movements, is particularly active in connecting questions of precarity and migration. The collective explains how current unemployment rates in Spain, low salaries, and the rise of 'mini-jobs' are causing an unprecedented number of youth to leave the country and frames the situation as 'labour exile', which also informs the main slogan: '*No nos vamos, nos echan*' (We are not leaving, they are kicking us out).

The campaign website states: '*#NoNosVamosNosEchan* is an initiative that denounces the situation of forced exile of precarious youth' making an explicit link between *exile* as forced migration and the language of precarity. A map of emigrants that have joined the campaign greets the website visitor with the title 'precarity, precarity everywhere!'. The website emphasizes that many emigrants are encountering precarious conditions in their countries of destination.

The colour maroon and luggage image were used in mobilization: 'la maleta' was brought into public spaces, to name meetings and actions, calling attention to the status of emigrants abroad as involuntary travellers.[18]

Also, graphics hacking airport imagery started to become visible in public spaces, both in Spain and abroad, where emigrant collectives were located, calling for specific days of actions and organizing meetings. The acronym JSF is used to parody the international airport of JFK, playing with imagery and paraphernalia of flights and major airports as icons of the growing emigration of youth with no jobs or hopping between short-term contracts.

Emigrants, immigrants, emigrant immigrants

Thus far, the political mobilization has focused on the movement abroad of primarily Spanish-born, Spanish citizens of Spanish decent. For example, a self-description of the *Marea Granate* reads:

> This organization struggles beyond borders against the causes that provoked the crisis to obtain a better future, especially for young Spaniards [...] [We want to] identify Spanish emigrants and form an organization that can maintain their contact with Spanish society and politics.

In this sense the emigration of recent immigrants into Spain, including those who may have obtained Spanish citizenship for themselves or their offspring, is not part of this discourse, despite the fact that at least in recent years, especially between 2008 and 2010, the largest number of emigrants from Spain was either recent immigrants or naturalized Spaniards (Banco de Espana 2014). This may be because building bridges takes time in social movements or also because there already are support networks for migrants who are 'returning'. However, it also points to a certain 'methodological nationalism' of emigrants' movements in Spain and elsewhere.[19]

Precarious offices

Towards the end of the last decade, several organizations working on precarity in Spain began to form *Oficinas de Derechos Sociales* [Offices of social rights]. These offered support for legal and direct action in particular cases (individual or collective) of people dealing with precarious conditions.[20] Inspired by this experience, *Oficinas Precarias* began popping up in other countries against precarious conditions abroad, where Spanish emigrants have recently arrived and were beginning to organize themselves. Assisting newly arrived emigrants in understanding labour legislation and access to services, there are currently *Oficinas Precarias* in London, Paris, Berlin, Prague and Vienna. In an explicit way, this organization is making a direct link between emigrant mobilizing and movements working on precarity prior to the recent emigration wave.

While primarily conceived to address recent Spanish emigrants, at least in the cases of the Berlin and Vienna offices, there is an explicit openness to migrants from other countries.[21] This need to address migration as a whole often comes from the very need to address increased racism and attempts to exclude migrants. In the case of the EU, currently talks are taking place on how to exclude not only non-EU migrants but also EU migrants from social programmes and benefits, in effect lumping all and every kind of migrant into one bag of 'threats'.[22]

Spaces of emigration, spaces of new identity?

The mobility expressed by the rise of emigration from Spain needs to be understood politically. Two trends in particular point to questions that need to be researched, but can serve as an initial contextualization of the struggle for the purpose of this chapter, so we will only mention them here. The first is the emergence of an understanding of hierarchies of mobility in Europe. Much emigration from Spain, particularly of Spanish youth, has been directed towards other European countries (EU and EFTA members). This has given rise to new debates about free movement within Europe, about a Western European identity of 'prosperity', and about the existence of hierarchies, centres and peripheries within the Union or the continent.[23] As countries such as Germany, Belgium, the United Kingdom and Switzerland consider putting limits to the entry or possibilities of residence of Southern and Eastern European Union citizens, in Spain people have begun to question what 'being European' means.

The second is a new dynamic between North and South at the global level. It is generally assumed that the majority of emigration to countries of the Global South involves immigrants who return to their countries of origin, and that Spanish nationals tend to migrate to other countries of the EU or North America. Spanish emigration not only involves other EU or OECD countries but also countries of the Global South, including those that have been Spanish colonies and traditionally sent migrants to Spain (Izquierdo *et al.* 2015).[24]

These new flows of Spanish citizens to the Global South require a renegotiation of presumed identities (post-colonial, developed, European). The current migration is not that of development professionals or tourists, but of people seeking employment in the destination country and sometimes moving there with a family. Groups of emigrants' coordination, like *Marea Granate* have formed in Uruguay, Peru, Central America and elsewhere.[25]

Towards a post-national freedom of movement?

Our appraisal of the current politics of emigration in relation to precarity has been two-fold: on the one hand, we identified the difficulty of turning Spanish emigration into a political issue when media and movements themselves have previously framed and politicized immigration to the EU through the image of the asylum seeker or the economic migrant from the Global South, going through the perils of crossing the Mediterranean or the Eurotunnel in Calais. The focus on the 'poor migrant' with racial underpinnings as a stereotyped *other* eschews the rethinking of European citizens having to move, not as tourists, students abroad or *expats*, but as precarious migrants themselves.

On the other hand, we suggest that when emigration is gradually being thought of and experienced through the gaze of precarity, mobility becomes a common ground. We signal how this common ground has the potential to act as a bridge to soften the divide between national and foreigner, bringing together the struggles of nationals (whether staying or leaving) and migrants (both in Spain and abroad). If precarity becomes the common ground, the demands of the current Spanish emigration movement may start loosening their current nation-state focus to amplify its vision and strategies in the pursuit of the broader demand for Freedom of Movement.

Existing and emergent intersections between emigrant and immigrant mobilizing may be pushed through a 'de-nationalized' struggle around precarity, understanding the legal category of nationality as an instrument of precarization upon which a set of social rights can be denied. Anderson's use of the concept of precarity in her work on migration controls points us in this direction (2013). Precarity is a way of moving beyond the framing of the 'national labour market' as a unitary space where the fundamental divide is between those who have a right to work (citizens) and those who do not (immigrants) (Anderson 2013: 71). In particular, Anderson shows how precarity as a concept pays attention to temporalities and vulnerabilities in employment and beyond, that while particularly acute among immigrant groups are not limited to nor mainly 'about' immigrants as such. The de-regulation of working conditions combines with an increasing over-regulation of migration to produce forms of precarity defined by a migrant's relationship to citizenship and rights of residence: 'Precariousness [...] facilitates an analysis that is more sensitive to the temporalities of labour markets and of immigration and migratory processes and how these interact' (Anderson 2013: 81). Anderson's observations help us focus on how migratory processes, immigration policy and labour market dynamics intersect in multiple ways to produce precarity.

Guy Standing's work on the notion of 'denizens' (2011, 2014) is yet another way to de-nationalize the emigrant movement while remaining sensitive to the hierarchies created via the instruments of nationality and citizenship. *Denizenship* is not a strict category but rather a 'layered system' (Standing 2011: 94) where one can witness a spectrum of different legal and subjective positions with varying degrees of access to different kinds of 'rights' granted by the sovereign. Among the many differences in types, 'a defining feature of all denizens is absence of rights' (Standing 2011: 158). A campaign such as *Yo si sanidad universal*, with explicit reference made to how both immigrants in an irregular situation and emigrants are singled out for their rights to healthcare in Spain to be curtailed signals how denizen status is being produced for those in precarious situations irrespective of their relationship to legal citizenship.

We can find further inspiration in Sandro Mezzadra and Brett Neilson's use of the notion of 'differential inclusion' as a way of examining how the dynamics of emigration, immigration, and the contexts of cutbacks (producing precarity by means of multiple types of 'border') are creating highly stratified and shifting forms of 'inclusion' (into countries, labour markets, etc.).

> The concept of differential inclusion attempts to come to grips with the undoing of the unitary figure of the citizen and the corresponding production of multiple conditions of 'partial citizenship' or denizenship. Migration [we would add emigration or immigration] is a crucial site of investigation from this point of view.
>
> (Mezzadra and Neilson 2013: 251)

El Devenir migrante del trabajo; el devenir (e)migrante del precario?[26]

The precarious conditions of work and life that have worsened since 2008, while affecting many sectors, were particularly harsh on migrants (Schierup *et al.* 2015). Youth employment also becomes increasingly precarious and in a sense reflects what some activists termed 'the becoming 'migrant' of work' (Toret and Sguglia 2006). This phrase captures the process whereby the mobile, intermittent and uncertain conditions faced by migrants spread to involve all labourers. When the crisis hit, migrants suffered unemployment the most, more than the overall unemployment rate for nationals. But when this is compared to youth unemployment, and those national citizens who were entering labour markets for the first time during the boom, we see there are very comparable rates of unemployment, sub-employment, and poor quality jobs between migrants and youth (or new workers). While this pairing in no way flattens the hierarchies between national youth and migrant labourers in terms of racialized policing, the exclusion based on visa categories, etc. it does provide a space where the national/foreigner divide can be rethought through the experience of precarity. In the same way that many of recent immigrants to Spain had to emigrate again due to economic conditions, we also see an uptake of emigration among the young, and one that has continued to rise.

We feel that bridging the emigrant/immigrant divide and building joint demands or campaigns will be essential to building an anti-racist politics of precarity and mobility. What would it mean to think through a de-nationalized set of rights, coming from the emigrant mobilizing as a kind of bridge between precarious (non-EU) migrants and precarious nationals (especially youth)? In what ways can, and are, the campaigns of the *Marea Granate* and other collectives – for reclaiming political and voting rights; for opening access to the healthcare systems; and for demanding a right to return to their home of choosing – thought of and demanded as rights for both mobile Spaniards and mobile non-EU citizens?[27] How can an expansion of these demands beyond legal citizens also lead to a way to short-circuit attempts to segment the population and the workforce through citizenship and racialization? Both pro-migrant rights movements and precarity struggles would gain a solid reconceptualization of the initial cry of: *Migrants and Precarious of the World, Unite!* By embodying the prec-mig hypothesis, these struggles around emigration are pointing to the fragile link between precariousness and citizenship. This realization might contribute powerfully to a necessary post-nationalized practice of political demands for Freedom of Movement.

Notes

1 From 2000 on, every May 1st, International Workers Day, precarity pride parades go viral and are celebrated across European cities under the name of *EuroMaydays*: 'EuroMayDay is a political day of action against precarity promoted by a network of feminist, anti-capitalist and migrant groups and collectives in mostly Western Europe. It takes place on the 1st of May each year, May Day, traditionally a celebration of solidarity among workers across the world. EuroMayDay has been promoted as an attempt to 'update' the traditional May Day by focusing on flex and temp workers, migrants and other 'precarious' people living in Europe. In 2005, the EuroMayDay network used the slogan Precarious people of the world let's unite and strike 4 a free, open, radical Europe.' http://maps.thefullwiki.org/EuroMayDay.

2 'Even seemingly simple issues like attending joint meetings could be problematic if immigrant attendees feared profiling in the neighbourhoods or times of the meeting' (Arribas Lozano 2012: 205).

3 Or even as the status of citizen is reduced to one of *denizenship* (Standing 2014). See also, for how precarity movements were articulating this reduction in rights for citizens in the early 2000s, Toret and Sguglia (2006).

4 As of July 2015 the unemployment rate was at 22 per cent, where it has approximately been for the past several years (INE 2015). Youth unemployment is currently about 53 per cent (EUROSTAT 2015). Temporary employment is at 25 per cent of the workforce (INE 2015). By point of comparison, the unemployment rate (harmonized, as a percentage of the total labour force) went from 7–8 per cent in 2007 to 26 per cent in 2013. In the same period, youth unemployment went from 19 per cent to 56 per cent (OECD 2015; Cobarrubias 2009).

5 As an example, by 2008 (during a historic economic boom and just before the crisis hit employment), Spain had become the country with the highest rates of temporary workers (around 30 per cent of the total workforce) of all 27-member states of the EU (Massarelli 2009).

6 This increase in migration is notable to the point that in the years 2006 and 2007, Spain ranked second, only after the US, in absolute number of migrants entering any country (OECD 2014).

7 On the Pan-European day of action *EuroMayDay* during May 1st since 2001, see Fernandez de Rota (2011).
8 On the campaign Cities without Borders, see www.museoreinasofia.es/fundacion-comunes/ciudades-sin-fronteras and www.trayectos.org/en/node/28
9 This mood of frustration is illustrated by a collective that formed just prior to the recent wave of mobilization called *Juventud Sin Futuro* (Youth without Future) whose slogan is: *Sin Curro, Sin Casa, Sin Pension... !Sin Miedo!* (Those without No Job, No House, No Retirement,...No Fear!) . Coincidentally, the recurrent use of 'SIN' (meaning without) is the same preposition as the one used by the first wave of undocumented migrants organizing in France in the 90s, the 'Sans Papiers' ('sin papeles' or 'those without papers'). This explicit use and reclaiming of 'not having' as an identity is used both by precarious extra-communitarian migrants and precarious Spanish youth.
10 Organized around the 'grandparents' identity (*yayo* in Spanish or *iaio* in Catalan). There are multiple associations of elderly activists involved in the occupy mobilizations: http://yayoflautasmadrid.org/ and www.iaioflautas.org/
11 http://mareagranate.org/?page_id=249
12 http://mareagranate.org/author/marea-granate-sanidad/
13 An interesting example of this is 15MGAS-Grupo de Accion Sindical (Group of Union Action). This group has developed relations with the Verdi union in Germany but focuses specifically on organizing and reaching out to recent Spanish emigrants in Germany and the work-related organizing needs (see www.accionsindical.org/).
14 Including networks such as *Marea Granate*, the *No nos vamos nos echan* mobilizations (we don't leave, they kick us out), and sector-based campaigns such as *yo también soy leyenda urbana* (I'm also an urban legend), and different local associations in Spain or countries of emigrant destination.
15 'Spain was an emigration country throughout most of the 20th century' (Izquierdo *et al.* 2015: 11). Until the 1960s the primary destination of these migrations was South America. In 1956, toward the middle of the dictatorship period, emigration began to be officially managed by the *National Institute of Emigration*, through which work contracts were negotiated in North Western European countries and emigrants became a source of official revenue for the national economy (Ochaita 2004). A large number of these seasonal emigrants were labourers from poorer rural areas working in French or West German industry. Flows out of Spain picked up pace in this period and were refocused towards the countries of the European Economic Community. While ideological disagreement with the Franco regime was one reason for emigration, political exile was aggravated by the post-civil war economic scarcity. The global economic crisis of the 1970s (starting with the 1973 oil crisis) coupled with the beginnings of the democratic transition led to many Spanish workers returning or being returned to Spain (La Caixa 2006). Yet Spain continued to be primarily an emigration country until the end of the 1980s.
16 International campaign collecting testimonies from emigrant Spanish researchers called 'I am also an urban legend' playing with the same words used by the Director of the National Scientific Research Council (CSIC) in reference to brain drain: www.aacte.eu/wp/blog/2014/12/08/leyendas-urbanas/
17 In a Foreign Land/En Tierra Extrana (Olías 2015) www.hollywoodreporter.com/review/a-foreign-land-en-tierra-736112
18 See http://mareagranate.org/en/
19 It should be noted that there are often clear messages of solidarity from emigrant organizations for migrant rights in Spain, and emigrant organizing of Spanish youth abroad has indeed included a focus on other migrants as well. This is a work in progress though, and both research and political work might benefit from paying close attention to how this develops.
20 See Arribas Lozano (2012) on *Oficinas de Derechos Sociales.*

21 The Precarity Office of Vienna has organized a series of events where attendees were asked to self-identify as 'Mobile' vs. 'Migrant' in order to work through these institutional and everyday-life categories. While opening an understanding of intra-EU immigration alongside immigration from outside the EU, the goal is to emphasize a shared condition – both of precarity and mobility. While acknowledging differences and hierarchies of rights and legal status, these experiments are focusing on what these struggles can mutually learn (see https://precarityoffice.wordpress.com/)

22 Example of these calls include: Germany www.eldiario.es/internacional/Alemania-planea-prohibir-parados-permanecer_0_242876298.html; or Belgium www.rtve.es/alacarta/videos/telediario/llevamos-ano-gobierno-belga-expulsado-300-espanoles-del-pais/2397485/. Also, recent debates on 'Brexit' highlight fears around the immigration of 'EU nationals'.

23 Even Pablo Iglesias, co-founder of the Podemos party, has phrased this provocatively as 'We don't want to be a colony of the North [of Europe]': www.lasexta.com/programas/sexta-noche/entrevistas/pablo-iglesias-candidato-podemos-espanoles-queremos-ser-colonia-norte_2014050400002.html

24 For this recent information we draw mainly on media reports, which point to migratory flows flipping directions. In the cases of Ecuador and Morocco, more people per year are leaving from Spain to these countries, reversing the trend of the past two decades: (http://economia.elpais.com/economia/2013/09/27/empleo/1380283340_251157.html; www.americaeconomia.com/politica-sociedad/mundo/ecuador-lidera-inmigracion-espanola-en-sudamerica-por-crisis-de-la-zona-euro).

25 See http://mareagranate.org/?cat=148

26 'The becoming-migrant of work; the becoming-migrant of the precarious.'

27 This could be translated into concrete practices by reframing some existing campaigns. For example, recently calls have come out to articulate a 'Derecho a Volver' (a right to return) for Spanish emigrants (http://mareagranate.org/2015/04/marea-granate-reivindicaciones-parlamento-europeo/). This understanding of a right to return could be expanded to include those recent immigrants that have had to leave Spain due to the crisis or even due to deportation. In this way, the current mobilizing on emigration could be linked to a common demand in the immigrant rights movement. This linking has incipiently emerged with campaigns around access to healthcare for immigrants and emigrants.

References

Alba Rico, S. (1992) *Viva el mal! Viva el capital!*. Barcelona: Virus Ed.

Anderson, B. (2010) Migration immigration controls and the fashioning of precarious workers. *Work, Employment & Society* 24(2): 300–317.

Anderson, B. (2013) *Us and Them: The Dangerous Politics of Immigration Control.* Oxford: Oxford University Press.

Arribas Lozano, A. (2012) Sobre la precariedad y sus fugas. La experiencia de las Oficinas de Derechos Sociales (ODSs). *Interface: A Journal for and about Social Movements* 4(2): 197–229.

Asamblea Ninguna Persona es Ilegal (2006) *Guia por la Libertad de Movimiento.* Madrid: El Ferrocarril Clandestino Ed.

Avila Cantos, D. (2012) *El Gobierno de La Diferencia: De Las Logicas de Gestion de Lo Social.* Doctoral Thesis. Facultad de Ciencias Politicas y Sociologia, Departamento de Antropologia Social, Universidad Complutense de Madrid. Available from: http://eprints.ucm.es/16373/1/T33918.pdf. [Accessed 2 August 2016].

Banco de Espana (2014) *Boletin Economico.* September. Madrid: Banco de Espana.

Casas-Cortés, M. (forthcoming) Precarity on the move?: The contested politics of immigration and emigration in Spain. *Interface Journal.*

Cobarrubias, S. (2009) *Mapping Machines: Activist Cartographies of the Border and Labor Lands of Europe*. PhD Dissertation. Department of Geography, University of North Carolina at Chapel Hill.

Corsín, J.A. and Estalella, A. (2011) #spanishrevolution. *Anthropology Today* 27(4): 19–23.

Daley, S. (2015) *For Many in Spain, a Heralded Economic Recovery Feels Like a Bust.* New York Times, 10 August. Available from: www.nytimes.com/2015/08/11/world/europe/for-many-in-spain-a-heralded-economic-recovery-feels-like-a-bust.html. [Accessed 2 August 2016].

De Genova, N. and Peutz, N.M. (2010) *The Deportation Regime: Sovereignty, Space, and the Freedom of Movement.* Durham, NC: Duke University Press.

EL PAÍS (2013) *Báñez Llama 'movilidad Exterior' a La Fuga Masiva de Jóvenes Del País.* Available from: http://economia.elpais.com/economia/2013/04/17/actualidad/1366187892_058898.html. [Accessed 2 August 2016].

EL PAÍS (2014) *Los Científicos Exiliados Claman Que No Son 'una Leyenda Urbana'.* Available from: http://elpais.com/elpais/2014/12/16/ciencia/1418757917_801968.html. [Accessed 2 August 2016].

Europa Press (2012) *El Gobierno cree que la emigración de jóvenes no se debe sólo a la crisis sino también a un 'impulso aventurero'.* Available from: www.europapress.es/epsocial/inmigracion-00329/noticia-gobierno-cree-emigracion-jovenes-no-debe-solo-crisis-tambien-impulso-aventurero-20121129190823.html. [Accessed 2 August 2016].

EUROSTAT (2015) Unemployment Rate by gender and age, 2007–2014. Available from: http://ec.europa.eu/eurostat/statistics-explained/index.php/File:Table_3_Unemployment_rate_by_gender_and_age,_2007-2014_%28%25%29.png. [Accessed 2 August 2016].

Fernandez de Rota, A. (2011) Un simbolo en disputa: Las politicas de la reinvencion y la reactualizacion precaria. *Tiempo de Espera en la Fronteras del Mercado Laboral: Nuevos Agentes Sociales en el Espacio Social.* Conferencia Nacional de Antropologia de Espana. San Sebastian.

Frassanito Network (2006) Precarious, precarisation, precariat?, *Mute Magazine* 2. Available from: www.metamute.org/editorial/articles/precarious-precarisation-precariat. [Accessed 2 August 2016].

INE (2014) *Notas de Prensa: Cifras de poblacion a 1 de Julio 2014.* Available from: www.ine.es/prensa/np917.pdf. [Accessed 2 August 2016].

INE (2015) *Notas de Prensa: Encuesta de Poblacion Activa Segundo Trimestre de 2015.* Available from: www.ine.es/daco/daco42/daco4211/epa0215.pdf. [Accessed 2 August 2016].

Izquierdo, M., Jimeno, J.F. and Lacuesta, A. (2015) Spain: From Immigration to Emigration? *Working Paper* 1503. Madrid: Banco de Espana.

La Caixa-Serveis d'Estudis (2006) La immigració esperona el creixement de l'economia espanola. *Informe Mensual* 288, February.

Martinez Veiga, U. (1999) Immigrants in the Spanish Labour Market. In Edwards, B. and Arango, J. (eds), *Immigrants and the Informal Economy in Southern Europe.* London: Frank Cass, pp. 105–28.

Martinez Veiga, U. (2006) Absolute poverty of illegal immigrants in Spain: A growing problem. In Petmesidou, M. and Papatheodorou, C. (eds), *Poverty and Social Deprivation in the Mediterranean Area: Trends, Policies and Welfare Prospects in the New Millennium.* Chicago: Zed Books, pp. 142–65.

Massarelli, N. (2009) Labour market latest trends. *EUROSTAT: Data in Focus*. Available from: http://ec.europa.eu/eurostat/documents/4168041/5944193/KS-QA-09-003-EN.PDF/774b3aea-cba5-4dc4-b252-b80e2c0eec11. [Accessed 2 August 2016].

Mezzadra, S. (2011) The gaze of autonomy: Capitalism, migration and social struggles. In Squire, V. (ed.). *The Contested Politics of Mobility: Borderzones and Irregularity*. London: Routledge.

Mezzadra, S. and Neilson, B. (2013) *Border as Method, Or, the Multiplication of Labor*. Durham: Duke University Press.

Observatorio Tecnológico del Estrecho (2006) Freedom of Movement - Freedom of Knowledge. Available from: http://straddle3.net/media/print/0609_fadaiat_book_txt.pdf [Accessed 2 August 2016].

Ochaita, J.O. (2004) Emigrantes-Inmigrantes: Movimientos Migratorios en la España del Siglo XX. Study supported by the Community of Madrid. Available from: http://sauce.pntic.mec.es/jotero/index.htm. [Accessed 2 August 2016].

OECD (2014) *International Migration Outlook*. Available from: www.oecd-ilibrary.org/social-issues-migration-health/international-migration-outlook-2014_migr_outlook-2014-en. [Accessed 2 August 2016].

OECD (2015) How does Spain compare? *OECD Employment Outlook 2015*. Available from: www.oecd-ilibrary.org/employment/oecd-employment-outlook-2015_empl_outlook-2015-en. [Accessed 2 August 2016].

Olías, L. (2015) Españoles 'en Tierra Extraña': Profesionales exiliados y en trabajos precarios. *Eldiario.es*. Available from: www.eldiario.es/sociedad/Espanoles-profesionales-preparados-trabajos-precarios_0_314618954.html. [Accessed 2 August 2016].

Oudenampsen, M. and Sullivan, G. (2004) Precarity and N/European identity: An interview with Alex Foti, ChainWorkers. *Mute Magazine*. Available from: www.metamute.org/editorial/articles/precarity-and-neuropean-identity-interview-alex-foti-chainworkers. [Accessed 2 August 2016].

Papadopoulos, D., Stephenson, N. and Tsianos, V. (2008) *Escape Routes: Control and Subversion in the Twenty-First Century*. London: Pluto Press.

Paratcha, D.S. (2009) Oficina de Derechos Sociales (ODS): Un Experimento de Organizacion entre Autoctonos y Migrantes. *Rebelion.org*. Available from: www.rebelion.org/noticia.php?id=93303. [Accessed 2 August 2016].

Schierup, C.U., Munck, R., Likić Brborić, B. and Neergaard, A. (2015) *Migration, Precarity, & Global Governance: Challenges and Opportunities for Labour*. Oxford: Oxford University Press.

Sitrin, M. and Azzellini, D. (2014). *They Can't Represent Us! Reinventing Democracy from Greece to Occupy*. London: Verso Books.

Standing, G. (2011) *The Precariat: The New Dangerous Class*. London: Bloomsbury Academic.

Standing, G. (2014) *A Precariat Charter: From Denizens to Citizens*. London: Bloomsbury Academic.

Suarez-Naval, L., Moreno Garcia, A. and Macia Preja, R. (2007) *Las Luchas de los Sin Papeles y la Extension de la Ciudadania: Perspectivas Criticas desde Europa y Estados Unidos*. Madrid: Traficantes de Suenos.

Toret, J. and Sguglia, N. (2006) Cartografiando el Exceso. Frontera y Trabajo en los Caminos del Movimiento. *Fadai'at: Libertad de Movimiento+Libertad de Conocimiento*, Malaga: Imagraf Impresiones, pp. 107–13.

Part III

Conceptual outlooks

14 Working for nothing

The latest high-growth sector?

Andrew Ross

In the years since the financial crash of 2008 we have seen the widespread proliferation of unpaid, or token-wage work in a broad variety of locations. Indeed, a cynic might well conclude that 'working for nothing' was the latest high-growth sector. Some of these tendencies are new, and are occurring as part of the ongoing mass transfer of work to digital platforms, where any of the solidity that was once attached to job-based employment is being pulverized beyond recognition. Others seem to be upgrades of existing patterns (more systematic wage theft, for example, or expanded use of prison labour), or they entail the conversion of formerly paid positions to unpaid ones, as is the case with white-collar and no-collar internships. Still others rest on the industrial uptake of 'working for exposure' as a normative career mentality, for youth in particular, who are encouraged to take on substantial upfront costs – weighed in time, labour, and debt – in order to win a stake in the lottery of the attention economy.

In the aggregate, the lost compensation might be statistically significant, though it would be a towering challenge, for any labour economist, to produce a reasonable estimate of all of that redistributed income. My task here is to ask whether these developments (many of which emerged under, or were deepened by, the exceptional circumstances of the post-crash recession) require us to re-think some of the critiques of precarity that emerged before 2008 (Beck 2000; Vishmidt 2005; Neilson and Rossiter 2005: Mitropoulos 2005). In those years, analysts promoted precarity as a paradigmatic explanation for the rapid undermining of *livelihoods* (understood as a vocational choice about how to sustain life) under neoliberal capitalism. These critiques were primarily sparked by the impact of casualization, which has marched its way steadily from low-wage temping to the liberalized sectors of the professions, but many of the characteristics of the post-2008 landscape seem to depart from the status quo ante. Is the more systematic expropriation of free labour outlined in this chapter simply an extension of this trend toward nonstandard employment, or are we seeing the birth of a durable transformation of work mentality, and, with it, a new dimension of precarious life?

When capitalist profit-taking in the present is thinned or exhausted, the quest to mine revenue turns toward the future. The new patterns of profit are tied, more and more, to lifelong financial extraction. Whether that takes the form of paper claims on the future, as is the case with debt instruments, or labour expended in hopes of securing forthcoming rewards, the outcome is the foreclosure of our lives to come. Whether it is the prisoner trying to earn his freedom, the unpaid intern building a resume for some unforeseen career, the student borrowing, and dedicating, wages she has not yet earned in order to prepare herself for employment, the migrant whose wages are withheld until her exit from the marketplace, or the online user volunteering monetizable data in pursuit of social network mobility, the beneficiaries are extracting value from our advance payments of time and labour, and are closing off life options in the years to come. In the pre-2008 paradigm of precarity, the dissolution of employment or career pathways through life was generating a radical uncertainty about the future. Today, increasingly, it looks as if profit is being extracted from the efforts of those who are trying to mitigate the uncertainty by pledging their labour upfront.

In the course of this chapter, I will describe some versions of free labour in more detail. But first, let me raise the question of whether the upsurge of unpaid labour can help us explain the gulf between the current inflation of corporate profits and high rates of underemployment. Two of the reasons for the gap between high earnings and joblessness seem to be beyond dispute. Corporations are still moving their operations offshore, especially jobs in high-skilled sectors where the largest savings in labour costs can be secured. In addition, these offshore activities allow them to dodge taxes by parking their profits overseas. A second explanation rests on increased productivity. Employees have been pressed by the stiff threat of layoffs, either to work harder and longer for the same pay check or to take a cut in wages. A third reason – and this is the unfamiliar quantum – is the growing reliance on new kinds of unpaid labour to supplement the balance sheet of employers that are canny enough to harvest it. Conclusive proof of this footprint is not so easy to muster but the strong anecdotal record and the available documented evidence suggest it is large enough to be a significant factor, especially in the high-velocity sectors of the financial and information industries.

As for the 'transformation of work mentality' that I referred to previously, the question I will ask is whether the systemic shift toward temping, which characterized the last three decades of job casualization, is being succeeded by an even more tenuous contractual relationship. Many of the new work arrangements I will be mentioning leave little trace of employment, and certainly nothing to implicate an employer in any legal or regulated network of obligations. Nor is the generalized musicians' profile of 'gigs' any longer adequate as a label. On the one hand, the patterns of expropriation may be more systematic than they are intermittent, and so they move the definition of a 'job' much closer to its etymological source – a discrete 'lump', or 'piece' of work that exists only for the duration of its fulfilment. On the other hand, and in cases where the arrangements are driven by the self-promotion of ordinary, unpaid individuals, the rewards for this labour are more typical of a preindustrial era, when the careful nurturing of attention from wealthy and powerful names or institutions were sources of considerable value and social mobility.

Seven varieties of free labour

(1) In the realm of digital labour, a substantial volume of unpaid labour is being extracted from sources such as the following: the establishment of free online media content as an industrial norm (taking a predictable toll on the pay scales of professional writers); extensive data mining from social media platforms like Facebook, Google, and Twitter, most often without the conscious knowledge of users; e-lance programmes like the Mechanical Turk, eLance, TaskRabbit, and oDesk, which allocate micro-tasks that may take no more than a few minutes to perform; crowdsourcing as an industrial principle, especially of creative or interesting work; and a host of other sophisticated digital techniques (involving the use of personalized algorithms) for extracting rents from users/participants (Scholz 2013). These are all forms of 'distributed labour' that tap the use of the Internet to mobilize the spare processing power of a widely dispersed crowd of discrete individuals. This should not to be confused with an older use of this term to describe the Business Process Outsourcing model for coordinating geographically dispersed workplaces, whether from telecommuting, or from distant nodes on a global production chain. So, too, the new model should be distinguished from the distributed workplace known today as the mobile office, whereby employers allow their employees to work anytime anywhere, whether in their homes, in Starbucks or in transit.

The new kind of distributed labour does not need to be performed by payroll employees in far-flung branch locations, or by laptop users in 'coffices', which have become the default workplace for a generation of contract freelancers who forsake the privacy of their homes to work in public view, braving, or feeding off, the gregarious hum of society. Rather, this labour is done either by users who do not perceive their interactive input as work at all, or else it is contracted out online – though a growing number of e-lance service sites – to the multitude of taskers who piece together lumps of income from motley sources. As in the offshore outsourcing model, the dispersion of this labour is highly organized but not dependent on physical relocation to cheap labour markets. Instead, cost savings can be derived either from the latent talent of the crowd or the micro-division of labour into puzzles, stints, chores, and bits which, if they amount to anything more than distractions, require only fitful bursts of concentration.

At the very least, the devising and parcelling-out of these micro-tasks is the latest development in a lineage of work management that derives from Taylorism. Taskers are effectively deskilled, dispersed, and deprived of any knowledge about the nature of the product to which their labour contributes. The coordinating manager, by contrast, is in complete control of the labour process. As for the donor labour of the crowd, this has a longer historical lineage since it owes a lot to the traditions of creative work where sacrifices in monetary compensation are commonly made in return for job gratification or the opportunity to test and advertise one's talent (Banks *et al.* 2013). This willingness to donate labour was referred to as self-exploitation when it first emerged as an industrial prototype in the formal employment offered by the New Economy or dot.com firms of the late

1990s, and for many researchers in the field it is a description that seems to sum up the mentality of passionate, or sacrificial, labour that drives the no-collar economy (Terranova 2010; Ross 2002; Hesmondhalgh and Baker 2010).

One of the ways to contextualize the rise of the 'creative industries' over the course of the last decade is to interpret it quite literally as an effort to industrialize creativity. Adapting the tempo of creative work to an industrial template is an acute managerial challenge, however, and, in a jackpot IP economy, the costs of competing are considerable (Rossiter 2007; Ross 2009). The turn to crowdsourcing offers a more impersonal solution that slices costs and delivers owners from any employer-type obligations. The crowd is not only smarter than trained employees, but employers don't need to offer health benefits or make social security contributions to take advantage of its wisdom, or put up with the wayward personalities of the creatives on payroll.

Even less recognizable as nonstandard employees are the users of social media platforms, yet they are sources of sizable revenue and profit to knowledge firms. One need only look at the ratio of earnings to payroll among leading information services firms like Google and Facebook to see one very influential model for twenty-first century capitalism: each firm posts billions of dollars of profits, while maintaining a very small paid workforce. This ratio of employees to revenue is unusual by any historical standards, but typical of firms that dominate the upper stratosphere of information services. Their astronomical earnings rest not on the surplus value created by paid employees, but on the unpaid input of users who are not consumers in any traditional sense of paying customers. The trade-off for users, of course, is free access to the platform and the software, but, from the company's perspective, the cost of hosting and maintenance is dwarfed by the tradeable value of the information it can extract from the daily churn on its site.

(2) Internships have become near-obligatory in almost every white-collar or no-collar sector. Our students are more familiar with the ubiquitous phrase, 'internship opportunities' than they are with 'job opportunities'. Internships are no longer a rite of passage into the professional service sector. For many, they are becoming a terminal limbo, not unlike the time spent by graduate students in teaching, which is no longer a term of apprenticeship, but, practically speaking, the end of their teaching career. In the last few years, unpaid internships have become the norm, especially for women (paid positions are disproportionately occupied by males) and according to an estimate from several years ago, they cumulatively provide a $2 billion subsidy to employers in the United States alone (Perlin 2011). As the market for internships develops, these unpaid positions are being openly sold, with the more sought-after placements generating large returns that will surely amplify this subsidy in the near-future. Much of this interning is off-the-books: neither counted nor recorded in any official estimates of labour activity. Like many of the other categories I cite here, interning has a sharp impact on the household debt burden. A large portion of internships are undertaken for college credit, and so, in the US at least, they are directly debt-financed. Most of the others are all-but-compulsory adjuncts of the collegiate quest for credentials. Inevitably, some of these stints can only be borne by taking on more debt. The

phenomenon of taking out loans simply to survive an unremunerated internship is more and more common and compounds the predicament of the intern, dedicating future wages in order to toil for free for a career placement that may never come.

(3) Wage theft has become a massive source of free labour for employers who routinely violate wages and hours laws, often by denying employees back pay, refusing to pay overtime, pocketing tips, paying below the minimum wage, or demanding off-the-clock hours. In 2008, at the onset of the recession, it was estimated that on average, low-wage workers in the US were losing 15 per cent of their annual income to wage theft in one form or another (Bernhardt *et al.* 2009), and wage theft was netting employers at least $100 billion a year (Bobo 2009). In the years since then, and especially in economic sectors which rely heavily on migrant labour, this illegal practice has become chronic. Downward pressure on the job market and stepped-up surveillance of immigrants has emboldened employers to deny pay to the more vulnerable members of their workforce. The rapid spread of tipping, from restaurant service to all kinds of in-person retail service jobs, is a recent innovation on the employers' efforts to pass on labour costs to customers. Once established, this practice becomes a legal rationale for paying the sub-minimum wage that many states set for tipped employees (in the US, as low as $2.13/hour by federal law). The most recent research, by the Economic Policy Institute, estimated that an aggregate of $50 billion is being stolen every year from the 30 million members of the US's low-wage workforce (Meixell and Eisenbrey 2014).

Wage theft is not just a gratuity for employers but also for the lenders that prey on the unbanked. These predominantly low-income earners are increasingly forced to pay fees simply to access the cash-value of their pay checks. The multitude of check cashers, pawnbrokers, payday lenders, and other sharks in the poverty business are committing a form of wage theft from people who are denied the full fruits of their labour because they cannot be members of a mainstream bank. According to one estimate, the working poor pay an effective surcharge of about $30 billion a year for the financial products they consume on Loan Alley, and more than twice that if you include subprime credit cards, subprime auto loans, and subprime mortgages (Rivlin 2011; Ehrenreich 2012).

(4) The pressure of import prices and recessionary drops in consumer demand has led American employers to seek out sharply discounted prison labour in ever greater quantities. The use of convicts in manufacturing and services has also been amplified by the decision of many state legislatures to outsource prisoners to private penitentiaries. As a result of the Prison Industries Act, pushed into law under the powerful auspices of the right-wing American Legislative Exchange, an estimated one million inmates are now employed at sub-minimum wages, and their labour is secured by the kind of disciplining of conduct that could not be enforced on the outside (Elk and Sloan 2011). Estimates of the median wage in state and federal prisons show that hourly compensation is between 20 and 31 cents. In addition, virtually all prisoners are engaged in 'institutional maintenance', in effect running the prisons for free; mopping cellblock floors, preparing and serving food in the dining hall, mowing the lawns, doing clerical work, and

laundering uniforms and bed linens. Prison labourers are not considered 'employees', so they have no protections under the law.

Notoriously, in the late nineteenth and early twentieth century, US prison inmates, especially in the South, were routinely leased out to private companies for labour under physically coercive circumstances. After long campaigning by the trade union movement, that system of convict-leasing was abolished, but the increasing use, by many companies, of today's prison industries programmes means that this practice is being revived in all but name. Last but not least, the efforts of many US states to lure home companies from cheaper offshore locations are being fronted by the promise of rock-bottom prisoner wages (Fraser and Freeman 2012). Workers in export-processing zones of South China are now competing with the even cheaper labour of US prisoners behind bars for petty drug offenses. For prisoners who elect to work in these programmes, it is informally understood (even though the promise may never be borne out) that their efforts will help in their quest for early release. In effect, they are working for (almost) nothing in hopes of earning their freedom.

(5) The 'sharing economy' has emerged as the 'next big thing'. It draws its inspiration from a host of sources: mutual aid and cooperative production; the ecological, cradle-to-grave drive to reduce waste; collaborative lifestyle consumption; the exercise of non-proprietary rights, etc. (Lovink and Scholz 2007). These roots are all quite progressive, and the non-profit sector of this economy has yielded many noble examples of commoning: time banking, horizontal resource and skill exchanges, and many other facets of alternative economies. But the commercial exploitation of these tendencies has opened up lucrative new markets that prey on the sharing of assets and labour. Companies like Airbnb, Uber, Lyft, and TaskRabbit extract vast profits from the monetization of our spare bedrooms, cars or down time even though they have contributed nothing to the acquisition or availability of these resources. Though participation is promoted as a source of supplementary income, for many it is increasingly becoming a primary source, and altering how people eke out a living. The companies in question employ a small staff and profit from the unpaid labour of all their micro-entrepreneurial 'community members', while avoiding any costs for benefits or unemployment insurance or workers' compensation. All of the risks are borne by the members, and competition drives down the prices and irregularizes the conditions under which their income is earned (Slee 2014). As this alternative economy grows, it destroys standard (and unionized) employment in the hotel, taxicab, and other service industries.

(6) The rise in household debt is an important inclusion in this list. For most people, debts are the wages of the future, to which creditors lay claim far in advance. As financialization penetrates many sectors of our lives, including access to vital social goods, the creditor class is taking an ever bigger bite out of the available labour surplus. In the US, this is most conspicuous in the case of education debt, which has surpassed $1.3 trillion. Amassing debt is a condition of students' entry to the workforce. Their wages, if they can access any, are more and more used to pay off loans taken out simply to prepare themselves for employability.

That is why some analysts have compared student debt to a form of modern indenture (Williams 2008). Indebtedness, in other words, is a necessary component of their labour, and it is not easily paid off in their working lifetimes. Alternately, student debt can be seen as a form of precocious wage theft (Ross 2014). Avoidance of student debt also has a significant labour impact. A sizable portion of the academic curriculum has long been taught by graduate employees looking for alternatives to the debt-financing of their studies, but campuses are now increasingly run on the back of their cheap undergraduate workforce. On many campuses, most of the clerical, landscaping, catering, and housekeeping duties are now performed by students trying to stave off taking on even more loans. In college towns, a variety of employers will take advantage of this desperation by treating the student body as a reserve army of cheap, temporary labour (Bousquet 2007). Not surprisingly, this debt burden has sharply limited the optional political imagination of young people, pre-empting their traditional capacity, and right, to devise alternative forms of social life.

(7) Last but not least, contestant volunteering has transformed many sectors of the entertainment industries into an amateur talent show, with jackpot stakes for a few winners and hard lumps for everyone else. The talent show/reality TV model has now become an industry standard, undercutting pay scales in all occupations. But given the powerful influence of popular entertainers over youth, the central principle of 'working for exposure' is becoming a normative career mentality for young people, with ominous economic consequences. Youth have accepted that this is the way of the world, and that they can only get ahead by offering their self-fashioned labour in advance and for free, in hopes of being noticed and favoured. For the current generation, the wages of industrialization have been replaced by the affective currency of attention and prestige. Under these circumstances, toil and effort buys the equivalent of a lottery ticket in the livelihood sweepstakes.

Is this new norm a significant shift beyond the more traditional use of 'casting' as an entry model for the entertainment workforce? If so, it may be because working for exposure is now regarded as part of the necessary upfront costs of stacking a resume for a livelihood based on gainful recognition. Just as student debts are taken on as a hedge against unemployability in the future, the donor labour given over to personal skill-building is a levy extracted in advance by industry employers, a gift of time and resources that employers would have devoted to job training, or the polishing of work personalities. But unlike membership dues, paid in advance to join an organization, there are no guarantees of benefits for the users. The only sure thing here is the extraction of free or discounted labour for employers who will take advantage of it.

Conclusion

At the time of writing, levels of unemployment in most northern countries are declining. In February 2016, the official US unemployment rate fell below 5 per cent for the first time since 2008. But labour under-utilization rates stood at 11.4 per cent, and the 'real' rate of unemployment remains much higher, because the prolonged duration of the recession meant that millions were no longer counted under the Bureau of Labour Statistics category of those who are available or looking for work; after 12 months, they drop off the roster. More notably, the official rates of youth unemployment were twice as high, at 10.5 per cent, and 'real' rates, for African Americans in particular, are as high as 51 per cent.

In austerity-squeezed countries like Italy, Spain and Greece, official youth unemployment levels were at 39 per cent, 45 per cent and 48 per cent respectively, with suicides on the rise. Meanwhile, most of the new jobs being created continue to be in sectors like restaurants, retail trade, and temporary help – among the lowest-paying positions, the least likely to offer benefits and any kind of job security. The acute predicament of the 'thousand-euro generation' is hardly unique to these Southern European economies, but it has been magnified by the Eurozone debt crisis and the loosening of labour laws in countries like Italy. As the foundations of the standardized wage labour economy have been systematically eroded, a good deal of daily work and effort went into alternative economies – skill-sharing, time banking, peer-to-peer production, and other forms of mutual aid. Much of that could be classified as labour for subsistence, and so it depends on the principle of *sharing by necessity*.

By contrast, much of the debate about 'free labour' has focused on the commercial exploitation of *volitional sharing* – whether within the vestigial gift economy at the core of digital labour or else as a basic commercial principle of the new sharing economy. In most of the categories I have outlined above, the uncompensated output is elective and unforced, even in the case of prison labourers seeking to 'earn' their freedom. In this regard, it can be distinguished from the dark history of labour exploitation governed by coercive regimes; indenture, debt peonage, human bondage, or 'wage slavery'. The new forms of unpaid labour are freely offered, just as the accompanying obligations are freely incurred. These self-imposed dimensions are intrinsic to the new kind of precarity, and may even be its hallmark.

Much of the public commentary about free labour has focused on the digital realm, in large part because journalists who write about the phenomenon have seen their own professional pay scales devastated by the transfer of reporting online platforms where free access is normative (Keen 2007: Anderson 2009). Understanding that the upsurge of unpaid work is not unique to the virtual economy can help us sidestep the fallacy of technological determinism – the belief, in other words, that the Internet came along and punched a big hole in the universe of standard employment, spilling the contents all over the place. Online technologies have certainly enabled, or facilitated some of the tendencies I have described, but they are not inherently responsible for them (Huws 2014).

In addition, what is distinctive about the foregoing survey is that some of the fastest developing trends in unpaid labour can be found in sectors of high-reward toil, especially in the creative industries, where amateur effort to win a niche in the attention economy can result in 'blockbuster hits'. In these sectors, there seem to be very few yardsticks for judging what fair labour is. Any attempt to draw a crisp equation between work and pay is increasingly difficult. Nor do most of the losing 'contestants' in this economy experience their thwarted efforts as a form of labour exploitation. Regardless of the income strata, however, the overall pattern seems to be an asymmetrical outcome for employer-owners on the one hand and worker-participants on the other. The cumulative result is a distribution of income that is even more skewed than that displayed by an industrial labour market where casual or contingent work predominates.

It should be noted that a variety of semi-organized initiatives have sprung up to counteract the erosion of fair labour standards in a few of the areas I mentioned (and they are described in other chapters of this book). Some of the remedies are aimed at bringing unpaid labour practices into line with existing laws and workplace regulations. Others are focused on pioneering and setting new standards. Few of them fall within the traditional orbit of the trade union movement, though some of them may well spark new forms of worker protection and organization, along the model of workers' centres, or pioneer alternatives such as the organizing of freelancers, fast food workers, fashion models, student debtors, interns, and teaching adjuncts.

Casualization took the best part of three decades to move from routinized low-wage sectors to high-wage services and professions. The reorganization of work that I have been describing appears to be happening at all skill levels, and at more or less the same time. Initially, at least, part of the explanation for this surely related to the severity of the recession. But the downturn has been so durable that some of these consequences may turn out to be permanent, rather than just the result of a temporary deficiency of economic activity. In the period following 2008, analysts in the business press advised firms to take advantage of new sources of free labour, far outside of the conventional workplace, in order to stay afloat and improve their market positions. Seven years later, it looks as if this tactic may be approaching a long-term business strategy. The social factory is no longer an avant-garde thesis proposed by the first generation of autonomous thinkers back in the mid-1970s. Today, we see it written all over the landscape of modern work.

References

Anderson, C. (2009) *Free: The Future of a Radical Price.* New York: Hyperion.

Banks, M., Rosalind, G. and Taylor, S. (eds) (2013) *Theorizing Cultural Work: Labour, Continuity and Change in the Cultural and Creative Industries.* London: Routledge.

Beck, U. (2000) *The Brave New World of Work.* Translation by P. Camiller. Cambridge: Polity Press.

Bobo, K. (2009) *Wage Theft in America: Why Millions of Working Americans Are Not Getting Paid – And What We Can Do About It.* New York: New Press.

Bernhardt, A., Milkman, R., Theodore, N., Heckathorn, D.D., Auer, M., DeFilippis, J., González, A.L., Narro, V. and Perelshteyn, J. (2009) *Broken Laws, Unprotected Workers: Violations of Employment and Labor Laws in America's Cities.* New York: National Employment Law Project.

Bousquet, M. (2007) *How the University Works: Higher Education and the Low-Wage Nation.* New York: New York University Press.

Ehrenreich, B. (2012) Preying on the Poor: How Government and Corporations Use the Poor as Piggy Banks. *Economic Hardship Reporting Project.* 17 May.
Elk, M. and Sloan, B. (2011) The hidden history of ALEC and prison labour. *The Nation.* 1 August.
Fraser, S. and Freeman, J. B. (2012) Locking down an American workforce. *Huffington Post.* 20 April. Available from: www.huffingtonpost.com/steve-fraser/private-prisons-_b_1439201.html [Accessed 20 July 2016].
Hesmondhalgh, D. and Baker, S. (2010) *Creative Labour: Media Work in Three Cultural Industries.* Abingdon and New York: Routledge.
Huws, U. (2014) *Labour in the Global Digital Economy: The Cybertariat Comes of Age.* New York: Monthly Review Press.
Keen, A. (2007) *The Cult of the Amateur: How Blogs, MySpace, YouTube, and the Rest of Today's User-Generated Media are Destroying Our Economy, Our Culture, and Our Values.* New York: Crown.
Lovink, G. and Scholz, T. (2007) *The Art of Free Cooperation.* New York: Autonomedia.
Meixell, B. and Eisenbrey, R. (2014) An epidemic of wage theft. *Economic Policy Institute.* 11 September. Available from: www.epi.org/publication/epidemic-wage-theft-costing-workers-hundreds/ [Accessed 20 July 2016].
Mitropoulos, A. (2005) Precari-Us? In Berry-Slater, J. (ed.), *The Precarious Reader.* London: Mute.
Neilson, B. and Rossiter, N. (2005) From precarity to precariousness and back again: Labour, life and unstable networks. *The Fibreculture Journal* 5. Available from: http://journal.fibreculture.org/issue5/neilson_rossiter.html. [Accessed 20 July 2016].
Perlin, R. (2011) *Intern Nation: How to Earn Nothing and Learn Little in the Brave New Economy.* New York: Verso.
Rivlin, G. (2011) *Broke USA: From Pawnshops to Poverty, Inc. — How the Working Poor Became Big Business.* New York: HarperBusiness.
Ross, A. (2002) *No-Collar: The Humane Workplace and Its Hidden Costs.* New York: Basic Books.
Ross, A. (2009) *Nice Work If You Can Get It.* New York: NYU Press.
Ross, A. (2014) *Creditocracy and the Case for Debt Refusal.* New York: OR Books.
Rossiter, N. (ed.) (2007) *My Creativity.* Amsterdam: Institute for Network Cultures.
Scholz, T. (ed.) (2013) *Digital Labour: The Internet as Playground and Factory.* New York: Routledge.
Slee, T. (2014) Sharing and Caring. *Jacobin.* 24 January. Available from: www.jacobinmag.com/2014/01/sharing-and-caring/ [Accessed 20 July 2016].
Terranova, T. (2010) Free Labour: Producing Culture for the Digital Economy. *Social Text.* 63(18/2): 33–58.
Vishmidt, M. (2005) Precarious straits. *Mute* 29 (February).
Williams, J. (2008) Student debt and the spirit of indenture. *Dissent* (Fall): 73–8.

15 Labour, (in-)dependence, care

Conceptualizing the precarious

Isabell Lorey
Translated by Aileen Derieg

One of the outstanding figures of European modernity is that of the autonomous individual. This figure is free because it devalues the reproduction of life. This negative freedom is profoundly gendered, as are, along with it, its conceptions of security and protection in contrast to feminized insecurity and need for protection. Efforts to single out and separate what is feminized about this figure of the autonomous individual, in order to preserve it as a masculine one, have marked our understanding of freedom, labour, reproduction and care since the seventeenth century, and had an impact on welfare protections in the second half of the twentieth century. Under neoliberal conditions, the autonomous individual now finds itself again in a process of fundamental change.

The historical genealogies and transformations of this gendered figure will be developed in this chapter on the basis of my political theory of precarization (Lorey 2015a). The modern domination logics of protection and security are to be breached and overcome through a multi-dimensional understanding of the precarious (Lorey 2011). These logics of protection and security make it so that fundamental precariousness, that is, the area of reproduction and thus mutual dependency and connection with others, is devalued, overlooked, or warded off as threatening.

This negation of precariousness constitutes not only the autonomous individual, but much more: the modern architecture of statehood, democracy and capitalism. This negation also structures central 'western' norms and parameters, such as freedom, equality, and property, which in turn influence the way in which the essential dichotomies of our bourgeois-capitalist societies are gendered through the separation between the public and the private sphere, self-determination and dependency, freedom and subjugation.

Historically, we owe the political idea of the individual and individual protection from insecurities and threatening fellow humans primarily to the Hobbesian conception of the security state. Here we find the beginnings of modern concepts of the individual in the history of ideas as the precondition for laws that sanction the protection of individuals and property. In the twentieth century, protection from existential insecurity, or precariousness, became the task of Fordist social welfare states (Castel 2003a). The central pillar of this protection was the heteronormative family with a male breadwinner. A gender-specific division of labour is the basis of the Fordist logic of social security. Yet neither Hobbes' Leviathan nor the social welfare state are able to eliminate the precarious; on the contrary, they engender the new historical forms of precarity and insecurities from which they are in turn supposed to provide protection. In *neoliberal* societies, however, social protection is remodelled, dismantled, individualized. Domination is legitimized less and less through social safeguards. In combination with one's responsibility for oneself, freedom is transformed into an instrument of domination.

To further develop my claim, I distinguish between three dimensions of the precarious: precariousness, precarity, and governmental precarization. *Precariousness* describes a socio-ontological level (Butler 2004, 2009). From birth onwards, bodies are dependent on the care and reproduction of others; in order to survive, they are dependent on social relationships. Living beings always exist relationally, a completely autonomous life is an illusion, and invulnerability a fantasy of omnipotence. However, despite care and reproduction, bodies remain precarious: it is inevitable that they become ill, suffer accidents, die. There is no complete protection from this precariousness. Precariousness is shared with others; it points out the fundamental connection with others, but does not make everyone the same. It designates no anthropological constant, because its degree is historically and geographically very differently determined. This is exactly the fundamental dimension of life that has been systematically devalued and warded off as threatening during the formation of bourgeois-liberal democracy and capitalist production conditions (Federici 2012).

The construction of precariousness as a threat already addresses the second dimension of the precarious: the dimension of *precarity*. This designates conditions of legal, political, economic and social inequality: hierarchizing categorizations, structural discrimination, belonging and exclusion. In short: precarity designates the conditions of domination that are divided up and distributed through protection, care, and safeguarding.

The third dimension is *governmental precarization*. This dimension of the precarious expands Michel Foucault's concept of governmentality: the techniques of governing he theorized to describe the birth of biopolitics. Against this background, governmental precarization emphasizes how the conduct of state governance and individualized self-governing are intertwined in a mode of governing that uses insecurity as its main tool. Understanding precarization governmentally as a processual term makes it possible to problematize the complex interactions between an instrument of governing, economic conditions of exploitation, and modes of subjectivation whilst appreciating the ambivalence between subjugation and freedom.

Independence and labour

John Locke, the founder of liberal thinking, derived the individual's right to self-determination not only from an idea of freedom linked to property in the late seventeenth century. Locke also understood labour as free labour. Within the framework of this free labour, the relationship to one's own body is a property relationship: 'Every man,' according to Locke, 'has a *property* in his own *person.* [...] The *labour* of his body and the work of his hands are properly his' (Locke 1689: 123–6). These thoughts were taken up again a hundred years later by Adam Smith, when he declared, '[t]he property which every man has in his own labour [...] is the original foundation of all other property' (1776: I.10.67). Smith was convinced that the freedom of productive labour would lead to the worker being able to feed not only himself as a 'free man,' (1776: I.8.40) but also a family, and that he is free and independent from charity provided by state or non-state institutions (1776: I.8.15).

In the second half of the eighteenth century, the idea of the freedom of labour as independence from conditions of feudal coercion intertwines with the bourgeois idea of freedom as voluntary submission to impersonal laws that apply to all, the self-decreed laws of political democracy. The new bourgeois laws replace 'the personal dependency and arbitrariness of the *ancien régime*' (Bensaïd 2011: 21). Yet the ideas of freedom, equality, independence and self-determination were based on contradictions from the outset. The bourgeois-democratic social contract is founded solely on the legal equality of the white male, free citizen. The equality and freedom of all (others) was postponed, in the best case, to the future.

In fact, to a large extent, the arrangement of bourgeois-male freedom and submission is based on the patriarchal subjugation of women in the private sphere, as Carole Pateman (1988) has highlighted. This involves a negative freedom from precariousness and from being constitutively connected with others. In the bourgeois-capitalist society, however, precariousness is no longer simply negated by means of a gender-specific division of social space. Instead, it is domesticated and enclosed in the private sphere. Care and reproduction are feminized, depoliticized, devalued (Federici 2012), structured by precarity on the basis of gender, sexuality, and 'race' (Stoler 1995).

This division of social space according to a gender-specific distribution of labour and the distribution of hierarchized subjectivations allows for the emergence of the new mode of governing of the bourgeois-capitalist society that Foucault called biopolitics (Foucault 1998, 2007, 2008). Power is no longer repressively exercised 'from above', but rather as governmentality through self-governing and exercising modes of behaviour. In a possessive-individualistic and simultaneously disciplining logic of individualization, every person of a population must learn, more or less self-responsibly, to have a body that is not independent from certain conditions of existence: they must learn to influence 'their' precariousness depending on how they live, take care of their health, work. These kinds of body relations served the production of a class-specific and heterosexual-racialized gender binary, which not only secured the maintenance of the labour force in a gender-segregating way, but also ensured generativity to strengthen the nation-state at the same time (Stoler 1995; Engel 2002; Lorey 2015b). In the nineteenth century, on the basis of ideas of one's own body and Christian practices of confession (Foucault 1998), biologistic and naturalized constructions of the disambiguation of gender and sexuality became manifest, along with constructions of a superior 'white race', which could not have emerged without the theory of 'possessive individualism' and the liberal ideas of freedom, autonomy and civilization.

Welfare-state (in-)dependence

For the (male) worker, however, precariousness could not be sufficiently domesticated through individualization, devaluation of the 'others', and feminization of reproduction in the private sphere. Smith's idea that free labour must be able to feed a family quickly turned out to be 'utopian capitalism' (Rosanvallon 1979). The freedom of labour capacity was no protection against precariousness: existential vulnerability due to illness, accidents or unemployment remained intact. The collective social welfare state institutions of insurance that had been fought for, were able to ensure relative independence – significantly for the male breadwinner. The welfare state and organizational structures of the (largely male) workers made it clear that the bourgeois logic of property could not be generalized, that autonomy and individualization was not possible for the workers in liberal democracies without collective protection and insurance systems. Legal claims and solidarity led to a social compromise that provided a welfare-state complement to Fordist individualization up until the 1970s (Castel 2003b). In this way, the idea of male freedom and independence through wage labour could be collectively supported and maintained through the consolidation of the gender-specific separations between paid productive and unpaid reproductive labour and between a public and a private sphere.

Social safeguarding had previously taken place on the basis of conditions of massive structural inequality in terms of origins, class and gender, that means precarity. In the *liberal* social-welfare-state governmental dynamics of safeguarding, the endeavour to control the fundamental precariousness shared by all, means that those constructed not only as 'abnormal', but also as dangerous 'others' are striated and marginalized at the 'peripheries' of society. In the liberal welfare state the logic of safeguarding is structured by precarity.

In their investigation of the discourse about welfare mothers in the 1980s and 1990s in the USA, Nancy Fraser and Linda Gordon have shown why the ambivalence of bourgeois-legal self-governing between freedom and subjugation can be persistently perceived as a paradox (Fraser and Gordon 1994). According to Fraser and Gordon, the independence of male white workers is based on their extensive lack of perception of subjugation in the conditions of production. The moment when white men were made politically and legally equal, 'by definition, then, economic inequality among white men no longer created dependency. [...] Thus *dependency* was redefined to refer exclusively to those noneconomic relations of subordination deemed suitable only for people of colour and for white women' (Fraser and Gordon 1994: 319). This male form of independence was thus based on the precarity of others, who were then further differentiated in their subordinate dependency: into those who appeared worthy of being protected and those who did not – into 'a 'good' household dependency, predicated of children and wives and an increasingly 'bad' (or at least dubious) charity dependency' (Fraser and Gordon 1994: 320).

Up to the present, it is due to the liaison between capitalism and liberal democracy that the 'social question' historically began as the 'worker question' (Sauer 1997: 127). The problem arising from this is not only that social democracy in Fordism was primarily based on the 'independence' of the male breadwinner safeguarded by the social welfare state. Rather, social rights in terms of health, education, housing or residency are substantially tied to wage labour still in the present. It is not possible to find an alternatively structured social form of democracy in Europe at this time.

Governing through precarization

What currently distinguishes neoliberalism is – despite assumptions that are still widespread – that the precarious are no longer solely those who can be marginalized to the peripheries of society. Due to the individualizing restructuring of the social welfare state, the deregulation of the labour market, and the expansion of precarious employment conditions, we currently find ourselves in a process of normalization of precarization, which also affects larger portions of the middle class. In this process of normalization, precarization has become a political and economic instrument of governing. At the same time, people continue to be legally, economically and socially marginalized and excluded through structural inequality, through precarity, which means that they are less protected than others or protection is altogether denied them (Lorey 2015b). This involves hierarchical classifications of the precarious in a new mode of governing through precarization. Due to the reduction and restructuring of collective safeguarding systems, an individualized risk management is required from everyone, regardless of gender, class and origins; depending on their social positioning on the scale of precarity, however, this is arranged in a very different way.

Governing through precarization is no longer fundamentally founded on the gender-hierarchical and heteronormative dichotomy of autonomy and dependency, which was still traditional in the Fordist social welfare state: the dichotomy between male individualization and female familization is breached (Hark and Laufenberg 2013). Paying for social safeguarding primarily through the Fordist family wages has been considered increasingly less financially feasible since the 1970s. Women's precarious (additional) income enables not only the incipient flexibilization of the labour market, but also supports an individualized social insurance tied to wage labour. In the course of this, however, collective insurance systems are not expanded, but rather restructured and reduced, and private insurance options are massively growing. Social safeguarding and thus social reproduction is increasingly de-collectivized, handed over to the responsibility of the individual and capitalized. The consequence of this is that for more and more people retirement provisions, health and education can only be financed through indebtedness (Lazzarato 2011; Lorey 2013). This de-secured individualization results in new inequalities. In this neoliberal precarity and the expansion of precarization, the possibility of experiencing precariousness as commonly shared vulnerability vanishes. Instead, the fear of precariousness has an individualizing effect and enhances governability within the framework of neoliberal governmentality.

Patriarchal heterosexual gender arrangements are not completely breached by these transformations, however, but instead only partially shifted. Old inequalities are manifested through, among other things, the still devalued care and reproduction work, which is additionally organized in an international distribution of labour, economically and ethnically differentiated and hierarchized (Hochschild 2000; Caixeta *et al.* 2004; Gutiérrez Rodríguez 2010). The internationalization of households reveals the shift of the patriarchal in the field of care, especially clearly in the migration of women, who undertake a movement in global capitalism away from one 'patriarchal system' (Parreñas 2001: 78) of a gender-specific distribution of labour in the direction of another.

Although the neoliberal flexibilization of working conditions signifies a flexibilization of family conditions, it does not necessarily change the hierarchically organized gendered distribution of labour. Where social reproduction is not monetarized, it is 're-privatized' (Hark and Laufenberg 2013) and is partly distinguished by a traditional heterosexual re-familization. Parallel to this, patriarchal gender relations are increasingly dissolving, the associated hegemonic masculinities eroding (Demirović and Maihofer 2013; Maihofer 2014). What is evident here is that neoliberal governing through precarization does not have to rely on a gendered distribution of labour and a heteronormative generativity, in the same way that was necessary for the formation of liberal capitalism and bourgeois society.

I suspect that the consequences of a sustained governing through precarization will be not only a conservative restructuring of the private sphere as a heteronormative protective space, but also that the politico-economic function of the 'family' will be strengthened at the same time beyond patriarchal heterosexual forms. Neoliberal governmentality needs only supportive, protective and reproducing relationships, which in this respect take over the governmental function of the heteronormative family.

Freedom and independence as neoliberal instrument of governing

Governing through precarization requires specific forms of freedom and independence, which are condensed in the concept of self-responsibility. Social safeguarding is newly transferred to the responsibility of single persons as autonomous individuals, no longer primarily with a gendered connotation, but with genealogies going back to the times before the formation of the European social welfare states, which now become recognizable as historical exceptions (Neilson and Rossiter 2008). With the call for self-responsibility, not only are the bourgeois biopolitics of neoliberal governmentality actualized, but the – morally supported – ideology of autonomy independent from the social welfare state also returns.

With the moral understanding of freedom and independence as responsibility over one's self, precarization, poverty, and dependency on the minimal social welfare state can be defamed as being solely self-inflicted. Securing one's own life continues to be based on wage labour. Neoliberal working conditions require workers to be completely available at all times, whilst simultaneously constraining labour and social rights. Time and capacities for care activities for others become scarce; self-care serves almost exclusively to (re-)produce a profitable and productive body. Reproduction as a mode of subjectivation is shifted into the realm of capitalist production.

Under the paradigm of mobility, flexibility and competition, not only are social rights reduced, but the labour relation is also structured by obligations to conformist engagement and performance agreements. New dependencies on state institutions, employers, creditors and banks emerge in precarious working and living conditions, where individuals seem to be left to fend for themselves with no possibility of demanding rights and no knowledge of them. Conformism and fear increase, as well as the acceptance of authoritarian-structured working conditions and institutions. Freedom as responsibility for one's self becomes a disciplining instrument of domination (Segal 2006; Sauer 2008). In this politico-economic regime, self-government and life conduct primarily serve political governability and capitalist valorization – and the anxiety of precariousness maintains this relation.

In North-Western Europe, the normalization of precarization is currently still being alleviated for the middle classes by family support and inheritances. The fear of biographical and generational social decline and the demands of privatized risk management still correlate with resentful isolation tendencies and demands for security against those declared as 'risk groups'. In the permanent race for the desired better safeguarding of one's own life and for social proximity against competing others, what is overlooked is that a sustainably better life cannot be an autonomous, individual matter.

Cuidadanía

This neoliberal link between autonomy and valorization is what has to be separated, which means at the same time a break with the predominant liberal understanding of how society is constituted and of belonging. The (neo)liberal governmental interplay of control, regulation and governing, which grants citizens their rights in the logic of the 'needs' of workers and the 'suitability of consumers' (Precarias 2014), is to be broken open.

To this end, the feminist theorists and activists of the group 'Precarias a la deriva' propose the concept of a 'care citizenship' (*cuidadanía*) (Precarias 2014: 102). The Spanish neologism *cuidadanía* conjoins (state) citizenship (*ciudadanía*) with care (*cuidado*) into a new form of socially, politically, legally, and economically living together beyond the (nation-)state border regime, in which the relationality with others is not to be broken off, but is instead considered fundamental (Precarias 2014; Hess and Kasparek 2010).

In the *cuidadanía* citizens' rights are no longer tied to the modern figure of the autonomous, independent individual; the ideal male-bourgeois subject of a nation-state, who stabilizes his superior position by outsourcing his own precariousness and shifting it as a deficit to the precarity of the devalued, subordinated, excluded, and invisible 'others', is divested of its foundation.

The Precarias are interested in sustainably breaching existing logics of security and insecurity. Their political and social strategy consists in enhancing the value of care, both at the individual level and at the level of society (Precarias 2014; Lorey 2015a; Lorey 2011). The focus on care has two strategic components: on the one hand it is intended to enhance the status of care activities and care needs in a new understanding, and on the other to make this the starting point for politico-economic considerations.

For the Precarias, the term 'care' covers all areas of social reproduction. The field of the needs and activities thus delineated goes beyond housework and care work as well as activities in the areas of health and education, and it takes fundamentally new forms of communicative and affective labour into consideration (Precarias 2014: 61). The Precarias situate care in the context of socially living with others. In this perspective of care, the social and political formation of community is not considered under the primacy of the security and protection of autonomous individuals (and their families).

In order to deconstruct the phantasm of independency and superiority, according to Precarias a la deriva, it is necessary to break with three fundamental dichotomies of liberal (state) citizenship. First it is necessary to break with the separation between a public and a private sphere and thus with the relationship of subordination between the genders. The second break that is needed is the break with the gender-specific division of labour, unequal pay, unpaid care work and its concomitant unequal access to social insurance, wealth and participation. Both breaks are decisive for the third break with the separation between autonomy and dependency, which permeates the understanding of self-determination and self-sustenance. For dependency means the 'incapacity to realize the project of individual emancipation' (Precarias 2014: 101). In this perspective, only those who are 'autonomous' are able to shape their own lives. The consequence of this is a very limited, 'one-sided and individualistic' understanding of care, in which dependents are cared for by those who are independent, 'healthy' and capable of self-care. Envisioning care differently consequently also means understanding emancipation and thus autonomy and self-determination in a new way – care ceases to be understood as a one-dimensional and individualized relation between dependents and those who are independent, when emancipation is no longer imagined as liberation from precariousness. But above all, this understanding of care is freed from moralistic elements. Care no longer depends on the private and contingent empathy of others; it no longer obligates one to gratitude. The phantasm of autonomy and supremacy, in which those in need of protection are viewed as victims in a paternalistic manner, is deconstructed.

In order to not negate the agency of those in need of care in the critique of independence and supremacy, the Precarias do not reverse these dichotomies. Instead, they propose 'a recognition of the tensions that permeate [these] concept[s]' (Precarias 2014: 104). For the relation between autonomy and dependency this means not denying the necessity of autonomy, not treating the tensions between these two poles through a hierarchizing separation, but rather taking into consideration 'that our autonomy and singularity are inevitably grounded in the interaction with others' (Precarias 2014: 105).

Even if private support is necessary for survival in situations of acute crisis, what is needed, according to the Precarias, is a general right to care for and to be cared for, which simultaneously means that obligations to perform care work do not follow one's positioning in society. *Cuidadanía* is based on this right, in which individuals are not understood as separate from one another, but as manifold, mutually relating singularities. It is a right that recognizes the commonly shared precariousness and is no longer based on a legal person, but on a legal singularity, according to which citizens' rights cease to be hierarchized.[1]

In order to articulate *cuidadanía,* what is needed therefore is a constituent process (Negri 1999), in which new subjectivities are invented to arrange shared precarious life in common, in which the security logics of precarity can be broken open, where the extreme differences in precarization and the commonness of precariousness simultaneously form a point of departure. With this fundamental change in perspective, *cuidadanía* begins in the present, in the 'Jetztzeit', and is not postponed to a future (Lorey 2016).

Note

1 Gerald Raunig and others give inspiration for thinking the concept of legal singularity further (Raunig 2016).

References

Bensaïd, D. (2011) Permanent scandal. In Agamben G. (ed.), *Democracy in What State?* New York: Columbia University Press.

Butler, J. (2004) *Precarious Life. The Powers of Mourning and Violence.* London/New York: Verso.

Butler, J. (2009) *Frames of War. When Is Life Grievable?* London/NewYork: Verso.

Caixeta, L., Gutiérrez Rodríguez, E., Tate, S. A., and Vega Solís, C. (eds) (2004) *Hogares, Cuidados y Fronteras/Home, Care and Borders/Haushalt, Sorge und Grenzen.* Madrid: Traficantes de Sueños.

Castel, R. (2003a) *From Manual Workers to Wage Laborers: Transformation of the Social Question.* Translated by R. Boyd. New Brunswick, New Jersey: Transaction Publishers.

Castel, R. (2003b) *L'insecurité sociale. Qu'est-ce qu'être protégé?* Paris: Édition du Seuil.

Demirović, A. and Maihofer, A. (2013) Vielfachkrise und die Krise der Geschlechterverhältnisse. In Heilmann, A. and Hildegard, M. N. (eds), *Krise, Kritik, Allianzen. Arbeits- und geschlechtersoziologische Perspektiven.* Weinheim/Basel: Beltz Juventa.

Engel, A. (2002) *Wider die Eindeutigkeit. Sexualität und Geschlecht im Fokus queerer Politik der Repräsentation.* Frankfurt M./New York: Campus.

Federici, S. (2012) *Aufstand aus der Küche. Reproduktionsarbeit im globalen Kapitalismus und die unvollendete feministische Revolution.* Translation by M. Henninger. Münster: Edition Assemblage.

Foucault, M. (1998) *The Will to Knowledge: The History of Sexuality, Vol. 1*. Translation by R. Hurley. London: Penguin Books.
Foucault, M. (2007) *Security, Territory, Population: Lectures at the Collège de France 1977–1978*. Translation by G. Burchell. New York: Palgrave Macmillan.
Foucault, M. (2008) *The Birth of Biopolitics: Lectures at the Collège de France, 1978–1979*. Translation by G. Burchell. London: Palgrave Macmillan.
Fraser, N. and Gordon, L. (1994) A genealogy of dependency. Tracing a keyword of the US welfare state. *Signs* 19(21): 309–36.
Gutiérrez Rodríguez, E. (2010) *Migration, Domestic Work and Affect. A Decolonial Approach on Value and the Feminization of Labour*. New York/London: Routledge.
Hark, S. and Laufenberg, M. (2013) Sexualität in der Krise. Heteronormativität im Neoliberalismus. In Appelt, E., Aulenbacher, B. and Wetterer, A. (eds), *Gesellschaft. Feministische Krisendiagnosen*. Münster: Westfälisches Dampfboot.
Hess, S. and Kasparek, B. (2010) *Grenzregime. Diskurse, Praktiken, Institutionen in Europa*. Berlin/Hamburg: Assoziation A.
Hochschild, A. R. (2000) Global care chains and emotional surplus value. In Giddens, A. and Hutton, W. (eds), *On the Edge. Living with Global Capitalism*. London: Jonathan Cape.
Lazzarato, M. (2011) *The Making of the Indebted Man*. Translation by Joshua David Jordan. Los Angeles: Semiotext(e).
Locke, J. (1689) *Two Treatises of Government*. Available from: http://press-pubs.uchicago.edu/founders/documents/v1ch16s3.html. [Accessed 3 August 2016]
Lorey, I. (2011) *Figuren des Immunen. Elemente einer politischen Theorie*. Zürich, Berlin: Diaphanes.
Lorey, I. (2013) Das Regime der Prekarisierung. Europas Politik mit Schuld und Schulden. In Blätter für deutsche und internationale Politik (ed.) *Demokratie oder Kapitalismus? Europa in der Krise*. Berlin: Edition Blätter.
Lorey, I. (2015a) *State of Insecurity. Government of the Precarious*. Translation by A. Derieg. London/New York: Verso.
Lorey, I. (2015b) Das Gefüge der Macht. In Bargetz, B., Ludwig, G. and Sauer, B. (eds), *Gouvernementalität und Geschlecht. Politische Theorie im Anschluss an Michel Foucault*. Frankfurt M./New York: Campus.
Lorey, I. (2016) Presentist Democracy. The Now-Time of Struggles. In Oberprantacher, A. and Siclodi, A. (eds), *Subjectivation in Political Theory and Contemporary Practices*. South Yarra/Sydney: Palgrave Macmillan.
Maihofer, A. (2014) Familiale Lebensformen zwischen Wandel und Persistenz. Eine zeitdiagnostische Zwischenbetrachtung. In Behnke, C., Lengersdorf, D. and Scholz, S. (eds), *Wissen - Methode - Geschlecht: Erfassen des fraglos Gegebenen*. Wiesbaden: VS Verlag für Sozialwissenschaften.
Negri, A. (1999) *Insurgencies. Constituent Power and the Modern State*. Minneapolis: University of Minnesota Press.
Neilson, B., Rossiter, N. (2008) Precarity as a political concept, or, Fordism as exception. *Theory, Culture & Society* 7–8.
Pateman, C. (1988) *The Sexual Contract*. Stanford: Stanford University Press.
Parreñas, R. S. (2001) *Servants of Globalization. Women, Migration, and Domestic Work*. Stanford: Stanford University Press.
Precarias a la deriva (2014) *Was ist dein Streik? Militante Streifzüge durch die Kreisläufe der Prekarität*. Translation by B. Mennel. Wien: Transversal texts. Available from: http://transversal.at/books/precarias-de. [Accessed 3 August 2016]

Raunig, G. (2016) *Dividuum. Machinic Capitalism and Molecular Revolution.* Los Angeles: Semiotext(e).

Rosanvallon, P. (1979) *Le capitalisme utopique. Critique de l'idéologie économique.* Paris: Ed. du Seuil.

Sauer, B. (1997) Krise des Wohlfahrsstaates. Eine Männerinstitution unter Globalisierungsdruck? In Braun, H. and Jung, D. (eds), *Globale Gerechtigkeit? Feministische Debatte zur Krise des Sozialstaats.* Hamburg: Konkret Literatur.

Sauer, B. (2008) Von der Freiheit auszusterben. Neue Freiheiten im Neoliberalismus. In Bidwell-Steiner, M. and Wagner, U. (eds), *Freiheit und Geschlecht. Offene Beziehungen – Prekäre Verhältnisse.* Innsbruck: Studien Verlag.

Segal, J. (2006) The Discipline of Freedom. Action and Normalization in Theory and Practice of Neo-Liberalism. *New Political Science* 3.

Smith, A. (1776) *The Wealth of Nations.* Available from: www.econlib.org/library/Smith/smWN4.html. [Accessed 3 August 2016].

Stoler, A. L. (1995) *Race and the Education of Desire. Foucault's History of Sexuality and the Colonial Order of Things.* Durham: Duke University Press.

16 Encoding the law of the household and the standardisation of uncertainty

Angela Mitropoulos

Maps

All maps involve subtractions from complexity – a condition that is both crucial for readability and, at the same time, a procedure that tends toward essentialism and obsolescence. Moreover, maps were, and are, anticipatory. If not quite the performance, then the script. According to J. B. Harley's notations in the margins of cartographic history, 'lands [were] claimed on paper before they were effectively occupied'. That is, 'maps anticipated empire. Surveyors marched alongside soldiers, initially mapping for reconnaissance, then for general information, and eventually as a tool of pacification, civilisation, and exploitation in the defined colonies' (2001: 57). As logical systems, maps are therefore not so much representational artefacts as propositions (Wood 2010: 41). This is especially so where mapping links laws and objects by encoding the defined properties of the latter in such a way that they are amenable to normative statements. This is why the history of the map is also the history of the concept of precariousness. The foundational incertitude of property rights is the protean circumstance that connects these two histories at the methodological juncture between property law and normative claims inferred from an assured knowledge about the enduring, unique properties of stuff. From imperial maps to cadastral records, the classical and modern cartographic ambition was to brush aside the irritant of epistemic uncertainty, to subtract from the semantic ephemera of (as Aristotle called them) accidents and anomalies, and in so doing to furnish a navigable and familiar *habitus* of scientific knowledge that was, at the same time, the construction of an intimate familiarity by way of mundane connections between 'the illusion of realistic and objective space' and the aesthetics of the intimate, habitable space of the home (Smith 2008: 62; Bachelard 1994). As Korzybski writes, 'the map is *not* the territory' (Korzybski 2000: xvii).

Herein lies the social cartographic significance of the concepts of *précarité* and precariousness. The somewhat paradoxical certainty that these concepts represent an unscripted truth disconnected from its provenance in government policy and statistics forgets that they arose from the faltering of two, crucial technical assumptions of statistical procedures and policy: the mathematical construction of a universal space of equivalence that makes comparability and ranking possible

(Desrosières 1998), and its capacity to yield propositions about stuff with some plausible modicum of rhetorical-scientific force. Together these describe the procedures upon which a claim for (social scientific) objectivity had been staked and from which it drew normative implications for government policy. For much of the nineteenth- and twentieth-centuries, these techniques preserved a methodological nationalism that scaled up from the familial household and scaled across as (national) populations, furnishing the enumeration of law-like regularities that converted propositional statements about the unique, enduring properties of classes and entities into persuasive rules and norms built on the expectation of a predictable future. They also enacted the rule-based procedural line that personifies and connects taxonomic ranks (such as family and nation), elaborated as the possession and transmission of unique, heritable properties, or essences) – which is to say *oikonomia*, or the (*nomos*) law of the (*oikos*) household.

While the concept of precariousness has not always been an explicit feature of policy, laws or statistical research, its reach has nevertheless been implicit in the 2009 standards issued by a group concerned with the universal engineering standards of organisations and systems. The concept of "uncertainty" has had a much longer conceptual history in economics and the (physical) sciences than "precariousness" has had in philosophy, sociology and the humanities, though "uncertainty" is also codified within ISO 31000, where it is defined as "an environment full of uncertainty" (International Organization for Standardization 2009). The ISO 31000:2009 was based on the AS/NZS ISO 31000:2004 issued by Standards Australia in 2004, at the same time as "casualisation" or zero-hour contracts had become not the exception but the standard wage contract (Mitropoulos 2005). Notably, the ISO insists that its acronym follows the French version of its name because "ISO" recalls Plato's esteem for isometric forms. The purpose of the ISO's codification of "uncertainty" is that it regulates accounting control systems whose aim it is to identify, measure, manage and – given the integration of actuarial practices – price risk, so as to optimise performance and maximise monetary returns. Risk, contra Ulrich Beck (1992), is not here understood as simply downside risk, but the analytical determination of a ratio, of more or less elaborate correlations, between possible gains and losses (Mitropoulos 2015). While some disciplines and researchers have used either "precariousness" or "uncertainty", for many and in the early literature they are often used interchangeably – this is not to say there are no differences, but it does suggest an epistemological orientation and research platform across disciplines.

Presented as the simple description of an existential truth and not as an overt system of accounting, the concept of precariousness – as Gaston Bachelard suggested of the figural, fragile nest – suggestively 'set us to dreaming of security'. When we dream, he went on to add, 'we are phenomenologists without realizing it', and 'in the very impetus of the imagination – we return to the sources of the oneiric house' (Bachelard 1994: 102–3). Of course, one person's nest is oftentimes another's place of work (Aguiar and Herod 2006; Mullally 2015) or, with some statistical regularity, is the scene not of repose but of intimate violence (Pleck 2004; Kelly 2003). Indeed, for some time now, the speculative inclination of national security doctrine and the imperative urge toward the remedial regulation of a phenomenal fragility have blended and forged a routine, hyperbolic violence around the sequential conflations of family, race and nation. This is the sense in which the inclination of "precarity", as *precor*, shifts so easily toward 'praying for guarantees and, at times, shields that often turn out to be fortresses' (Mitropoulos 2005).

Précarité and precariousness

In the early 1980s, French Government statisticians began using the category of *précarité* in labour force surveys (Barbier 2002; French Ministry of Labour 1992). That history was preceded by its use in studies of rural-to-urban migration and Agnès Pitrou's ethnographic studies of *les solidarités familiales* (1978, 1992). Research such as that undertaken by Josef Gugler on labour migration in Sub-Saharan Africa is indicative of the ways in which "precarious" had come to describe not the 'precarious (property) title' referred to in the earliest codification of civil law in the first century (Scott 1973), but the porosity and scattering of the boundaries of a disciplinary object from whose regularities (policy) norms were conventionally derived – or, as Gugler put it, such a study would 'provide excellent data for answering central sociological questions such as: How do changing economic forces and social norms interact?' (Gugler 1968: 463). Over later decades, the concept of *précarité* would become the phenomenological description of an existential condition, having slipped its relegation to the margins of sociological objectivity. In reconsidering this history and its implications, this chapter extends and modifies two arguments made elsewhere: that "precarity" pertains to the dynamics and displacement of a specifically capitalist uncertainty (Mitropoulos 2005); and that contemporary welfare, social and economic policy treats contingency as (capitalist) necessity, whose policy implications are more or less explicitly shaped according to an *oikonomia* (law of the household) construed as the necessary, dispositional fundament of capitalist futurity (Mitropoulos 2012).

Overall, this chapter theorises the link between the phenomenological concept of precariousness and the statistical category of *précarité* in the context of a broader, partial turn to theories of "spontaneous order". It does so by critically reading Hayekian theories of 'spontaneous order' not as arguments for deregulation but, on the contrary, as normative claims for the endogenous regulation of uncertainty by means of encoding rules of selective conservation. Those rules pertain to methods for handling 'life' according to universal standards and the managerial gain of 'investment' in categorical forms (Thévenot 2009), and investment in categorical forms is weighted in policy and scripted through rules so as to guide the strategic calculations of risk-bearing subjects. This has entailed a renewed emphasis on a phenomenological "parts-whole" paradigm. It is a reformulated epistemology that reluctantly admits the inferential weaknesses of macro-scaled, probabilistic distributions and categorical "incompleteness". Yet whether it does so to salvage a metaphysics of forms from the incapacitation of normative inferences and prediction, or because the total elimination of anomaly does away with scientific and creative invention, is an arguable point. It depends to some extent on whether the reconstruction of a framework follows invention. Inasmuch as it does, the recourse to local-scaled ethnographic knowledge of the non-correspondence between universal standards and forms, the creative fuzziness that aesthetic imagination contributes by stretching probabilities into a modal range of possibilities, or the simplification of complexity by clustering data sets is perhaps far less indicative of a jump into a different eigenstate than the reformation up of "parts-whole" Platonism along the way.

In the case of the statistical category of *précarité*, the argument here is that it involved a shift from statistical measures of national labour capacity to a metrics of uncertainty based on Pitrou's indicators of risk absorption and the cost of inter-generational transactions (*solidarités familiales*), along with the statistical clustering of non-uniform contract durations undertaken by government statisticians at the government's statistical bureau. The informational yield of these indices is not the national unemployment rate or Gross Domestic Product (GDP) as it was in earlier research on the rate of unemployment but, first, the feasibility and cost of transferring risk from governments and corporations to households and, secondly, the ratio of risk (flexibility-disorder) in the system. It is the ratio (of the ratio) between flexibility and disorder that furnishes a new metrics of social volatility. As Dirac claims: 'a measurement always causes the system to jump into an eigenstate of the dynamical variable that is being measured' (Dirac 2004: 36).

These metrics signal the abandonment of the premise that the wage corresponds to a quantum of labour and instead underline the role of the contract as a mechanism for the allocation of risk (Mitropoulos 2012, 2015). For instance, in André Masson's modelling of precarious work, labour is not measured as a stock of energy (a "lump of labour") but as the 'virtual risk' contained in a 'demographic flows-stock' system (1983: 28). Such arguments follow the trend from classical to modern physics in successive understandings of the properties of energy – from the elemental phlogiston, through Antoine Lavoisier's substances, to kinetic energy (statistical distribution and error rates), and on to the energetic vortices of quantum physics. This parallels a shift in concepts of labour: from labour as form-giving fire, to a substance, to a focus on the ratio of employment to unemployment as a statistical measure of entropy (i.e. as the statistical rate of the unavailability of energy for conversion into "useful work"), to a current emphasis on measuring the degree of disorder or randomness in the system. The difference between the metrics of GDP and those set to marking degrees of randomness or disorder is not as subtle as it might seem.

While the push to predictability was integral to the early use of statistics in policy, it could not account for stochastic processes that troubled categorical neatness and, at the same time, implied the destruction of entrepreneurial risk: for early neoclassical economists such as Frank H. Knight, the unbounded elimination of uncertainty would mean the elimination of above-average profits and losses, the mythic quality of entrepreneurialism (Knight 2006; Mitropoulos

2015). Furthermore, an emphasis on the degree of disorder and not entropy sets aside the substantive distinctions and polarities of "the reserve army of labour" and "full employment", so as to both uphold the personalised, customisable tenets of human capital theory and put the category of unemployment to work. Significantly, this supersedes Michał Kalecki's contention – which drew upon Rosa Luxemburg's theory of capitalist dynamics (2004) – that "full employment" would be corrosive of discipline in a labour market but feasible under conditions of involuntary or forced labour (Kalecki 1971). Workfare, zero-hour contracts and below-subsistence wages blur the categorical distinctions between employment and unemployment (as well as employer and welfare agency, welfare recipients and the working poor). Importantly, they do this while maintaining a high degree of discipline.

For management, however, there is a downside risk of maintaining discipline through intermittence and related measures of "flexibility", namely disorder. This is why it is important to emphasise a proportional concept of risk. Risk management is a consideration of this ratio (Mitropoulos 2015). It is notable that, in both Pierre Bourdieu's and Richard Sennett's ethnographic studies of younger workers (the first discusses '*précarité*' and the second downside 'risk'), disorder is presented as a lack of attachment of workers to employers, a prospect that Bourdieu and Sennett present as a matter of grave concern for maintaining social cohesion in the face of "globalisation" and, in Sennett's account, a degeneration of the normative character traits of loyalty and trust (Bourdieu 1993; Sennett 1999).

In actuarial-fiscal terms, welfare policy and social insurance are questions about which (and whose) transaction costs (or contracts) should be underwritten, the means by which the risks of contracting are pooled, spread, and priced. The institutional setting of these calculations are generic combinations of government, non-government and corporate systems, including those of welfare, such as in the case of pension funds (Clark 2000), the financial instruments of social investment schemes (Mitropoulos and Bryan 2015), and the practices of punishing (non-corporate) welfare recipients for transgressions of behavioural codes of conduct set by joint public-private agencies (Stoesz 1999). Caution is required when using privatisation rather than risk management as the lens through which to understand these changes. It makes sense to talk of privatisation to describe the transfer of risk from government to households in one regard, particularly insofar as it can entail the reduction of transaction costs by calling upon unpaid labour in the home. Yet the sweeping juxtaposition of states and markets is an insufficient guide for considering the history and current terms of welfare and other policy, not least because it neglects the ways in which laws, codes, contracts and universal standards (including money as a universal equivalent) have always linked and shaped any salient differences along those lines. The concept of privatisation can often neglect the crucial difference between strategies which decrease transactional costs by calling upon unpaid labour, as in Becker's human capital theory and New Household Economics (1962), and those which transfer revenue to corporations to carry out compliance or risk-shifting, as in outsourcing.

The precarious form of value

The form of value (or value-form) of the classical scientific paradigm – that is, the valid form of reasoning that infers norms or rules (or what is right and proper) from the common properties of classes – has been supplanted by an emphasis on the endogenous regulation of properties through selective conservation, or in other words, the evaluative rules of self-regulatory systems based on the conservation of unique properties and their patterned advance. This entails an emphasis on mechanisms of risk-shifting and selective conservation, where the attachment to categorical forms is recast as the strategic calculations of risk-bearing subjects. In practice, the risk of some transaction costs are underwritten, others are not. This is the terrain of post-welfare social management theory, setting the protocols to guide and underwrite decisions as investments in human capital and households, and to do so where the meaning of decision itself is rendered precarious according to the patterning of legal protections (Mitropoulos 2016).

The blows to the classical paradigm delivered by Kurt Gödel's theory of the undecidability of forms illustrates the extent to which this was an epistemological, mathematical problem within the categorical certitude of statistical methods, even though those blows would not have landed as they did without a range of struggles that Gilles Deleuze and Félix Guattari described as the 'flight from the enclosures' (see Deleuze and Guattari 1988). Gödelian 'undecidability' means, briefly put, that the inclusion of statements of a system's consistency within that system makes that system inconsistent (Gödel 1962). The implication is that any language or formal semantic system which involves mathematics, syntactical formulae of classes, ranking and number or computations is 'incomplete'. The insight of Gödel's mathematical theorem of formal undecidability is, in this chapter, extended to suggest that systems of classification cannot include an account of the validity of their predicates without breaking down and, subsequently, responding to that breakdown by resorting to metaphysics (such as universal standards) so as to stake an *a priori* claim on categorical necessity (as Gödel himself did). Alternately, they are compelled to reach beyond syntax to context and thereby to non-necessary (historical) explanations of categorical forms and their methods (as the approach in this chapter does). The point is that the concept of precariousness identifies and transfers the risks of deciding on what (in the Gödelian sense) is 'undecidable' – a procedure that among other things reconstructs decision as a matter of attachment to and selective conservation of categorical forms or, as Laurent Thévenot would say, the 'investment in forms' (Thévenot 1984).

Spontaneous orders and selective conservation

The assumptions behind the concept of "spontaneous order" are often obscured by, on the one hand, its associations with one side of Cold War polemics over "free trade versus state planning" (Hayek 1960) and, on the other hand, the eclipse of earlier polemics within Marxism over "spontaneous organisation" (Luxemburg 2006; Lenin 1902). This has obscured the meaning of positions taken on calculative reason. Despite the usual reading of the first set of arguments, Friedrich Hayek's argument for "liberty of contract" followed the Spanish Scholastics, from whom concepts of contract freedom and the *ius communes* (the just distribution of the common good) were borrowed. Moreover, despite their differences, both Hayek and Karl Polanyi dispensed with "freedom of contract" at the front door of the familial household and at the edge of presumably archaic tradition. For the Spanish Scholastics, freedom of contract found its limit-case in the proper, categorical orders of *oikonomia* (the law of the household), and the *ius communes* took its form of "right reasoning about properties" from a natural law understanding of the *oikos* (Schermaier 2009). In Hayek's terms, this is pattern recognition and pattern prediction (1994). Unlike Hayek, Luxemburg, trained in mathematics and statistics, treated (statistical) patterns as the operational effects of a methodological apparatus and its metrics and not as naturally occurring forms of providential design. Indeed, Luxemburg put forward a theory of the spontaneous emergence of order and dynamic complexity well before Hayek (Mitropoulos 2016). It is also worth recalling that the so-called Socialist Calculation Debates, which raged between those influenced by Luxemburg and Hayek's predecessors, understood calculation as a debate about the *political regularities* of economic processes and the extent to which the state (or *polis*) could or should regulate economics (*oikos*). Those debates involved a range of positions, including Oskar Lange's socialist arguments for state planning as 'programming under conditions of uncertainty' (1971: x).

That said, theories of "spontaneous order" *derived from Hayek* involve, first, an argument for the endogenous regulation of properties through selective conservation (or qualification), and second, an argument that the circumstances in which this occurs are (paradoxically) necessarily uncertain. Put in more classical Scholastic terms, this implies that contingency is necessity (Mitropoulos 2012: 27–9). In more contemporary, Hayekian-derived terms, this implies a theory of selective conservation in the face of inevitable uncertainty. A 1991 working paper from the Santa Fe Institute defined it in this way:

> This new body of thought implies that the poised coherence, precarious, subject to avalanches of change, of our biological and social world is inevitable. Such systems, poised on the edge of chaos, are the natural talisman of the adaptive order.
>
> (Kauffman 1991: 2)

This is not the subordination of qualities by quantification that is so often decried in ongoing, neo-Kantian conflicts between the faculties of the humanities and the sciences – an assumption that continues to shape understandings of neoliberalism as deregulatory and preoccupied in the main with the subordination of political, moral and ethical values by 'economic calculation' (Brown 2005: 46).

From the angle of Hayekian spontaneous order, the question posed by these concepts of welfare policy is not one of evolutionary biology ("How do things change?") but, on the contrary, "How does capitalism undergo changes while staying the same?" In Aristotelian logic, this is called the problem of entelechy. Where selective conservation diverges from the evolutionary (Darwinian) theory of "natural selection" is in the emphasis the former accords to the preservation of the ostensibly regular properties of uniquely existing entities. For Charles Darwin, by contrast, the encounter between transmissible variations and uncertainty is the non-teleological condition of adaptation. The point is not that Darwin's theory is without its problems, even less socio-biology, which amounts to the recapture of Darwinian evolution by Aristotelian teleology. It is that the Darwinian theory of evolution is the inverse of Pitrou's argument that 'family solidarity' acts as a shock absorber in dealing with happenstance (1978, 1992). In other words, it is instructive that the proposition of an 'environment full of uncertainty' precipitates an argument for the preservation and solidification of ostensibly universal forms and not for, say, the diversification that in Darwinian theories of evolution increases the range of chances and possible futures. The emphasis on shock-absorption is moreover the source of later concepts of "resilience", and in this sense less biopolitical in its "politicisation of life" than it is oikonomic in its conflation of national security doctrine with the financial securitisation of the household.

Moreover, Pitrou's concept of familial solidarity, and its corollary focus on inter-generational solidarity and population policy were used with increasing frequency by conservatives in France precisely because of how they diverged from Darwinian concepts of non-teleological evolution and adaptation. Indeed, by 1999 the Juppé Government had established a Ministry for Solidarity Between Generations. There is a similar conjuncture between the concept of 'fragile families' (Kowaleski-Jones and Wolfinger 2007) and conservative welfare policy elsewhere. This is because these concepts pose a question about the transactional costs of such things as pension schemes, aged care – as questions about the flows of insecure migrant care workers and/or the 'gift economy' of family solidarity – because they are concerned with the selective preservation of categorical properties rather than the variability that is integral to adaptation. This is not quite the "parts-whole" neo-Platonism of G. W. F. Hegel or Edmund Husserl, though it travels in both their shadows. Instead, the training of statisticians places an increasing emphasis on the default, conventionalist Platonism of social and political engineers seeking to encode a link between ideal and phenomenal forms of life through universal standards (or laws). The implications it holds for the transfer of risk from corporations to households are immense, as noted by the International Monetary Fund's 2005 *Global Financial Stability Report*, which observed that 'the household sector has increasingly and more directly become the "shock absorber of last resort" in the financial system' (IMF 2005: 5).

Regulating precarious life and universal standards

The recurrent syntactical use of an adjective (*précarité*, precarious) as a concept underlines its status as an operating function within a larger formulation. Cutting across this, the entwined histories of sociology and property law are crucial reminders that the systematic use of grammatical operators involves a history. On the one hand, the emergence of the classical sociological paradigm (of Auguste Comte, Adolphe Quetelet, Emile Durkheim, Max Weber) occurs at those moments where the unique coherence of its object – society – is deemed to be at risk of being rent asunder by divisions and, at the same time, to be a necessary and natural whole whose contours just happen to accord with those of nation-states (Mitropoulos 1999). On the other hand, the earliest effort at legal codification – the Byzantine Empire's compendium of civil laws (Scott 1973) – is replete with mentions of 'precarious *title*' over land and slaves. The dropping of the explicit referential (to property title) points toward the Early Modern Lockean redefinition of contractual personhood as "property-in-one's-self" (Macpherson 1983) and, furthermore, underscores the sense in which the demand for (property) rights are often couched in somewhat Byzantine terms as the restoration of a lost empire.

The link between norm or law and systems for classifying the properties of things is crucial. Firstly, the use of these concepts suggests an effort to reorient social-scientific conventions from the mapping of known probabilities to a cartography of the 'non-standard', anomalous or stochastic. This accords with the trajectory from classical to neoclassical paradigms in the natural and physical sciences, not least since Thomas Kuhn pointed out that scientific invention turns on the assimilation of that which was previously deemed as being anomalous or accidental (1970). Indeed, without exploiting this frontier of the anomalous or stochastic (and in contemporary terms, "the household frontier") by translating it into universal, categorical forms, the machinery of universal equivalence and classification comes to a tautological, non-generative standstill. As in Marx's depiction of the circuit of capital, without this exploitation, 'C does not become C''.

Secondly, the concepts of *précarité* and precariousness describe again the familiar *habitus* of (national) statistical space in emphatically aesthetic terms. Prediction comes to rely more on imagined scenarios, speculative estimates, qualitative ethnography and fuzzy categories than on the extensive enumeration of past frequencies into the future. Where neoclassical economics multiplied objective probabilities by way of the concept of preference, so too phenomenology and associated ethnographic studies shifted the emphasis from known probabilities to the range of all that can be imagined and is possible, often at lower scales. Scenario planning and game theory, for instance, incorporate aesthetic and phenomenal possibilities into tools of statistical modelling. Statistics responds to the challenge of randomness by scaling-down, clustering, or plotting the relationship between the 'poised coherence' of categories and Hilbert space so as to model inter-generational household assets in systems whose borders are porous. In the reorganisation of the faculties as a division of labour between the conscription of researchers and the use of an implicit methodological script, phenomenology can function just as well through the aesthetic, roughly encoded and local-scaled part of this 'parts-whole' methodology as it can fuel a philosophical firewall against the corrosive implications of categorical undecidability.

Thus the epistemological assumption of a "parts-whole" relationship between objects readily converts variety into a Platonist question about an entity's "participation" in universal, eternal forms. Judith Butler's discussion of 'precarious life', wherein 'open-ended and plural cohabitation' is framed as a species of 'global ethics' is an elegant case in point (2012: 144). Where classical statistics frowned upon 'deviations from the average' (as in Comte), in contemporary phenomenology, after a brief ethnographic detour through the margins, those "deviations" are translated back into universal law as an approximate case. Similarly, the debate between Erin Manning and Jodie McNeilly over whether bodily movements outrun the metastable, precarious equilibria of subjectivity is a debate between processual and phenomenological paradigms of variation, one that underscores the theological affiliations of the latter (Manning 2014; McNeilly 2014). This echoes previous debates about the ways in which the concept of precarity sought to enjoin a faltering movement to the task of reconstructing a measure of a general rule (Mitropoulos 2005). Phenomenology, of course, involves a more or less tacit question about eternal Being's appearance in, by its view, the messy sensorium (Hegel 1977; Husserl 1970; Janicaud 2000). In the phenomenological view, nothing "of substance" changes, except the modes, which as modes of a metaphysical substance are conceived as amenable to measure and comparability. And 'unruly specificities'' – to borrow a phrase (Law 2009: 8) – are thereby treated, at best, as either modal multiplications of this metaphysical whole, or as an index of divergences from ideal forms (of labour, polity, community, nation and so on) whose existence, as uniquely existing entities, is routinely given in languages, rhetoric and histories as an idea, but always falls short in any attempt at empirical verification. This is a strict philosophical idealism in that its impetus is to convert ostensibly unformed matter into ideal forms. In this way, the implicit question is much like – and often simply just is – the classical theological concern with the preservation or dissolution of the immortal soul (Elkaisy-Friemuth and Dillon 2009), and universal standards and codes are the abstract scripture which guides the risk-bearing subject's prudential reckonings or risk-taking calculations of transactional costs. The propositional yield of arithmetic-phenomenological co-operation are codes of conduct in which regulation (or conformity to a rule) means the operationalisation of the formal rules of semantic systems that are framed by the vital qualifying point of ostensibly eternal and uniquely existing forms or, in more explicitly vitalist accounts, by the ideal form of life encompassing all forms. That is, *up to* the ranking qualifications (the borders) of the categorical forms of 'species-genus' reasoning that recalls Aristotle and Carl Linnaeus far more than Darwinian a-teleological, evolutionary time or Donna Haraway's recombinant, a-categorical speciation.

Thévenot's argument in *Governing Life by Standards* and elsewhere, by which he meant 'the deployment of standards throughout our lives and the lives of all living entities' (2009: 793), is an argument made in close proximity to the development of the concept of *précarité*. At the beginning of the 1980s, government statisticians at the Institut National de la Statistique et des Études Économiques (INSEE) began discussing modifications to the statistical classes used in national surveys of the labour force (Eymard-Duvernay 1981: 68). From the late 1970s, the INSEE had taken a robust interest in exploring the history of statistical axioms beyond the usual administrative questions of operationalisation and interpretation. While politically diverse in some respects, most of its staff had been trained at the École Nationale de la Statistique et de l'Administration Économique (ENSAE). Michel Aglietta, who would come to be associated with the post-Marxist Regulation School, studied at the ENSAE and worked at the INSEE for some time (1964–75). Bourdieu, who positioned himself within the libertarian tradition of the Left, taught at the ENSAE briefly between 1963 and 1966. While the regulationist approach emphasised regularities at different scales, Bourdieu's cultural sociology took its cues from Ruth Benedict's cultural anthropology, wherein each individual is a fractal, scalar instance of a larger-scale culture that, in turn, is both figuratively personified and understood as having a personality. These more or less isometric, scalable "parts-whole" constructions reflect a statistical training and concept of properties. Yet unlike in Benedict's argument, where she contended that it was possible to infer from a comparison of 'primitive' cases what is 'specific to local cultural types and those that are general to mankind' (1934: 20), in late 1960s France, this "parts-whole" edifice was reconstructed from both angles: by way of localised ethnographic research, often about young workers (Bourdieu 1993), and the propositional certainties of universal standards (Thévenot 2009). Categories became clusters, informed on the one hand by qualitative, ethnographic research and, on the other, accorded the weight of validity in policy terms through the rule-based formalism of the conventionalist approach.

The conventionalist approaches of Thévenot and Luc Boltanski came to the fore in the early 1980s, often in sharp contrast to Bourdieu's cultural sociology, which placed the emphasis on political norms, and still further from Marxism. They were also reminiscent of earlier influences on the ENSAE, including a concern with the engineering of standards and the codification of 'life' (Thévenot 2009, 1983a, 1983b). The emphasis on reflexivity and convention in this approach created a link between understanding the historical limits, imprecision and artifice of particular techniques and applying them nevertheless. The conventionalist approach at the ENSAE could, then, be viewed as a moving bridge between the pragmatic Platonism of mathematicians (for whom the axioms and techniques through which statistical space is constructed are based on theorems, subject to dispute, reformulation and experiment) and the pragmatic realism of the statistical professions (for whom the construction is an occupational necessity).

From the late 1970s there was, as Bernard Mériaux put it, 'a specific question [posed] regarding the reasons and above all forms of [employment] segmentation in the French case, inspiring several research programs, frequently across axes exploring the variety of forms of precarious employment' (1978: 133). Mériaux cites Michael Piore (visiting from MIT), whose theory and study of labour market segmentation in France – that is, a growing gap between stable, well-paid jobs and a secondary 'sector … manned by women, youth, minority groups, migrants, part-time peasants and other groups which we tend to think of as marginal or "disadvantaged"' – appeared in the same 1978 edition of *Revue Économique* (1978). Piore makes no mention of precariousness, though the essay is subtitled 'A Response to Uncertainty and Flux'. From the late 1970s, statistical surveys increasingly classified the labour market through the explicit criteria of contracts: *formes particulières d'emploi* (FPEs) and *contrats à durée indéterminée* (indefinite contracts). This new nomenclature was used in an increasing number of statistical surveys and outlined in the 1979 Report of the Planning Commission (Michon and Germe 1979; Barbier 2002: 7). Within a decade, the non-standard work contracts which had been statistically aggregated as FPEs were redefined as *statuts précaires* in labour force surveys from as early as 1982, as *situations précaires* in statistical tables, and subsequently as *précarité* in the Labour Code, in the minimum income (RMI) law of 1988, and across all government and administrative departments (Barbier 2002). The FPE clustered data on temporary agency work, apprenticeships, seasonal work and short-term contracts together with housework and *aidex familiaux* (work undertaken for a familial relative whose data was enumerated in another class, i.e. as self-employed).

In the history of statistics and particularly its computations, the practice of clustering arose as a means to combine entities deemed to be not of the same property but of approximate resemblance (Ammar *et al.* 2015), or: more like than unlike, rather than the same. Cluster analysis involves the explicit use of logical steps (algorithms), and is often used in machine learning, pattern recognition and information retrieval systems. It is one of the most prevalent tools of social scientific research on precariousness (e.g., O'Rand 2011; Scherer 2001; Muntaner *et al.* 2012; Herman 2014; Verd and López-Andreu 2012). Yet while clustering enhances the complex view of multivariate data, without the superposition of a qualitative hierarchy (ordinal rankings of value) it wears out the inferential force of norms and laws.

It is against this backdrop that Thévenot's remarks on the generational 'flouting' of species-genus (syllogistic) reasoning are instructive:

> Statistical coding as a scientific activity is ... regulated by logical principles which determine the *correct forms* of classification. But when a statistician is required to classify [an occupational] post or status which has not already received technical, administrative or legal coding, these logical principles are flouted, and this is the case with young people whose family situations and occupational status are often ill-defined.
>
> (Thévenot 1984:1)

Thévenot explains this as a problem of an 'ill-defined' generation and the flouting of categorical rules. Not as the technical limit of 'correct forms' which infers propositions from the properties of classes. What he does not quite say is that the syllogism deals in absolute all-or-nothing classes, and not the proportional-probabilistic statements of statistics or the modal logic of possibilities. But no matter.

The point is not that there is an inherent problem with abstraction, numbers or classification as such. This chapter makes no such suggestion. It argues for rethinking operational concepts as something like rough encoding for machine learning let loose through the wild complexity of an eponymous field, rather than as necessary forms of knowledge and practice calling upon a managerial investment in the ideal forms of universal standards. It is not, then, that abstraction, imagination or enumeration should be jettisoned for claims of noumenal authenticity, as if this were not already encompassed in the phenomenological form-matter dichotomy. It is that the elementary insistence on 'parts-whole' reasoning of 'correct forms' greets variation, mutability and undecidability with a recurrent, metaphysical question about the ways in which forms of life "participate" in universal, eternal forms (Welton 2002). It does so, ultimately, as a means of re-affirming a faith in 'the total [idealizable] form encompassing all forms' (Husserl 1970: 35), as the trope of international law, the engineering of organisational systems, or as a more explicit theology of natural law that stakes its ground on the reconstruction of the law of the household. It is a faith that forgets 'that rules and procedures do not actually rule' (Law 2009: 5). But in proceeding from a question of forms (and their scaling and ranking), it glosses over the ineradicable difference between processes and forms, between indefinite processes and objectified classifications. The appeal of the latter draws the emphasis from the processes through which forms are given form, and therefore away from contextual, indefinite questions about infrastructure to the dream of rules that do not rule without violence.

Back to class and the leap beyond classification

Earlier debates over the use of "precarity" among radical scholars and movements often turned around the extent to which the neologism could be leveraged around the recomposition and identification of a new class and, moreover, the implications of treating this as a shared ontological circumstance given the material weight of differences between those newly arrived to the experience of, say, zero-hour contracts and those for whom the standard-issue Fordist wage had never been a reality (Vishmidt 2005; Mitropoulos 2005; Gill and Pratt 2008). Since then, others have pointed to the feigning of shared feelings across such divisions that the uptake of concepts such as precarity and precariousness has furnished within and around the university (Gregg 2011). These debates occurred in an institutional context where the standardisation of uncertainty had become an encoded convention of organisational engineering and, moreover, where the social sciences were increasingly being invested by the practices and analytics of risk management. While the Hegelian-Marxist concept of class was imbued with an ahistorical teleology of a universal spirit manifested in imperfect, modal appearances, it can instead be critically understood as the incomplete effect of mundane and methodical *processes of classification*, including those derived from neo-Platonism. The argument here as to the history of the concepts of *précarité* and precariousness is that, when those procedures of classification were confronted with their own mathematical, technical limits while, at the same time, there were struggles against the limits of those categorical forms, the statistical categories of GDP and rate of unemployment came to be replaced by sociologists first with a tentative risk-absorption metrics of selective conservation and the law of the household and, secondly, by sociologists and government statisticians preoccupied with the flexibility-disorder ratio of *précarité*. The broader point is that what is being mapped can never be mapped completely.

References

Aguiar, L. L. M. and Herod, A. (2006) *The Dirty Work of Neoliberalism: Cleaners in the Global Economy*. Malden, MA: Blackwell.

Ammar, A., Elouedi Z. and Lingras, P. (2015) Semantically segmented clustering based on possibilistic and rough set theories. *International Journal of Intelligent Systems* 30 (6): 676–706.

Bachelard, G. (1994) *The Poetics of Space*. Translated by M. Jolas. Massachusetts: Beacon Press.

Barbier, J-C. (2002) A survey of the use of the term *Précarité* in French economics and sociology. *Document de Travail* 19. CNRS/Centre d'etudes de l'emploi.

Beck, U. (1992) *Risk Society: Towards a New Modernity*. London: Sage Publications.

Becker, G. S. (1962) Investment in human capital: A theoretical analysis. *Journal of Political Economy* 70(5): 9–49.

Benedict, R. (1934) *Patterns of Culture*. Boston: Houghton Mifflin Company.

Bourdieu, P. (ed.) (1993) *La misère du monde*. Paris: Éd. du Seuil.

Brown, W. (2005) *Edgework: Critical Essays on Knowledge and Politics*. Princeton: Princeton University Press.

Butler, J. (2012) Precarious life, vulnerability, and the ethics of cohabitation. *The Journal of Speculative Philosophy* 26 (2): 134–51.

Clark, G. L. (2000) *Pension Fund Capitalism*. Oxford: Oxford University Press.

Deleuze, G. and Guattari, F. (1988) *A Thousand Plateaus*. Trans. Brian Massumi. Minneapolis, MN: University of Minnesota Press.

Desrosières, A. (1998) *The Politics of Large Numbers: A History of Statistical Reasoning*. Cambridge: Harvard University Press.

Dirac, P. A. M. (2004) *The Principles of Quantum Mechanics*. Oxford: Clarendon Press.

Elkaisy-Friemuth, M. and Dillon, J. M. (eds) (2009) *The Afterlife of the Platonic Soul: Reflections of Platonic Psychology in the Monotheistic Religions*. Leiden: Brill.

Eymard-Duvernay, F. (1981) Les secteurs de l'industrie et leurs ouvriers. *Économie et statistique* 138: 49–68.

French Ministry of Labour (1992) France: First assessment of the 1990 law on precarious employment. *European Industrial Relations Review* 222: 21–22.

Gill, R.. and Pratt, A. (2008) In the social factory? Immaterial labour, precariousness and cultural work. *Theory, Culture & Society* 25(7–8): 1–30.

Gödel, K. (1962) *On Formally Undecidable Propositions of Principia Mathematica and Related Systems*. New York: Basic Books.

Gugler, J. (1968) The impact of labour migration on society and economy in Sub-Saharan Africa: Empirical findings and theoretical considerations. *African Social Research* 6: 463–86.

Harley, J. B. (2001) *The New Nature of Maps: Essays in the History of Cartography*. Baltimore: Johns Hopkins University Press.

Hayek, F. A. (1960) *The Constitution of Liberty*. Chicago: University of Chicago Press.

Hayek, F. A. (1994) A theory of complex phenomena. In Martin, M. and McIntyre, L. C. (eds), *Readings in the Philosophy of Social Science* 55–70. Cambridge: MIT Press.

Hegel, G. W. F. (1977) *Phenomenology of Spirit*. Translated by Miller, A. V. and Findlay, J. N. Oxford: Clarendon Press.
Herman, E. (2014) Working poverty in the European Union and its main determinants: An empirical analysis. *Engineering Economics* 25(4): 427–36.
Husserl, E. (1970) *The Crisis of European Sciences and Transcendental Phenomenology. An Introduction to Phenomenological Philosophy*. Evanston: Northwestern University Press.
International Monetary Fund. (2005) *Global Financial Stability Report* (April).
International Organization for Standardization (2009) *ISO 31000: Risk Management: Principles and Guidelines - Management du risque: Principles et lignes directrices*. Geneva: ISO.
Janicaud, D. (2000) *Phenomenology and the 'Theological Turn:' The French Debate*. New York: Fordham University Press.
Kalecki, M. (1971) *Selected Essays on the Dynamics of the Capitalist Economy 1933–1970*. Cambridge: University Press.
Kauffman, S. A. (1991) The sciences of complexity and 'origins of order'. SFI Working Paper: 199104-021. California: Santa Fe Institute.
Kelly, K. A. (2003) *Domestic Violence and the Politics of Privacy*. Ithaca: Cornell University Press.
Knight, F. H. (2006) *Risk, Uncertainty and Profit*. Mineola: Dover Publications.
Korzybski, A. (2000) *Science and Sanity: An Introduction to Non-Aristotelian Systems and General Semantics*. Brooklyn: Institute of General Semantics.
Kowaleski-Jones, L. and Wolfinger, N. H. (2007) *Fragile Families and the Marriage Agenda*. New York: Springer.
Kuhn, T. S. (1970) *The Structure of Scientific Revolutions*. Chicago: University of Chicago Press.
Lange, O. (1971) *Optimal Decisions: Principles of Programming*. New York: Pergamon Press.
Law, J. (2009) The Greer-Bush test: On politics in STS. *Heterogeneities.net*. Available at: www.heterogeneities.net/publications/Law2009TheGreer-BushTest.pdf (Accessed 3 August 2016).
Lenin, V. I. (1902) *What Is to Be Done?: Burning Questions of Our Movement*. London: Lawrence.
Luxemburg, R. (2004) *The Accumulation of Capital*. London: Routledge.
Luxemburg, R. (2006) Leninism or Marxism? In Buhle, P. (ed.) *Reform or Revolution and Other Writings*. Mineola: Dover.
Macpherson, C. B. (1983) *Property: Mainstream and Critical Positions*. Toronto: University of Toronto Press.
Manning, E. (2014) Wondering the world directly. Or, how movement outruns the subject. *Body & Society* 20(3–4): 162–88.
Masson, A. (1983) Estimation du risque à terme de chômage. *Annales de l'Inséé* 52: 23–53.
McNeilly, J. (2014) A phenomenology of/with total movement: Response to Erin Manning. *Body & Society* 20(3–4): 208–21.
Mériaux, B. (1978) Point de vue sur les recherches françaises en économie du travail. *Revue Économique* 29 (1): 120–40.
Michon, F., and J. F. Germe (1979) 'Stratégies des entreprises et formes particulières d'emploi' rapport pour le Commissariat Général du Plan. 2. Paris: SET, Université de Paris I.

Mitropoulos, A. (1999) Discipline and labour: Sociology, class formation and money in Australia at the beginning of the twentieth century. *Journal of Sociology* 35(1): 77–91.

Mitropoulos, A. (2005) Precari-Us? In Berry-Slater, J. (ed.) *The Precarious Reader*. London: Mute.

Mitropoulos, A. (2012) *Contract and Contagion: From Biopolitics to Oikonomia*. Brooklyn: Minor Compositions/Autonomedia.

Mitropoulos, A. (2015) Archipelago of risk: Uncertainty, borders and migration detention systems. *New Formations* 84: 163–83.

Mitropoulos, A. (2016) *Infrastructures of Uncommon Forms*. Forthcoming.

Mitropoulos, A. and Bryan, D. (2015) Social benefit bonds: Financial markets inside the state. In Meagher, G. and Goodwin (eds), *Markets, Rights and Power in Australian Social Policy*. Sydney: Sydney University Press.

Mullally, S. (2015) *Care, Migration, and Human Rights: Law and Practice*. London: Routledge.

Muntaner, C., H. Chung, Benach, J. and Ng, E. (2012) Hierarchical cluster analysis of labour market regulations and population health: A taxonomy of low- and middle-income countries. *BMC Public Health* 12(1): 1–15.

O'Rand, A. M. (2011) 2010 SSS Presidential Address: The devolution of risk and the changing life course in the United States. *Social Forces* 90(1): 1–16.

Piore, M. J. (1978) Dualism in the labor market: A response to uncertainty and flux. The case of France. *Revue économique* 29(1): 26–48.

Pitrou, A. (1978) *La vie précaire des familles face à leurs difficultés*. Paris: Caisse nationale des allocations familiales, Caisse nationale des allocations familiales, Laboratoire d'économie et de sociologie du travail.

Pitrou, A. (1992) *Les solidarités familiales : vivre sans famille?* Toulouse: Privat.

Pleck, E. H. (2004) *Domestic Tyranny: The Making of American Social Policy against Family Violence from Colonial Times to the Present*. Urbana: University of Illinois Press.

Scherer, S. (2001) Early career patterns: A comparison of Great Britain and West Germany. *European Sociological Review* 17(2): 119–44.

Schermaier, M. J. (2009) *Res Communes Omnium*: The history of an idea from Greek philosophy to Grotian jurisprudence *Grotiana* 30(1): 20–48.

Scott, S. P. (ed.) (1973) *The Civil Law, Including the Twelve Tables, the Institutes of Gaius, the Rules of Ulpian, the Opinions of Paulus, the Enactments of Justinian, and the Constitutions of Leo*. New York: AMS Press.

Sennett, R. (1999) *The Corrosion of Character: The Personal Consequences of Work in the New Capitalism*. New York: WW Norton.

Smith, D. K. (2008) *The Cartographic Imagination in Early Modern England: Re-Writing the World in Marlowe, Spenser, Raleigh and Marvell*. Aldershot: Ashgate.

Stoesz, D. (1999) Unravelling Welfare Reform. *Society* 36(4): 53–61.

Thévenot, L. (1983a) A propos d'une définition des couches moyennes et de la nouvelle nomenclature des professions et catégories socioprofessionnelles. *Revue Française de Sociologie* 24(2): 56–79.

Thévenot, L. (1983b) L'économie du codage. *Critiques de L'économie Politique* 23–24: 188–222.

Thévenot, L. (1984) Rules and implements: Investment in forms. *Social Science Information* 23(1): 1–45.

Thévenot, L. (2009) Postscript to the Special Issue: Governing life by standards. *Social Studies of Science* 39(5): 793–813.

Verd, J. M. and López-Andreu, M. (2012) La inestabilidad del empleo en las trayectorias laborales. un análisis cuantitativo / Employment Instability in Labour Trajectories. A Quantitative Analysis. *Reis* 138 (April): 135–48.

Vishmidt, Marina (2005) Precarious straits, in *Mute* Vol 1, No. 29. The Precarious Issue. Available at: www.metamute.org/editorial/articles/precarious-straits [Accessed 1 December 2016].

Welton, W. A. (ed.) (2002) *Plato's Forms: Varieties of Interpretation*. Lanham: Lexington Books.

Wood, D. (2010) *Rethinking the Power of Maps*. New York: Guilford Press.

Index

A4E 74
academic careers 82–97
activism 7, 26, 113, 123–5, 130–2, 149–52, 158–9, 165, 171, 174–6, 180, 205
adaptation 217
Africa 6, 15–30, 86, 212
Aglietta, M. 220
agriculture 15, 20–1, 24–5, 31, 33, 38, 102, 107, 116, 161
Airbnb 194
Alcoholics Anonymous 164
alienation 53, 61, 78, 92, 94, 99, 165
All China Federation of Trade Unions (ACFTU) 39
Allegri, G. 153
Amamiya, K. 129–31
Amateur's Revolt 130–2
American Legislative Exchange 193
Anderson, B. 171–2, 179
Andræ, G. 24
apartheid 22
Arab Spring 26, 138, 142, 152, 174
Aristotle 210, 217, 219
Armano, E. 1–12, 47–59
Asia 130
aspiration 77–9, 82, 88
'Association nationale des Coopératives d'Activité et d'Entrepreneurs' (COPEA) 63
asylum seekers 179
austerity 16, 24–5, 47, 99, 143, 152–3, 160, 170–1, 173, 175, 196
Australia 6–7, 82, 86–94, 211
autonomy 6, 47, 56–7, 60–9, 125–7, 141, 165, 202–7

Bachelard, G. 211
Bank of England 152
banking 32, 152, 174, 193, 205
Barchiesi, F. 6, 15–30
Baumol, W.J. 41
Beck, U. 93, 211
Becker, G.S. 214
Beckman, B. 24
Belgium 178
Benedict, R. 220
Bentley, P.J. 88
Berardi, F.B. 141, 161–2
Berg, L.D. 94
Berlant, L. 162
Bexley, E. 84
biofinancialisation 140–3
biopolitics 77, 200–1, 204, 217
Blockupy movement 151
blogs 103, 111, 130
Boggs, C. 157–8
Bologna, S. 52
Boltanski, L. 220
Bost, E. 60, 62
Bourdieu, P. 214, 220
bourgeoisie 104, 128, 151, 154, 199–202, 204–5
Bove, A. 1–12
Brazil 27
Bureau of Labour Statistics 196
Bureau, M.-C. 6, 60–9
bureaucracy 72, 74, 82–5
Business and Employment Cooperative (BEC) 6, 60–9
Business Process Outsourcing 191
Butler, J. 4, 16, 128, 218
Byzantine Empire 218

cadastral records 210
call centres 110
callings 83, 95

Calvinism 75
Cameron, D. 75–6
Canada 164
Candeias, M. 124
Candida TV 110
CAP Services 62
capitalism 4–6, 15–18, 47, 50–1, 53; and academic careers 85; and caregiving 199–205, 212, 214, 216; and destabilisation 19–27; and employability 73, 78; and Europe 141; and France 61, 70–1; and free labour 189, 192; and Greece 99, 107; and Japan 125, 128; and PhD graduates 111, 113; and prefigurative practices 158, 161–3, 165–6; and workers' movements 152, 154
care/caregiving 57, 199–209, 217
Carrot Workers Brigade 54
Cartmel, F. 94
cartography 210, 218
Casas-Cortés, M.I. 8, 170–85
Cassegård, C. 127, 129–31
Castel, R. 34
Castoriadis, C. 68
casualisation 19–22, 33, 82, 86–92, 99, 189–90, 197, 211
Ceausescu, N. 114, 117, 119
cell phones 54–5, 71
Central America 179
ChainWorkers Crew 137, 149–51
Charlemagne Prize 150
children 18, 23, 36–7, 86, 107, 119, 202
China 6, 27, 31–46, 194
Chinese Communist Party (CCP) 32, 39
Chinese Dream 31–46
Christians 201
Ciccarelli, R. 153
citizenship 3, 5, 8, 57, 139; and Africa 15, 23; and caregiving 201, 205–7; and China 35, 40; and Greece 99, 105; and Spain 171, 177, 179–81
class 1–2, 5, 8, 138, 143; and academic careers 85, 90–1, 93–4; and Africa 15–17, 19–20, 22, 25–7; and caregiving 201–3, 205; and employability 70–1; and Europe 149, 151–2, 154; and Greece 104, 108; and household law 222; and Italy 56–7; and Japan 123, 125, 129; and prefigurative practices 157, 161
Climate Justice Action 152
cluster analysis 213, 218, 220–1
co-research 65
Cobarrubias, S. 8, 170–85
codes of conduct 214, 219
cognitariat 164–5
Cohen, P. 83
Cold War 215
collective enterprises 65–8, 103–6
collectivisation 42–3, 165, 203
collegiality 84–5, 95
Collini, S. 84
Colombia 164
colonialism 6, 15–24, 128, 178, 210
commodification 18, 57, 72, 77–8, 99, 126
communism 31–2, 34, 116, 119, 151
communities of practice 90, 94, 107
Comte, A. 218–19
Congo, Democratic Republic of 27
contracts 3, 5, 8, 74, 140; and academic careers 87–9, 93; and Africa 20, 23–4; and China 33; contractualisation 33; and Europe 153; and France 60–1, 64, 66; and free labour 190–1; and Greece 100; and household law 213, 216, 218, 221; and Italy 48–9, 51–7; and Japan 122, 126, 129; and PhD graduates 110, 112–13, 116, 119; social contracts 17, 35, 201; and Spain 170–1, 173, 177; zero hours contracts 4, 92, 98, 211, 214, 222
convict-leasing 194
Coopaname 61, 63–8
Cooper, F. 21
cooperative movement 6, 60–9
'Coopérer pour entreprende' network 63
COOPTIS 61
Corbyn, J. 144
corporations 23, 27, 82, 85, 93, 100, 107, 130, 149, 190, 213–14, 217
Corsani, A. 6, 60–9
counter-conduct 78
counterfeiting 27
creative industries 25, 31, 50, 54–6, 125–6, 131–2, 149, 191–2, 196, 213
Cremin, C. 77–8
criminality 21–2, 26, 77, 151
crowdsourcing 191–2
cuidadanía 205, 207

Dardot, P. 165
Darwin, C. 217, 219

Darwinism 55
deadlines 52
debt 73, 101, 104, 113, 139; and caregiving 203; and Europe 151; and France 62; and free labour 189–90, 192, 194–7; and Italy 53; and prefigurative practices 158, 164
Debtors Anonymous 164
decolonisation 18, 20–2
dehumanisation 15
Deleuze, G. 52, 215
Delfanti, A. 157
Delvolvé, N. 66
democracy 26, 65, 104–6, 124, 153, 158, 199–200, 202–3
Deng Xiaopeng 34
denizenship 171, 180
Denmark 164
dependence 199–209
Derieg, A. 199
desire 77–9
Dewey, J. 65
differential inclusion 171, 180
diplomés chômeurs 26
Dirac, P.A.M. 213
discipline 3, 5, 73–6, 78, 99; and academic careers 90, 94; and Africa 15, 17, 19, 21; and caregiving 201, 205; and free labour 193; and household law 212, 214; and Italy 52, 55; and prefigurative practices 161
disorder 213–14, 223
distributed labour 191
division of labour 85, 119–20, 154, 191, 201, 206, 218
domestication 52
Durkheim, E. 218

e-lance programmes 191
East 150
East Asia 130
Eastern Europe 178
École Nationale de la Statistique et d l'Administration Économique (ENSAE) 220
economic exile 170, 176–7
economic growth 2–3, 32–4, 42
Economic Policy Institute 193
education 7, 24–6, 33, 39, 41; and academic careers 82–3, 85–7, 91–2, 94; and caregiving 203, 206; and employability 70, 72–6, 78; and free labour 194; and Italy 51; and PhD graduates 119–20; prefigurative practices 164, 166; and Spain 174
Edwards, D.88
efficiency 72, 85, 87, 107
Egypt 152, 158
Ehrenreich, B. 74
elites 18–19, 74, 89, 125, 138, 143, 150, 153–4
Elyachar, J. 25
emigration *see* migrants
employability 70–81
enclosures 107, 215
England 107
entelechy 217
entrepreneurship 3–4, 6, 23–7, 60, 140; and employability 71, 73–4, 77; and France 62–7; and free labour 194; and Greece 103; and household law 213; and industrial workers 31–46; and Japan 126
entropy 213–14
epistemology 5, 9, 211–12, 215, 218
Ernst and Young 89
ERT 100–1, 103, 105, 107
essentialism 210
ethics 4, 17, 19, 21, 24; and academic careers 82, 94–5; and Africa 27; and employability 75; and Greece 104, 107–8; and household law 216, 219; and Italy 56; and prefigurative practices 166
Euro May Day 7–8, 124, 137, 149–56, 160, 171, 174
Eurocentrism 6, 17
Eurocracy 150
Europe 5, 7, 123, 137–8, 143; and Africa 17, 19–22, 24; and caregiving 199, 204–5; Euro May Day 149–56; and media 98, 101; and PhD graduates 110–11; and prefigurative practices 157, 163; and Spain 170, 178–9
European Central Bank 99, 151
European Foundation for the Improvement of Living and Working Conditions (Eurofound) 2
European Health Card 175
European Parliament 176
European Social Strike Network 154
European Union (EU) 2, 17, 114, 116–17, 150, 152, 170–3, 175–6, 178–9, 181
Eurostat 100, 153

Eurotunnel 179
Eurozone 153, 170, 196
evolution 216–17, 219
existential issues 4–5, 16, 18, 20, 50, 162, 199, 202, 211–12
experts 24, 119, 124
Expósito, M. 152
extrospection 157–69

Facebook 191–2
feminism 110, 113, 138, 205
Ferguson, J. 25
financial crises 38, 122–3, 138, 140, 142; and Europe 152, 154; and free labour 189, 193, 197; and Greece 100–2, 104; and Italy 49; and prefigurative practices 164; and Spain 171, 174–5
financialisation 8–9, 61, 140–3, 194
Finland 153
flexibility 2–3, 24, 138, 154, 173; and caregiving 203–5; and China 34; and employability 70–1, 77; and Europe 154; flexploitation 7, 82–97; and France 62, 65; and Greece 99, 102, 107; and household law 213–14, 223; and Japan 125, 128; and PhD graduates 110–11, 116; and Spain 173
Fordism 2–3, 5, 16, 49, 142; and academic careers 85, 94; and caregiving 199–200, 202–3; and employability 73; and Europe 149; and France 61–2; and household law 222; and Italy 51, 55; post-Fordism 71, 93, 111, 125, 127
formes particulières d'emploi (FPEs) 221
Foti, A. 8, 149–56
Foucault, M. 52, 61, 72, 78, 127, 161, 200–1
Fourier, C. 67
France 1, 6, 20–1, 60–9, 98, 152–4, 212, 217, 220
Franco, F. 174
Fraser, N. 202
free air 103
free labour/work 9, 52–4, 56–7, 189–91, 193, 196–7, 200, 202
free movement 178–9, 181
freelancers 6, 47–52, 54, 56, 93–4, 129, 152–3, 191, 197
Fumagalli, A. 52
Furlong, A. 94
future research 171, 180

game theory 218
gaze 20
gender 5, 7, 110, 115, 119, 199–204, 206
generational issues 7, 88, 122–3, 126, 143–4, 152, 213, 217–18
Gerbaudo, P. 153
Germany 1, 98, 115, 153–4, 178
Ghana 22
gift economy 196, 217
Global Financial Stability Report 217
globalisation 25, 70, 123, 149–50, 152, 158, 160, 214
Gödel, K. 215
Google 191–2
Gordon, L. 202
governance 4–5, 7, 9, 15–20, 22, 26, 61, 150, 200
governmentality 127–8, 158, 163, 200–5
graduates 73, 75, 77, 82, 88, 90–3, 95, 113–15, 122, 192, 195
Graeber, D. 158
Graziano, V. 8, 157–69
Great British Class Survey 154
Great Depression 21
Greece 6–7, 98–109, 144, 154, 160, 174, 196
Gross Domestic Product (GDP) 40, 87, 118, 213, 222
Guangdong 31, 33–5, 37–42
Guattari, G. 215
Gugler, J. 212
Guiheux, G. 32, 41–2
guild systems 84–5
Gulf of Guinea 20

habitus 210, 218
Hall, S. 94
Handy, C. 93
Haraway, D. 219
Hardt, M. 150
Harley, J.B. 210
Hayek, F. von 212, 216
healthcare 120, 175, 180–1, 203, 206
Hegel, G.W.F. 196, 217, 222
hegemony 123, 129–30, 204
Hidden Agenda 132
high-growth sectors 189–98
Higher Education Academy (HEA) 72
Hobbes, T. 127, 129, 199–200
Holland 153
homelessness 129, 131–2

homo oeconomcus 72, 77
Hong Kong 132
household law 210–26
Hugo, G. 88
human capital 3–4, 50, 71, 73, 78, 214–15
Hungary 115
Husserl, E. 196, 217
hybrid work areas 47–59

I Quaderni di San Precario 2
Ichimura, M. 132
ideology 2, 70–3, 75–8, 130, 142–3; and Africa 17, 21; and caregiving 204; and Europe 149, 153; and Greece 99; and Italy 47; and PhD graduates 119; and prefigurative practices 161
Impaction 123–5, 127, 129
imperialism 210
indenture 195–6
independence 199–209
India 27
Indignados 150, 152, 174
individualisation 6, 61, 71–2, 77, 139; and academic careers 90, 92, 94; and caregiving 200–4, 206; and China 41, 43; and Italy 50, 56; and PhD graduates 104
industrial relations 16, 22, 66, 89, 128
industrial workers 31–46
industrialisation 16, 18, 31–46, 71, 195
inequalities 6–7, 47–51, 53–7, 99, 110, 119, 123, 128, 153, 200, 202–4
informal economy 2, 4, 8, 15, 17–27, 33–4, 56–7, 98, 140, 171, 194
informationalism 149
Institut National de la Statistique et des études économiques (INSEE) 219
institutionalisation 16, 24, 39, 98, 123
institutions 2, 61, 66–8, 83, 85–8; and academic careers 93; and Africa 17–18, 23, 25; and caregiving 201–2, 205; and China 34; and employability 70–1, 76–8; and free labour 190, 193; and household law 214, 222; and instability 35, 42; and Italy 57; and Japan 125; and PhD graduates 120; and Spain 176
insurance 35–7, 60, 116, 194, 202–3, 206, 214
intellectual property 61
internalisation 6, 52–3, 71, 77, 99, 161
International Labour Organisation (ILO) 2, 17, 24, 32
International Labour Review 1
International Monetary Fund (IMF) 18, 23, 26, 99, 196, 217
International Workers' Day 149, 151
internet 131, 191, 196
interns 4, 54, 118, 151, 189, 192–3, 197
intersectionality 172, 179
investment 25, 27, 101, 104, 140, 176, 212, 215, 222
Iron Rice Bowl 32, 34
Islam 24, 26
ISO 211
Israel 164
Italy 1, 5–7, 137, 142, 149–51; and France 65; and free labour 196; and hybrid work areas 47–59; and Japan 123; and PhD graduates 110, 118; and prefigurative practices 160; and workers' movements 153–4
ius communes 216

Japan 6–7, 122–34
Jiang Zemin 32
job security 2, 15, 26, 35, 37; and academic careers 87–9, 92–4; and caregiving 199; and employability 70; and free labour 196; and Greece 98–9; and Japan 122, 126; and PhD graduates 114–15
Jobcentres 77
Jobseeker's Allowance 75–6
Junor, A. 88
Juppé, A. 217
Juventud sin Futuro (JSF) 174–5, 177

Kalecki, M. 214
Kant, I. 216
Katanga mines 20, 27
Key Performance Indicators (KPIs) 84
Keynesianism 2–3, 16
Knight, F.H. 213
Kohso, S. 125
Korzybski, A. 210
Kuhn, T. 218

Labour Question 2
Lange, O. 216
Latin America 176
Laval, C. 165

Lavoisier, A. 213
legislation 6, 22, 175, 190, 193, 201
liberalisation 18, 23, 25–7
liberalism 4, 19, 26, 61, 128, 200, 202–6
Linnaeus, C. 219
livelihoods 33, 125, 189, 195
Locke, J. 200–1, 218
Lonmin Marikana mine 27
Lordon, F. 165
Lorey, I. 9, 123, 127–9, 131, 199–209
lost generations 7, 88, 122–3, 126
lumpenproletariat 1
Luxemburg, R. 214, 216
Lyft 194

machine learning 221
McNeilly, J. 219
macroeconomics 27
Makori, T. 27
managerialism 7, 57, 82–6, 89, 91, 94, 192, 212, 222
Manning, E. 219
Mao Zedong 31–2
maps 1–12, 210–12, 223
marabout 24, 27
Marchant, O. 126–7, 129
Marea Granate 174–7, 179, 181
market mechanisms 6, 35, 37, 42
marketing 71, 77–8, 87, 126, 129
Marx, K. 1, 72, 218, 222
Marxism 107, 154, 165, 215, 220
Massive Open Online Courses (MOOCs) 87
Masson, A. 213
Matsumoto, H. 130–1
May Day 7–8, 124, 137, 149–57, 160, 171, 174
May, R. 88
media 75, 77, 137–8, 149, 151; and Greece 98–109; and Japan 124–5, 129, 132; and PhD graduates 118; social media 152–4, 174, 176, 191–2; and Spain 173, 179
Mediterranean 153, 179
Mériaux, B. 220
meritocracy 50
Merkel, A. 150
metaphysics 212, 215, 219, 222
Mezzadra, S. 171, 180
migrants 2, 8, 137–8, 149, 152; and Africa 17, 20–2, 25, 27; and China 32, 34, 37; and free labour 190, 193; and household law 212, 217, 220; and Japan 129; and PhD graduates 118; and prefigurative practices 160; and Spain 170–85
mining 18, 20, 22, 27, 114
Mitropoulos, A. 9, 210–26
mobilisations 16, 137–9, 142, 149–51, 158–60; and China 43; and Europe 149–51; and free labour 191; and Greece 103; and Italy 57; and prefigurative practices 158–60; and Spain 170–1, 173–4, 177–9, 181
modernisation 31–2, 42, 82, 84, 86, 125, 131
Moore, M. 41
Moore, P. 72
Morgan, G. 7, 82–97
Morice, A. 24
Morocco 26, 176
Moulier Boutang, Y. 143
multinational corporations 23, 107
Mulvaney, K 122
Munck, R. 17
Murgia, A. 1–12, 47–59, 94
Muridiyya 24
mutualism 57, 63–5, 67, 196, 207

National Social Security Institute (INPS), Italy 48
National Tertiary Education Union (NTEU), Australia 88
nationalism 19, 177, 211
negotiations 2, 22, 36
Negri, A. 150, 159, 161, 167
Neilson, B. 16, 171, 180
neoclassical economics 213, 218
neoliberalism 2–4, 6, 99, 107, 158–9; and academic careers 82, 84, 86, 90–1, 93–5; and Africa 15, 17, 22–7; and caregiving 199–200, 203–5; and employability 72–5, 77–8; and Europe 149, 152–4; and France 60–4, 67; and free labour 189; and household law 216; and Italy 47, 49–50, 52, 55–7; and Japan 128, 130–1
neuro-linguistic programming 74, 163
New Deal 75
New Household Economics 214
Nigeria 22, 24
non-governmental organisations (NGOs) 17, 25
norms 2, 16–17, 19, 24, 32; and academic careers 93; and caregiving 199, 203; and

China 34; and employability 70, 73; and free labour 189, 191–2, 195–6; and household law 210–15, 218, 220–1; and Italy 53, 56; and Japan 128
North 8, 140, 164, 178
North America 153, 178
Norton, A. 89

Occupy movement 142, 158–60, 174, 177
OECD 86–7, 153, 178
Offices of Social Rights 171–2, 178
offshoring 23, 190–1, 194
Ogawa, T. 132
oikonomia 211–12, 216–17
oil 22, 27, 116
oligarchy 153–4
oligopoly 154
ontology 4, 9, 27, 142, 200, 222
Operaismo 65
outsourcing 18, 23, 61, 93, 191, 193, 206, 214
Oxalis 63

Papadopoulos, D. 8, 137–48
parts-whole paradigm 212–13, 217–18, 220, 222
passions 52–3, 57, 67, 79, 83–4, 113, 192
Pateman, C. 201
paternalism 84, 206
patriarchy 18, 201, 204
patronage 24–5, 92
peasants 20, 22, 220
pedagogy 66, 73, 84, 160, 163, 166
pensions 37, 61, 73, 115, 214, 217
Pentecostals 26
performance 51, 71, 74, 82–5, 87, 90, 95, 120, 126, 159–62, 205, 210–11
Peru 179
PhDs 82, 90, 92
phenomenology 51, 196, 211–12, 217–19, 222
Piore, M. 220
Pitrou, A. 212–13, 217
Plato 196, 211, 213, 217–18, 220, 222
Polanyi, K. 216
police 23, 27
political economy 1, 19, 204–6
Poncin, B. 60, 63
portfolio workers 93
Portugal 153–4
post-Fordism 71, 93, 111, 125, 127
post-wage era 23
postcolonialism 6, 15–30, 172, 178
postmodernism 24, 93, 99
poverty 34, 41–2, 70, 76, 88; and Africa 24–5; and caregiving 204; and free labour 193; and Greece 107; and Japan 122–3, 126–7, 129; and PhD graduates 110, 117; and prefigurative practices 164; and Spain 173
power relations 67, 73–4, 89
practice firms 163
prec-mig hypothesis 171–3, 181
Precarias a la Deriva 128
precariat 5, 7–8, 16–17, 83, 92; and academic careers 94–5; and caregiving 206–7; and Euro May Day 149–56; and Greece 98–9, 107; and Japan 123–4, 126, 129; and PhD graduates 119
precariedad 170–85
precariousness 1–12, 57, 86, 93, 210; and Africa 15–30; categories 9; classification 222–3; conceptualizing 199–209; and Greece 98–109; and household law 211–14; and Italy 47–59; and Japan 122–34; movements 137–8, 142–4, 149–56; and PhD graduates 110–21; regulation 217–22; and Spain 170–89; trajectories 55–6; transformation 47–59; two endings 137–48
precarisation 9, 62, 86, 137–8, 142; and caregiving 199–200, 203, 207; and Europe 154, 157; and Japan 123–9; and Spain 171, 179
precarity 9, 22–7, 71, 137–8, 140–2; and academic careers 87, 93; and Africa 16; and caregiving 200–3, 206–7; classification 222–3; definitions 34–5, 111; and employability 70–81; and Europe 150, 152–4; extrospection of 157–69; and free labour 189–90, 196; and Greece 99; and household law 210, 212–14, 219; and Italy 48; and Japan 125–8, 130; and PhD graduates 113, 119–20; plateau 31–46; and prefigurative practices 157–69; rethinking 170–85
prefigurative practices 157–69
prison labour 6, 189–90, 193–4, 196
privatisation 26, 116, 125, 139, 204–5, 214
profit 41, 76, 99, 113, 140, 154, 165, 189–90, 192, 194, 205, 213

project work 47–50, 52, 54–5
proletarianisation 6, 19–20, 35, 41
proletariat 15, 18, 71, 149, 151, 154
property rights 61, 139, 199–202, 210, 217–18
protests 1, 32, 101, 123, 137, 151–3, 158, 160, 162, 174
psychopathologies 162
public opinion 8, 137
push factors 35, 37, 170, 175

Quetelet, A. 218

racialisation 15–19, 172, 179, 201
racism 152, 160, 178, 181
Radical Education Forum Clinic 166
raw materials 15, 22–3, 25
recessions 23, 154, 189, 193, 196–7
reflexivity 106, 127, 167, 220
refugees 115, 160, 173
regulation 2, 4, 9, 140, 143; and Africa 27; and caregiving 205; free labour 190, 197; and household law 212, 215–22; and Italy 47, 54; and Spain 172, 179
relationality 54–5, 57, 200, 205
religion 24, 26, 75
representationalism 142–4
reproduction 189–98
Research Commission 64–5
resilience 25, 217
resistance 1–12, 19, 34, 57, 135; and academic careers 84, 86, 91; and employability 71–2, 77–8; and France 64, 66–7; and Greece 100, 105; and Japan 132; and prefigurative practices 162
retirement 6, 21, 35–7, 40, 42, 60, 87, 203
Richardson, J. 7, 110–21
Richter, S. 7, 122–34
risk 3, 5–6, 8, 27, 32; and academic careers 87, 91; and caregiving 203, 205; and China 34; and employability 75; and France 66–7; and free labour 194; and Greece 98; and household law 211–15, 217–19, 222; and Italy 50, 55; and Japan 126, 128, 131; and PhD graduates 112
Romania 6–7, 110–21
Ross, A. 8–9, 157, 189–98
Rossiter, N. 16
rosu jene 122–3, 129
rule of law 74
Russia 27

salaries 1, 37, 39, 48–9, 51; and academic careers 94; and France 60–8; and Greece 104, 108; and Japan 125; and PhD graduates 110–11, 113, 116–17; and prefigurative practices 163; and Spain 171, 177
Santa Fe Institute 216
Sarkozy, N. 150
scholars/scholarship 1, 16, 23, 72, 75, 82–6, 90–1, 94–5, 171, 222
Scholastics 216
Scotland 144
segregation 19, 201
selective conservation 215–17
self-employment 6, 15–16, 18, 21, 23–7, 47–54, 56–7, 62, 71, 77, 100, 221
self-exploitation 24, 52, 71, 94, 191
Senegal 24–5, 27
Sennett, R. 214
September 11 2001 4
shareholders 64, 103–4
Shoe Zone 76
Shunsuke, S. 123
Sicily 1
silk industry 61
Simondon, G. 162
slavery 17, 20, 75–6, 94, 196, 218
Smith, A. 201–2
smuggling 26–7
social compacts 15–16, 18
social construction 50
social contracts 17, 35, 201
social democracy 4, 6, 143, 151, 203
social management theory 215
social media 152–4, 174, 176, 191–2
social mobility 18, 33, 35, 41, 190
social movements 1–2, 5, 7–8, 16, 137–8; and Africa 26, 33; and Europe 151, 154; and prefigurative practices 157–60, 166–7; and Spain 170–1, 173, 175–6, 179
socialism 19, 31, 114, 119, 216
Socialist Calculation Debates 216
Société de Manutention de Travaux et Service (SMTS) 62
sociology 5, 15–16, 65, 93, 98, 123, 138, 212, 217–18, 220, 222–3
solidarity 5, 8, 83, 85, 89, 92, 150, 152, 160, 172–4, 202, 217
Sommer, B. 6, 31–46
South 8, 17, 178

South Africa 19–20, 22, 27
South Korea 132
Southwood, I. 7, 70–81
sovereignty 19, 127
Spain 6, 8, 138, 142–4, 152–4; and caregiving 205; and emigration 170–85; and free labour 196; and household law 216; and Japan 123, 128; and PhD graduates 118; and prefigurative practices 158, 160
Spinoza, B. 165
spontaneous order theories 212, 215–17
Spyridakis, M. 7, 98–109
standard employment relation (SER) 2–3, 6, 33–4
standardisation 3, 9, 52, 210–26
Standards Australia 211
Standing, G. 5, 8, 16–17, 57, 93, 98–9, 149, 154, 171, 180
Starbucks 191
Start and Improve Your Own Business (SIYB) programme 32
state 3, 127, 129, 132, 150; and Africa 15–16, 18, 21–5; and caregiving 199–202, 204–6; and China 31–2, 34–5, 41–2; and employability 76; and free labour 193; and Greece 108; and household law 212, 214–16, 218; and PhD graduates 112, 114, 116, 119
State Owned Enterprises (SOEs) 31, 34, 41
statistics 5, 9, 38, 98, 124, 189, 196, 210–13, 215, 217–23
Stop précarité 137, 154
strikes 27, 36–7, 39–40, 100–1, 103–4, 116, 159, 162, 167, 173
structural adjustment programmes 17–18, 23, 25–6, 107
students 1, 82–97, 111–12, 115, 118; and Africa 26; and employability 72–6, 79; and Europe 152–3; and free labour 190, 192, 194–5, 197; and Japan 125; and prefigurative practices 157; and Spain 179
Sub-Saharan Africa 86, 212
subcontractors 23
subjectivities 1–12, 139–40, 157, 160–2, 165–6; and Africa 19, 26; and caregiving 200–1, 207; and China 35; counter-subjectivities 1; and employability 78; and France 61–2, 67; and household law 219; and Italy 47–59; and Japan 123, 126–7, 130–1
subsidies 23, 32, 89, 100, 192
subsistence 3, 18, 22, 32, 196, 214
Sufis 24
Supreme Council of Scientific Research, Spain 176
surveyors 210
Sweden 153
Switzerland 178
Sylos, P. 1

Taiwan 37, 132
talibé 24, 27
task-oriented logic 51–2
TaskRabbit 191, 194
taxation 19, 60, 113, 190
Taylor, F. 85
Taylorism 83–6, 191
technocrats 24
Terranova, T. 162
textile industry 61, 110
Thévenot, L. 215, 219, 221
think-tanks 70, 77
Thompson, E. 51
Tiffen, R. 87
Toret, J. 152
tourism 23, 179
Toyotism 125
traineeships 76
transaction costs 213–15, 217, 219
transnational corporations 27
tribalism 21
Tunisia 152
Twitter 191

Uber 194
umbrella companies 60
uncertainty 98–109, 140–1, 180, 190, 210–26
undecidability 215, 218, 222
underclass 21, 88, 154
Underearners Anonymous (UA) 163–6
underemployment 21, 138, 176, 190
unemployment 6, 8, 21, 26, 38; and academic careers 86; and caregiving 202; and Europe 151–3; and France 60–2; and free labour 194–6; and Greece 98–101, 107; and household law 213–14, 222; and Italy 49; and Japan 126; and PhD graduates 114–15; and

prefigurative practices 163; and Spain 170, 173–4, 176–7, 180; and unemployability 73–9
unions 4–5, 112, 116–17, 124, 137; and academic careers 88, 90–1, 93; and Africa 19, 22; and China 35, 39–40; and employability 71; and Europe 149, 151–2; and free labour 194, 197; and Greece 102, 105, 107; and Italy 49; and Japan 130–1; and Spain 171, 173
United Kingdom (UK) 6–7, 20–1, 54, 70–1, 74, 98, 144, 163–4, 178
United Precarious of Europe 152
United States (US) 1, 4, 6, 24, 74, 90, 153, 164, 174, 192–6, 202
universal standards 217–22
universities 82–97, 110–21
urban labour preference policy 22
urbanisation 20–2
Uruguay 179

value extraction 55–6, 159, 161, 165, 190, 215
value production 138–9, 141, 143
Veyer, S. 66
visas 171–2, 180
vocation 83–6, 91, 94–5
volunteering 195
Vosko, L.F. 34
vulnerability 4, 16, 19–20, 23, 27; and academic careers 84; and caregiving 200, 202–3; and China 36; and employability 79; and free labour 193; and Greece 99; and Italy 57; and prefigurative practices 162; and Spain 171, 179

wages 3, 31, 33–4, 37–43, 138; and academic careers 92; and Africa 15–19; and caregiving 202–3, 205; and employability 73, 76; and Europe 149–50, 153; and France 60–1; and Greece 100–1, 104, 108; and household law 211, 213–14, 222; and Italy 57; and Japan 128; and PhD graduates 111, 117, 119; post-wage era 23; working for nothing 189–98
war zones 27
Watson, I. 88
Weber, M. 1, 26, 218
welfare provision 6–7, 18, 34, 49, 137; and caregiving 199–200, 202–5; and employability 70, 74; and Europe 149; and household law 212, 214–17; and Italy 57; and Japan 125; and prefigurative practices 157, 160; and Spain 173, 176
West 18, 23–5, 33–4, 86, 93, 110, 123, 128, 199
West Africa 20
Western Europe 110, 178
White, L. 20
Whyte, W. 93
women 2–3, 7, 18, 21–3, 137; and Africa 25; and caregiving 202; and China 33, 36; and Europe 149, 152; and France 64; and free labour 192; and Greece 100, 107; and household law 220; and PhD graduates 110–21; and prefigurative practices 157
Wong Ah-Kok 132
Wood, J. 7, 82–97
work 70, 73–6, 98, 106, 137; beyond employment 57; and caregiving 206; and employability 78; free 52–3, 189–98; and prefigurative practices 157, 162; refusal of work 15–19; and Spain 172; working poor 49, 122, 126, 131, 164, 173, 193, 214
workfare 75–7, 173, 214
World Bank 18, 23
World War II 21

xenophobia 154
Xi Jinping 32

youth 22, 26–7, 86, 94, 100; and Europe 149–54; and free labour 189, 195–6; and household law 214, 220–1; and Japan 125, 127; and Spain 170–3, 176–7, 180–1
Yue Yuen 36–7

Zambia 22